ISBN: 9781314030778

Published by:
HardPress Publishing
8345 NW 66TH ST #2561
MIAMI FL 33166-2626

Email: info@hardpress.net
Web: http://www.hardpress.net

A

GEOGRAPHICAL AND HISTORICAL

DESCRIPTION

OF

ASIA MINOR;

WITH A MAP.

BY

J. A. CRAMER, D.D.

PRINCIPAL OF NEW INN HALL, AND PUBLIC ORATOR OF THE
UNIVERSITY OF OXFORD.

IN TWO VOLUMES.

Νῦν δ' αὖ παρραλίης 'Ασίης πόρον ἐξενέποιμι
Ὅς ῥά τε πρὸς νότον εἰσιν, ἐφ' Ἑλλήσποντον ὁδεύων
Καὶ ποτὶ μηκίστου νότιον ῥόον Αἰγαίοιο.
DIONYS. PERIEG. V. 799.

VOL. I.

OXFORD.
AT THE UNIVERSITY PRESS.
MDCCCXXXII.

—6

PREFACE.

THE present volumes complete the plan I had originally proposed to myself of illustrating the geographical antiquities of the three countries, which offered the greatest interest to the classical student. Asia Minor presents a field of inquiry hardly inferior to the other two in historical importance, since it exhibits a nearly unbroken chain of events, from the siege of Troy to the downfall of Constantinople; and it possesses moreover one point of peculiar interest, from being so closely connected with the name and labours of St. Paul.

With respect to the comparative geography of this extensive and diversified country, our information on several points, more especially in the interior, is still inadequate and defective. Much certainly has been done by that eminent geographer and antiquary

Col. Leake, in his work on Asia Minor[a], and some further light has since been derived from the journals of Mr. Arundell and Major Keppel, and from foreign sources ; but still our knowledge of Anatolia is in many respects incomplete.

The late celebrated Major Rennell had apparently bestowed much time and labour on the comparative geography of Western Asia, and had he lived to complete the work, he would certainly have produced a valuable map of those extensive regions. But the two volumes which have been published from his papers contain little that was not known before ; and present rather a series of detailed notes and observations, than a systematic and organized work[b].

Such being the state of our information respecting the comparative geography of Asia Minor, I cannot pretend to offer the map

[a] Journal of a Tour in Asia Minor, with Comparative Remarks on the Ancient and Modern Geography of that country, by W. L. Leake. 8vo. Lond. 1824.

[b] A Treatise on the Comparative Geography of Western Asia, accompanied with an Atlas of Maps, in two vols. 8vo. Lond. 1831.

which accompanies these volumes as at all equal in truth and accuracy to those of Italy and Greece, but I may express the hope that it will be found superior to any that have preceded it. And I think considerable credit is due to Mr. Findlay for the manner in which he has put together and arranged the different materials within his reach.

CONTENTS

OF

THE FIRST VOLUME.

SECTION I.

ASIA MINOR.

———◆———

Preliminary observations on the name of Asia—Principal geographical features of the peninsula commonly called Asia Minor—Inquiry into the origin of the various nations by which it was peopled—Divisions.

As EARLY as the time of Herodotus we find the name of Asia employed to designate the vast continent situated to the east of Europe, and almost entirely subject at that period to the Persian dominion. The Greeks, as we learn from that historian, pretended that it was derived from Asia, the wife of Prometheus, but the Lydians, on the other hand, affirmed that its origin was to be sought for in their country. For that Asius, from whom it was deduced, was the grandson of Manes, one of their earliest monarchs; and, to corroborate this assertion, they adduced the fact of the name of Asias having been originally attached to a Sardian tribe [a]. (IV. 45.) The evidence which can be brought forward in favour of the Lydian tradition, leaves little doubt respecting the issue of this question. It may be ob-

[a] Bochart derives the name from *Asi,* a Phœnician word signifying *a middle part,* or something intermediate; according to which etymology Asia would signify the continent situated between Europe and Africa. Geogr. Sacr. IV. 33. p. 298.

served that Homer applied the name of Asia to a small district of Mæonia, or Lydia, situated near the river Caystrus,

'Ασίῳ ἐν λειμῶνι, Καϋστρίου ἀμφὶ ῥέεθρα.

IL. B. 461.

a passage which Virgil has imitated in his Georgics :

. . . . quæ Asia circum
Dulcibus in stagnis rimantur prata Caystri.

I. 383.

Euripides also evidently restricts the appellation to a portion of Lydia, where he says,

'Ασίας ἀπὸ γᾶς
ἱερὸν Τμῶλον ἀμείψασα—

BACCH. 64.

(Cf. Dionys. Perieg. 836. et Eustath. Comm.)

By what process this specific name came to be applied generally to the whole peninsula, and after that to the entire Asiatic continent, it is not easy to determine. But it is probable that the Ionian Greeks, on their first arrival on the banks of the Mæander and Caystrus, adopted the name which they found already attached to the country, and communicated it to their European countrymen. These gradually learned to apply it first to that maritime portion with which they were most familiar, then to the interior also, and finally to all those countries which were situated to the east of Greece. This final extension had already taken place, as I have before observed, in the time of Herodotus, who employs the division of Upper and Lower Asia. The latter of these answers in fact to what we now call Asia Minor, while the former denotes the vast tract of country situated to the east of the Euphrates. Notwithstanding, however, this wide acceptation given to the name, it appears clearly that it always remained attached in a peculiar and restricted sense to a portion of Asia Minor, which strongly confirms the notion that the appellation originated in that district. In proof of the above assertion it is only necessary to refer to the title of Asia Propria, ἡ ἰδίως καλουμένη Ἀσία, given to the Roman proconsular province forming a part only of the Asiatic peninsula. (Strab. XIII. p. 626. II. p. 188.) It is in this sense too that we always find the word used in the New Testament, as in the Acts ii. 9. where Asia is distinguished from Cappadocia, Pontus, Phrygia, and Pamphylia ; and xvi. 6. it is said, " Now when they had gone through- " out Phrygia and the region of Galatia, and were " forbidden of the Holy Ghost to preach the word " in Asia." From the book of Revelations, which is addressed to the seven churches in Asia, it is further seen that the name was strictly confined to that portion of ancient Lydia which contained Ephesus, Smyrna, Pergamus, Sardis, &c.[b] It is not exactly known when the peninsula came to be designated by the name of Asia Minor, now generally used by the European nations ; but it does not, I believe, appear in any author prior to Orosius, who employs it, (I. 2.) as well as Constantine Porphyrogenetes, (de Themat. I. 8.) The term *Anatolia*, used by the Turks to denote this portion of the Ottoman

[b] See Cellarius Dissertatio de Sept. Eccles. Asiæ inter Dissert. Academ. p. 412.; also archbishop Usher's Geogr. and Hist. disquisition touching the Asia properly so called. Oxford, 1643.

empire, is evidently of Greek origin, and answers to the Frank word *Levant*. Towards the decline of the Roman empire we find Asia Minor divided into two dioceses, or provinces, called Asiana and Pontica, (Notit. Imper. I.) each governed by a lieutenant termed *Vicarius*. (Cod. Theod. V. tit. 2.) Other divisions were afterwards adopted by the Byzantine emperors, but these do not come within the scope of a work especially intended to illustrate classical geography.

Asia Minor is bounded on the north by the Pontus Euxinus, or *Black sea*, which communicates with the Propontis, or *sea of Marmara*, by means of the Bosphorus, or *straits of Constantinople;* and this again with the Ægæum Mare by the Hellespontus, now *straits of the Dardanelles*. The Ægean sea, called *Archipelago* in modern geography, forms its western boundary, while on the south its shores are washed by that inland sea to which the name of Internum or Mediterraneum was more particularly applied. In order to define the eastern limit of the peninsula, we must follow the river sometimes called Acampsis, at others Apsarus, now *Tchorok-sou*, which divides Pontus from Colchis, from its termination into the Euxine, to where it meets the great chain of Armenian mountains formerly called Scydisces. This ridge, running in a south-westerly direction from the Acampsis to the Euphrates, then forms one boundary as far as the latter river, the course of which, dividing the two Armenias, traces the line of separation as far as the little district of Melitene, belonging to Cappadocia. At this point the great chain of mount Taurus, running from west to east, is intersected by the river. Our line, therefore, leaving the Euphrates, follows Taurus to the west, till it meets mount Amanus, which, branching off from the central ridge in a south-westerly direction, closes upon the Cilician sea at the defile called the Syriæ Pylæ, and thus completes the angular line which joins the two seas, and forms the fourth side of the Asiatic peninsula.

Were we to form our notions of the shape and extent of Asia Minor from the measurements transmitted to us by the geographers of antiquity, we should be led into numerous errors, and those of no trifling kind. This will be at once evident by merely attending to those of Strabo; for being a native of the country, and, generally speaking, the best informed writer on the subject of which he treats, he may fairly be considered as affording the best criterion of the accuracy of the ancients on the point in question.

Now with respect to the northern coast of Asia Minor, Strabo's want of accuracy is rendered apparent, by his supposing the shore of the Euxine to form nearly a straight line from Byzantium to Amisus; (II. p. 74.) whereas it advances in a northerly direction nearly the whole way, from the Thracian Bosphorus to the *Cape Inje,* formerly Syrias, above Sinope; so that the difference of latitude between this promontory and Byzantium is more than one degree. From Sinope it bends to the south again as far as Amisus, which is nearly forty miles below the parallel of the former town. From Chalcedon to Sinope, Strabo reckons 3500 stadia, and 900 from Sinope to Amisus, in all 4400; and for the southern coast about 5000, from Rhodes to Issus in Cilicia. Thus Issus would be 600 stadia to

the east of Amisus, and yet Strabo himself elsewhere looks upon these two places as situated under
the same meridian. (II. p.126. XIV. p.678.ᶜ) With
regard to the southern coast, the same geographer, when he affirms that it extended from Rhodes
to Tarsus in a south-easterly direction, does not
appear to have been aware of the great sweep it
takes, first round the province of Lycia to the great
gulf of *Attalia*, the ancient Mare Pamphylium, and
round Cilicia to the mouth of the Cydnus. With
respect to the breadth of the peninsula, Strabo has
given us no positive statement; but from his measurement of the western coast, and the too great
elevation he assigns to Byzantium, it appears he
considered it to be much broader than it is. He informs us, however, that Eratosthenes reckoned 3000
stadia between Issus and Amisus, where the neck of
the isthmus is the narrowest. This statement comes
very near the truth; for the best modern maps allow
about 330 miles from one sea to another in this
part. It may be here observed, that Herodotus was
very wide from the mark, when he estimated the
distance from the coast of Cilicia to Sinope to be
only five days' march for a person lightly equipped.
(II. 34.ᵈ) The peninsula is widest between capes
Anemurium, *Anemur*, in Cilicia, and Carambis,
Kerempe, in Paphlagonia.

Asia Minor contains numerous chains of mountains,
some of which attain to a great elevation. The most

ᶜ Gosselin, Géogr. des Grecs
Analysée, p. 95.

ᵈ The ancients themselves
were aware of the error made
by Herodotus in this matter,
for Scymnus of Chios corrects
his statement, and observes,
that the distance is not less
than seven days' journey.
Fragm. v. 885.

considerable is that of mount Taurus, which, commencing at the Sacrum Promontorium on the Lycian
and Pamphylian coast, stretches in a north-easterly
direction through Pisidia, Isauria, and Cappadocia,
till it is intersected by the Euphrates near Melitene.
It extends, however, much further, according to
Strabo, as that geographer connects it with the
great Indian ridge of Imaus, or Emodius, now
Himalaya. (XI. p. 511.) He looks, indeed, upon
this great chain as forming the belt of the entire
Asiatic continent for the space of 4500 stadia, (XI.
p. 490.) whilst its breadth in some parts is not less
than 3000 stadia. That part of mount Taurus
which belongs to Asia Minor, and with which we
are alone concerned at present, is called by the
Turks *Sultan dagh*. To the west it is connected
with the chain of lofty mountains known to the
ancients by the name of Cragus, and which rises
precipitously above the coast of Lycia throughout
nearly the whole of its extent. To the north-east
Taurus sends out one of its ramifications under the
name of Anti-taurus, through Cappadocia and Armenia Minor; the highest point of this ridge was
mount Argæus, its summit, as Strabo affirms, being
covered with perpetual snow. (XII. p. 538.) Further north, Anti-taurus is connected with the inferior
chains which traverse Paphlagonia and Pontus;
such as mount Teches, Scydisces, Paryadres, and
others, uniting afterwards with the central Armenian range of which Ararat forms the highest point;
and stretching also into Colchis, where it meets the
no less elevated ridge of Caucasus. In the north-
western parts of Asia Minor we have the celebrated
chain of Ida, which rises above the coast of the an-

cient Troad, and unites to the north-east with the
high range of the Mysian, and Bithynian Olympus ;
this again is connected with several chains which
form the principal basons and valleys of Phrygia
and Galatia.   To the south of Ida, and in the ancient kingdom of Lydia, we have the parallel chains
of Sipylus and Tmolus running from west to east,
and uniting with the different ranges which sur-
round Phrygia on every side.   From these and
other mountains, which will be specified in the
course of this work, descend numerous rivers, forming large and fertile valleys, and finally discharging
their waters into the several seas which wash the
shores of the peninsula.   Of those which fall into
the Ægean sea the principal are the Caicus, now
Bakir-tchai, Hermus, *Kodus*, Caystrus, now *Lesser
Mendere*, and the Mæander, *Greater Mendere*.
All these, with the exception of the first, which rises
in Mysia, come from the mountains of Phrygia,
together with their numerous tributary streams, and
have their course generally parallel to each other.
The rivers which flow into the Propontis from
mount Ida and Olympus are the Granicus, *Sataldere*, Æsepus, *Boklu*, or *Guimenen-tchai*, and Rhyndacus, *Edrene-sou*.   Those which discharge their
waters into the Euxine are the Sangarius, now
Sakaria, which rises in Galatia and traverses a
great portion of Phrygia and Bithynia, the Billæus,
Filbas, and Parthenius, or *Bartan*.   But the largest
of these rivers, and indeed of all Asia Minor, is the
Halys, now *Kizil-ermak*, which consists of two
branches, one rising in the Cappadocian mountains
on the frontiers of Cilicia, the other in Armenia
Minor on the borders of Pontus, and after a long

and tortuous course, in which it nearly traverses the peninsula from south-west to north-east, falls into the Euxine to the south-east of Sinope. Beyond is the Iris, formed by the junction of the Scylax, Lycus, and other streams; its mouth is a little to the east of *Samsoun*, the ancient Amisus. The rivers which discharge their waters into the Pamphylian and Cilician seas are much less considerable, owing to the proximity of mount Taurus, from which they descend, to the coast. They are the Catarrhactes, now *Duden*, Calycadnus, *Ghiuk-sou*, Cydnus, *Tersoos*, Sarus, *Sihoun*, and Pyramus, now *Gihoun*.

Asia Minor contains several lakes, but most of them are inconsiderable, and unnoticed by classical writers. Those which can be identified are the Aphnitis, Dascylitis, Miletopolitis, and Apolloniatis, in Mysia; the Ascanius and Sophon, in Bithynia. In Phrygia we find the great salt lake Tattæus, noticed by Strabo, (XII. p. 568.) now *Tuzla*, together with the Palus Trogitis and Caralitis, besides several others, whose ancient names are unknown.

Few countries present such a diversity of soil and climate as the great peninsula to which our attention is at present directed. The genial temperature of Ionia, Lydia, and Caria, and indeed, generally speaking, of the whole of western Asia, together with the extreme fertility of those provinces, are proved beyond dispute by the number and opulence of the towns they contained, especially those founded by Grecian colonists. Herodotus affirms, that the climate of Ionia surpassed that of every country with which he was acquainted, (I. 142.) and the testimony of antiquity is in this respect fully confirmed by the accounts of modern travellers and geogra-

phers.   On the other hand, large tracts of country
were very thinly inhabited, from the coldness of the
climate and the unproductiveness of the soil.   This
was more especially the case in the mountainous
districts of Lycia, Pisidia, Cilicia, and Cappadocia,
where the land is very elevated, and the snow remains for a considerable part of the year.   Many
parts of Phrygia and Galatia were also nearly deserted, from the barrenness of the ground, which
was strongly impregnated with salt, and exhibited,
besides, other indications of volcanic agency.   This
was principally observed in that part of Lydia
called Catacecaumene, or *the burnt*, and near the
Mæander.   Several other provinces presented similar appearances, though in a less degree; but the
whole country appears to have been subject at an
early period to violent earthquakes, which destroyed
or damaged many flourishing cities. (Strab. XII.
p. 578.)

Nevertheless, taken collectively, Asia Minor was
one of the most productive and opulent countries
of which antiquity has left us any account.   The
wealth of the kings of Phrygia and Lydia had become proverbial at a time when Greece and the rest
of Europe were yet without civilization or commerce.   Under the empire of the Persians, Asia
Minor was divided into five nomes or districts, if
we include the tribes which belong to the province
commonly known by the name of Pontus; these
poured annually into the royal treasury the sum of
2060 Euboic silver talents, or little short of one
seventh of the whole revenue, which is estimated
by Herodotus at 14,560 talents.   Of this sum it
should be observed, that India alone furnished in

gold ore the value of 4680 silver talents, and Assyria 1000 talents. (Herod. III. 90.) So that if we
deduct the produce of these two satrapies from the
whole amount, it will reduce the proportion of the
revenue of Asia Minor to that of the remaining 18
satrapies as 2 to 9. And it may be seen by the
map that Asia Minor does not constitute one tenth
part of the Persian empire in the time of Darius.
It was by means of the great resources which the
younger Cyrus derived from this country, that the
Lacedæmonians, whom he befriended, were enabled
to conquer Athens, and to put an end to the Peloponnesian war. By the help of the same resources
that prince had nearly succeeded in his ambitious
enterprise against the throne of his brother Artaxerxes. Persia may be said to have been already
conquered when the battles of the Granicus and
Issus secured to Alexander the possession of Asia
Minor. Its annexation to the crown of Syria, after
the death of that prince, in consequence of the defeat and death of Antigonus in the battle of Ipsus,
threw a degree of weight in the political scale in
favour of the Seleucidæ, which might have proved
prejudicial to the independence of the surrounding
countries, or at least have served to check the rapa-
cious designs of the Romans, if the sovereigns of
that house had been gifted with greater energy and
powers of mind. One battle, however, wrested it
from the feeble grasp of Antiochus, and annexed it
to the empire of his enterprising and restless foes.
In their hands Asia Minor became a source of vast
profit and wealth ; and we have the authority of
Cicero for stating, that the Roman treasury derived
its largest and surest revenues from that great pro-

vince. (Orat. pro Leg. Manil. §. 2, 6.) " Certissima
" populi Romani vectigalia, et maxima." And, (§. 6,
1.) " Asia vero tam opima est et fertilis, ut et uber-
" tate agrorum, et varietate fructuum et magni-
" tudine pastionis, et multitudine earum rerum,
" quæ exportantur, facile omnibus terris antecellat."
With regard to mineral productions, we know that
the mountains of Lydia, Phrygia, and Mysia, in
ancient times, produced gold. Pontus furnished
silver, iron, and sandarach. Phrygia, Mysia, and
Caria supplied several sorts of marble highly prized
by the Romans for the beauty and variety of their
colours. In Cappadocia were to be found quarries
of alabaster, onyx, and crystal, and rich veins of
the earth called sinope. The vegetable produce
consisted ' in corn, millet, and every other sort of
grain, which were grown in the greatest abundance,
not only in the extensive valleys and plains, but even
on some of the elevated lands in the chain of mount
Taurus. The Hellespontine district, the islands of
Lesbos and Chios, and some parts of Ionia and
Caria, furnished wines highly esteemed by the ancients. Pontus, Bithynia, and Galatia abounded in
fruit-trees of different sorts ; Cilicia supplied saffron
and the gum storax ; and the olive and fig-tree flourished in almost every part of the peninsula. The
forests of Ida, Tmolus, Olympus, and Taurus grew
timber for the construction of ships, and other purposes, as well as fuel in the greatest abundance.
The rich pastures of the provinces watered by the
Halys, Thermodon, Sangarius, and Mæander, supported numerous herds and flocks. Paphlagonia
was celebrated for its mules as early as the days of
Homer ; and the steeds of Cappadocia were reserved

for the royal studs of Persia and Byzantium. The fleeces of Ionia were unrivalled throughout the world for the softness of their texture; and the Persian monarchs drew from Cilicia annually a tributary supply of white horses.

If to these physical advantages we add others, presented by the great extent of coast and the number of excellent harbours it afforded, it will appear, that no country was so much favoured by nature, and so well calculated for becoming the centre of a mighty and perhaps universal empire. But the moral condition and character of its population has never kept pace with the physical resources of the country. From the earliest period, under the kings of Assyria, the dynasties of Lydia and Persia, under the empires of Rome and Byzantium, down to the present day, Asia Minor has been peopled by a race fitted, as it were, by nature for slavery and bondage. Effeminacy and luxury have been the prevailing habits of the inhabitants from the times of the soft and voluptuous Lydians to those of the indolent Turk; and this will probably always be the case as long as the softness of the climate and the fertility of the soil continue to exercise an enervating influence over the character of the people; an influence which has shewn itself so strikingly, first in the change it wrought upon the Greek colonists, who, from being brave and hardy like the parent race, became proverbially soft and effeminate; then upon their Persian conquerors; and, lastly, on the warlike and fierce Osmanlis.

There is only one short period in the history of Asia Minor during which it may be seen how the genius and energy of one man, even with such a

population as we have here described, and the resources of less than half the peninsula, could grapple
with the giant strength of Rome, and even shake
her power to the very centre. The noble stand
made by Mithridates, though finally unsuccessful,
serves at least to prove, that if Asia Minor had been
united under the sole command of such a prince, it
never would have remained a province of the Roman empire.

The origin of the first tribes who peopled Asia
Minor, like that of almost every nation of antiquity,
is a question involved in obscurity, and beset with
doubts and perplexities ; from which we are not
likely to extricate ourselves with ease and readiness
at the present day. Where history supplies no ade-
quate information on the subject, the language of a
people has always been considered as affording the
best clue for discovering its primary seat and origin.
Here, however, that resource is denied us ; since,
with the exception of a few detached words, preserved by the Greek grammarians and lexicograph-
ers, we are left in entire ignorance as to the prevailing dialects among the indigenous tribes of Asia
Minor[e]. I use the word *indigenous*, in contradis-
tinction to the colonies established by the Greeks, in
times which are well authenticated. It appears then
that we are obliged, in this question, to glean from

[e] These will be found nearly all brought together in a
learned and elaborate dissertation of professor Jablonsky, entitled, Disquisitio de Lingua
Lycaonicâ, and which has been
printed in the 3d vol. of his
Opusc. Acad. published by prof.
Te-Water, at Leyden, 1809.
Other dissertations on the same
subject by different learned men
have been brought together in
a work, entitled, Thesaur. Nov.
Dissert. ex Musæo Hasæi et
Ikenii, tom. II. p. 625—661.

history such scattered notices and hints as it has placed within our reach. Scanty and imperfect as that source is found to be, it is so far satisfactory, that it does not present us, as in the cases of Greece and Italy, with conflicting systems and opinions scarcely reconcilable with each other. It may be remarked, in the first place, that the ancients did not look upon any of the tribes of Asia Minor as autochthonous. In the next place, all those writers whose testimony is thought to have most weight, agree in deriving the origin of those tribes from two principal sources or channels, though diametrically opposed to each other, considered geographically; I mean the nations of Upper Asia and the Thracians of Europe: the former penetrating into the peninsula by the Syrian gates and the upper valleys of the Euphrates; the latter, by the straits of Byzantium. This being premised, we have now to consider by which of these two routes Asia Minor received its first settlers. Taking then the Mosaic account as the basis of our investigation, it will be seen at once that the descendants of Noah, after their dispersion in the plains of Mesopotamia, would, from their proximity to Asia Minor, have had time, not only to occupy its nearest provinces, but to spread over the whole country, before their more northern brethren could reach the Bosphorus by the slow and circuitous journey round the Palus Mæotis and the shores of the Euxine. Not to mention that the process of crossing an arm of the sea, in order to occupy a country, implies necessarily a state of things somewhat removed from a rude and primitive order of society, and supposes consequently a period much subsequent to the primeval dissemination of mankind recorded in the book of Genesis.

Probability then alone would lead us to derive the origin of the primary settlers in Asia Minor from the plains around the Euphrates and Tigris. But this ceases to be even a matter for inquiry, when we find how strongly it is confirmed by the testimony of history. We are assured by Herodotus, that in the time of Crœsus all the tract of country to the east of the Halys was occupied by a race of Syrians, whom the Greeks termed Leuco-Syri, or the White Syrians, in order to distinguish them from their more sunburnt kinsmen, who occupied the country to the S. E. of the Amanus and the shores of the Mediterranean as far as Palestine. Herodotus affirms, that the Cappadocians, a name derived from the Persians, were Syrians; and by extending their country to the shore of the Euxine, it is evident that he included the people of Paphlagonia and Pontus under the same denomination and race. (I. 72. 76.) Under the Cappadocians too we must range the inhabitants of Lycaonia and Isauria, who, though speaking a dialect of their own, are classed by Strabo with the former people. (XII. p. 533.) The Cilicians are spoken of as a nation distinct from the Cappadocians, but it is highly probable that they were only another branch of the same eastern stock. Herodotus states that they were originally called Hypachæi, but had taken the name which they then bore from Cilix, the son of Agenor, (VII. 91.) which is saying, in other words, that they received a Phœnician colony. The presence of this most ancient and remarkable people in

several parts of Asia Minor, at a very remote period, is too well attested, by the direct as well as the
indirect testimony of antiquity, to be called in question, even if we should not be disposed to go so far
as Bochart and his followers have done in the etymological system. If we range along the southern
coast of Asia Minor from Cilicia, we · shall find
traces of the Phœnicians in Pamphylia, though that
name is certainly Greek, but indicative, at the same
time, of a mixed and heterogeneous population ; we
find traces of them beyond Pamphylia, in the country of the ancient Solymi, who are always spoken
of as the first inhabitants of what was afterwards
called Pisidia. Still further to the west, we hear of
them on the coast of Caria, and in the island of
Rhodes, under the names of Telchines and Heliades.
There is little doubt that the Cilices of Homer, who
occupied the plain of Thebe in the Troad, as well
as the Dactili of mount Ida, were also Phœnicians.
We have the authority of Thucydides for believing
that the same people had, at a very early period,
settled in several of the Greek islands. (I. 8.) Herodotus affirms, that they colonized Thasus. Other
authorities speak of their establishments on the
shores of the Propontis and Hellespont. And there
is every reason to believe, with Bochart[f], that the
worship of the Cabiri, and the Samothracian mys-
teries, were first introduced by them, and afterwards
adopted by the Pelasgi. According to Strabo, Cadmus and his Phœnicians[g] had first occupied Eubœa
before they colonized Bœotia. It is also highly probable that the Carians and Pelasgi, the earliest

[f] Geogr. Sacr. I. 12. p. 394.
[g] Strabo calls them Ara-
bians, (X. p. 447.) Cf. Plut.
Thes. tom. I. p. 1

people among the Greeks who made any proficiency in nautical affairs, derived their instruction from this enterprising race.

Thus we have seen that the whole coast of Asia Minor was covered with Phœnician establishments at a period of remote antiquity, while a branch of the same people occupied, in land, the whole of the country which lies between the Halys and the Euphrates. But however the former river might have been the boundary of the Leuco-Syrians to the west, in the time of Crœsus, it is not to be supposed that this had always been the limit of the Asiatic colonists of the peninsula. On the contrary, it is plain, as we have before stated, that they must have had time to spread over the whole country before the Thracian tribes had become strong and populous enough to cross the Bosphorus, and occupy the shores of the Propontis. It is probable too that the Syrians of Cappadocia and Cilicia were the last and most recent influx of Asiatic tribes, those who preceded them having become blended with the hordes which successively crossed over from Europe, and thus preserving but faint and imperfect traces of their primary origin[h].

Having thus brought forward what evidence we possess of the population of Asia Minor having been derived in the first instance from more eastern coun-

[h] Most of the commentators on the book of Genesis suppose Asia Minor to have been occupied by the immediate descendants of Gomer, Askenaz, whose name is thought to bear some resemblance to that of Ascania, and Riphath and Togarmah. Others, however, have imagined, that it was peopled by the descendants of Shem, among whom Aram would be the progenitor of the Syrians, and Lud of the Lydians. Bochart, Geogr. Sacr. III. 8 and 9. p. 171. II. 12. p. 83.

tries, we may pass on to consider summarily what
additions were subsequently made to it from Europe. I have stated already, that according to the
concurrent testimony of antiquity we must admit
the European origin of several extensive tribes in
Asia Minor. Of these, the earliest and most numerous appear to have been the Phrygians, who, as
we learn from Herodotus, on the authority of traditions preserved by the Macedonians, once dwelt
in their country under the name of Bryges; but
having crossed into Asia at a period of which we
cannot now form any accurate notion, they changed
that appellation to the form under which it was
ever after known. (I. 72.) The testimony of Herodotus is confirmed by that of Strabo, who quotes
from Xanthus, the Lydian historian, and Menecrates, of Elæa, (XII. p. 572. Cf. VII. p. 295. XII.
p. 550.) and Conon. (ap. Phot. Narrat. I. p. 424.
Cf. Plin. V. 32.) It may be observed also, that
there existed a people named Brygi in Macedonian
Thrace, in the time of Herodotus[i], (VI. 45. VII.
185.) and the same historian alludes to traditions
which represented that country as the original abode
of the Phrygian Midas. (VIII. 138.) On such evidence it seems impossible to deny the fact of a migration of these Thracian Bryges into Asia at an
uncertain epoch, but certainly prior to the Trojan
war, since the Phrygians are clearly mentioned by
Homer as a people of Asia Minor. (B. 862. Γ. 184.)
As to those traditions which assign to the Phrygians a date anterior even to the formation of the
Ægyptian nation, (Herod. II. 2.) if any credit is due

[i] The word *briga* appears to
have belonged to the ancient
Thracians as well as to the
Celts. Strabo VII.

to them, they must apply, I conceive, to that indigenous race who occupied this rich and fertile country before the Thracian ᐧ migration, and became
united by conquest with their successful invaders.
Herodotus, too, clearly recognises an affinity between
the Phrygians and the Armenians; (VII. 73.) and
though I suspect that the fact is exactly the reverse
of what he states, and that the Armenians were the
progenitors of the Phrygians rather than descended
from them, the tradition seems to strengthen the
idea of what may be called an Asiatic foundation in
the Phrygian stock.

Antiquity is not less positive respecting the Thracian origin of the Lydians, Carians, and Mysians,
though there are many questions which render the
early history of these nations intricate and perplexing; these will be considered more at length when
we come to examine the origin of each people separately. At present it will be sufficient to state generally, that the three nations above mentioned acknowledged a common origin, (Herod. I. 172. Strab.
XIV. p. 659.) and if it be true that the Mysi in particular were the same as the Mœsi of Thrace, and
came from that country, (Strab. XII. p. 571. VII.
p. 303.) it will follow, that the Carians and Lydians
had also their primary seats in the same part of the
European continent.   ᐧ

From the southern position occupied by the Carians, it is reasonable to suppose that they came first
in the order of migration. Herodotus has stated,
that this people occupied first of all the Cyclades,
and other islands, under the name of Leleges; but
that having been driven from thence by Minos, on
account of their piracies, they passed over to the

Asiatic continent. The historian, however, observes, that the Carians themselves affirmed that their nation had always been possessors of the province which derived its name from them. (I. 171.) The first account, however, confirmed as it is by Thucydides, (I. 4.) and other weighty testimonies, has doubtless superior claims to our attention. Amongst these must not be forgotten that of Homer, who brings together the Carians, Leleges, Pelasgi, and Caucones, people all apparently of Thracian origin, and of wandering habits. (Il. K. 480.)

Next in order to the Carians are the Lydians, or, as they are more anciently called, the Mæones; at least it appears to have been the more general opinion among the ancients that they ought to be identified. Some writers, however, as Strabo affirms, looked upon them as two distinct nations. (XII. p. 571. XIII. p. 625.) Homer appears to have known only the name of Mæones, which, according to Herodotus, was also the more ancient appellation. (VII. 74.) It must be confessed, however, that this change of name, as well as the whole account of the Lydian dynasties, together with the celebrated tradition of the Tyrrhenian migration, recorded by that historian, are all alike unsatisfactory, and beset with great difficulties, especially in regard to chronology. These will be fully discussed when we come to treat of Lydia in particular; but I will only observe by the way, that when we find among the Lydian kings of the Heraclid dynasty the names of Ninus and Belus, it is impossible not to admit that there must have been some connexion, though Herodotus was not aware of it, between Lydia and the ancient kingdom of Assyria;

a circumstance which tends to confirm our hypothesis of an Asiatic *substratum* in the population of the
entire peninsula.

The Mysi, whose Thracian origin appears least
subject to dispute, if we may judge from their more
northern position, settled in Asia posterior to the
Mæonian migration. Indeed Herodotus affirms, that
they were a colony (ἄποικοι) of the Lydians. (VII. 74.)
This people always retained, as it should seem, a
footing in the European continent; and it is to that
more ancient and considerable part of the nation
that we must perhaps refer that great invasion of
Pæonia and Macedonia recorded by Herodotus as
having taken place before the Trojan war, though
it is certain that the historian expressly states that
they crossed over on that occasion from Asia into
Europe in conjunction with the Teucri. (VII. 20.
75.)   The latter people, who are probably the ancestors of the Trojans, certainly formed settlements
on the Asiatic shores of the Hellespont, with the
Mysi and Dardani, at an early period ; but we must
look for the original seat of all these tribes in the
great Pannonian and Mœsian plains, south of the
Danube.   It must be observed, that Herodotus himself supposes that the Pæonians were descendants
of the Teucri, (V. 13.) but this could hardly be true
of the Trojan Teucri.   And when we find that the
Dardani, who were certainly Illyrians, and contiguous to the Mœsi, boasted of having anciently
been masters of all Pæonia, (Liv. XLV. 29.) it is
natural to suspect that the Teucri belonged to the
same European stock, whether of Thracian or Illyrian origin.

The Bithynians are another Thracian people, but

belonging apparently to a different family from that
of the three important tribes we have just mentioned.   Herodotus affirms, that they were originally called Strymonii, from the great Macedonian
river on whose banks they were settled.   But having been disturbed by the irruption of the Teucri
and Mysi, they finally crossed over into Asia, and
took the name of Bithyni. (VII. 75.)   The Thracian origin of the Bithyni is also attested by Xenophon, (Anab. VI. 4, 1.) and Strabo, (XII. p. 511.)
And I should imagine that Homer alludes to this
people under the name of Hellespontine Thracians,
in his account of the Trojan forces and their allies.
(Il. B. 844.)   To the great Thracian family belong
also the Mariandyni, Bebryces, Doliones, Caucones,
and other early and obscure tribes, which once had
a separate political existence on the shores of the
Propontis and Euxine, but became merged afterwards in the general nomenclature of Mysians and
Bithynians. (Strab. XII. p. 542.)   Respecting the
Paphlagonians, who follow next in the same line of
coast, it is not so easy to form an opinion ; as the
writers of antiquity seem to be silent on the question of their origin.   According to Strabo, they
were certainly a different people from the Cappadocians, and yet he allows that there were many
words common to the two nations ; whence it might
be inferred, that the Paphlagonians were a mixed
people, formed from the Leuco-Syri, or Cappadocians, and some other race ; which, if not Thracian,
came most probably from Scythia.   The Amazons,
who settled on the Paphlagonian coast, were believed by many to have come from that vast country, as well as the Halizones and Heneti, ranked

by Homer among the Paphlagones. (Il. B. 851. Strab. XII. p. 543.) And it is not improbable that some of the minor tribes which occupied the coasts and mountainous regions of Pontus, as far as Colchis, might trace part of their population to a Scythian source; the rest being derived, more especially in the case of the Chalybes and Chaldæi, from Armenia and Assyria.

Having thus endeavoured to analyse succinctly the probable elements of what may be called the barbarian population of Asia Minor, I shall proceed to give a brief and general history of Greek colonization in that extensive country.

If we are to allow the Pelasgi the honour of being considered the progenitors of the Hellenic race, we may then look upon their settlements in Asia Minor before the siege of Troy, as the first attempts to establish Grecian colonists in that country. Next to the Pelasgic migrations, we must place the settlements formed by Minos, who seems to have reigned, not only over Crete and the Cyclades, but to have had possessions on the coast of Caria and Lycia. In the former country, Sarpedon, his brother, is said to have founded Miletus; in the latter, the same chief established his Cretan bands, named Termilæ, after having driven from the coasts or exterminated the Milyæ and Solymi, the first possessors of the country, and descended, as appears most probable, from the Phœnicians or Syrians. But a fresh change was again introduced on the arrival of Lycaon, or Lycus, son of Pandion king of Athens, and the whole population was thenceforth designated by the name of Lycians. (Herod. I. 173. Strab. XII. p. 573.)

We must likewise place before the siege of Troy the colonization of Rhodes and Cos by the descendants of Hercules, (Il. B. 655. Strab. loc. cit.) and that of Mysia by Telephus. (Strab. XIII. p. 615.) Some of the Hellespontine towns, such as Abydos and Cyzicus, owed their foundation to Greek or Pelasgic colonists before the same era. Other cities on the coast of Pamphylia, Cilicia, and Cyprus, are supposed to be nearly coeval with the downfall of Troy. But the most numerous and important migrations from the Grecian continent were posterior to that celebrated event. The first of these was the Æolic colony, led, as we learn from Strabo and Pausanias, by some descendants of Orestes, after the death of that prince, through Thessaly and Thrace to the Hellespont; whence they crossed over into Asia, and occupied the shores of the ancient Troas, and the island of Lesbos. (Strab. XIII. p.582. Pausan. Lacon. 2.) Other descendants of Agamemnon shortly after crossed over from Thessaly, with a fresh body of Æolian colonists, and founded Cumæ, south of the Caicus. Strabo places these events about 60 years after the fall of Troy, and not long before the return of the Heraclidæ into the Peloponnesus.

The Ionian migration was four generations later, or 1130 B. C. It was composed principally of Ionians from Attica and Ægialus, subsequently called Achaia; but Herodotus affirms, that a large portion of the colony was composed of people who had nothing in common with the Ionian name. These settled on the coast of Asia Minor, then occupied by the Carians and Leleges, whom they expelled; and having founded twelve principal cities, formed themselves into a federal government, which held its meetings in the temple called Panionium. (I. 146. Strab. XIV. p. 633. Pausan. Achaic. 2.)

The coast of Caria, to the south of Cape Posidium, was occupied by Dorian Greeks, who migrated at different periods from Megara, Trœzene, Argos, and other cities of the mother country. The principal colonies then formed were Halicarnassus and Cnidus, with the islands of Rhodes and Cos, which together constituted the Dorian confederacy; whose meetings were held at Triopium. (Herod. I. 144.) Besides these, numerous single settlements were from time to time formed by the Greeks, both on the shores of the Euxine and those of the Cilician and Pamphylian seas. Insensibly also they spread themselves in the interior of the peninsula, as well in Lydia and Phrygia as in Galatia and Cappadocia; so that finally there was not a province, from the Ægean to the Euphrates, which could not boast of possessing more than one Greek colony. It is this circumstance which gives to Asia Minor its classical character and principal historical interest, and causes it to be associated, in the mind of the scholar and the antiquary, with all that we admire in Grecian genius and taste. It is true, that the Greeks of Asia Minor, owing to the softness of the climate, and the debasing influence of a despotic government, afford us no such recollections as the glorious achievements of the sons of Hellas recall to the mind; yet it is certain, that in refinement, and the cultivation of the arts, they were at least equal, if not superior, to their European brethren. If Asia Minor cannot boast of having given birth to warriors and statesmen, she glories justly in her poets,

her historians and philosophers, her sculptors, painters, architects, and musicians. And in the three
first departments she may more especially boast of
having rather served as a guide to the mother country than followed in her train [k].

We learn from Herodotus, that subsequent to the
establishment of the Greek colonies Asia Minor was
overrun consecutively by large bodies of Cimmerians and Scythians; the former being propelled,
as we often find was the case with barbarian migrations, and pursued by a more powerful horde of
Scythians from the Caspian and over mount Caucasus, to the shores of Pontus, whence they afterwards penetrated into Lydia, and took Sardis. (Herod. I. 6. and 15. IV. 1. 11. 12.) But this irruption was of short duration, as the barbarians, being
unable to secure a permanent footing in the country, were soon expelled by Alyattes, king of Lydia.
(Herod. I. 16.) Many centuries after, another barbarian horde, coming from the west of Europe, arrived, after traversing several countries, and expe-
riencing various vicissitudes of fortune on the Byzantine territory. These were a body of Gauls,
who had left their country under the banners of
Brennus; and having survived the disasters which
befell their countrymen in Greece and Thrace, reached the Hellespont, whence they crossed over into
Asia, at the instigation of Nicomedes, king of Bithynia, and finally settled in that part of the peninsula which took from them the name of Gallo-

[k] In poetry Asia lays claim
to Homer, Hesiod, Sappho,
Alcæus, Anacreon, Mimner-
mus, Hipponax, and Nicander.
In philosophy, to Thales, Pythagoras, Anaxagoras, Bias,
and Pittacus. In history, to
Hecatæus, Charon, Hellanicus, Xanthus, Herodotus, Ctesias, and Ephorus.

Græcia, or Galatia. (Liv. XXXVIII. 16. Strab.
XII. p. 566.) This was the last important addition made to the population of Asia Minor; and on
looking back to the mixed character of its inhabitants, and the many revolutions it has experienced
from the earliest period, we must feel how hopeless
a task it would be, even with less scanty materials
than those which we possess, to trace the languages
and dialects of the peninsula to a common primitive
source.

In the description of Asia Minor, the geographers
of antiquity appear to have adhered to no fixed plan
of arrangement, but to have followed that order
which accorded with their whole system. Thus
Strabo begins his description with Cappadocia, and
proceeds through the remaining provinces from east
to west, because he had been led by his periegesis
of northern Asia to Armenia. Scylax and Scymnus, of Chios, set out from Colchis, and so make the
circuit of the peninsula from Pontus to Cilicia.
Pomponius, Mela, and Pliny, on the contrary, begin with Cilicia, and proceed round the whole of
the coast to the river Phasis. Ptolemy takes first
the north coast from the Hellespont to the extremity
of the Euxine, and then returns to the Hellespont
to describe the western and southern coasts.

This method of description being evidently arbi-
trary, I have preferred adhering to that of D'Anville,
as being both most simple and natural in itself, and
as agreeing better with the practice I have generally
observed in my other geographical works, of commencing the periegesis or periplus of a country from
west to east, and from north to south. D'Anville
has, with great perspicuity, divided the peninsula

into three parallel strips, each containing four sections. According to this arrangement, Asia Minor will comprise twelve principal provinces, which are as follows: 1. Mysia, including the Hellespontine district and the Troad, with the Æolian colonies. 2. Bithynia. 3. Paphlagonia. 4. Pontus. 5. Lydia, including the Ionian towns and islands. 6. Phrygia, including Lycaonia. 7. Galatia. 8. Cappadocia, together with Armenia Minor. 9. Caria, with its islands. 10. Lycia. 11. Pamphylia, including Pisidia. 12. Cilicia. The last section will be devoted to the island of Cyprus.

SECTION II.

MYSIA AND TROAS.

Origin and history of the Mysians—The Hellespont and Propontis—Interior of Mysia—The Teucri and Dardani—Ancient Ilium and the Homeric topography—The Troad—Æolian colonies—Kingdom of Pergamus—Island of Lesbos.

I<small>T</small> was the prevailing opinion of antiquity that the Mysians were not an indigenous people of Asia, but that they had been transplanted to its shores from the banks of the Danube, where the original race maintained itself under the name of Mœsi, by which they were known to the Romans for several centuries after the Christian era. (Strab. VII. p. 303. Artemid. ap. eund. XII. p. 571.) Nor is that opinion at variance with the tradition which looked upon this people as of a kindred race with the Carians and Lydians, since these two nations were likewise supposed to have come from Thrace ; (Herod. I. 172. Strab. XIV. p. 659.) nor with another which regarded them in particular as descended from the Lydians, in whose language the word *mysos* signified *a beech*, which tree it was further observed abounded in the woods of the Mysian Olympus. Strabo, who has copied these particulars from Xanthus the Lydian and Menecrates of Elæa, states also on their authority that the Mysian dialect was a mixture of those of Phrygia and Lydia. (Strab. XII.

p. 572. Steph. Byz. v. Μυσία) We may collect from Herodotus that the Mysians were already a numerous and powerful people before the Trojan war, since he speaks of a vast expedition having been undertaken by them, in conjunction with the Teucri, into Europe, in the course of which they subjugated the whole of Thrace and Macedonia as far as the Peneus and the Ionian sea. (VII. 20. 75.) Subsequent, however, to this period, the date of which is very remote and uncertain, it appears that the Mysi were confined in Asia Minor, within limits which correspond but little with such extensive conquests. Strabo is inclined to suppose that their primary seat in that country was the district which surrounds mount Olympus, from whence he thinks they were afterwards driven by the Phrygians, and forced to retire to the banks of the Caïcus, where the Arcadian Telephus became their king. (Eurip. ap. Aristot. Rhet. III. 2. Strab. XII. p. 572. Hygin. Fab. CI.) But it appears from Herodotus that they still occupied the Olympian district in the time of Crœsus, whose subjects they had become, and whose aid they requested to destroy the wild boar which ravaged their country. (I. 36.) Strabo himself also recognises the division of this people into the Mysians of mount Olympus and those of the Caïcus. (XII. p. 571.) These two districts answer respectively to the Mysia Minor and Major of Ptolemy. Homer enumerates the Mysi among the allies of Priam in several passages, but he nowhere defines their territory, or even names their towns ; in one place indeed he evidently assigns to them a situation among the Thracians of Europe.

Νόσφιν ἐφ' ἱπποπόλων Θρῃκῶν καθορώμενος αἶαν,
Μυσῶν τ' ἀγχεμάχων, καὶ ἀγαυῶν Ἱππημολγῶν,
Γλακτοφάγων, ἀβίων τε, δικαιοτάτων ἀνθρώπων.

Iʟ. N. 5.

(Cf. Strab. VII. p. 303.)

The Mysians of Asia had become subject to the Lydian monarchs in the reign of Alyattes, father to Crœsus, and perhaps earlier ; as appears from a passage of Nicolaus Damascenus, who reports that Crœsus had been appointed to the government of the territory of Adramyttium and the Theban plain during the reign of his father. (Creuzer. Hist. Frag. p. 203.) Strabo even affirms that Troas was already subjected in the reign of Gyges. (XIII. p. 590.) On the dissolution of the Lydian empire they passed, together with the other nations of Asia, under the Persian dominion, and formed part of the third satrapy in the division made by Darius, (Herod. III. 90. VII. 74.) After the death of Alexander, they were annexed to the Syrian empire ; but on the defeat of Antiochus, the Romans rewarded the services of Eumenes, king of Pergamus, with the grant of a district, situated so conveniently with regard to his own dominions, and which he had already occupied with his forces. (Polyb. XXII. 27, 10. Liv. XXXVIII. 39.) At a later period Mysia was annexed to the Roman proconsular province ; (Cic. Ep. ad Qu. Frat. I. 8.) but under the emperors it formed a separate district, and was governed by a procurator. (Athen. IX. p. 398. E.) It is to be observed also, that St. Luke, in the Acts, distinguishes Mysia from the neighbouring provinces of Bithynia and Troas. (XVI. 7. and 8.)

The Greeks have stigmatized the Mysians as a cowardly and imbecile race, who would suffer themselves to be injured and plundered by their neighbours in the most passive manner. Hence the proverbial expression Μυσῶν λεία, used by Demosthenes (Cor. p. 248, 23.) and Aristotle (Rhet. I. 12, 20) ; to which Cicero also alludes when he says, " Quid " porro in Græco sermone tam tritum atque celebra- " tum est, quam, si quis despicatui ducitur, ut My- " sorum ultimus esse dicatur." (Orat. pro Flacc. c. 27.) Elsewhere the same writer describes them as a tribe of barbarians, without taste for literature and the arts of civilized life. (Orat. c. 8.)

It is extremely difficult, as Strabo had already observed, to assign to the Mysians their precise limits, since they appear to have varied continually from the time of Homer, and are very loosely marked by all the ancient geographers from Scylax to Ptolemy. Strabo conceives that the Homeric boundaries of the Lesser Mysia were the Æsepus to the west, and Bithynia to the east ; (XII. p. 564.) but Scylax removes them considerably to the east of this position by placing the Mysians on the gulf of Cius. (Peripl. p. 35.) Ptolemy, on the other hand, has extended the Mysian territory to the west as far as Lampsacus, while to the east he separates it from Bithynia by the river Rhyndacus. The more eligible arrangement in this difficulty will be to look to the physical division of the coast, and to neglect distinctions which appear so variable and uncertain. I propose, therefore, to subdivide the whole extent of coast belonging to this section into three portions ; the former comprising what is situated on the Propontis between the Rhyndacus and the headland of

Priapus, now *Karaboa*, where the Hellespont commences; the second, the Hellespontine shore from
the last mentioned point to the promontory of Sigeum, where the strait terminates; the third and
last part will include Troas and the Æolian colonies
as far as the Caïcus, together with the islands of
Tenedos and Lesbos.   In the interior we shall have
to examine what belongs to the two Mysias, and we
shall conclude the section with the history of Pergamus and its kingdom, and the Æolian towns near
the mouth of the river Hermus.

Propontis.   The Greeks gave the name of Propontis to that
minor bason which lies betwixt the Ægean and the
Euxine, and communicates with those seas by means
of two narrow straits, the Hellespont and Bosphorus.
Herodotus estimates its breadth at 500 stadia, and
its length at 1400. (IV. 85.)   Modern navigators
reckon about 120 miles from one strait to another,
while its greatest breadth from the European to
the Asiatic coast does not exceed forty miles.   Towards its south-eastern extremity it forms a deep
bay, at the end of which was situated the ancient
town and harbour of Cius; and immediately to the
north of this another, formerly called Astacenus
Sinus, from the port of Astacus placed on its shores.
The modern appellation of *Marmara* which has
been given to the Propontis is derived from the
island of that name, anciently called Proconnesus [a].

Priapus.   The first town to be noticed on entering the Propontis from the Hellespont is Priapus, founded, as

[a] For a description of the
sea of *Marmara*, see Belon, Observations sur plusieurs singu-
larités et choses memorables
trouvées en Grèce, Asie, &c.
II. 1. Thevenot, Voyages au Levant, p. I. l. i. c. 15. Walpole's
Turkey, vol. II. p. 46.

Strabo reports, by a colony from Miletus, or, as others relate, by the inhabitants of Cyzicus. The god Priapus, whom it was said a nymph had borne to Bacchus, gave his name to this town, whose territory produced excellent wine, a circumstance which sufficiently accounts for the worship paid to him there. (Strab. XIII. p. 587. Schol. Theocr. I. 21.) Thucydides speaks of Priapus as a naval station. (VIII. 107.) It surrendered to Alexander before the battle of the Granicus. (Arrian. Exp. Alex. I. 13. Cf. Strab. loc. cit. Scyl. Peripl. p. 35. Plin. V. 40. Steph. Byz. v. Πρίαπος.) The modern name is *Karaboa* [b]. A little to the east was a spot called Harpagium, or Harpagia, where, according to mythologists, Ganymede was snatched away by the eagle of Jove. (Strab. loc. cit. Athen. XIII. p. 601. Steph. Byz. v. Ἁρπάγια.) Thucydides notices it in conjunction with Priapus (loc. cit.) The surrounding district was known by the name of Adrastea, which is also that of a small town situated to the west of Priapus. Homer has spoken of this little tract of country in his Catalogue of the Trojan forces. (Il. B. 828.) Strabo, on the authority of Callisthenes, reports that it took its name from king Adrastus, who erected there a temple to Adrastea, or Nemesis. (XIII. p. 588. Steph. Byz. v. Ἀδράστεια.) Through the Adrasteian plain flowed the Granicus, which, according to Demetrius of Scepsis, had its source in mount Cotylus, belonging to the chain of Ida. (Strab. XIII. p. 602.) The Table Itinerary marks twenty-seven miles between its mouth and Priapus. Homer enu-

Marginal notes: Harpagium. Adrastea regio. Granicus fl.

b There are both autonomous and imperial coins of Priapus. The legend is ΠΡΙΑ. ΠΡΙΑΠ. and ΠΡΙΑΠΗΝ. Sestin. Mon. Vet. p. 73.

merates the Granicus with the other streams which
descended from Ida [c].

Δὴ τότε μητιόωντο Ποσειδάων καὶ Ἀπόλλων
Τεῖχος ἀμαλδῦναι, ποταμῶν μένος εἰσαγάγοντες,
Ὅσσοι ἀπ᾽ Ἰδαίων ὀρέων ἅλαδε προρέουσι,
Ῥῆσός θ᾽, Ἑπτάπορός τε, Κάρησός τε, Ῥοδίος τε,
Γρήνικός τε, καὶ Αἴσηπος, διός τε Σκάμανδρος.

This torrent is celebrated in history on account of
the signal victory gained on its banks by Alexander
the Great over the Persian army 334 B. C. (Arrian.
I. 13. Plut. Alex. c. 24. Diod. Sic. XVII. 19.)

The Granicus is the river of *Dimotiko,* mentioned
by Chishull [d]. " At this place," says the traveller,
" occurs a moderate river with a wooden bridge ;
" and an hour beyond the town, a large one with a
" fair bridge of stone." The small river which here
met the Granicus was thought by some to be the
Rhesus of Homer. (Demetr. Sceps. ap. Strab. XIII.
p. 602.) Strabo places on its banks an ancient city

Sidene. named Sidene, which once possessed an ample territory, and was governed by a prince named Glaucias ;
but having been taken and destroyed by Crœsus, it
never rose from its ruins. (XIII. p. 587. 601.) *Di-
motico,* as Chishull supposes, answers probably to a

Didymi-
teiche. town named Didymi-teiche, which Polybius places
in this part of Mysia. (V. 77.)

Æsepus fl. The Æsepus flowed also from mount Cotylus,
and after a course of 500 stadia emptied itself in the
Propontis, to the east of the Granicus. (Demetr.
Sceps. ap. Strab. XIII. p. 602.) Strabo conceives
that Homer extended the boundaries of Priam's

[c] Mannert is therefore mistaken when he says that Homer
was not acquainted with the
Granicus, vol. VI. p. iii. p. 523.
[d] Travels in Turkey, p. 60.

kingdom to this river, (XIII. p. 582.) It is now
called *Boklu*, as appears from Chishull, who crossed
it on his way from *Mihalick* to *Lampsaki*. He
came, he says, " to *Bozaegee*, seated in the Adras-
" tian plains ; and at the same place to a large and
" fair river, named by the Turks *Boclew*, which `
" we leave on our left hand, till in two hours we
" cross it by a dangerous wooden bridge near *Sor-*
" *ricui*[e]." Chishull, however, mistook the Æsepus for
the Rhyndacus. Mons. Gosselin calls the Æsepus
Sataldere[f]. The Barenus, or Varenus, of Anna
Comnena, is probably no other than the Æsepus.
She describes it as flowing from a mountain named
Ibibus, from whence spring also several other rivers,
such as the Scamander, Angelo-Cometes, and Empe-
lus. The Ibibus I take to be the Cotylus of Demetrius Scepsius. (Ann. Comn. p. 439. B.)

At the distance of eighty stadia from the mouth of Zeleia.
the Æsepus, and 190 from Cyzicus, Strabo places
the ancient Zeleia, the city of Pandarus.

> Οἱ δὲ Ζέλειαν ἔναιον ὑπαὶ πόδα νείατον Ἴδης,
> Ἀφνειοὶ, πίνοντες ὕδωρ μέλαν Αἰσήποιο,
> Τρῶες· τῶν αὖτ' ἦρχε Λυκάονος ἀγλαὸς υἱὸς,
> Πάνδαρος, ᾧ καὶ τόξον Ἀπόλλων αὐτὸς ἔδωκεν.
>
> IL. B. 824.

Here it may be observed that the poet describes
the subjects of Pandarus as Trojans, but Strabo
remarks that elsewhere he designates them as Lycians, alluding probably to the line

> Οὐδέ τις ἐν Λυκίῃ σέογ' εὔχεται εἶναι ἀμείνων.
>
> IL. E. 172.

[e] Travels in Turkey, p. 59.
[f] Note to the French Strabo, tom. IV. p. 187.

D 3

which, however, might only be meant to express,
that even the archers of Lycia, a country celebrated
for its bowmen, could not equal the skill of Pandarus.   However, some lines above, that chief himself speaks of Lycia as his mother country;

.   .   .   .   εἰ ἐτεόν με
ʼΏρσεν ἄναξ, Διὸς υἱὸς, ἀπορνύμενον Λυκίηθεν.
Il. E. 105.

but how or when this colony came to settle on the
Trojan territory, Homer has never informed us.
The epithet of ʼΑφνειοὶ, given to the same people,
was thought to be derived, as Strabo informs us,
from the lake Aphnitis, otherwise called Dascylitis.
(XIII. p. 587.)   Homer elsewhere terms Zeleia " the
" sacred city."

Οἴκαδε νοστήσας ἱερῆς εἰς ἄστυ Ζελείης.
Il. Δ. 103.

Zeleia is mentioned by Arrian as the head quarters of the Persian army prior to the battle of the
Granicus; (I. 13.) and it is evident from Strabo
that it still existed in that geographer's time. (Cf.
Plin. V. 40. Steph. Byz. v. Ζέλεια.)   Chishull must
have passed near the site of this town between
Bozaegee and *Sorricui* [g].   Mons. Gosselin calls it
Biga [h].   Above Zeleia was a mountain named Pirossus, where the sovereigns of Lydia and the Persian monarchs had a park, for the diversion of hunt-
ing. (Strab. XIII. p. 589.)   Some geographers identified it with the Terea of Homer.   Not far from
the mouth of the Æsepus, Strabo places the tomb of
Memnon, son of Aurora, and near it a small town
of the same name as that hero. (XIII. p. 587. Pau-

Pirossus mons.

Memnonis tumulus et vicus.

[g] Travels in Turkey, p. 59.
[h] French Strabo, tom. IV. p. 149. marg.

san. Phoc. c. 31, 2.) Beyond Zeleia is the river Tarsius fl.
Tarsius, which, as Strabo asserts, travellers had to
pass twenty times ; but he does not state on what
route. Chishull, who crossed it once only, describes
it as " a fair and broad river, now called *Tarza* by
" the Turks." He was informed that it fell into a
neighbouring lake, and afterwards into the sea [i].

We must now return to the coast, to speak of Cy- Cyzicus.
zicus, the largest and most celebrated city on the
shores of the Propontis. Its first foundation is
ascribed by Conon to a colony of Pelasgi from Thessaly, under the conduct of Cyzicus, son of Apollo,
and Aristides speaks of the god himself as the founder of the city. (Orat. Cyzic. I. p. 414.) In process
of time the Pelasgi were expelled by the Tyrrheni,
and those again made way for the Milesians, who
are generally looked upon by the Greeks as the real
settlers to whom its foundation is to be attributed.
(Conon. Narrat. XLI. Strab. XIV. p. 635.) According to several ancient writers, the first inhabitants of the Cyzicene district were the Doliones, a Doliones.
people of great antiquity and uncertain origin.
(Strab. XII. p. 575. Apollod. ap. eund. XIV. p. 681.)

> Ἰσθμὸν δ' αὖ πεδίον τε Δολίονες ἀμφενέμοντο
> Ἀνέρες· ἐν δ' ἥρως Αἰνήϊος υἱὸς ἄνασσε
> Κύζικος.   APOLLON. RHOD. I. 947.

They occupied the tract of country which lay between the Æsepus and the lake Dascylitis. (Strab.
loc. cit.) They are not mentioned by Homer, nor
has he spoken of Cyzicus. Herodotus informs us,
that Cyzicus had become subject to the Persian empire in the reign of Darius, having surrendered to

[i] Travels, p. 58, 59.

Œbares, satrap of Dascylium. (VI. 33.) After the
battle of Mycale, it appears to have been wrested
from Xerxes, with the other Hellespontine cities, by
the Grecian fleet, and with them it became after-
ward tributary to Athens. Having revolted from
that city in consequence of the disasters of Sicily, it
was recovered by her fleet after the battle of Cynossema, being then, as we learn from Thucydides,
without fortifications. (VIII. 107.) Not long after,
Alcibiades completely defeated the Lacedæmonian
fleet under Mindarus off Cyzicus, and again entered
that city which had been occupied by the Lacedæmonian admiral and Pharnabazus. Alcibiades, on
this occasion, levied a heavy fine on the inhabitants.
(Xen. Hell. I. 9.) After the battle of Ægospotami,
Cyzicus received a Spartan harmost ; (Xen. Anab.
VI. 2. VII. 3.) but at the peace of Antalcidas it
once more reverted to the Persians. Alexander took
possession of it after his victory on the banks of the
Granicus, and caused the island on which it was
built to be connected with the main land by means
of a bridge. (Plin. V. 32.) After the death of that
prince, we find this city retaining its independence,
and powerful enough to interpose its mediation between Ptolemy Philopator and Antiochus. (Polyb.
V. 63, 5.) The Cyzicenes were also allied to the
kings of Pergamus, and through their means secured
the favour and protection of Rome. (Polyb. XXVI.
6, 13. XXXIII. 11, 2.) At this period their city
was at the height of its prosperity. Florus says of
it, " nobilis arce, mœnibus, portu, turribusque mar-
" moreis, Asiaticæ plagæ litora illustrat." (III. 5.)
Cicero styles it, " urbem Asiæ clarissimam, nobis-
" que amicissimam." (pro Leg. Manil. 8.) Strabo

assures us that it equalled the most renowned cities of Asia in extent and beauty, as well as in the wisdom of its political institutions, and the firmness of its government in time of war or peace. The Cyzicene commonwealth resembled those of Rhodes, Marseilles, and Carthage. They elected three magistrates, who were curators of the public buildings and stores. They possessed extensive arsenals and granaries, and care was taken to preserve the wheat by mixing it with Chalcidic earth. Owing to these wise and salutary precautions, they were enabled to sustain an arduous and memorable siege against Mithridates, king of Pontus, both by sea and land. (74 B. C.) In order that the reader may be better enabled to follow the operations of the siege as they are detailed by Appian and Plutarch, it will be necessary first to give a brief chorographical description of the city and its vicinity.

Cyzicus was placed in an island which is nearly triangular, and about 500 stadia in circuit; its base being turned towards the Propontis, while the vertex advances so close to the continent, that it was easy to connect it by a double bridge. This, as Pliny reports, was accomplished by Alexander. The city was situated partly in the plain which extended to the bridges, and partly on the slope of mount Arcton-oros, which rose above it, towards the north. Another mountain, named Dindymus, overhung the city also in the direction of the Propontis, having on its summit a temple, said to have been erected by the Argonauts in honour of Cybele, who was worshipped by the Cyzicenes with peculiar veneration. (Strab. XII. p. 575.)

Ἔστι δέ τις αἰπεῖα Προποντίδος ἔνδοθι νῆσος,
Τυτθὸν ἀπὸ Φρυγίης πολυληΐου ἠπείροιο
Εἰς ἅλα κεκλιμένη, ὅσσον τ' ἐπιμύρεται ἰσθμὸς,
Χέρσῳ ἐπιπρηνὴς καταείμενος· ἐν δὲ οἱ ἀκταὶ
Ἀμφίδυμοι, κεῖνται δ' ὑπὲρ ὕδατος Αἰσήποιο.
Ἄρκτων μιν καλέουσιν ὄρος περιναιετάοντες.

APOLL. RHOD. I. 936.

Terra sinu medio Pontum jacet inter et Hellen
Ceu fundo prolata maris ; namque improba cæcis
Intulit arva vadis, longoque sub æquora dorso
Litus agit, tenet hinc veterem confinibus oris
Pars Phrygiam, pars discreti juga pinea montis.
Nec procul ad tenuis surgit confinia ponti
Urbs placidis demissa jugis : rex divitis agri
Cyzicus.   VAL. FLACC. II. 630.

(Cf. Ovid. Trist. I. 9. Aristid. Orat. Cyzic.)
It had two ports, which could be closed, and might
contain 200 galleys. One of these harbours was
called Chytus,

Ἡοῖ δ' εἰσανέβαν μέγα Δίνδυμον, ὄφρα καὶ αὐτοὶ
Θηήσαιντο πόρους κείνης ἁλός· ἐν δ' ἄρα τοίγε
Νῆα Χυτοῦ λιμένος προτέρου ἐξήλασαν ὅρμου.

APOLL. RHOD. I. 985.

the other Panormus, as we learn from the Scholiast.
(I. 954.) The latter still retains the name of *Pa-
normo*. The same poet names the two fountains
Artacie and Cleite. (I. 958. 1068.)

Mithridates having assembled an immense force,
estimated by Appian at 300,000 men, by Strabo at
150,000 infantry, with a numerous cavalry, proceeded to invest Cyzicus on the land side by occupying
mount Adrastea, opposite to the town, while he
blockaded it by sea with a fleet of 400 vessels. The
Cyzicenes, who had lost 3000 men and ten galleys

in a naval engagement fought previously near Chalcedon, (Plut. Lucull. c. 9.) were not intimidated by these formidable preparations, but resolved to defend their city to the last extremity. The siege was then pressed with the greatest vigour, and Mithridates, having succeeded in throwing troops into the island itself, brought up his engines, and began to batter the walls and towers on ten different points. One of these machines is said to have been 100 cubits high, and this sustained another tower, from which darts and missiles of every description might be discharged. It was the work of Nicomedes, the Thessalian. But a violent wind, raised, as it was supposed, by Proserpine, in favour of the besieged, blew with such force as to hurl this huge mass, and other engines, to the ground. This loss was however soon repaired, and other machines again shook the walls; whilst secret attacks were directed against the town by means of the sap and mine. These were, nevertheless, vigorously and dexterously repelled by the besieged, who had even nearly seized Mithridates in one of the mines which he was directing in person.

Meanwhile, however, Lucullus, the Roman general, having assembled an army for the relief of the town, posted himself at a place called Thracia in the vicinity of Cyzicus, and in the rear of the enemy's camp. From thence he greatly harassed Mithridates by cutting off his supplies, and destroying whole divisions of his army, and throwing reinforcements into Cyzicus, which was plentifully supplied with provisions, whilst the besiegers were reduced to the greatest distress. Famine and disease made such ravages amongst them, that Mithridates

was finally obliged to break up his camp and raise
the siege with the greatest loss and disgrace. Lucullus then entered the town, and was received with
every demonstration of gratitude and joy. (Appian.
Bell. Mithr. c. 73. seq. Plut. Lucull. c. 9. seq. Strab.
XIII. p. 575.) The Romans, in acknowledgment of
the bravery and fidelity displayed by the Cyzicenes,
guaranteed to them their independence, and besides
granting them several privileges and immunities,
extended their territory towards Troas, and as far
as the lake Dascylitis in the direction of Bithynia.
(Strab. loc. cit.) Under the Roman emperors Cyzicus continued to flourish and prosper greatly. Aristides, who lived in the reign of Hadrian, has left us
an Oration he composed expressly in honour of this
city, from which the following passages may be
selected as most illustrative of its greatness and flourishing condition. " Its plains," says the orator,
" would suffice, not for a city merely, but for na-
" tions : and as for rivers and lakes, and pools and
" dells, there are so many, that if any one chose to
" form settlements around them all, it would be pos-
" sible to have many cities on the banks of the
" lakes ; many too on the shore of the sea, and not
" a few inland." The forum was consecrated to
all the gods, and also a temple within it, which
appears to have been one of the most magnificent
and extensive buildings of the kind recorded in antiquity. " The temple," says Aristides, " supplies
" the place of heights, and you alone require neither
" lights, nor beacons, nor watch-towers for those
" who arrive in your ports ; but the temple, which
" fills the whole sight, exhibits at once to the view
" both the city, and the noble spirit of its inhabit-

" ants. You might say, that each of the stones of
" which it was built was equal to a temple ; and
" the temple itself to the whole peribolus of such an
" edifice ; the peribolus again to the circumference
" of an entire city. The parts below ground, as
" well as the upper and the middle, are worthy of
" admiration. And there are also subterraneous,
" as well as other walks, raised all round the build-
" ing, which appear, not as a secondary object, but
" as if they alone had constituted the original plan."
From an epigram preserved in the Anthology, it
appears to have been dedicated to Hadrian. Xiphilinus affirms, that it was the largest and most beautiful of all temples. The columns being four yards
in thickness, and fifty cubits high, and each formed
out of one piece. This magnificent edifice, according to the same writer, was destroyed by an earthquake, which caused great damage at Cyzicus, and
several other towns on the Hellespont. (p. 799.)

Pliny speaks of a temple at Cyzicus in which
golden threads were inserted in all the joints of the
marble blocks of which it was built ; which contrivance diffused a rich and soft colouring over the
pictures and statues which adorned the edifice.
The same writer notices a remarkable echo near the
gate called Trachia. Also the fugitive stone, as
it was called, from its always moving from the pry-
taneum, where it was kept as a curiosity, having
been left by the Argonauts, who used it as an
anchor. The Cyzicenes, to prevent its escaping, at
last fastened it down with lead. The senate-house
was a vast edifice, in the construction of which no
iron had been employed, and the blocks with which
it was built were so arranged, that any of them

might be removed and replaced without the use of
props. (Plin. XXXVI. 15. Vitruv. IV. 10.) Great
facility was afforded for the erection of these and
other important public buildings, from the extensive
quarries of marble with which the island of Cyzicus
and that of Proconnesus abounded. (Strab. XIII.
p. 589. Plin. V. 32.) The games, and other festivals celebrated at Cyzicus, were commensurate with
the greatness and wealth of the city. We hear of
Olympian games held every five years; of others in
honour of Lucullus, to commemorate the deliver-
ance of the town by that general; of the Hierome-
nia; the festival of Cybele, and others. (Aristid.
Collect. Hist. Vit. Appian. Bell. Mithr. c. 76.) Cyzicus was also famous for its golden staters, which
were beautifully executed, as we learn from Suidas.
Xenophon often speaks of them in the Anabasis,
and Demosthenes states that they were worth twenty-
eight Attic drachmæ [k]. Under the Byzantine emperors this city continued to flourish as the metropolis of the Hellespontine province, (Hierocl. Synecd. p. 661. Jo. Mal. Chron. I. p. 364.) and its see
furnished several bishops to the Christian church [l].
Having been often taken by the Turks, and recovered by the Greek emperors, it was nearly destroyed by an earthquake A. D. 943. Cyzicus
gave birth to several historians, philosophers, and
other writers, whose works are quoted by Athe-

[k] For a full account of the
gold and silver staters of Cyzicus, the reader may be referred
to a special work of Sestini,
(Descrizione degli Stateri An-
tichi. Firenze 1817. p. 45.) The
autonomous coins are rare, but
the imperial series extends from
Augustus to Justinian. Sestin.
Mon. Vet. p. 72.

[l] Geogr. Sacr. Car. S. Paol.
p. 238. Le Quien, Oriens Chris-
tianus.

næus, the Scholiast to Apollonius, and Suidas; such as Agathocles, Neanthes, Deilochus, Eudoxus, and others [m]. The remains of this celebrated city have been described at some length by Pococke [n], and Lucas [o], and still more recently by Sestini, in a journey made there in 1779.[p] Pococke points out a large area, about 100 paces broad and 400 long, with the remains of an extensive building, having a Corinthian portico and several passages underground; it is also described by Sestini; but neither of these travellers seems to have suspected that these were the ruins of the celebrated temple, the theme of Aristides' panegyric: this is however evident from the subterraneous works, and its position in the forum. The modern name of *Atraki*, which attaches to these ruins, recalls to mind the little town of Artace, spoken of by Herodotus, Scylax, and Strabo. Artace. The former, in relating the history of the impostor Aristæus of Proconnesus, mentions Artace as a town in the vicinity of Cyzicus. (IV. 14.) In another place he says, it was burnt by a Persian fleet, together with Proconnesus. (VI. 33.) Scylax says it was within the isthmus. (Peripl. p. 35.) But Strabo speaks of it as a mountain of the peninsula covered with thick woods, and having a little island opposite to it. (XII. p. 576.) Elsewhere, however,

[m] See a full list of these Cyzicene writers in a learned and elaborate note to Thucydides VIII. 107. by Wasse, from which I have derived much information.

[n] T. II. p. ii. p. 114. seq.

[o] Second Voyage, t. I. c. 4.

[p] Viaggio per la penisola di Cizico a Nicea fatto dall' Abbate Domenico Sestini Livorno, 8vo. 1789. This antiquary observes, that the island is now completely united to the land, and that there are no indications of the bridges mentioned by Strabo. The isthmus is a flat, about a mile and a half in length, and three furlongs broad. Lett. VI. p. 502. seq.

the same geographer acknowledges a town or place
of that name in the Cyzicene territory, opposite to
Priapus, and colonized by the Milesians. (XIII. p.
582. XIV. p. 635.) Timosthenes, a writer cited by
Steph. Byz. v. Ἀρτάκη, gave this name both to a
mountain of Cyzicus and a little island about one
stadium from the land. The mountain bending
round the shore, makes a haven capable of receiving
eight ships. Sophocles alluded to Artace in a verse
preserved by Steph. Byz.

Τί μέλλετ' Ἀρταχεῖς τε καὶ Περκώσιοι ;

and Demosthenes, the Bithynian poet,

Νάσσατο δ' Ἀρταχίοισιν ἐφέστιος αἰγιαλοῖσιν.

Pliny calls the island Artacæon, and places the town
in it. (V. 32.) In the time of Procopius, Artace
was considered to be a suburb of Cyzicus. (Bell.
Pers. I. 25.)

Melanos promontorium.

Cape Melanos, which Strabo places in a ship's
course from Cyzicus to Priapus, is probably the
western extremity of the Cyzicene peninsula. More
to the north, and nearly opposite to the mouth of

Proconnesus insula et urbs.

the Æsepus, is the island called Proconnesus, or isle
of stags, by the ancients, now *Marmara*, whence
the modern name of the Propontis is also derived.
Proconnesus was much celebrated for its marble
quarries, which supplied most of the public buildings in Cyzicus with their materials. (Strab. XIII.
p. 588.), as also the palace of king Mausolus. (Vitruv.
II. 8.) The marble was white, with black streaks
intermixed [q]. From Herodotus we collect that there
was a town of the same name with the island, of

[q] Blasius Caryoph. de Marm. Antiq.

which Aristeas, who wrote a poem on the Arimas-
pians, was a native. (IV. 14. Strab. XIII. p. 588.)
This town was burnt by a Phœnician fleet, acting
under the orders of Darius. (Herod. VI. 33.) Strabo
distinguishes between an old and new Proconnesus ;
and Scylax, besides Proconnesus, recognises another
island, named Elaphonesus, with a good harbour : Elaphonesus insula.
it was dependent on the former. (Peripl. p. 35.)
Pliny seems to consider Elaphonesus as a more ancient name for Proconnesus. (V. 32.) Pausanias
reports that Proconnesus was conquered by the Cyzicenes, who removed from thence the statue of
Dindymene. (Arcad. c. 46.) Mention is made of
this island as a bishopric in the ecclesiastical historians and the Acts of the Council of Chalcedon [r].
Pliny names several other islets in this part of the
Propontis : Ophiusa, Acanthus, Phœbe, Scopelos,
Porphyrione, Halone, with a town, Delphacia, and
Polydora. (V. 44.) Of these, Halone is the only
one which can be identified with the modern *Alonia*,
a little to the west of the peninsula of *Artaki* [s].
Polydora is placed by Steph. Byz. in the vicinity of
Cyzicus.

Returning to the mainland we have to mention
Antigonea, a fortress belonging to the latter city, Antigonea.
about fifty stadia from the sea, (Steph. Byz. v. Ἀν-
τιγονεία,) as well as Scyrmus, which the same geogra- Scyrmus.
pher ascribes to the Doliones. (v. Σκύρμις.) Continuing along the coast from Cyzicus, we may notice
Scylace and Placia, named by Herodotus among the Scylace.

[r] Geogr. Sacr. S. Paol. p.
239. There are some few autonomous coins belonging to
this island with the epigraph
ΠΡΟΚΟΝ. Sestini Mon. Vet. p.
75.

[s] Pococke, tom II. part iii.
c. 22.

few settlements belonging to the ancient race of the
Pelasgi which existed in his time. The inhabitants
of these towns spoke a language which was entirely
different from that of the neighbouring people.
(I. 57.) Scylax names only Placia. (Peripl. p. 35.)
Mela and Pliny both towns. (I. 19. V. 32.) The
latter notices also an obscure place called Ariacos.
Further on we come to the mouth of the river
Rhyndacus, which separates Mysia from Bithynia.
Strabo reports that it took its source in Azanitis,
a district of Phrygia ; and after receiving the waters
of the Macistus, and other streams of Mysia, discharged itself into the Propontis, opposite to
the little island of Besbicus. (XII. p. 576.) Pliny
states that the Rhyndacus was formerly called Lycus, and took its source in the lake Artynia, near
Miletopolis ; that it received the Macestus, and
other rivers, and separated the province of Asia
from Bithynia. (V. 32.) It is easy to see that this
account is quite at variance with that of the Greek
geographer. The latter, however, is confirmed by
other writers, and especially by modern geographers, so that he is alone to be followed. The lake
which Pliny calls Artynia is the same to which
Strabo gives the name of Miletopolis, from a neighbouring town so called. (XII. p. 575.) But there
is another lake further to the east, through which
the Rhyndacus flows before it reaches the Propontis. It was called Apolloniatis, from the town of
Apollonia, situated at its northern extremity, and
near the point where the river issues again from it.
Hence Apollonia was usually distinguished by the denomination of ad Rhyndacum, from other towns of the

Marginal notes:
Placia.
Ariacos.
Rhynda-
cus fl.
Artynia
sive Mile-
topolitis
palus.
Apollonia-
tis palus.

same name [t]. With respect to the assertion of Pliny that the Rhyndacus was once called Lycus, I do not find that it is supported by any other authority; but all from Scylax to Ptolemy give it only the former name. Polybius, indeed, mentions a river Lycus in this vicinity, (V. 77.) which may have united with the Rhyndacus; and this might account for Pliny's mistake. The Scholiast to Apollonius Rhodius is equally in error, when he says the Rhyndacus was called, in his time, Megistus; (ad Argon. I. 1165.) for the Megistus, or Macestus, is clearly distinguished from that river by Strabo and Pliny. The former describes it as rising in the district of Abasitis, near a place called Ancyra, and after flowing through Abrettene, a part of Mysia, as uniting with the Rhyndacus. (XII. p. 576.) Polybius also mentions the Megistus in his narrative of an expedition of king Attalus into Mysia, which I shall have occasion to notice presently. (V. 77.) From the information communicated by modern travellers, it appears that the Macistus is the stream which the Turks call *Mikalick*, and which, after receiving the waters of the lake Miletopolis, now called *Minias*, joins the Rhyndacus, or river of *Lubad*, a little below that town. Chishull, on his way from Smyrna to the Hellespont, crossed this river, which he mistook for the Æsepus, at the village of *Mandahora* [u]; and he informs us, "that he came to it again at a "place called *Susegierlick*, and that he could trace "the whole of its remaining course almost as far as "*Mikalick*, where it enters the sea:" in the latter assertion, however, his information is not correct.

---

[t] See a description of the coins of Apollonia in Eckhel and Sestini.

[u] Pag. 58. and p. 52.

The same traveller describes the lake of Miletopolis
as being " about thirty miles in circumference,
" always full of water, and stored with plenty of
" fish. A river empties itself into this lake, from
" whence by a new channel it takes its course to
" *Mikalick*. Directly beyond this lake," he adds,
" we then beheld the fair exalted hills of Cyzicus,

Miletopo-
lis. " and the peninsula Cyzicena [x]." Miletopolis, as
its name implies, must have been a colony of the
Cyzicenes, who themselves came from Miletus. The
earliest writer who mentions it is Apollodorus,
quoted by Strabo. (XIV. p. 681. Id. XII. p. 575.
Plin. V. 32.) Stephanus Byz. places it between Cyzicus and Bithynia, near the Rhyndacus. (v. Μιλη-
τούπολις.) Mention is made of the bishops of Miletopolis in ecclesiastical writings [y], and its coins shew
that it was a place of some note [z]. In the Synecdemus of Hierocles (p. 663.) it is probable, that for
Μόλις we should read Μιλητόπολις. The Table Itinerary reckons twenty miles from this place to Apollonia. Sestini says, its ruins are to be seen at a place
called *Milet*, or *Melté*, by the Turks [a]. The site of

Apollonia
ad Rhyn-
dacum. the ancient Apollonia is occupied, as we are informed by modern travellers, by the Turkish town
of *Abulliona*, situated in a peninsula about five
miles in circuit, which advances into the lake towards its north-western extremity. Near it are
scattered two or three small islands. The lake is a
fine piece of water, nearly fifty miles round and ten
long ; it is well stocked with fish [b]. Apollonia on

---

[x] P. 59.

[y] Geogr. Sacr. S. Paol. p.
239.

[z] Sestini Mon. Vet. p. 73.
The imperial series extends

from Tiberius to Otacilia.

[a] Viaggio per Brusa, p. 82.

[b] Sestini Viaggio p. 86. Chishull, p. 51.

the Rhyndacus is noticed by Strabo, (XII. p. 575.)
Pliny, (V. 30.) Ptolemy, and Steph. Byz. (v. Ἀπολ-
λωνία.) Plutarch reports that a division of the forces
of Mithridates was defeated in this vicinity by Lucullus. (Lucull. c. 164.) The Rhyndacus is now
called the river of *Ulubad*, from a Turkish town of
that name, situated on its left bank a little below
the point where it issues from the lake. *Ulubad* does
not represent Apollonia, as Chishull imagined, but
Lopadium, a Greek town of the Byzantine empire, Lopadium.
said to have been built by one of the Comneni
against the Turks of Nicæa. It is often mentioned
by the historians of the lower empire, and appears
to have been a bishop's see. (Nic. Chon. p. 186.
Ann. Comn. p. 177. C.) The ruins of *Ulubad* consist in massive walls, with turrets placed at inter-
vals. The Rhyndacus is navigable at this point,
and ships often come up to *Ulubad* from Constantinople and the Black sea [c]. Anna Comnena mentions a river called Lampes, near Lopadium, which Lampes fl.
is either the Rhyndacus, or some branch of it.
(p. 177. C.) The poet Apollonius places at the
mouth of the Rhyndacus the tomb of the giant
Ægæon, or Briareus.

> Ἀλλ' ὅτε δὴ Μυσῶν λελιημένοι ἠπείροιο,
> Ῥυνδακίδας προχοὰς μέγα τ' ἠρίον Αἰγαίωνος
> Τυτθὸν ὑπ' ἐκ Φρυγίης παρεμέτρεον εἰσορόωντες.
>   ARG. I. 1164.

This spot, according to Bacchylides, cited by the
Scholiast, was properly called Rhyndacus. (Cf. Steph.
Byz. v. Ῥυνδακός.) The little island now called *Ka-
lolimno*, situated in the Propontis, about two miles
from the mouth of the river, answers to the Besbi- Besbicus
insula.

c Sestini Viaggio, p. 83.

E 3

cus of the ancients. Pliny says it once formed part
of the mainland, but that it was separated from it
by an earthquake. (II. 88.) According to the same
writer it is eighteen miles in circumference. (V. 32.)
Other traditions relative to this island will be found
in Steph. Byz. v. Βέσβικος. This part of the Propontis abounded with the zoophyte called halcyo-
nium. (Dioscor. V. 136.)

Little is known respecting the interior of Mysia,
since even the ancient geographers were but imperfectly acquainted with it, there being no towns of
any importance situated in that part of the province,
and the country possessing no features sufficiently
attractive to deserve a particular description. The
information obtained by modern travellers is almost
exclusively confined to the tract which lies between
Bergamah and *Ulubad,* the road between these two
towns being the only one which appears to be frequented at present. The country to the south of
Lopadium and the lake of Apollonia was mountainous and difficult, and it required three days' march
to make the circuit of the latter. (Mich. Duc. p. 93.)

That portion of Mysia which lies around the
sources of the river Macistus, and between it and
Abrettene the Rhyndacus, was called Abrettene, as we learn
regio. from Strabo, who informs us, that in the reign of
Augustus it formed part of a principality granted
by that emperor to Cleon of Gordiu-come, a bandit
chief, who had rendered him some service in his
wars against Antony. Strabo adds, that Cleon was
also priest of Jupiter Abrettenus, and lord of Morene, another Mysian district, noticed by no other
writer. (XII. p. 575.) The Abretteni are mentioned
by Pliny. (V. 30. Cf. Steph. Byz. v. Ἀβρεττίνη. The

road mentioned above as leading from Pergamus and along the Caicus by *Gelembe,* near the sources of that river to *Mandrakhora, Susugherli,* and *Ulubad,* must have traversed part of Abrettene. The country is described as wild, desolate, and mountainous by Chishull[d], Lucas[e], and Sestini[f]. The only remains of antiquity which appear to have been there noticed by Chishull are at *Mandrakhora;* they consist in seven large pillars, of coarse porphyry, which support the roof of the *khan,* or inn, at that place. This may have been the Μάν- Mandra. δρα ἵπποι, or Μάνδρα ἵππων, of Hierocles Synecd. (p. 663.) Joannes Malala speaks of a place called Mandra, or Mandro, where Priam sent Paris to be nursed. The word Μάνδρα signifies simply a stall or stable. The river which runs by *Mandrakora* is probably the Lycus of Polybius[g]. It flows towards the Propontis, as Chishull, Sestini, and other travellers represent. Polybius, in describing an expedition of king Attalus into Mysia, with a large body of Gallo-Græci, or Galatæ, (V. 77.) says, that having crossed the river Lycus, he advanced to- Lycus fl. wards the settlements of the Mysians; from thence he directed his march towards Carscæ, which is probably the Caresus of Strabo, and placed by that writer in Troas. Carseæ and Didymoteiche having surrendered, the king moved onwards, and ravaged the plain of Apia. Now the plain of Apia Apiæ cam- is placed by Strabo above Thebe and Adramyttium, pus. and north of mount Temnus, (XIII. p. 616.) exactly where it was observed by Chishull in 1701.

[d] P. 47.
[e] 3me Voyage, tom. I. p. 133.
[f] Viaggi Diversi, p. 136-8.

[g] See the map to col. Leake's Asia Minor. It is by mistake made to fall into the Caicus.

E 4

" In somewhat more than six hours we had passed
" the Temnus, and enter into a rich plain, extended
" all along the backside of Ida, now *Cordag;* at the
" foot of which, about four miles distant from the
" road, we descry the agreeable seat of *Balihisar*."
From the Apian plain Attalus crossed over a mountain named Pelecas, and arrived on the banks of
the Megistus, where the Gauls having refused to
proceed further, he settled them on the Hellespont,
and returned with his own forces to Pergamos. The
Pelecas of Polybius is probably that continuation of
mount Temnus which separates the valley of the Æsepus from that of the Megistus. This ridge appears
in the Byzantine historians under the name of Lentiani montes; at least it is the only range in the
vicinity of Cyzicus and Lopadium, which seems to
answer to Anna Comnena's narrative of the capture
of the latter city by a Turkish army, and their subsequent retreat over these hills by a defile named
Aorata, in which they were attacked by Camytzes,
a general who had been detached in their pursuit
by the emperor Alexius. In the immediate vicinity
of these hills, but nearer Cyzicus, as we learn from
the same narrative, was Pœmanenus, a Mysian town
of some note, and a place of great strength, (πολίχ-
νιον ἐρυμνότατον.) Ann. Comn. p. 440. A. Aristides
also informs us, that it had a temple, sacred to
Æsculapius, which was held in great veneration.
(Sacr. Orat. IV. p. 569.) The orator passed through
Pœmanenus on his way to the hot baths of the Æsepus, which had been recommended to him for the
cure of a complaint to which he was subject. He
was then coming from Hadriani, his native town,
which we know to have been situated in Bithynia,

Marginal notes:
Pelecas mons.
Lentiani colles.
Aorata saltus.
Pœmanenus.

at the foot of mount Olympus, and near the Rhyndacus. He seems to reckon 160 stadia, or somewhat less than 20 miles, from thence to Pœmani-
non; but there is reason to suppose either that this
number is corrupt, or that it is not reckoned from
Hadriani, but from some nearer spot. At all events
we shall be justified in placing Pœmanenus between
the Rhyndacus and the Æsepus. The Table Itinerary
will furnish us another indication of its position;
for we find in it a place laid down on the road from
Pergamus to Cyzicus, under the name of Phemenio,
which, as Mannert judiciously observes, can be no
other than the town in question[h]. It is evident indeed, from Anna Comnena, that it was not far from
Cyzicus; and Stephanus Byz. terms it expressly
Χωρίον Κυζίκου[i], (v. Ποιμάνινον.) Hierocles calls it Pœ-
manentus, and enumerates it with other towns belonging to the Hellespontine province. (Synecd. p.
662. Cf. Plin. V. 32.) In the Geographer of Ra-
venna, (p. 761.) the name is written Pomenion,
which comes nearest to the Phemenio of the Table.
Mannert is inclined to identify the site of this town
with some ruins on a hill observed by Pococke at a
place called *Doulokcui*[k], to the S. E. of Cyzicus,
and on the road from that city to *Mikalitzka*. But
I think it could not have been to the north of the
lake of Miletopolis; I should rather look for its
ruins above the *Hamanlee* of Chishull, among the
hills which overhang the Tarsius.

[h] Geogr. tom. VI. part. iii.
p. 543.

[i] There are autonomous coins
belonging to this town with the
head of Jupiter crowned with
laurel; on the reverse, a thun-
derbolt, and the inscription,

ΠΟΙΜΑΝΗΝΩΝ. There are
others also struck in the reign
of Trajan. Sestini Lett. Numism. tom. VI. p. 76.

[k] Geogr. tom. VI. part. iii.
p. 543.

I shall conclude this article on Pœmanenus, by reminding the reader, that according to ecclesiastical documents it was a bishopric[1], and that its church was dedicated to the archangel Michael. (Georg. Acrop. p. 19.) The Byzantine historian just quoted seems to speak of Lentiana as a tract of country about Pœmanenus and Lopadium, and between the latter and the Hellespont. (p. 6. C.) In another passage he distinctly refers to a town of the same name. (p. 15. C.) This is perhaps the same town which Hierocles calls Σκέλεντα, (Synecd. p. 662.) and which itself may be a corruption of Πελεκάντα. (Polyb. V. 77.)

The Tabula Theodosiana lays down, immediately after Pœmanenus, on the road to Pergamus, and at the distance of thirty miles from the former, and thirty-five from the latter, a station, under the name of Argesis, which Mannert is inclined to identify with the Ergasteria observed by Galen on the same route[m]; but that writer reckons 440 stadia, or about fifty Roman miles, from Pergamus to Ergasterion; consequently it must have been situated fifteen miles beyond Argesæ, towards Cyzicus. (Simpl. Med. IX. 22. p. 127.) There can be little doubt that Argesæ is the Argiza of Hierocles, (Synecd. p. 663.) and that writer, by distinguishing it from Ergasterion, which he also names, throws a further obstacle in the way of Mannert's conjecture. It is not improbable that Argiza is the same town as the Erezii of Pliny, which he seems to place about Pœmanenus and Miletopolis. (V. 32.) The road from

Argiza.

Ergasterion.

Erezii.

[1] Geogr. Sacr. S. Paol. p. 238. Le Quien Oriens Christ. p. 769.
[m] Geogr. tom. VI. part. iii. p. 543-4.

Pergamus to Cyzicus led probably along the valley
of Tarsius, and if so, according to Strabo, must
have crossed it no less than twenty times. (XIII.
p. 587.) It is in this valley, which no modern traveller seems to have explored, that I would seek for
Argiza or Erezii and Ergasterion; the latter might
easily be found from the scoria and other metallic
appearances indicative of ancient mines noticed by
Galen, (loc. cit.)

Germe, or, as Ptolemy terms it, Hiera Germe, a *Germe.*
name which also appears on its coins[n], is classed by
that geographer among the towns of the Lesser
Mysia, and by Stephanus Byz. is said to be near
Cyzicus and the Hellespont, (v. Γέρμη. Hierocl. Syn-
dec. p. 662.) Socrates, the ecclesiastical writer,
reports, that it was in great measure destroyed by
an earthquake in the reign of Valens; but the
Byzantine historians speak of it as still existing in
their time; (Georg. Pachym. p. 295.) and one of
its bishops is known to have sat in the council of
Chalcedon[o]. From the mention of the Germian
mountains in Anna Comnena, (p. 464,) we collect,
that this town was situated in a hilly country, and
in the vicinity of Lopadium; and it is in this direction that Leunclavius[p], Holstenius[q], and D'Anville[r], point out a small town, named *Ghirmasti* by
the Turks, as occupying the ancient site. In the
same direction I would look for the remains of Oca, *Oca.*
or Occa, a town mentioned only by later writers,

---

[n] The epigraph is sometimes
IEPA . ΓΕΡΜΗ, and sometimes
IEPA ϹΥΝΚΛΗΤΟϹ ΓΕΡΜΗΝ-
ΩΝ. Sestini Mon. Vet. p. 73.
  [o] Geogr. Sacr. Car. S. Paol.

p. 239.
  [p] Ap. Car. S. Paol. loc. cit.
  [q] Annot. ad Geogr. Car. S.
Paol. p. 239.
  [r] Geogr. Anc. p. 96.

such as Hierocles, Synecd. (p. 662.)[s] and the ecclesiastical notices, which record the fact of its being a bishopric in the reign of the emperor Leo[t]. I

Acrocon saltus. take Oca to be the same as the Acrocon, i. e. Ἄκρα Ὀκῶν of Anna Comnena, (p. 441. A.) from whom we collect also, that to the south of it was a defile leading to Philadelphia, in Lydia, (p. 443. A.) We may conjecture, that this pass traversed the mountains which divide the valleys of the Megistus and Rhyndacus from those of the Hermus and its tributary streams. Another pass appears to have led from Lopadium to Thyatira. (Mich. Duc. p. 45.)

Ptolemy names three obscure tribes in the interior of Mysia, which are unknown, I believe, to the

Temeno-thyritæ. Myso-Ma-cedones. Pentade-mitæ. other geographers. Of these the Temenothyritæ occupied the west of the province, the Myso-Macedones the centre, and the Pentademitæ the south, p. 126.

HELLESPONTUS.

The narrow strait which separates the Thracian Chersonnese from the coast of Asia, and by which the waters of the Propontis are poured into the wider bason of the Ægæan, had in fabulous times received its name from the fate of Helle, daughter of Athamas, who was supposed to have perished there in her voyage to Colchis.

Ὅσσον ἐπὶ στεινωπὸν ὕδωρ Ἀθαμαντίδος Ἕλλης.

DIONYS. PER. 515.

Ἔνθα σφὶν λαιψηρὸς ἄη νότος· ἱστία δ᾽ οὔρῳ
Στησάμενοι, κούρης Ἀθαμαντίδος αἰπὰ ῥέεθρα
Εἰσέβαλον.   APOLL. RHOD. I. 926.

[s] It should be observed, that I adopt Wesseling's correction of ΟΚΗ, ΣΙΔΗΡΟΝ for Ο ΚΙΣΙ-ΔΗΡΟΝ.

[t] Geogr. Sacr. Car. S. Paol. p. 239.

(Cf. Apollod. I. 9,1.) The tomb of Helle was placed, as Herodotus reports, on the shores of the Chersonnese, near the city of Cardia. (VII. 58.) The narrowness and length of this celebrated channel, together with the sinuosities of its shores, and the rapid and powerful current which is constantly flowing through them, are sufficient reasons to justify Homer in the epithets of Πλατὺς, which he applies to it, if we regard the epithet as bestowed upon what might be viewed rather as a mighty river than a winding arm of the sea.

Ὄφρα ἑ ταρχύσωσι καρηκομόωντες Ἀχαιοὶ,
Σῆμά τέ οἱ χεύσωσιν ἐπὶ πλατεῖ Ἑλλησπόντῳ.

IL. H. 86.

(Cf. Il. P. 432. Od. Ω. 82. Æsch. Pers. 880.) It will not be necessary, therefore, to seek for an explanation of the word in the remote signification of brackishness, which has by some critics been attached to it, (Athen. II. p. 41. B.) more especially if we take into the connexion the analogous epithets of ἀγάρροος and ἀπείρων, which are elsewhere used by the poet.

Ὅσσους Ἑλλήσποντος ἀγάρροος ἐντὸς ἐέργει.

IL. B. 845.

Καὶ Φρυγίη καθύπερθε, καὶ Ἑλλήσποντος ἀπείρων.

IL. Ω. 545.

It may be worth while to adduce, in confirmation, the remarkable expressions of δολερὸς καὶ ἁλμυρὸς ποτάμος, which Herodotus puts into the mouth of Xerxes, as applied to the Hellespont. (VII. 35.[u])

The straits begin properly a little to the south of cape *Karaboa*, where the ancient town of Pria-

[u] See the word πλατὺς, in the glossary of Bloomfield's edition of the Persæ, v. 880.

pus stood, and terminate with cape Sigeium, now
C. *Kumkalé*. Some ancient geographers, however,
supposed them to commence only at Sestos and
Abydos; they consequently extended the shores of
the Propontis, in a south-westerly direction, to the
vicinity of those towns. (Strab. XIII. p. 583. Cf.
Ptol. p. 126.) When Herodotus states that the
breadth of the Hellespont is seven stadia, (IV. 85.)
he must be considered to mean in the narrowest
part; which is between Sestos and Abydos, where
Xerxes built his famous bridges. (Cf. VII. 34.) The
same historian reckoned 400 stadia for the length
of the strait, without however stating from what
point he measured his distance. Modern measurements give about sixty miles from *Kamares*, where
the straits of *Gallipoli*, or the *Dardanelles*, as they
are now called, fairly commence, to the Sigeian promontory. The mean breadth seems to be not less
than three miles[x].

The name of Hellespont, though properly belonging to the sea straits, in process of time was applied
to the land on each side, and to the cities founded there
by the Greeks. (Thuc. VIII. 86.) Not unfrequently also the Persian satrap, of whose government
these cities formed a part, on the Asiatic side, was
designated by the title he derived from this celebrated channel. The importance of the passage, in
a political and commercial point of view, was as
much felt in ancient times as at present; and the
possession of it was always considered by the Athenians as indispensable to the preservation of their

[x] See a particular Memoir on
the Hellespont by D'Anville,
inserted in the Mémoires de
l'Académie des Belles Lettres,
LXXVIII. p. 318.

naval ascendency, and the security of their commerce. It was here, in fact, that the struggle between them and their enemies was long carried on
with alternate success, each making the greatest
efforts to drive the other from the sea, till at last
the decisive battle of Ægospotami deprived Athens
of her fleet, and, by closing the Hellespont to her
ships, stripped her of her best resources, and left
her no alternative but to surrender. I shall commence the Hellespontine periplus from the point
where the shores of the Propontis begin to be strait-
ened, that is, somewhat to the south-west of Priapus, which town has been considered as belonging
to that sea.

Parium, founded by the Milesians, the Erythræ- Parium.
ans, and the Parians, of Paros, (Strab. XIII. p.
588.) is mentioned for the first time by Herodotus,
in the reign of Darius. (V. 117.)   Under the kings
of Pergamos it became a city of some extent and
opulence, having been enlarged by those princes at
the expense of the neighbouring towns of Adrastea
and Priapus. (Strab. XIII. p. 588.)   Its harbour
was secure and capacious, being able to contain a
fleet of more than eighty ships. (Xen. Hell. I. 1, 8.)
At a later period, it was dignified by Augustus with
the title of a Roman colony. (Ulpian. Digest. L. tit. 5.
Plin. V. 32.ʸ)

The ruins of this town are pointed out by travellers at *Kamares.* " The walls of the city, which
" fronted the sea, still remain, and are built of large

ʸ Coins and inscriptions give
it the title of Colonia Julia and
Colonia Antonia. The series
of the former extends from Julius Cæsar to Saloninus. The
autonomous coins are also very
numerous. Sestin. Mon. Vet.
p. 73.

" blocks of squared marble, without mortar. We
" saw ruins of an aqueduct, reservoirs for water,
" and the fallen architraves of a portico. There are
" also some subterranean buildings, whose arched
" roofs incline or dip from the horizontal level. As
" Καμάρα means both *arch* and *aqueduct*, we can be
" at no loss for the derivation of *Camaris*, the modern
" name of the town. The circuit of Parium has
" been about four miles[z]."

Linum.   Linum was a spot situated on the coast between
Parium and Priapus, and well known for a sort of
shell-fish caught there. (Strab. XIII. p. 588.) More
Pityea.   inland was the town of Pityea and the district of
Pityus re- Pityus, which derived its name from a hill covered
gio et mons. with firs. The town is named by Homer, with
other places in this vicinity,

Οἳ δ' Ἀδρήστειάν τ' εἶχον καὶ δῆμον Ἀπαισοῦ,
Καὶ Πιτύειαν ἔχον, καὶ Τηρείης ὄρος αἰπύ.
Τῶν ἦρχ' Ἄδρηστός τε καὶ Ἄμφιος λινοθώρηξ,
Υἷε δύω Μέροπος Περκωσίου.   ILIAD. B. 828.

and by Apollonius Rhodius, Argon. I. 933.

. . . ζαθέην τε παρήμειβον Πιτύειαν.

Some writers, however, identified Pityea with Lampsacus. (Schol. Apoll. ad loc. cit. Steph. Byz. v. Λάμψακος.)

Adrastea.   Pliny was of opinion that the Adrastea of Homer
had made way for Parium, (V. 32.) but Strabo expressly asserts, that it stood between the latter city
and Priapus; and that it possessed a temple and

z Walpole's Turkey, tom. I.   p. 439. B. The bishop of Pa-
p. 88. from Dr. Sibthorp's Pa-   rium is named among the pre-
pers. It appears from Anna   lates who sat in the council of
Comnena that Parium still re-   Chalcedon. Geog. Sacr. S. Paul.
tained its name in her time,   p. 240.

oracle of Apollo Actæus. This building was, however, afterwards demolished, and the materials were
removed to Parium, and employed there in the construction of a magnificent altar. (XIII. p. 580.) In
the vicinity of Parium there was said to exist a race
of men, named Ophiogeneis, who were supposed to
have some affinity with serpents, and to be able to
cure persons who had been bit by those reptiles.
(Strab. ibid.) Iliocolone, according to Strabo, was Iliocolone.
a place situated in the Parian territory. (XIII.
p. 589.)

Apæsus, or Pæsus, for Homer employs both Apæsus
names, sive Pæsu:
urbs et fl.

Οἳ δ' Ἀδρήστειάν τ' εἶχον καὶ δῆμον Ἀπαισοῦ.

Il. B. 828.

Καὶ βάλεν Ἄμφιον, Σελάγου υἱὸν, ὅς ῥ' ἐνὶ Παισῷ
Ναῖε πολυκτήμων, πολυλήϊος. Il. E. 612.

was situated to the south of Parium, on a rivulet of
the same name, now called *Beiram-dere*[b]. It had
been founded by the Milesians, but they afterwards
deserted it for the more flourishing colony of Lampsacus. (Strab. XIII. p. 589.) Pæsus, however, existed in the time of Herodotus, who records its
occupation by a Persian general at the time of the
Ionian revolt excited by Histiæus and Aristagoras
(V. 117. Steph. Byz. v. Ἀπαισός.)

Lampsacus, one of the most celebrated of the Hel- Lampsacus.
lespontine cities, was known to have existed under
the name of Pityusa before it received colonies from
the Ionian towns of Phocæa and Miletus. (Strab.
XIII. p. 589. Steph. Byz. v. Λάμψακος. Plut. de Virt.
Mul. 18. P. Mel. I. 19.) It was situated opposite

---

[b] Chevalier, Voyage dans la Troade, p. I. ch. 5.

to Callipolis, in the Thracian Chersonnese, the
strait which separated the two cities being only
forty stadia in breadth, and it possessed an excellent
harbour.

Herodotus relates, that the first Miltiades, who
settled in the Chersonnese, made war upon the
Lampsacenes, who surprised him in one of his attacks, and took him prisoner. Being threatened,
however, with the vengeance of Crœsus, who favoured Miltiades, they released their captive. (VI.
37.) The same historian informs us, that Lampsacus fell into the hands of the Persians during the
Ionian revolt. (V. 117.) The territory of this city
produced a great abundance of excellent wine, a circumstance which induced the Persian monarch to
bestow it on Themistocles, when that illustrious
Athenian sought refuge in his dominions, in order
that his table might be furnished with that beverage
from thence. (Thuc. I. 138. Athen. I. p. 29. F.) It
continued, however, under the government of a native prince or tyrant, named Hippocles. His son,
Æantides, married Archedice, the daughter of Pisistratus, whose tomb, with an inscription comme-
morative of her virtues, was to be seen at Lampsacus when Thucydides wrote. (VI. 59.) Athenæus
has recorded the attempt of another citizen, named
Euagon, to obtain possession of the citadel, and seize
thereby the sovereign power. (XI. 508. F.) It became tributary to Athens after the battle of Mycale,
and revolted on the failure of the Sicilian expedition ;
but, being unfortified, was easily reconquered by a
small fleet under Strombichides. (Thuc. VIII. 62.)
After the death of Alexander, we find the Lamp-
sacenes defending their city against the attacks of

Antiochus, (Liv. XXXIII. 38. XXXV. 42. Polyb. XXI. 10.) voting a crown of gold to the Romans, and received by them into their alliance. (Liv. XLIII. 6.) Strabo reports that Lampsacus was yet a flourishing city in his day. It had produced several distinguished literary characters and philosophers, such as Charon the historian, Anaximenes the orator, and Metrodorus a disciple of Epicurus. That celebrated philosopher had himself resided many years there, and had reckoned some of its citizens amongst his most intimate friends. (Strab. XIII. p. 589. Diog. Laërt. Epicur.)

Lampsacus had been adorned by a remarkable statue, executed by the celebrated Lysippus, representing a prostrate lion ; but it was removed by Agrippa to decorate the Campus Martius at Rome, (Strab. loc. cit.)   It is well known that Priapus was worshipped with peculiar reverence in this city. (Athen. I. 30. B. Lucian. I. 275.)

> Et custos furum atque avium cum falce saligna
> Hellespontiaci servet tutela Priapi.   GEORG. IV. 110.

> Et te ruricola Lampsace tuta deo.   OVID. TR. I. 11.

Other passages relating to the history of Lampsacus, will be found in Xenophon. (Anab. VII. 8, 1. Polyb. V. 77. Steph. Byz. v. Λάμψακος. Polyæn. VIII. 38. Plin. V. 32. Arrian. I. 5, 16.) The name of *Lamsaki* is still attached to a small town near which Lampsacus probably stood, as *Lamsaki* itself contains no remains or vestiges of antiquity. A modern traveller assures us besides, that " its " wine, once so celebrated, is now among the worst " that is made in this part of *Anatolia* [b]."

---

[b] Dr. Sibthorpe, in Walpole's Turkey, tom. I. p. 91.   There are gold and silver staters of Lampsacus in different

Abarnis was a promontory belonging to the Lamp-sacenes, as we learn from Hecatæus and Ephorus, cited by Steph. Byz. (v. Ἄβαρνος) and Xenophon in the Hellenics, who reports that Conon, the Athenian general, having escaped from the defeat of Ægos-potami, carried off from thence the sails left there by the Lacedæmonian fleet under Lysander. (II. 1, 19.) It is also noticed by Apollonius Rhodius. (Argon. I. 932.)

Περκώτην δ' ἐπὶ τῇ, καὶ 'Αβαρνίδος ἡμαθόεσσαν
'Ηϊόνα—

Stephanus Byz. ascribes it to Parium, whence we may conclude that it lay between that town and Lampsacus. Theophrastus, in a passage cited by Athenæus, says, that the trufle called " Iton" was found there. (II. 62. C. Plin. XIX. 13.) Theo-phrastus also says, that there were gold mines near Lampsacus, in which a gem was found of such beauty and rarity, that the Lampsacenes presented it to Alexander. (de Lapid. Plin. XXXVII. 74.) We have yet to notice, in the territory of this city,

Colonæ, a Milesian settlement, at some distance from the sea, and which must not be confounded with another town of the same name in the Troad. (Strab.

XIII. p. 589. Arrian. I. 5, 16.) Gergithium, a dis-trict planted with numerous vineyards, and distinct from Gergis, or Gergitha, a Trojan town, of which we shall have occasion to speak hereafter. (Strab.

loc. cit.) Myrmissus, or Mermessus, said to be the birthplace of the Erythræan sibyl, who is also sometimes called Gergithia and Hellespontiaca, was placed by Polemo near Lampsacus. (ap. Steph. Byz.

numismatical collections. The imperial medals have been traced from Augustus to Gal-lienus. Sestini Mon. Vet. p. 73.

v. Μυρμισσός. Id. v. Μερμεσσός. Lactant. de Fals.
Rel. I. c).

Mount Terea, the name of which occurs in the Terea
Homeric topography, was identified by some writers mons.
with a hill, distant forty stadia from Lampsacus.
Hermæum, according to Polyænus, was a spot Hermæum.
between that city and Parium, seventy stadia from
the latter. (VI. 24.) Continuing along the shore of
the Hellespont we come to the Practius, a small Practius fl.
river, which has a place in the Homeric topography,
together with Percote, an ancient town, situated Percote.
apparently on its banks.

Οἳ δ᾽ ἄρα Περκώτην καὶ Πράκτιον ἀμφενέμοντο.

IL. B. 835.

Charon of Lampsacus, cited by Strabo, (XIII. p.
583.) reckoned 300 stadia from Parium to the Practius, which he looked upon as the northern boundary of the Troad. This distance serves to identify
that stream with the river of *Bergaz,* or *Bergan,* a
small Turkish town situated on its left bank, and which
probably represents Percote. The situation is thus
described by a traveller : " A river called *Chiergee*
" runs near Lampsacus, and two hours from thence
" we met another winding stream, which falls into
" the Hellespont at a point projecting very far to-
" wards the European coast. We then passed a
" village called *Beergan,* on the banks of this river.
" Its situation on a sloping hill, with clumps of
" trees left in picturesque spots round it, and a clear
" stream running in the valley, formed a very beau-
" tiful landscape. Indeed the whole of this shore
" furnishes a continual succession of the richest

c See the notes of Berkelius to Steph. Byz. v. Γέργις, and Sal-
masius, Exercit. Plin. p. 79.

F 3

" scenery[d]." Percote is mentioned again by Homer,
(Il. O. 548.) when speaking of Menalippus, son of
Priam ;

> . . . ὁ δ' ὄφρα μὲν εἰλίποδας βοῦς
> Βόσκ' ἐν Περκώτῃ, δηΐων ἀπονόσφιν ἐόντων.

and Λ. 229. from which latter passage it is apparent
that Percote was on the sea, or very near it. (Cf.
Xen. Hell. V. 1, 23.)

> Τὰς μὲν ἔπειτ' ἐν Περκώτῃ λίπε νῆας ἐΐσας·
> Αὐτὰρ ὁ πεζὸς ἐὼν, εἰς Ἴλιον εἰληλούθει.

Percote continued to exist long after the Trojan
war, since it is spoken of by Herodotus, (V. 117.)
Scylax; (Peripl. p. 35.) Apollonius, (Rh. I. 932.)
Arrian, in his account of Alexander's expedition,
(I. 13.) Pliny, (V. 32.) and Steph. Byz. (v. Περκώτη.)
It was named by some writers among the towns
given to Themistocles by the king of Persia. (Athen.
I. 29. Plut. Themistocl. c. 30.)   Somewhat fur-
Arisbe.   ther south we find Arisbe, mentioned also by Homer,
together with the river Selleis.

> Οἳ δ' ἄρα Περκώτην καὶ Πράκτιον ἀμφενέμοντο,
> Καὶ Σηστὸν καὶ Ἄβυδον ἔχον, καὶ δῖαν Ἀρίσβην·
> Τῶν αὖθ' Ὑρτακίδης ἦρχ' Ἄσιος, ὄρχαμος ἀνδρῶν,
> Ἄσιος Ὑρτακίδης, ὃν Ἀρίσβηθεν φέρον ἵπποι
> Αἴθωνες, μεγάλοι, ποταμοῦ ἀπὸ Σελλήεντος.

IL. B. 835.

(Cf. Z. 13. Φ. 43.) Arisbe, according to Steph. Byz.,
had been founded by the Mitylenæans, in whose
island there was a town of the same name.   Other
traditions are to be found in the same lexicographer
under Ἀρίσβη.   It was here, according to Arrian,
that Alexander stationed his army immediately
after crossing the Hellespont at Abydos. (I. 12.)
When the Gauls passed over into Asia, some centu-

---

[d] Dr. Sibthorpe's Journal in Walpole's Turkey, tom. I. p. 91.

ries after, they also occupied Arisba, but were totally
defeated by king Prusias. (Polyb. V. 111.) A rare
coin belonging to this town shews that it still existed in the reign of Trajan [e]. Pliny also names it;
(V. 32.) and if it is the same as the Barispe of
Hierocles, (p. 663.) we should be able to trace its
history some years later. Wesseling, in his notes
to that writer, quotes a passage from the Acts of
St. Parthenius of Lampsacus, in which mention is
made of Arisba as a place near Abydos. If Barispe again is the Bares of the ecclesiastical writers,
it will follow that Arisbe was a bishop's see, under
the metropolitan church of Cyzicus, about that
period [f]. The Selleis is probably the river called
Moussa-tchai by the Turks, and Arisbe may
have stood at *Gangerlee*, where Dr. Sibthorp observed " the ruined wall of some ancient Greek
" town [g]."

Further south, and on the promontory now called Abydos.
Nagara, are to be seen the inconsiderable remains
of the once rich and flourishing city of Abydos.
We learn from Strabo that it had been founded by a
colony of Milesians, with the consent of Gyges, king
of Lydia, to whom the whole of the surrounding
country was subject ; but it is evident that the name
of Abydos had long been attached to the spot, since
it occurs in Homer in conjunction with Sestos,
with which it seems naturally united :

Καὶ Σηστὸν καὶ ῎Αβυδον ἔχον, καὶ δῖαν ᾿Αρίσβην.

IL. B. 836.

[e] Imperatorius unicus cum
capite Trajani. Epigraphe APIC-
BEΩN. Æ. Autonomi Epi-
graphe. AP. API. Æ. Sestini
Mon. Vet. p. 76.

[f] Car. S. Paol. Geogr. Sacr.
p. 239.

[g] Walpole's Turkey, tom. I.
p. 92.

F 4

elsewhere the poet mentions it as celebrated for its
breed of horses.

> 'Αλλ' υἰὸν Πριάμοιο νόθον βάλε Δημοκόωντα,
> "Ος οἱ 'Αβυδόθεν ἦλθε, παρ ἵππων ὠκειάων.

> IL. Δ. 499.

After the siege of Troy, Abydos was occupied by
some Thracians, and then finally by the Milesians.
Strabo asserts that it was burnt by order of Darius,
together with some other cities on the Hellespont,
on his return from Scythia, as he feared lest the
Scythians should in return be disposed to invade
his dominions, and seek to effect a passage in this
direction. (XIII. p. 591.)   Herodotus, however, has
omitted all mention of this circumstance ; and it is
evident, from his subsequent history of the operations of Xerxes, that Abydos was then in a flourishing condition.   But even before that, he states, that
in the Ionian revolt it was taken by Daurises, a
general of Darius, with other Hellespontine towns.
(V. 117.)   On this occasion the city, perhaps, suffered from fire, and this may have given rise to the
report followed by Strabo.

It was at Abydos that Xerxes, seated on an eminence, where an ivory throne had been prepared for
him, surveyed his mighty fleet which covered the
Hellespont, whilst the neighbouring plains swarmed
with his innumerable troops. (Herod. VII. 44.)   The
bridge, destined for the passage of these multitudes
into the opposite continent, was placed in the narrowest part of the straits, where the breadth did not
exceed seven stadia, whence it was usually called Hep-
tastadium.   The point immediately opposite to Abydos was called Zeugma, and that to which the bridge
had been fixed, Apobathra.   Sestos stood further

to the north, the distance between it and Abydos
being not less than thirty stadia. (Strab. XIII. p.
591.)

Tales fama canit tumidum super æquora Xerxem
Construxisse vias, multum cum pontibus ausus,
Europamque Asiæ, Sestonque admovit Abydo.

                                LUCAN. II. 672.

Abydos became dependent upon Athens after the
Persian war, together with Sestos, which secured to
that power the passage of the Hellespont. It recovered its liberty for a short time, when the failure
of the Sicilian expedition had shaken the empire of
the Athenians, (Thuc. VIII. 61.) but was recovered
afterwards by Alcibiades, who appears to have spent
much of his time there in the midst of pleasures.
(Antiph. ap. Athen. XII. p. 525. B. Cf. XIII. p.
574. E.)   The Abydenes, indeed, are noted by ancient writers in general for their voluptuous and
sensual habits. (Hermipp. et Aristoph. ap. Athen.
loc. cit. Steph. Byz. v. Ἄβυδοι.)   The Athenians
once more lost Abydos, after the battle of Ægospotami, but it was again conquered by Thrasybulus;
the Lacedæmonians afterwards sent a force under
Anaxibius to occupy it, but he was defeated and
slain by Iphicrates. (Xen. Hell. IV. 8, 35.)   Antalcidas, the Spartan admiral, having however assembled a considerable fleet, occupied Abydos, and
drove the Athenians from the Hellespont, which
finally brought on the peace to which he has given
his name. (Hell. V. 1, 23.)   Some centuries after,
this city sustained a memorable siege against the
forces of Philip, the son of Demetrius, king of Macedon, who, after reducing many Thracian towns,
and the whole Chersonnese, summoned the inhabit-

ants to open their gates to his troops. The Abydenes, however, courageously refused, and, though
unsupported by any allies, defended themselves with
the greatest obstinacy, till their walls were in many
places laid open. Even then they continued fight-
ing to the last ; and though the principal inhabitants
agreed to surrender to the king, the people preferred
to perish, with their wives and children, rather than
fall into his hands. (Polyb. XVI. 30. Liv. XXXI.
16.) On the defeat of Philip at Cynoscephalæ, that
prince was compelled by the Romans to evacuate
Abydos, (Polyb. XVIII. 27, 4.) It was not long
after occupied by Antiochus, and vainly besieged by
C. Livius, commander of the Roman fleet. (Liv.
XXXVII. 9—12. Appian Syr.) The defeat which
Antiochus sustained at Magnesia compelled him,
however, to give up the whole of Asia Minor on
this side Taurus, and Abydos was ceded by the
Romans, together with the other Hellespontine
cities, to Eumenes, king of Pergamus. (Polyb. XXII.
27, 10.) Beyond this period it makes but little
figure in history, though from its coins it is known
to have flourished in the reign of the emperor Maxi-
minus [h] ; and still later we can trace its existence
through the Byzantine historians, to the close of
the Greek empire. (Cedren. p. 699.)

Abydos has derived some celebrity from the romantic story of Hero and Leander, which cannot
be said to exist merely in the fictitious poem of
Musæus [i], since Virgil and Ovid confirm the tale ;

[h] Imperatorii ab Augusto usque ad Maximinum Autonomi
Anepigraphi Aurei et Argentei — Autonomi Inscripti AB.
ABY. ABYΔ. Insignes Tetra-
drachmi argentei inscripti ABY-
ΔHNΩN. Sestini Mon. Vet. p.
76.

[i] For an account of this
poet, see Fabricius Biblioth.

(Georg. III. 260. Heroid. Epist. 18 and 19.) and Strabo speaks of an edifice near Sestos which was commonly known by the name of Hero's tower, (XIII. p. 591.) and some of the imperial medals have inscribed on them the names of the lovers [k].

The situation of Abydos was not so advantageous, in a commercial point of view, as that of Sestos, since the latter was nearer the Propontis, and above the current which set in from that sea; whence a ship might with great facility work its way in that direction towards the Bosphorus or Euxine, and also descend with the stream into the Ægean; whereas a vessel setting out from Abydos, had great difficulty in making way against the current which set in strongly from the European shore. (Strab. XIII. p. 591. Polyb. IV. 44.)

Σηστὸς ὅπη καὶ Ἄβυδος ἐναντίον ὅρμον ἔθεντο.

DIONYS. PERIEG. 516.

Pontus et ostriferi fauces tentantur Abydi.

GEORG. I. 207.

Seston, Abydena separat urbe fretum.

OVID. TRIST. I. 9, 28.

Near Abydos, and in a plain among the mountains which rose behind the city, were some gold mines, as we learn from Xenophon, belonging to the Abydeni; the precise spot was called Cremaste. Cremaste. (Hell. IV. 8, 37.) It is probable that these mines are the same as those of Astyra, mentioned by Strabo. (XIII. p. 591.) Astyra had been once an Astyra. independent and flourishing town, but in the geo-

Græc. tom. I. p. 105; also a dissertation in the Mém. de l'Academie des Belles Lettres, tom. VII. by Mons. de la Nauze.
[k] Sestini loc. cit.

grapher's time it was in ruins, and its territory belonged to Abydos. (Cf. Steph. Byz. v. Ἄστυρα.)

South of cape *Nagara*, on which the ancient Abydos stood, a considerable torrent, called *Scultanie* by the Turks, and more commonly known as the river of the *Dardanelles*, empties its waters into the sea opposite to Cynossema, in the Chersonnese.

Rhodius fl. This, according to Strabo, is the Rhodius of Homer. (XIII. p. 595.)

> Ῥῆσός θ', Ἑπτάπορός τε, Κάρησός τε, Ῥοδίος τε.
>
> Il. M. 20.

But Demetrius of Scepsis supposed the Rhodius to be a rivulet which rose at the back of Ida, and joined the Ænius; a tributary stream of the Æsepus. (ap. Strab. XIII. p. 603.)

DARDANIA.

We now enter upon that portion of ancient Troas to which the name of Dardania had been attached long before the existence of Troy, from Dardanus, universally acknowledged as the founder of the Trojan dynasty. This celebrated hero, whom fabulous accounts represent as the son of Jupiter and Electra, came, according to some accounts, from Arcadia, according to others, from Italy; but all agree in fixing upon Samothrace as the spot in which he had formed his first principality, before he migrated to the foot of mount Ida. (Apollod. Bibl. III. 12, 1. Strab. Epit. VII. p. 331. Virg. Æn. VII. 207.) We may reconcile this variety of opinions respecting the native country of Dardanus, by supposing that he was a chief of that early race, who, under the name of Pelasgi, were so widely diffused, and more especially in those very countries, each of which separately claimed to be the birth-place of the Trojan prince. The epoch of the arrival of Dardanus on the coast of Asia is too re-mote to be ascertained at present with accuracy[1]. Plato, as we learn from Strabo, (XIII. p. 592.) placed his arrival in the second epoch after the universal deluge, when mankind began to leave the summits of the mountains to which fear had driven them, and where they led a barbarous and savage life in caves and grots, like the Cyclopes of Homer. The Athenian philosopher deduced his reasoning from the passage in that poet in which Dardania, the town founded by Dardanus, is stated to have been built, at the foot of Ida.

Δάρδανον αὖ πρῶτον τέκετο νεφεληγερέτα Ζεύς·
Κτίσσε δὲ Δαρδανίην ἐπεὶ οὔπω Ἴλιος ἱρὴ
Ἐν πεδίῳ πεπόλιστο, πόλις μερόπων ἀνθρώπων,
Ἀλλ' ἔθ' ὑπωρείας ᾤκεον πολυπιδάκου Ἴδης.

IL. Υ. 215.

Dardanus, however, was not the first settler in the Trojan plains, since he found the country already occupied by a people whose name of Teucri was de-rived from that of Teucer, their king. This sove-reign gave Dardanus his daughter Batieia in mar-riage, and ceded to him a part of his territories. (Apollod. Bibl. III. 12, 1. Steph. Byz. v. Ἀρίσβη. Eust. Il. B. 813.)

It is remarkable that Homer has never once men-tioned the Teucri, who are so often identified with the Trojans by Virgil, and other Latin poets : but their existence in this part of Asia at a very early period

[1] Homer reckons five gene-rations between Dardanus and Priam. Il. Υ. 230. Cf. Apol-lod. Bibl. III. 12, 3.

is certified by historians of great authority. From
Herodotus it appears that they were once a very numerous and powerful people, as he speaks of a great
expedition undertaken by them, in conjunction with
the Mysi, into Europe, before the Trojan times. (VII.
20. 43.)   This is a point of history which appears
particularly intricate, and seems to involve the origin
of the Teucri in great obscurity.   I think it much
more probable that the great migration alluded to
by Herodotus, and by him only, took place from the
great plains around the *Danube*, where the Mysians
undoubtedly had their first seat, and with whom
the Teucri may have been originally connected.
From thence they may have spread themselves into
Macedonia and Illyria, while a portion of their wandering hordes may have crossed the Hellespont, and
settled in the valleys of mount Ida.   The Pæonians,
as we learn from Herodotus, gave out that they
were descended from the Teucri : now the Pæonian
nation appears to have been one of the most ancient
and widely spread of all the tribes which were to
be found between Greece, properly so called, and
the Danube north and south, and the Euxine and
Hadriatic west and east ; and it is hardly credible
that this people, bearing every mark of the highest
antiquity, and closely connected with the surrounding Thracian and Illyrian nations, should have
owed its origin to an obscure nation occupying a
small district on the coast of Asia Minor.   It certainly does appear from Homer that the Pæonians
of Macedonian Thrace were allied to the Trojans,
and that they sent an auxiliary force to the aid of
Priam ; but it is nowhere said that they were the
subjects of that prince.   This only tends to shew

that there was a strong affinity between the tribes
of Macedonia and Thrace and those of Asia, which
may easily be accounted for on the supposition of
their common origin. It is a curious circumstance
that the Dardani, a very primitive race, apparently
of Illyria, (Strab. VII. p. 316.) but who are only
known to us in the latter period of the Macedonian
history, claimed the sovereignty of Pæonia as their
ancient right ; (Liv. XLV. 29.) and I am strongly
inclined to imagine that the connexion of the Darda-
nians and Teucrians was not formed in the valleys
of Ida and the shores of the Hellespont, but in the
plains of the Danube, and the Illyrian and Pæonian
Alps. The Teucri probably came first into Asia,
as all accounts seem to establish their greater antiquity ; (Apollod. Bibl. loc. cit. Diod. Sic. IV. 75.)
but they would present us with a most singular
anomaly in the history of nations, if they were to be
looked upon as of a different race from the Mysians,
Phrygians, Bithynians, and other nations, avowedly
of Thracian origin, by which they were surrounded.
It was from Thrace that the tide of population was
then setting very strong towards Greece, Italy, and
across the Bosphorus and Hellespont into Asia, and
it is very improbable that a counter current should
have been formed, such as Herodotus describes, to
throw back these Thracian hordes from the shores
of the Hellespont and Propontis, to those countries
from whence their forefathers had themselves first
migrated. Upon the whole it appears probable,
that though some such great migration, as Herodotus has recorded, did take place, he was misinformed
as to one principal fact, namely, that it did not, as
he relates, take place from Asia into Europe, but

vice versa. As the Teucri in his time were known only as an Asiatic people, it is easy to understand how he was led into the mistake, upon hearing that a very extensive migration had been formed by this people in the north of Greece, as far as Illyria and the shores of the Adriatic. When the historian wrote, Gergis, or Gergithæ, was the only city of the Troad which preserved some vestige of the ancient Teucrians. (V. 122.) This primitive appellation had first given way to that of Trojans and Troas, just as the older name of Graii, or Greeks, had been superseded by the more recent denominations of Hellenes and Achivi ; and it is somewhat curious, that in both cases the older name should have been more commonly used by the Latins, whilst they were scarcely known to the Greeks.

According to the Homeric topography, the Dardani, who were subject to Anchises, and commanded by his son Æneas during the siege, occupied the small district which lies between the territory of Abydos and the promontory of Rhœteum, beyond which point the Trojan land, properly so called, and the hereditary dominions of Priam, commenced.

Δαρδανίων αὖτ᾽ ἦρχεν, ἐῢς παῖς Ἀγχίσαο,
Αἰνείας· τὸν ὑπ᾽ Ἀγχίσῃ τέκε δῖ᾽ Ἀφροδίτη.

IL. B. 819.

Towards the mainland, Dardania extended to the summit of Ida, and beyond that chain to the territory of Zeleia, and the plains watered by the Æsepus on the north, and as far as the territories of Assus and Antandros, Æolian colonies on the Adramyttian gulf, to the south. (Strab. XIII. p. 592. 606.) It was more particularly in this inland district that the descendants of Æneas are said to have

maintained themselves as independent sovereigns
after the siege of Troy ; and even during the Persian empire we read in the Hellenics of Xenophon
of a Dardanian princess, named Mania, who held
under the satrap Pharnabazus a principality possessed by her husband Zenis during his lifetime.
On the death of this lady, by the hands of Meidias,
her son-in-law, the latter seized on her fortresses
and treasures, and usurped the sovereignty ; but
by the interference and skilful management of Dercyllidas, the Lacedæmonian general, who then commanded a Greek force on the Hellespont, he was
stripped of the possessions he had so unjustly acquired, and reduced to the rank of a private individual.   The Greek towns held by Mania were then
declared independent. (III. 1.)   After this digres-
sion on the history of Dardanus and Dardania, we
may now resume our description of the coast of the
Hellespont from the mouth of the river Rhodius,
where we last halted.

South of Abydos, Strabo mentions the promon- Dardanis
tory Dardanis, or Dardanium, (XIII. p. 587, 595.) nium pro-
which answers to the headland named *Kepoburun* rium.
by the Turks, and *Punta dei Barbieri* by the
Franks.   Pliny speaks of another promontory called
Trapeza, between Dardanium and Abydos, eighteen
miles from the former, and ten from the latter ; but
these numbers are faulty.   It is probable that Pliny's
cape is the Dardanis of Strabo.   Near it was the
town of Dardanus, distant from Abydos about seventy Dardanus.
stadia.   Though of great antiquity, it was not to be
identified, as Strabo remarks, with the ancient city
founded by Dardanus ; since this, as we collect from
Homer, was situated more inland, and at the foot of

Ida. (XIII. p. 592.) By whom the second Dardanus was built is uncertain; we know, however, that
it existed in the time of Herodotus, who mentions
its capture by the Persians in the reign of Darius.
(V. 117.) In the narrative of Xerxes's march he
describes it as close to the sea, and conterminous
with Abydos. (VII. 43.) Scylax styles it a Greek
town, and places it first in his periplus of the
Troad. (p. 35.) Strabo reports that the inhabitants
were often compelled to change their abode by the
successors of Alexander; he reports also, that peace
was concluded here between Sylla and Mithridates.
(XIII. p. 595. Cf. Plut. Syll. c. 24.) Livy states
that it had been declared a free city by the Romans
after the defeat of Antiochus, in memory of their
Trojan origin. (XXXVIII. 39. Cf. XXXVII. 9,
37. Steph. Byz. v. Δάρδανος [m]. Plin. V. 32.) The
ruins of Dardanus are to be found between *Kepos-
Burun* and *Dervend Tchemeh Burun*. The name
of *Dardanelles*, which has in the first instance been
applied to the Turkish castle erected to defend the
passage of the straits, and next to the straits themselves, is confessedly derived from this ancient town.

Ophry-
nium.
        In the vicinity of Dardanus we may notice Ophry-
nium, where was a grove, consecrated to Hector,
on an eminence, which might be seen from all the
Pteleos la-
cus.
surrounding country; also a little lake, named Pteleos. (Strab. XIII. p. 595. Lycophr. v. 1200.)
Ophrynium is mentioned by Herodotus, in his account of the march of Xerxes, (VII. 43.) and by

---

[m] The imperial coins of Dardanus are numerous, from the
reign of Augustus to that of Severus. The name of the river
Rhodius appears on a medal of
Domna. Sestin. Mon. Vet. p.
76.

Xenophon, who passed through it with the 10,000 on his way from Lampsacus to Pergamus, and offered there a sacrifice of swine. (Anab. VII. 8.) Strabo is the only writer who speaks of the lake, but Steph. Byz. places a town called Pteleos in Troas.

Further south was Rhœteum, situated on a hill, Rhœteum. or promontory, (Orus ap. Steph. Byz. v. 'Ροίτειον.) whence commences the Trojan bay, and the interesting scenery, so familiar to every one who is acquainted with the poem of Homer. At a little distance from the town, on the sea shore, might be seen the Æanteum, or tomb of Ajax, with a temple and statue erected to the memory of that hero by the Rhodians. (Plin. V. 30. Strab. XIII. p. 595.) Mention of Rhœteum occurs in Herodotus, (VII. 43.) Thucydides, (IV. 52. and VIII. 107.) and several other writers.

> . . ἐννύχιοι 'Ροιτειάδος ἔνδοθεν ἀκτῆς
> Μέτρεον, 'Ιδαίην ἐπὶ δεξιὰ γαῖαν ἔχοντες.
> Δαρδανίην δὲ λιπόντες ἐπιπροσέβαλλον 'Αβύδῳ.
>
> APOLL. RH. I. 929

> Teucrus Rhœteas primum est advectus in oras.
>
> ÆN. III. 108.

> Tunc egomet tumulum Rhœteo in litore inanem
> Constitui—   ID. VI. 505.

It is generally supposed that the Turkish village of *Et-Ghelme*, where there are some vestiges of antiquity, represents the town of Rhœteum[n], and that the Æanteum was at *Intepé*[o]. The statue had been removed, and sent to Egypt, with many other

[n] There are some few coins extant belonging to this place. Sestini Mon. Vet. p. 76.

[o] Pococke's Travels, vol. II. part ii. p. 104. Le Chevalier's

Description of the Plain of Troy, ch. 13. p. 102. Leake's Asia Minor, p. 275. Walpole's Turkey, vol. I. p. 96.

works of art, by Marc Antony; but they were all
restored by Augustus to the several places from
whence they had been taken. (Strab. XIII. p. 595.)

The interior of Dardania offers yet for our notice
some ancient sites to which interesting recollections
Gergis sive are attached. The first is Gergis, or Gergitha,
Gergitha. which we know from Herodotus to have been a
remnant of the ancient Teucri, and consequently a
town of very great antiquity. (V. 122. VII. 43.)
Cephalo, an early historian, who is cited by Dionysius of Halicarnassus, Athenæus, and others, as
having written a history of Troy, was a native of
this place. (Dion. Hal. Ant. Rom. I. p. 180. Athen.
IX. p. 393. Strab. XIII. p. 589. Steph. Byz. vv.
Ἀρίσβη, Γραικός.) Gergis, according to Xenophon,
was a place of strength, having an acropolis and
very lofty walls, and one of the chief towns held by
Mania, the Dardanian princess. (Hel. III. 1, 12.)
It had a temple sacred to Apollo Gergithius, and
was said to have given birth to the sibyl, who is
sometimes called Erythræa, from Erythræ, a small
place on mount Ida, (Dion. Hal. 1. 55.) and at others
Gergithia. In confirmation of this fact it was observed, that the coins of this city had the effigy of the
prophetess impressed upon them. (Phlegon, ap. Steph.
Byz. v. Γέργις.q) It appears from Strabo that Gergitha having been taken by Attalus, king of Pergamus, he removed the inhabitants to the sources of the
Caicus, where he founded a new town of the same
name. (XIII. p. 616.) The Romans, according to

q Some of these coins are
still extant, and accord with
the testimony of Phlegon.
They are thus described by numismatic writers : Caput mu-
liebre adversum laureatum cum
stola ad collum R. ΓΕΡ. Sphinx
alata sedens Æ. 3. Sestini
Lett. Numism. t. I. p. 88.

Livy, made over the territory of the old town to the Ilienses. (XXXVIII. 39.) Herodotus, in describing Xerxes' march along the Hellespont, states that he had the town of Dardanus on his left, and Gergitha on his right; it is evident, therefore, that the latter must have been situated inland, and towards mount Ida. (VII. 43.) The name of Marcæum was particularly applied to that portion of the ridge which overhung Gergitha and its territory. (Steph. Byz. v. Μάρκαιον.)

Marcæum mons.

Palæscepsis, so called to distinguish it from the more recent town simply known by the name of Scepsis, was a city apparently of the highest antiquity, since the latter even dated its origin from the time which immediately succeeded the Trojan war. Demetrius, a native of Scepsis, and who had written largely on the topography of the Troad, considered that city as the capital of Æneas's dominions; and affirmed it was his son Ascanius, who, together with Scamandrius, the son of Hector, transferred the inhabitants of the old to the site of the new town, distant about sixty stadia from each other. The Dardanian princes long held sway at Scepsis; but afterwards the government assumed the form of an oligarchy, and finally that of a democracy: the latter event dates from the union of a Milesian colony with the Scepsians; yet the title of sovereign was still preserved by the descendants of the royal family. (Strab. XIII. p. 607. XIV. p. 635.) Scepsis, as we learn from Xenophon, was the chief city belonging to Mania, the Dardanian princess, already spoken of. After her death it was seized, together with the treasures and stores deposited there, by Meidias, who had married her daughter; but Der-

Palæscepsis.

Scepsis.

cyllidas, having obtained admission into the town
for the purpose of holding a conference with Meidias,
and sacrificing in the acropolis, expelled him, and
gave up the authority to the citizens. (Hell. III. 1.)
Under the Macedonian kings, Scepsis underwent
several vicissitudes. Antigonus transferred the inhabitants to Alexandria Troas, on account of their
wars and disputes with their neighbours the Cebrenians, but Lysimachus restored to them their
former abode : subsequently it became subject to
the kings of Pergamus. (Strab. XIII. pp. 597. 607.)
These did not prevent, however, philosophy and
science from flourishing there ; and Scepsis especially deserves a place in the annals of literature for
the discovery of the books of Aristotle and Theophrastus, which occurred there about the time of
Sylla. Strabo, who gives an interesting account of
this curious circumstance, relates that Neleus of
Scepsis, a disciple of Aristotle, and intimate friend
of Theophrastus, having been presented by the latter
with his own books, and those he had inherited
from their great common master, brought them
from Greece to his native town. On his death, this
valuable collection came into the possession of his
relations, who being illiterate persons, and unacquainted with their real worth, suffered the MSS.
to remain heaped together, without any care being
taken to preserve them. But what was still more
to be lamented, on hearing that the king of Pergamus was busily employed in searching for rare and
curious books, to add to his library, they immediately buried the MSS. of Neleus in a deep pit,
where they of course sustained serious injury from
damp and worms. At length, however, they were

rescued from this state, and sold to an amateur, named Apellicon, of Teos, for a considerable sum of money. This person endeavoured to supply the *lacunæ*, and make corrections; but being incompetent to execute such an undertaking, he published copies which abounded in errors. After the death of Apellicon, Sylla took possession of his books, and caused them to be removed to Rome. (XIII. p. 608.) Besides Demetrius, a distinguished writer and commentator on Homer, who is often quoted by Strabo and Athenæus, Scepsis gave birth to Metrodorus, who published also several works, and was high in favour with Mithridates, being employed by that prince in various public functions and important commissions. (Strab. loc. cit. Plut. Lucull. c. 22.) Scylax has erroneously ranked Scepsis among the maritime cities of Troas. (Peripl. p. 35.) It is evident, from Strabo and Demosthenes, (Contr. Aristocr. p. 671, 9.) that it stood at some distance from the coast. From the former it appears that Palæscepsis was situated near the source of the Æsepus, and the highest part of mount Ida and Scepsis about sixty stadia lower down. (XIII. p. 607.) In Pliny's time there existed no longer any vestige of the former; (V. 30.) but the latter is mentioned by Hierocles, (Synecd. p. 664.) and the ecclesiastical notices of bishoprics [r]. According to Mannert, it still retains the name of *Eskiupschi* [s]. Around Palæscepsis were several places, for the knowledge of which we are indebted to the researches of De-

---

[r] Geogr. Sacr. p. 239. The autonomous coins have the epigraph ΣΚΗΨΙΩΝ and ΣΚΑ-ΨΙΩΝ, sometimes with ΔΑΡΔ. for ΔΑΡΔΑΝΙΩΝ: this is more frequently the case in the imperial money. Sestin. Mon. Vet. p. 77.

[s] Geogr. tom. VI. part. iii, p. 471.

metrius the Scepsian, to illustrate the topography of the Iliad. Strabo, who has communicated them to us, places, in the upper valley of the Æsepus, Polichna, then Palæscepsis and Halizonium; the latter he supposes to be an imaginary city, brought there solely for the purpose of accounting for the Halizones, reckoned by Homer among the allies of Priam. (Il. B. 856.) Polichna is acknowledged by Steph. Byz. as a town of Troas, (v. Πολίχνα,) and also by Pliny; (V. 32.) but it must not be confounded, as some critics have done, with the Polichna mentioned by Thucydides. (VIII. 14. 23.) Beyond these the Æsepus received the waters of the Caresus, which gave its name to a small town, and a rich and populous valley through which it flowed. This stream derived further celebrity from being recorded by Homer.

Ῥῆσός θ', Ἑπτάπορός τε, Κάρησός τε, Ῥοδίος τε.

Il. M. 20.

The district of Caresus was conterminous to the territory of Zeleia; but the town was in ruins and deserted in the time of Demetrius of Scepsis, whose words to that effect are cited by Strabo. (XIII. p. 602.) It is probable, however, that the Carseæ, of which Polybius has made mention in the expedition of Attalus into Mysia, (V. 77.) is no other than the town in question. The Caresus, according to the same writer, had its source near Mallus, or Malus, a spot situated between Palæscepsis and Achæium; the latter place was opposite to the island of Tenedos. On the right bank of the Æsepus, and between Polichna and Palæscepsis, Demetrius placed Ænea, or Nea-Come, at the distance of fifty stadia from the latter site. Pliny reports, that the rain

Marginal notes: Polichna. · Halizonium. · Caresus fl. · Caresene regio. Caresus urbs. · Mallus. · Ænea sive Nea-Come.

was never observed to fall round the image of Minerva preserved in this town. (II. 96. Steph. Byz. v. Νέα.) I think it probable that the name of Ænea was first given to it in honour of Æneas, but that it was afterwards corrupted to Nea. It has been supposed by some travellers, that the Turkish village called *Ené* occupies this ancient site ; but this is too far from the Æsepus, and answers better to Neandria[t]. In the vicinity of Nea were some silver mines, which in the system of Demetrius corresponded with the Alybe of Homer. (ap. Strab. XII. p. 551. XIII. p. 603.) These mines were observed by Pococke at *Eskupi*[u]. It is uncertain whether the Ænius, a small river named by Strabo, without Ænius fl. any indication of its course, should be connected with the Ænea or Nea of the same geographer. (XIII. p. 603.) D'Anville seems to have been of this opinion, since in his map of the country around Troy he supposes it to fall into the Æsepus.

TROJA, ET TROJANUS AGER.

I must now turn to the topography of Troy itself; a subject which will always be interesting to the classical reader, but which has been so much discussed and minutely inquired into by modern travellers and antiquaries, that no additional light can be expected to be derived from subsequent researches. To bring together all that has been said on this point by the ancients as well as the moderns, would be to form a very voluminous work in it-

[t] Le Chevalier, Voyage dans la Troade, p. iii. c. 3. Chandler's Travels in Asia Minor, ch. 12. and Inscr. Ant. p. 4. Choiseul Gouffier supposes it to be Neandria.

[u] Tom. II. part iii. p. 107.

self; and as many of the latter have only repeated what their antecessors have stated before them, and most of them agree in all the principal and material points, I shall better consult the reader's convenience by presenting him with a brief summary of what I have collected from the different authors who have expressly written on the subject; referring at the same time the student, who is desirous of investigating it more deeply, to the works enumerated at the bottom of the page [x].

This, the most classical of all lands, has been so completely trodden and examined, that it may be truly said that the ancient writers who wrote on the subject were much less acquainted with the actual topography of the Trojan plain, than our best informed modern travellers. The researches of these intelligent men have not only confirmed the great historical facts connected with the fate of Troy, which few persons indeed either in ancient or modern times have ventured to question, and those evidently for the purpose of maintaining a paradox; but they have served beautifully to illustrate the noblest poem of antiquity, and to bear witness, with due allowance for poetical exaggeration, to the truth and accuracy of Homer's local descriptions.

[x] A Comparative View of the ancient and present State of the Troad, by Rob. Wood ; subjoined to the essay on the Genius and Writings of Homer. Description of the Plain of Troy, by M. Chevalier, Edinburgh, 4to. 1791. Le Chevalier, Voyage dans la Troade, Paris, 8vo. 1802. Observations on the Topography of the plain of Troy, by James Rennell, Lond. 1814. 4to. Chandler's History of Ilium, or Troy, Lond. 1802. 4to. Voyage Pittoresque de la Grece, par Choiseul Gouffier, tom. II. Gell's Topography of Troy, fol. Lond. 1804. Dr. Clarke's Travels, tom. III. Col. Leake's Geogr. of Asia Minor, ch. 6., and some memoirs in Walpole's Turkey, vol. I.

They have proved, that as in every other point he was the most close and happy delineator of nature, so here he has still copied her most faithfully, and has taken his descriptions from scenes actually existing, and which must have been familiar to his eyes. In order that this may be proved to the reader's satisfaction as far as it is possible, without an actual inspection of the country, I purpose first to lay before him all the general and most striking features in the Homeric chorography, and then to illustrate them by a continued reference to modern travellers and antiquarians. It will be seen then from the Iliad that the Greeks, having arrived on the coast of the Hellespont, and effected a landing, drew up their vessels in several rows on the shore of a small bay confined between two promontories.

Πολλὸν γάρ ῥ' ἀπάνευθε μάχης εἰρύατο νῆες
Θῖν' ἐφ' ἁλὸς πολιῆς· τὰς γὰρ πρώτας πεδίονδε
Εἴρυσαν, αὐτὰρ τεῖχος ἐπὶ πρύμνῃσιν ἔδειμαν.
Οὐδὲ γὰρ οὐδ', εὐρύς περ ἐὼν, ἐδυνήσατο πάσας
Αἰγιαλὸς νῆας χαδέειν· στείνοντο δὲ λαοί.
Τῷ ῥα προκρόσσας ἔρυσαν, καὶ πλῆσαν ἁπάσης
Ἠϊόνος στόμα μακρὸν, ὅσον συνεέργαθον ἄκραι.

Il. Ξ. 30.

Elsewhere he states, that Achilles was posted at one extremity of the line, and Ajax at the other. (Θ. 224. Λ. 7.) He nowhere names the two promontories which enclosed the bay and the armament of the Greeks: but all writers, both ancient and modern, agree in the supposition that these are the capes Rhœteum and Sigeum, between which tradition attached to different spots the names of Naustathmus, the port of the Greeks, and the camp of

the Greeks. (Strab. XIII. p. 595.)   According to
Pliny, the distance from headland to headland was
thirty stadia. (V. 33.)   Strabo reckoned sixty stadia
from Rhœteum to Sigeum, and the tomb of Achilles
close to the latter; (loc. cit. y) and these distances
agree sufficiently well with actual measurements z.
Considerable changes, however, have taken place
during the lapse of so many ages in the appearance
of the coast.   The promontories remain; but the
bay has been completely filled up by the deposit of
rivers and the accumulation of sand and soil, and
the shore now presents scarcely any indenture between the headlands : but we are assured by Choiseul Gouffier, and others, who have explored the
ground, that there is satisfactory proof of the sea
having advanced formerly some way into the land in
this direction a.   The next great feature to be examined in the Homeric topography, is the poet's account of the rivers which flowed in the vicinity of
Troy, and discharged their waters into the Hellespont.
These are the Xanthus, or Scamander, and the
Simois, whose junction is expressly alluded to. (Il.
E. 774.)

> Ἀλλ' ὅτε δὴ Τροίην ἷξον, ποταμώ τε ῥέοντε,
> Ἧχι ῥοὰς Σιμόεις συμβάλλετον ἠδὲ Σκάμανδρος,
> Ἔνθ' ἵππους ἔστησε θεὰ λευκώλενος Ἥρη.

y Le Chevalier was not correct in charging Strabo with
inaccuracy in his statement of
this distance.   He supposes
that Strabo spoke of cape Rhœteum, whereas he, no doubt,
meant the town, which is some
way from it.

z Note to the French Strabo,
tom. IV. p. 170.
a Voyage Pittoresque, tom.
II. p. 216. Col. Leake's Sketch
to explain the supposed alteration in the coast and rivers of
Troy. Asia Minor, p. 273.

And again, (Z. 2.) where it is said, that the conflict between the Greeks and Trojans took place in the plain between the two rivers.

Πολλὰ δ' ἄρ' ἔνθα καὶ ἔνθ' ἴθυσε μάχη πεδίοιο,
'Αλλήλων ἰθυνομένων χαλκήρεα δοῦρα,
Μεσσηγὺς Σιμόεντος, ἰδὲ Ξάνθοιο ῥοάων.

One of the first questions then to be considered, in reconciling the topography of ancient Troy with the existing state of the country, is this : Are there two streams answering to Homer's description, which unite in a plain at a short distance from the sea, and fall into it between the Rhœtean and Sigean promontories? To this question it certainly appears, from recent observations, that we must reply in the negative. There are two streams which water the plain, supposed to be that of Troy, but they do not meet, except in some marshes formed principally by the *Mendere*, the larger of the two, which seems to have no exit into the Hellespont; while the smaller river partly flows into these stagnant pools, and partly into the sea near the Sigean cape[b]. It appears, however, from Strabo, or rather from Demetrius, whom he quotes, that when he wrote, the junction did take place; for he says, " The Sca-" mander and Simois advance, the one towards Si-" geum, the other towards Rhœteum, and after unit-" ing their streams a little above New Ilium, fall " into the sea near Sigeum, where they form what " is called the Stomalimne." (XIII. p. 597. Cf. p. 595.) Pliny also, when he speaks of the Palæscamander, evidently leads to the notion that the channel of that river had undergone a material alteration.

[b] Choiseul Gouffier.

(V.32.) The observations of travellers afford likewise evidence of great changes having taken place in regard to the course of these streams ; and it is said that the ancient common channel is yet to be traced under the name of *Mendere,* near the point of *Kum-kale.* The ancients themselves were aware of considerable alterations having taken place along the whole line of coast ; for Histiæa, of Alexandria Troas, a lady who had written much on the Iliad, affirmed, that the whole distance between New Ilium and the sea, which Strabo estimates at twelve stadia, had been formed by alluvial deposit; (XIII. p. 598.) and recent researches prove that this distance is now nearly double[c]. The great question, however, after all, respecting the two rivers alluded to, and on which the whole inquiry may be said to turn, is, which is the Scamander and which the Simois of Homer? If we refer for the solution of this question to Demetrius of Scepsis, who, from his knowledge of the Trojan district, appears to have been best qualified to decide upon it, we shall find, that he looked upon the river now called *Mendere* as corresponding with the Scamander of Homer, a supposition which certainly derives support from the similarity of the two names ; while he considered the Simois to be the stream now called *Gi-umbrek-sou,* which unites with the *Mendere* near the site of *Paleo Aktshi,* supposed to represent the Pagus Iliensium, and which Demetrius himself identified with ancient Troy. But it has been rightly observed by those modern writers who have bestowed their attention on the subject, that the simi-

[c] Col. Leake's Asia Minor, ch. vi. p. 295.

larity of names is not a convincing reason in itself,
since they have often been known to vary; and that
after all we must refer to the original account,
where we find the characteristics of the two rivers
described in a manner which must eventually settle
the whole question, as far as regards their identity.
A reference to the Iliad itself is the more necessary,
as Demetrius does not appear to have satisfactorily
explained, even to himself, certain doubts and difficulties which naturally arose from comparing his
system of topography with that suggested by the
perusal of the poet.   Now it appears from more
than one passage that the Simois, according to
Homer, had its source in mount Ida ;

"Ενθ' ἔβαλ' 'Ανθεμίωνος υἱὸν Τελαμώνιος Αἴας
'Ηΐθεον θαλερὸν, Σιμοείσιον· ὅν ποτε μήτηρ
"Ἰδηθεν κατιοῦσα παρ' ὄχθῃσιν Σιμόεντος
Γείνατ', ἐπεί ῥα τοκεῦσιν ἅμ' ἕσπετο μῆλα ἰδέσθαι.   -

IL. Δ. 475.

Δὴ τότε μητιόωντο Ποσειδάων καὶ 'Απόλλων
Τεῖχος ἀμαλδῦναι, ποταμῶν μένος εἰσαγάγοντες,
"Οσσοι ἀπ' 'Ιδαίων ὀρέων ἅλαδε προρέουσι,
'Ρῆσός θ', 'Επτάπορός τε, Κάρησός τε, 'Ροδίος τε,
Γρήνικός τε, καὶ Αἴσηπος, δῖός τε Σκάμανδρος,
Καὶ Σιμόεις, ὅθι πολλὰ βοάγρια καὶ τρυφάλειαι
Κάππεσον ἐν κονίῃσι, καὶ ἡμιθέων γένος ἀνδρῶν.

IL. M. 22.

and though in the latter passage the same thing is
affirmed of the Scamander, it will be seen elsewhere,
that the sources of that river are so plainly described
as situated close to the city of Troy, that they never
could be said to rise in the main chain, unless Troy
itself was placed there likewise.   When speaking of
the pursuit of Hector by Achilles beneath its walls,
he says,

. . . . τρέσε δ' "Εκτωρ
Τεῖχος ὕπο Τρώων, λαιψηρὰ δὲ γούνατ' ἐνώμα.
Οἱ δὲ παρὰ σκοπιὴν καὶ ἐρινεὸν ἠνεμόεντα
Τείχεος αἰὲν ὑπ' ἐκ κατ' ἀμαξιτὸν ἐσσεύοντο·
Κρουνὼ δ' ἵκανον καλλιρρόω, ἔνθα δὲ πηγαὶ
Δοιαὶ ἀναΐσσουσι Σκαμάνδρου δινήεντος.
Ἡ μὲν γάρ θ' ὕδατι λιαρῷ ῥέει, ἀμφὶ δὲ καπνὸς
Γίνεται ἐξ αὐτῆς, ὡσεὶ πυρὸς αἰθομένοιο·
Ἡ δ' ἑτέρη θέρεϊ προρέει εἰκυῖα χαλάζῃ,
Ἡ χιόνι ψυχρῇ, ἢ ἐξ ὕδατος κρυστάλλῳ.
Ἔνθα δ' ἐπ' αὐτάων πλυνοὶ εὐρέες ἐγγὺς ἔασι
Καλοὶ, λαΐνεοι, ὅθι εἵματα σιγαλόεντα
Πλύνεσκον Τρώων ἄλοχοι, καλαί τε θύγατρες,
Τὸ πρὶν ἐπ' εἰρήνης, πρὶν ἐλθεῖν υἷας Ἀχαιῶν.

IL. X. 143.

These marks, which point out the double sources of the Scamander, are so peculiar and so striking, that the discovery of them would, it seems, be decisive of the question, not only as far as regards the Trojan rivers, but also, in all probability, as to the situation of Troy itself, which, according to the poet, must have stood in the immediate vicinity of the sources. It is in tracing this remarkable and most distinguishing feature of the Homeric description, that modern research and industry have been particularly conspicuous, and have enabled us to solve a question, which the ancients, from their want of similar information, could never understand. It is to Mons. Choiseul Gouffier that the merit of first discovering the springs of the Scamander undoubtedly belongs; and though the phenomena of heat and cold, described by Homer, have not been so convincingly observed by subsequent travellers as by himself, yet, by taking the positive testimony of the natives themselves, who repeatedly corroborated the statement made by the poet, as well as the several experiments made by M. Choiseul Gouffier, and subsequently by Mons. Dubois [d], we cannot refuse to acknowledge at least that there is very sufficient foundation for the poetical picture formed of the spot by Homer. M. Choiseul describes the hot source " as one abundant stream, which gushes out " from different chinks and apertures, formed in " an ancient structure of stone work. About 400 " yards higher up are to be seen some more springs, " which fall together into a square stone bason, " supported by some long blocks of granite. These " limpid rills, after traversing a charming little " wood, unite with the first sources, and together " form the Scamander [e]." The latter, which are the cold springs of Homer, are called *Kirk Guezler*, or the *Forty Fountains*, by the Turks [f]. If we besides look to the general features which ought to belong to the Scamander and the Simois of Homer, we shall find that the former agrees remarkably with the beautiful little river of *Bounarbachi,* which is formed by the sources above mentioned, while the rapid Simois finds a fit representative in the impetuous *Mendere-sou,* which descends from the summits of Gargara, and fills its bed with trees torn from their roots, and huge fragments of rock. The former is described as a copious, rapid, and clear stream, whose banks are spread with flowers, and shaded with various sorts of trees.

ἈΑλλ' ὅτε δὴ πόρον ἷξον εὐρρεῖος ποταμοῖο
Ξάνθου δινήεντος, ὃν ἀθάνατος τέκετο Ζεύς. IL. Φ. 1.

[d] Voyage Pittoresque, p. 267, 268. Col. Leake's Asia Minor, ch. vi. p. 283.

[e] Voyage Pittoresque, p. 228.
[f] Ibid. p. 268.

. . . . .   ἀλλὰ Σκάμανδρος
Οἴσει δινήεις εἴσω ἁλὸς εὐρέα κόλπον.   Il. Φ. 124.

Ἔσταν δ’ ἐν λειμῶνι Σκαμανδρίῳ ἀνθεμόεντι
Μυρίοι.   Il. B. 467.

Καίοντο πτελέαι τε, καὶ ἰτέαι, ἠδὲ μυρῖκαι,
Καίετο δὲ λωτός τ’, ἠδὲ θρύον, ἠδὲ κύπειρον,
Τὰ περὶ καλὰ ῥέεθρα ἅλις ποταμοῖο πεφύκει·
        Il. Φ. 350.

According to Mr. Chevalier, the river of *Bounar-bachi* " is never subject to any increase or diminu-
" tion ; its waters are as pure and pellucid as cry-
" stal ; its borders are covered with flowers ; the
" same sort of trees and plants which grew near it
" when it was attacked by Vulcan, grow there still ;
" willows, lote-trees, ash-trees, and reeds, are yet to
" be seen on its banks, and eels are still caught in
" it[g]." It was doubtless on account of the beauty
and copiousness of its stream that divine honours
were paid to the Scamander by the Trojans. (Il. E.
77. Cf. Æschin. Epist. X. p. 680.)

The Simois, on the contrary, bears all the marks
of a mighty torrent, rushing down from the mountains with furious haste and resistless force. This is
evident from the address of the Scamander to his
brother god, invoking his aid against Achilles ;

Φίλε κασίγνητε, σθένος ἀνέρος ἀμφότεροί περ
Σχῶμεν, ἐπεὶ τάχα ἄστυ μέγα Πριάμοιο ἄνακτος
Ἐκπέρσει, Τρῶες δὲ κατὰ μόθον οὐ μενέουσιν·
Ἀλλ’ ἐπάμυνε τάχιστα, καὶ ἐμπίπληθι ῥέεθρα
Ὕδατος ἐκ πηγέων, πάντας δ’ ὀρόθυνον ἐναύλους·

g Description of the Plain of Troy, p. 83.   See also Voyage
Pittoresque, tom. II. p. 228.

"Ιστη δὲ μέγα κῦμα· πολὺν δ' ὀρυμαγδὸν ὄρινε
Φιτρῶν καὶ λάων, ἵνα παύσομεν ἄγριον ἄνδρα.

IL. Φ. 308.

and all modern travellers and topographers concur
in allowing that this is precisely the character of
the *Mendere*, which takes its rise in a deep cave
below the highest summit of mount Ida, and, after
a tortuous course between steep and craggy banks,
of nearly thirty miles, in a rugged bed, which is
nearly dry in summer, finds its way into the plain
of *Bounarbachi*.   It is true, that when Demetrius
of Scepsis wrote, which is some years after the defeat of Antiochus by the Romans, (Strab. XIII. p.
593.) the *Mendere* certainly bore the name of Scamander, for he describes the source of that river in
mount Ida very accurately, (ap. Strab. XIII. p. 602.)
I should admit also, that the Scamander, which, according to Herodotus, was drained by the army of
Xerxes, (VII. 42.) is the *Mendere :* Hellanicus likewise was of this opinion, (ap. Schol. Il. Φ. 242.) But
this objection may be fairly disposed of, by supposing, that the name of Scamander, which is certainly
much oftener mentioned in Homer, had in process
of time been transferred to the river whose course
was longer, and body of water more considerable ;
whereas it is impossible, I conceive, to get over the
difficulty presented by Homer's description of the
double sources of the Scamander.   The question
may be fairly summed up in this way : either we
must allow that Homer drew his local descriptions
from real scenes, or that he only applied historical
names to fanciful and ideal localities ; in the latter
case, all our interest in the comparative topography
of Troy ceases, and it is a fruitless task to look for

H 2

an application of the imagery traced by the poet to
the actual face of things.   But if a striking resemblance does present itself, we are bound, in justice to the poet, to take our stand on that ground,
and, without regarding any hypothesis or system
which may have been advanced or framed in ancient
times, to seek for an application of the remaining
local features traced in the Iliad in the immediate
vicinity of the sources of *Bounarbachi*.   Here then
travellers have observed, a little above these springs
and the village of the same name, a hill rising from
the plain, generally well calculated for the site of a
large town, and in particular satisfying many of the
local requisites which the Homeric Troy must have
possessed ; such as a sufficient distance from the
sea, and an elevated and commanding situation.
This is evident from the epithets of ἠνεμόεσσα, αἰ-
πεινή, and ὀφρυόεσσα, which are so constantly applied
to it.   If we besides have a rock behind the town,
answering the purpose of such a citadel as the Pergamus of Troy is described to have been, " Πέργα-
" μος ἄκρη," rising precipitously above the city, and
presenting a situation of great strength, we shall
have all that the nature of the poem, even in its
historical character, ought to lead us to expect[h].
With respect to minor objects alluded to by Homer
in the course of his poem, such as the tombs or
mounds of Ilus, Æsyetes, and Myrina, the Scopie
and Erineus, or grove of wild fig-trees, it is perhaps too much to seek to identify them, as the
French topographers have somewhat fancifully

[h] For a detailed decription
of the heights of *Bounarbachi*,
I would refer the reader to the
Voyage Pittoresque, tom II. p.
238, where an accurate plan is
given.

done, with present appearances[i]. It is certain that
such indications cannot be relied upon, since the inhabitants of New Ilium, who also pretended that
their town stood on the site of ancient Troy, boasted that they could shew, close to their walls, these
dubious vestiges of antiquity. (Strab. XIII. p. 599.)
With respect to the objection which may be brought
against the situation here assigned to ancient Troy,
that it would not have been possible for the flight
of Hector to have taken place round the walls, as
the poet has represented it, since the heights of
Bounarbachi are skirted to the N. E. by the deep
and narrow gorge of the *Mendere*, which leaves no
room even for a narrow footpath along its banks ; I
agree with those commentators and critics who are
of opinion that we ought not to take the words of the
poet in the sense which has commonly been assigned
to them, but that it is better to suppose, that Hector and Achilles ran only round that portion of the
city which fronts the plain from the Scæan gates
to the sources of the Scamander, and back again[k].
The difficulty in that case will be satisfactorily removed, and there will then remain, I conceive, no
valid objection to the system which recognises the
hill of *Bounarbachi* as the representative of the
ancient city of Priam, and which has been almost
universally embraced by modern travellers and scho-
lars.

There remain only two or three sites to be noticed, in order to complete this short view of the

[i] I allude to Messrs. Choiseul Gouffier and Le Chevalier.

[k] Choiseul Gouffier, Voyage
Pittoresque, tom. II. p. 238—
240; Le Chevalier's Description
of the Plain of Troy, p. 135;
Leake's Asia Minor, ch. vi. p.
304.

H 3

Homeric topography of the plain of Troy. The

Throsmos
collis.

hill called Throsmos by the poet, and which was a favourite station of the Trojan army in advance of their city towards the Grecian camp, is supposed to correspond with some rising ground on the left bank

Callicolone
collis.

of the Scamander. That of Callicolone, on the other hand, where Mars took his stand, for the purpose of encouraging the Trojan troops, was near the Simois, and towards the left of the Greek encampment.

Αὖ δ᾽ Ἄρης ἑτέρωθεν, ἐρεμνῇ λαίλαπι ἴσος,
᾽Οξὺ κατ᾽ ἀκροτάτης πόλιος Τρώεσσι κελεύων,
Ἄλλοτε πὰρ Σιμόεντι θέων ἐπὶ Καλλικολώνῃ.   Il. Υ. 51.

According to Strabo, who probably copies Demetrius, Callicolone was ten stadia from the Pagus Iliensium, and five from the Simois. From whence it appears to answer to a hill near the site called *Eski Aktchi-kevi;* (XIII. p. 597.) but, as this arrangement is entirely deduced from the hypothesis which Demetrius had adopted with respect to the Simois and Scamander, it has not been adhered to by modern critics, who place Callicolone on the left bank of the *Mendere* or Simois; some opposite to the heights of *Bounarbachi,* others nearer the sea. Demetrius, in placing ancient Troy on the site of

Pagus Ili-
ensium.

the Pagus Iliensium, said to have been built by Ilus, (Strab. XIII. p. 593.) was obliged to seek for a representative of the Simois in one of those small streams which, flowing from east to west, fall into the *Mendere* on the right bank of that river. And if we fix the Pagus of Demetrius at *Eski Aktchi-kevi,* as most modern critics have done, his Simois will be the *Kamar-sou,* the most considerable of the streams alluded to, and which joins the *Mendere*

about three miles below *Bounarbachi:* the plain
situated between the two rivers would also seem to
be the Simoisius campus of the same ancient writer.
But according to the modern system, the *Kamar-
sou* is the river Thymbrius, and the plain that of
Thymbra, alluded to by Homer, in the account of Thymbra.
the Trojan forces, and their different positions, supposed to be disclosed by Dolon :

Πρὸς Θύμβρης δ' ἔλαχον Λύκιοι, Μυσοί τ' ἀγέρωχοι,
Καὶ Φρύγες ἱππόδαμοι, καὶ Μήονες ἱπποκορυσταί.

IL. K. 430.

There is another river, however, which now falls
into the Hellespont, near the tomb of Ajax, but
which appears formerly to have joined the *Mendere,* and, from the name of *Tumbrek,* which it
bears, may be thought to have a better claim to
be considered as the Thymbrius of Strabo, though
not that of Homer; for it must not be forgotten,
that in the geographer's time the inhabitants of
New Ilium had confounded all the Homeric topography by adapting the names of places mentioned
in the Iliad to the localities of their own district
and city. Apollo had a temple at Thymbra, as we
further learn from Strabo, which accounts for the
epithet of Thymbræus applied to that god by
Virgil :

Da propriam, Thymbræe, domum: da mœnia fessis.

ÆN. III. 85.

and before him by the author of Rhesus, v. 224.

Θυμβαῖε καὶ Δάλιε, καὶ Λυκίας
Ναὸν ἐμβατεύων
Ἄπολλον.

It was in this temple that Achilles is said to have
been mortally wounded by Paris. (Eustath. ad

H 4

Il. K. 433. Serv. ad Æn. loc. cit. Steph. Byz. v.
Θύμβρα.)

Ilium No-
vum.

Whatever traces might remain of the ruins of the
city of Priam, after it had been sacked and burnt
by the Greeks, these soon disappeared, as Strabo
assures us, by their being employed in the construction of Sigeum, and other towns founded by the
Æolians, who came from Lesbos, and occupied nearly the whole of Troas.   On their arrival in that
country, they had found it possessed by the Treres,
a barbarian tribe of Thracian origin, who are supposed to have come into Asia with the Cimmerians.
(XIII. p. 599. XII. p. 573.)   The first attempt to
restore the town of Troy was made by some Asty-
palæans, who, having first settled at Rhœteum, built,
near the Simois, a town they called Polium, but
which subsisted only a short time; the spot, however, still retained the name of Polisma when Strabo
wrote.   Some time after, a more advantageous site
was selected in the neighbourhood, and a town, consisting at first of a few habitations and a temple,
was built under the protection of the kings of Lydia,
the then sovereigns of the country.   This became a
rising place; and in order to ensure the prosperity
of the colony, and to enhance its celebrity, the inhabitants boldly affirmed that their town actually
stood on the site of ancient Troy, that city having
never been actually destroyed by the Greeks.   There
were not wanting writers who propagated this false-
hood, in order to flatter the vanity of the citizens,
(Strab. XIII. p. 601.) and when Xerxes passed
through Troas, on his way to the Hellespont, the
pretensions of New Ilium were so firmly established,
that the Persian monarch, when he visited their acro-

polis, and offered there an immense sacrifice to Minerva, actually thought that he had seen and honoured the far-famed city of Priam. (Herod. VII. 42.) In the treaty made with the successor of Xerxes, Ilium was recognised as a Greek city, and its independence was secured; but the peace of Antalcidas restored it again to Persia. Some years after, it was momentarily in the hands of Charidemus, a Greek partisan, at the head of some mercenary troops hired by Artabazus, satrap of the Hellespont, to defend himself against the attack of Autophradates, governor of Lydia. Charidemus obtained possession of the town and citadel by a stratagem, but being besieged by the forces of the victorious Autophradates was unable to hold out, and obtained permission to withdraw. (Demosth. in Aristocr. p. 671. Æn. Tact. c. 24. Polyæn. Stratag. III. 14.)

On the arrival of Alexander in Asia Minor, (Arrian. Exp. Alex. I. 11, 12,) or, as some say, after the battle of the Granicus, (Strab. XIII. p. 593.) that prince visited Ilium, and after offering a sacrifice to Minerva in the citadel, deposited his arms there, and received others, said to have been preserved in the temple from the time of the siege of Troy. He further granted several rights and privileges to the Ilienses, and promised to erect a more splendid edifice, and to institute games in honour of Minerva; but death prevented the execution of these designs. (Arrian. loc. cit. Strab. loc. cit. Diod. Sic. XVIII. p. 589.) Lysimachus, however, to whose share Troas fell on the division of Alexander's empire, undertook to execute what had been planned

by the deceased monarch. He enclosed the city
within a wall, which was forty stadia in circumference ; he also increased the population by removing thither the inhabitants of several neighbouring towns. (Strab. XII. p. 593.) At a subsequent
period Ilium further experienced the favour and
protection of the kings of Pergamus ; and the Romans, on achieving the conquest of Asia Minor,
sought to extend their popularity by securing the
independence of a city from which they pretended
to derive their origin, and added to its territory the
towns of Rhœteum and Gergitha. (Liv. XXXVII.
37. XXXVIII. 39.) And yet it would appear, that
at that time Ilium was far from being a flourishing
city, since Demetrius of Scepsis, who visited it about
the same period, affirmed that it was in a ruinous
state, many of the houses having fallen into decay
for want of tiling. (ap. Strab. loc. cit.) During the
civil wars between Sylla and Cinna, Ilium was
besieged and taken by assault by Fimbria, a partisan of the latter. This general gave it up to plunder, butchered the inhabitants, and finally destroyed
it by fire. Not long after, however, Sylla arrived
in Asia, and having defeated Fimbria, who fell by
his own hand, restored Ilium to the surviving inhabitants, reinstated them in their possessions, and
restored the walls and public edifices. (Appian. Bell.
Mithr. c. 53. Plut. Vit. Syll. Strab. XIII. p. 594.)
The Ilienses received Lucullus in their city when
that general had compelled Mithridates to raise the
siege of Cyzicus, and paid him distinguished honours. (Plut. Vit. Lucull.) After the battle of
Pharsalus, Ilium was visited by Julius Cæsar, who

explored, if we may believe Lucan, all the monuments and localities which claimed any interest
from their connexion with the poem of Homer.

Sigeasque petit, famæ mirator, arenas,
Et Simoëntis aquas, et Graio nobile busto
Rhœtion, et multum debentes vatibus umbras.
Circuit exustæ nomen memorabile Trojæ,
Magnaque Phœbei quærit vestigia muri.
Jam silvæ steriles, et putres robore trunci
Assaraci pressêre domos, et templa deorum
Jam lassâ radice tenent : ac tota teguntur
Pergama dumetis : et jam periêre ruinæ :
Adspicit Hesiones scopulos, silvasque, latentes
Anchisæ thalamos ; quo judex sederit antro ;
Unde puer raptus cœlo ; quo vertice Naïs
Luxerit Œnone : nullum est sine nomine saxum.
Inscius in sicco serpentem pulvere rivum
Transierat, qui Xanthus erat : securus in alto
Gramine ponebat gressus ; Phryx incola manes
Hectoreos calcare vetat.   Discussa jacebant
Saxa, nec ullius faciem servantia sacri ;
Herceas, monstrator ait, non respicis aras ?

PHARS. IX. 961.

Cæsar, in consequence of this visit, and his pretended descent from Iulus, conceded fresh grants to
the Ilienses, and added Sigeum, Dardanus, and other
towns, to their territory; he likewise instituted
those games which Virgil has alluded to in the
Æneid, and which the Romans called " Ludi Tro-
" jani." (Æn. V. 602. Suet. Cæs. 39. Dio. Cass.
XLIII. 23.)   We hear of the Ilienses having been
fined by Agrippa for not paying proper respect to
Julia, when that princess visited their city ; but the
fine was remitted, owing to the intercession of Herod,
king of Judæa. (Nicol. Damasc. Exc. p. 418.)   We

further trace the history of Ilium through the reign
of Tiberius, when it was visited by Germanicus,
but refused permission to erect a temple to the emperor. (Tacit. Ann. II. 54. IV. 55.) It preserved
its privileges and freedom under Trajan, as we learn
from Pliny, who styles it, " Ilium immune, unde
" omnis claritas." (V. 30.) It subsisted under Dio-
cletian, and it is even said that Constantine had entertained serious thoughts of transferring thither the
seat of empire. (Sozom. Hist. Eccl. II. 3. Zosim. II.
34.) The last records we have of its existence are
derived from Hierocles, (Synecd. p. 663.) the Itineraries, and the Notices of Greek bishops under the
Byzantine empire. It became afterwards exposed
to the ravages of the Saracens, and other barbarians, who depopulated the Hellespont and Troad :
it sunk beneath their repeated attacks, and became
a heap of ruins. The surrounding villages are yet
filled with inscriptions, and fragments of buildings
and monuments, which attest its former splendour
and magnificence. According to the account of a
modern traveller, who has minutely explored the
whole of Troas, New Ilium occupied a gently rising
hill about seventy feet high, above the adjacent
plain, in which the waters of the *Tumbrek-tchai*
and *Kamar-sou* form some marshes. On the south
side are to be seen the foundations of the acropolis,
and the lines of the walls may be traced along the
whole of their circuit, though the Turks have removed the stones to construct their habitations.
They call the site *Hissardjick*, or *Eski Kalafatli* [1].

[1] Choiseul Gouffier, tom. II.
part iii. p. 381. Barker Webb,
Osservazioni intorno l'Agro

Trojano Bibl. Ital. No. 67.
Luglio, 1821.

New Ilium was twenty-one miles from Abydos, or
170 stadia, (Strab. XIII. p. 591.) and about eleven
miles from Dardanus. (Itiner. Anton. p. 334.)   According to Strabo, New Ilium was not more than
twelve stadia from the Portus Achæorum, and twenty
from the mouth of the Scamander. (XIII. p. 598.)
Pliny reckons a mile and a half. (V. 30.)   It is uncertain where we should place the small town of
Scamandria, mentioned by the latter author, and Scaman-
also by Hierocles, who calls it Σκάμανδρος. (Synecd. dria.
p. 663.) An inscription has been discovered, record-
ing a treaty for the sale of corn between the Ilienses and Scamandrians [m].

Sigeum was founded posterior to the siege of Sigeum.
Troy by an Æolian colony, headed by Archæanax
of Mytilene.   He is said to have employed the
stones of ancient Ilium in the construction of his
town.   The Athenians, some years afterwards, sent
a body of troops there headed by Phrynon, a victor
at the Olympic games, and expelled the Lesbians.
This act of aggression led to a war between the
two states, which was long waged with alternate
success.   Pittacus, one of the seven sages, who commanded the Mityleneans, is said to have slain Phrynon, the Athenian leader, in single fight.   The poet
Alcæus was engaged in one of the actions that took
place, and, by his own confession, fled from the
field, leaving his arms to the enemy.   At length
both parties agreed to refer their dispute to Periander of Corinth, who decided in favour of the Athenians. (Strabo XIII. p. 599. Herod. V. 95. Diog.
Laert. I. 74.)   The latter people, or rather the Pi-
sistratidæ, remained then in possession of Sigeum,

[m] Voyage Pittoresque, tom. II. p. 288.

and ͵Hippias, after being expelled from Athens, is known to have retired there, together with his family. (Herod. V. 65.)

The town of Sigeum no longer existed when Strabo wrote, having been destroyed by the citizens of New Ilium. (XIII. p. 600. Plin. V. 30.) The *Sigeum promonto-rium.* promontory was especially celebrated in antiquity, as the spot on which the ashes of Achilles had been interred; and such was the reverence with which *Achilleum.* it was regarded, that a small town, named Achilleum, appears to have grown up around the tomb, as early as the time of Herodotus. (V. 94.) Strabo, on the authority of Demetrius of Scepsis, reports that it was fortified by the Mitylenians in their war with Athens. (XIII. p. 600.) The tomb of Achilles was successively visited by Alexander, (Arrian. Exp. Alex. I. 12. Cic. pro Arch. c. 10.) Julius Cæsar, and Germanicus; and the mound which overtops it is still visible at the present day, together with those of Patroclus and Antilochus [n].

Ἐν τῷ τοι κεῖται λεύκ' ὀστέα, φαίδιμ' Ἀχιλλεῦ,
Μίγδα δὲ, Πατρόκλοιο Μενοιτιάδαο θανόντος·
Χωρὶς δ', Ἀντιλόχοιο· τὸν ἔξοχα τῖες ἁπάντων
Τῶν ἄλλων ἑτάρων, μετὰ Πάτροκλόν γε θανόντα.
Ἀμφ' αὐτοῖσι δ' ἔπειτα μέγαν καὶ ἀμύμονα τύμβον
Χεύαμεν Ἀργείων ἱερὸς στρατὸς αἰχμητάων,
Ἀκτῇ ἔπι προὐχούσῃ, ἐπὶ πλατεῖ Ἑλλησπόντῳ·
Ὡς κεν τηλεφανὴς ἐκ ποντόφιν ἀνδράσιν εἴη
Τοῖς, οἳ νῦν γεγάασι, καὶ οἳ μετόπισθεν ἔσονται.

Od. Ω. 76.

The cape of Sigeum is now called *Yeni-cher*. A little to the south of it is another headland, with some ruins, which may possibly belong to the little

[n] Chevalier, Descr. of the Plain of Troy, chap. xxi. p. 142. Voyage Pittoresque, tom. II. p. 330.

town of Agamia °, said to have been so called from Agamia.
the adventure of Hesione, who was there exposed to
the sea-monster, and delivered by Hercules. (Steph.
Byz. v. 'Αγάμεια. Cf. Hesych. ead. v.) In Hierocles
it is not unlikely that for 'Αρτέμεια we ought to read
'Αγάμεια. (Synecd. p. 663.) Opposite to the headland are some little islands, or rocks, which may be
the Lagussæ of Pliny ; (V. 38. Cf. Eustath. Il. B. Lagussæ
insulæ.
p. 306.) but this is uncertain, as the same geogra-
pher enumerates with those on the coast of Troas
several others; Ascaniæ, Plateæ III., Lamiæ, Pli-
taniæ II., Plate, Scopelos, Getone, Arthedon, Cœlæ,
Didymæ. The largest of these islets is now called
Taushan. Somewhat to the south is the more conspicuous and celebrated island of Tenedos, whither Tenedos
insula.
the Greeks retired, as Virgil relates, in order to surprise the Trojans.

> Est in conspectu Tenedos, notissima fama
> Insula, dives opum, Priami dum regna manebant ;
> Nunc tantum sinus, et statio male fida carinis ;
> Huc se provecti deserto in littore condunt.
> ÆN. II. 21.

> Et jam Argiva phalanx instructis navibus ibat
> A Tenedo, tacitæ per amica silentia lunæ,
> Littora nota petens. IBID. 254.

This island was formerly called Leucophrys, from
its white cliffs ; (Eustath. Il. A. p. 33. Lycophr.
346.)

> Τοῖς εἰς στενὴν Λεύκοφρυν ἐκπεπλευκόσι.

and it took the name of Tenedos from Tennes, the
son of Cycnus, whose adventures are related at
length by Heraclides Ponticus, (Polit. p. 209.) ·
Strabo, (VIII. p. 380. XIII. p. 604.) Pausanias, (Phoc.

° Voyage Pittoresque, tom. II. p. 331.

14.) Conon. (Narrat. pp. 24. 130.) Tenedos received a colony of Æolians, (Herod. I. 149. Thuc. VII. 57.) which flourished for many years, and became celebrated for the wisdom of its laws and civil institutions. This we collect from an ode of Pindar inscribed to Aristagoras, prytanis or chief magistrate of the island. (Nem. XI.) Aristotle is known to have written on the polity of Tenedos. (Steph. Byz. v. Τένεδος.) Apollo was the principal deity worshipped in the island, as we know from Homer. (Il. A. 37.)

Κλῦθί μευ, 'Αργυρότοξ' ὃς χρύσην ἀμφιβέβηκας,
Κίλλαν τε ζαθέην, Τενέδοιό τε ἶφι ἀνάσσεις,
Σμινθεῦ—

According to the same poet, Tenedos was taken by Achilles during the siege of Troy. (Il. Λ. 624.) When the prosperity of Tenedos was on the decline, the inhabitants placed themselves under the protection of the flourishing city of Alexandria Troas. (Pausan. Phoc. 14.) At a still later period it derived again some importance from the granaries which Justinian caused to be erected there, for the purpose of housing the cargoes of corn brought from Egypt and intended for Constantinople, but which were frequently delayed by contrary winds blowing from the Hellespont. (Procop. Æd. Justin. V. 1.) Strabo estimates the circuit of Tenedos at eighty stadia, and its distance from the mainland at forty, which is pretty correct; but the little islands called Calydnæ, which the same geographer places between cape Lectum and Tenedos, are not to be found in that direction. (XIII. p. 603.) In Choiseul Gouffier's map, they are laid down between Tenedos and Sigeum. There were several proverbs con-

nected with the history of Tenedos which may be
found in Steph. Byz. (v. Τένεδος.) It may be worth
while to remark, that Nymphodorus, a geographical
writer quoted by Athenæus, affirmed that the women
of Tenedos were of surpassing beauty. (XIII. p. 60.)
When Chandler visited this island, which retains its
ancient name, " he found there but few remains of
" antiquity worthy of notice; in the streets, the walls
" and burying-grounds, were pieces of marble and
" fragments of pillars, with a few inscriptions P."
Homer places between Imbros and Tenedos the sub-
marine cave, in which Neptune rested his horses
while he proceeded to aid the Greeks.

> Ἔστι δέ τι σπέος εὑρὺ βαθείης βένθεσι λίμνης,
> Μεσσηγὺς Τενέδοιο καὶ Ἴμβρου παιπαλοέσσης·
> Ἔνθ' ἵππους ἔστησε Ποσειδάων ἐνοσίχθων.   IL. N. 32.

Opposite to Tenedos, on the Trojan coast, was a
spot named Achæium, (Strab. XIII. p. 603, 4.) and Achæium.
immediately after followed Larissa and Colonæ, two
towns of great antiquity, but which made way, together with several others, for the rising city of
Alexandria Troas.   Colonæ was the city of Cycnus, Colonæ.
already mentioned as the father of Tennes, and
stood at a distance of 140 stadia from Ilium. (Strab.
XIII. p. 589. Pausan. Phoc. 14. Xen. Hell. III. 1,
10.)   Larissa, a name always indicative of a Pelasgic origin, had probably been founded by one of
those wandering tribes, which settled in different
parts of the Asiatic coast before the siege of Troy;
but Strabo is of opinion, and apparently on good
grounds, that this was not the Larissa spoken of by Larissa.
Homer, (Il. P. 301.) as that is expressly said to have
been far from Troy. (Strab. XIII. p. 620.)   This

P Travels in Asia Minor, p. 22. Inscr. Ant. pp. 3, 4.

town is alluded to by Thucydides (VIII. 101.) and
Xenophon (III. 1, 10.) Cf. Scyl. p. 36. But Stephanus Byz. looks upon it as the Homeric town.
(v. Λάρισσα.) Athenæus mentions some hot springs
near Larissa in Troas, (II. p. 43.) which are still

Alexandria known to exist a little above the site of Alexandria
Troas.
Troas [q]. The latter city, which was so called by
Lysimachus, had been first named Antigonia, from
Antigonus, another of Alexander's generals, who
was its first founder. Antigonus had already increased its population by sending thither the inhabitants of Cebrene, Neandria, and other towns; and
it received a further increase under the auspices of
Lysimachus: under the Romans it acquired still
greater prosperity, and became one of the most
flourishing of their Asiatic colonies. (Strab. XIII.
pp. 593, 604. Cf. Plin. V. 30.) It was thus distinguished by the Romans on account of the fidelity
it had displayed in the war which they waged
against Antiochus. (Liv. XXXV. 42. Polyb. XXI.
10, 3. Cf. V. 78, 6. 111, 3.) In the Acts of the
Apostles it is simply called Troas, and it was from
its port that St. Paul and St. Luke set sail for Macedonia, (xvi. 11.) and it was there, on his return
from Macedonia, that the apostle restored to life
Eutychus, who had been killed by a fall from an
upper story whilst asleep. (xx. 9.) Of this town
were Hegesianax and Hestiæa, who wrote com-
mentaries on Homer, and Hegemon, an epic poet.
(Strab. XIII. p. 599. Steph. Byz. vv. Τρωϊας et Ἀλεξ-
άνδρεια. Athen. IX. p. 393.) The site of Alexandria
is called *Eski Stamboul*, and numerous ruins attest
its former magnificence. According to Chandler, "it

[q] Voyage Pittoresque, tom. II. p. 438.

" was seated on a hill sloping toward the sea, and
" divided from mount Ida by a deep valley. On
" each side is an extensive plain, with water courses.
" The city wall is standing, but with gaps, and the
" battlements ruined. It was thick and solid, had
" square towers at regular distances, and was seve-
" ral miles in circumference. Besides houses, it has
" enclosed many magnificent structures ; but now
" appears as the boundary of a forest or neglected
" park." The principal buildings, according to the
same diligent and learned traveller, were a public
gymnasium, or stadium, a theatre and odeum, several temples, and a magnificent aqueduct built by
Herodes Atticus. There are also some vestiges of
the port and mole [r].

Strabo affirms, that the site on which this city
was built had borne the name of Sigia. (XIII. p. 604.)
More to the south was the town of Chrysa, surnamed Dia, and celebrated for the worship of Apollo
Sminthius, so called from σμίνθος, which in the Æolic
dialect signifies a *rat*. Tradition ascribed the origin
of the name to the circumstance of this animal's
having appeared in great numbers, when the Teucrians landed in Troas from Crete, and having
gnawed the leather of their arms and utensils. Various other fabulous tales respecting these rats are
to be found in Strabo, who observes, that there were
numerous spots on this coast to which the name of
Sminthia was attached. The temple itself was called

Chrysa quæ et

[r] Chandler's Travels in Asia Minor, p. 32. The reader will find also a detailed account of the ruins of Alexandria, toge- ther with a plan of them, in the splendid work of Choiseul Gouffier, so often referred to. tom. II. p. 434. The coins of Alexander Troas are to be found in almost every collection. The earliest bear the name of Anti- gonia. Sestin. Mon. Vet. p. 76.

Sminthi-
um.

Sminthium. He does not however allow, as Scylax does, (p. 36.) that this edifice, or the Chrysa here mentioned, were those to which Homer has alluded in the first book of the Iliad, as the abode of Chryses, the priest of Apollo. He places these more to the south, and on the Adramyttian gulf. (XIII. pp. 604, 612.)

Halesium.

Tragasæ.

Continuing along the coast, we find a plain of some extent, anciently called Halesium, from the salt springs with which it abounded. These furnished a great supply of salt from works established in the spot called Tragasæ. And it was affirmed, that when Lysimachus had laid a duty on this article, the springs suddenly failed, but reappeared on the tax being withdrawn. (Athen. III. p. 73. Strab. XIII. p. 605. Steph. Byz. vv. Ἀλήσιος, Τράγασαι.) The salt of Tragasæ is mentioned by Galen, (de Temp. Medic. Simpl. t. II. p. 151.) Hesychius, (v. Τραγασαῖοι,) and others. The works are still in existence, and are known to the Turks by the name of *Tuzla*, which precisely corresponds with the Latin Salinæ [s]. Near these works we must look

Hamaxi-
tus.

for the ruins of Hamaxitus, an ancient town, probably of Æolic origin, noticed by Scylax, (p. 36.) Thucydides, (VIII. 101.) and Strabo, (XIII. p. 605.) as situated on the Trojan coast. (Cf. Plin. V. 33. Apollod. ap. Steph. Byz. v. Ἀμαξιτός.) The pro-

Lectum
promonto-
rium.

montory of Lectum was the southernmost point of Troas, the towns situated beyond it, on the Adramyttian gulf, being considered as belonging to Æolis. (Strab. XIII. p. 605. Plin. V. 32.) Homer, in

[s] Le Chevalier, Voyage dans la Troade, tom. I. ch. 2. Col. Leake states, that the neigh- bouring hills are composed of rock salt. Asia Minor, ch. vi. p. 274.

his account of the deceit practised upon Jupiter by
Juno, makes it part of the chain of Ida, and the
spot where the goddess landed, together with her
auxiliary the god of sleep:

Τὼ βήτην, Λήμνου τε καὶ Ἴμβρου ἄστυ λιπόντε,
Ἥρα ἐσσαμένω, ῥίμφα πρήσσοντε κέλευθον·
Ἴδην δ᾽ ἱκέσθην πολυπίδακα, μητέρα θηρῶν,
Λεκτὸν, ὅθι πρῶτον λιπέτην ἅλα· τὼ δ᾽ ἐπὶ χέρσου
Βήτην· ἀκροτάτη δὲ ποδῶν ὑπ᾽ ἐσείετο ὕλη.

IL. Ξ. 281.

Herodotus relates, that after the battle of Mycale
the Greek fleet took up their station near Lectum,
on their way to the Hellespont, the wind being ad-
verse. (IX. 114.)   It is also alluded to by Thucydides, (VIII. 101.) Livy, (XXXVII. 37.) and Plutarch, in the life of Lucullus.   Athenæus reports,
that the purple shellfish was found here, as well as
near Sigeum, and of a large size. (III. p. 88.)   The
modern name is Cape *Baba*.

In the interior of Troas there remain yet a few
places to be pointed out.   Among these, Neandria is Neandria.
frequently mentioned in history as an Æolian colony
of some note. (Scyl. p. 36.)   Its territory appears
from Strabo to have included a fertile and extensive
plain, named Samonium; (II. p. 106. XI. p. 472.) Samonius
and the same geographer affirms that it was situated Campus.
between Hamaxitus and New Ilium, at a distance
of 130 stadia from the latter.   These circumstances
concur in fixing the site of this ancient town near
the modern village of *Enai*, or *Ene*, where there
are many vestiges of antiquity, and above which
the valley of the *Mendere*, or Simois, opens into a
broad and well cultivated plain, now called *Baira-*

misch [t]. Neandria, as we learn from Xenophon, had belonged to the Dardanian princess Mania; but on her death it was declared independent by Dercyllidas. (Hell. III. 1, 13.) After the dissolution of Alexander's great empire, Antigonus obtained for a short time possession of Troas, and Neandria and other small towns were destroyed, to make way for the city which that general founded on this coast under the name of Antigonia, but which afterwards was called Alexandria Troas. (Strab. XIII. p. 604. Cf. Steph. Byz. v. Νεάνδρεια. Antigon. Caryst. c. 187. Cedren. Compend. p. 126. Plin. V. 30.) A little to the south of *Ene*, and between it and *Eski Stamboul*, or Alexandria, a small place named *Kutchu-*

Cocylium. *lan* [u] is thought to represent Cocylia, or Cocylium, a Greek town mentioned by Xenophon, in connexion with Ilium and Neandria, in the passage above referred to. In Pliny's time it no longer existed. (V. 33.)

On the left bank of the *Mendere*, and to the south of *Ene*, or Neandria, is a ruined fortress called *Tchigri* by the natives; this may have been

Cenchreæ. Cenchreæ, a town of Troas, where Homer was said to have resided some time, to make himself acquainted with the Trojan topography. (Steph. Byz. v. Κεγχρέαι.) Some even pretended that the poet was born there. (Suid. v. Ὅμηρος.) Under the Greek emperors, Cenchreæ is mentioned as a fortress in which state prisoners were confined. (Pachymer.

---

[t] Voyage Pittoresque, tom. II. p. 285. Leake, Asia Minor, ch. vi. p. 274. Some topographers have identified *Enai* with Nea or Neacome, but this was near the Æsepus. There are some few coins of Neandria, with the legend NEAN. Sestini, p. 77.

[u] Voyage Pittoresque, Carte de la Troade, tom. II. p. 201.

tom. I. p. 331.) It was besieged and taken by the
Turks in the fourteenth century. (Pach. tom. II.
p. 334.) According to Choiseul Gouffier, the walls
and gates of this town are yet standing [x]. Higher
up the river *Mendere*, and not far from its source
in mount Ida, are some extensive ruins denoting
an ancient town of importance. The site is called
Kutchulan-tepe, and its topographical situation agrees
with that which ancient writers assign to Cebrene, Cebrene.
capital of a small district named from it Cebrenia. Cebrenia
But it was affirmed by some, that the name was regio.
derived from Cebriones, the natural son of Priam,
and charioteer of Hector. Strabo reports, that the
district of Cebrenia was separated by the Scamander
(the Simois of Homer) from the territory of Scepsis,
with which town the Cebrenians were almost constantly at war. This state of discord was at length
put an end to by Antigonus, who removed the inhabitants of both towns to Antigonia, afterwards Alexandria Troas. (XIII. p. 597.) According to Ephorus, Cebrene had received a colony from the Æolian
Cyme. (ap. Harpocr. v. Κέβρηνα. Cf. Scyl. Peripl.
p. 36.) Xenophon affirms that it was a place of
great strength. It resisted for some time the attack
of Dercyllidas, the Lacedæmonian commander, but
at length submitted to his authority. (Hell. III.
1, 14.) Cebrene is also noticed by Demosthenes.
(contr. Aristocr. p. 671.) We learn from Apollodorus that there was a river named Cebren, which
probably flowed near the town. (Biblioth. III. 5, 6.
Steph. Byz. v. Κεβρήνια.) It is now called *Kaz-
dagh-tchai*, and falls into the *Mendere* a little above
the ruins of *Kutchunlu-tepe* [y].

[x] Voyage Pittoresque, tom. II. p. 201.   [y] Ibid. p. 284.

The *Mendere* receives on its right bank, some
miles below, a larger torrent, called *Lidjick-Deressi-*
Andrius fl. *tchai,* which is probably the river Andrius, which,
according to Strabo, flowed from Caresene. (XII.
p. 602.) It was from the number of the streams
which descend from its sides into the Hellespont
and Propontis that Homer gives to mount Ida the
epithet of πολυπίδαξ; and, according to modern travellers, it still preserves that feature, as well as the
accompanying one, of being the haunt of numerous
beasts, expressed by the poet in the same line :

"Ίδην δ' ἵκανεν πολυπίδακα, μητέρα θηρῶν.   Il. Θ. 47.

Strabo compares the whole chain to a scolopendra,
on account of the great number of subordinate hills
which branched off from it in various directions.
Of these, the highlands about Zeleia were the most
northern; while the headland of Lectum formed
the extreme point to the south-west.   Two other
subordinate ranges, parting from the principal summit, and terminating, the one at cape Rhœteum, the
other at the Sigean promontory, might be said to
enclose the territory of Troy in a crescent; while
another central ridge betwixt the two, separating
the valley of the Scamander from that of the Simois, gave to the whole the form of the Greek letter ε. (Demetr. ap. Strab. XIII. p. 597.) The highest
summit, which Homer calls Gargara, is now called
Kaz-dagh.   Its elevation has been ascertained to
be 775 toises, or about 5000 English feet, above the
level of the sea.   Those travellers who have ascended
this lofty mountain give an animated description of
the extensive prospect over the Hellespont, Propontis, and the whole surrounding country, which they

enjoyed from it [z], and which fully justifies the expressions of the poet :

Ἴδην δ' ἵκανεν πολυπίδακα, μητέρα θηρῶν,
Γάργαρον, ἔνθα δέ οἱ τέμενος, βωμός τε θυήεις·
Ἔνθ' ἵππους ἔστησε πατὴρ ἀνδρῶν τε θεῶν τε,
Λύσας ἐξ ὀχέων, κατὰ δ' ἠέρα πουλὺν ἔχευεν.
Αὐτὸς δ' ἐν κορυφῇσι καθέζετο κύδεϊ γαίων,
Εἰσορόων Τρώων τε πόλιν καὶ νῆας Ἀχαιῶν.   IL. Θ. 47.

Several ancient writers have spoken of a remarkable coruscation of light which was to be observed before sunrise around this elevated summit :

Quod genus Idæis fama est e montibus altis
Dispersos igneis orienti lumine cerni :
Inde coire globum quasi in unum, et conficere orbem.
LUCRET. V. 662.

(Cf. Diod. Sic. XVII. 7. Pomp. Mel. I. 18.) Various explanations of this phenomenon have been suggested by modern naturalists, which will be found in Choiseul. The sources of the *Mendere* are to be seen in a remarkable cavern above the village of *Audgelar*, at the foot of the mountain. Besides Gargara, we hear of three other summits ; Cotylus, which has already been mentioned, Pytna, and Dicte, in the territory of Scepsis. (Strab. XIII. p. 472.) Other passages relating to this celebrated mountain will be found in Homer's Hymn to Venus ; Ovid's Epistles, XVI. 53 ; Dionys. Perieg. 814.

On rounding cape Lectum, the coast is seen to stretch far to the east, when it again bends to the south-west, so as to form a deep bay, which took its name from the once flourishing city of Adramyt-

Adramyttenus Sinus.

z Voyage Pittoresque, tom. II. p. 281. Clarke's Travels, tom. II. p. 134. Dr. Hunt's Journal, in Walpole's Turkey, tom. I. p. 120.

tium, situated at the head of it, at a little distance from the coast. The shores of this beautiful gulf had at an early period been peopled by those wandering tribes who, under the name of Leleges, are so often mentioned in the barbarous age of Grecian history. Homer enumerates them among the Trojan forces, (Il. K. 432.) and assigns to them the town of Pedasus, on the river Satnioeis :

Pedasus.

Ἄλτεω, ὃς Λελέγεσσι φιλοπτολέμοισιν ἀνάσσει,
Πήδασον αἰπήεσσαν ἔχων ὑπὸ Σατνιόεντι.   Il. Φ. 86.

Ναῖε δὲ, Σατνιόεντος ἐϋῤῥείταο παρ' ὄχθας,
Πήδασον αἰπεινήν.   Il. Z. 34.

The situation of this Homeric town remains undefined ; it appears indeed from Pliny, that some authors identified it with Adramyttium. (V. 32.) There was another Pedasus in Caria, which must not be confounded with it. The Satnioeis is generally supposed to be a small stream which falls into the Ægean sea, some miles to the north of cape Lectum, and near the salt works of *Tuzla*, from whence it derives its present name[a]. Strabo informs us, that some critics wrote the word Saphnioeis. (XIII. p. 605.) The first city of note to the east of cape Lectum is Assus, founded, according to Myrsilus and Hellanicus, the Lesbian historians, by a colony from that island. (Ap. Strab. XIII. p. 610.) It is celebrated in the annals of Grecian philosophy as the birthplace of Cleanthes the Stoic, the successor of Zeno. Aristotle resided also some time at Assus, having married, it is said, the niece of Hermias, a eunuch, who had made himself tyrant of the city. Hermias, however, having fallen into the

Satnioeis fl.

Assus.

[a] Choiseul Gouffier, tom. II. p. 438. Leake's Asia Minor, p. 273.

hands of Memnon, the Persian general, was put to
death, and Assus was taken possession of by the
Persian forces. (Strab. XIII. p. 610. Cf. Diog. Laert. V. 3.) Assus occupied a commanding situation,
at some distance from the coast, and was fortified
with strong walls ; but the road which led to it
from the port was so steep, that Stratonicus the
musician humorously applied to it this verse of
Homer ;

Ἄσσον ἴθ', ὥς κεν θᾶσσον ὀλέθρου πείραθ' ἵκηαι.

IL. Z. 144.

The port was chiefly formed by a great mole. We
learn from the Acts of the Apostles that St. Luke,
and the other companions of St. Paul, here rejoined
with their ship the apostle, who had left them at
Alexandria Troas, and had crossed on foot from
that city to Assos : (xx. 13.) "And we went before
" to ship, and sailed unto Assos, there intending to
" take in Paul : for so had he appointed, minding
" himself to go afoot. And when he met with us at
" Assos, we took him in, and came to Mitylene."
Pliny seems to say Assus was once called Apollonia.
(V. 32.) The same writer informs us, that a stone
was found in the territory of this city which had
the peculiar property of wasting the flesh of bodies
entombed in it ; hence it was called " sarcophagus."
(XXXVI. 17. Vid. Salmas. Cf. Steph. Byz. v. Ἄσ-
σος.) Col. Leake, who visited the remains of this
ancient city, on the site now called *Beriam Kalesi*,
observes, " that they are extremely curious. There
" is a theatre in very perfect preservation ; and the
" remains of several temples lying in confused heaps
" upon the ground. On the western side of the
" city, the remains of the walls and towers, with a

" gate, are in complete preservation; and without
" the walls is seen the cemetery, with numerous
" sarcophagi still standing in their places, and an
" ancient causeway leading through them to the
" gate. Some of these sarcopahgi are of gigantic
" dimensions. The whole gives perhaps the most
" perfect idea of a Greek city that any where ex-
" ists [b]." Strabo places between Assus and cape
Lectum, at forty stadia from either, a fortress named

Polyme-
dium.

Polymedium; (XIII. p. 606.) but Pliny perplexes
us by naming in this vicinity Palamedium and Po-
lymedia: his text is probably not without error.
(V. 32.) Sixty stadia beyond Assus, and 140 from

Gargara.

cape Lectum, we must place Gargara, a colony of
the former, and situated on a cape which probably
took its name from the celebrated summit of mount
Ida. It was from this cape that the Adramyttian
gulf, called also by some the bay of Ida, properly
commenced. (Strab. XIII. p. 606.) Gargara had
been an Æolian colony, but it afterwards received
an increase of inhabitants from the town of Miletopolis, so that the town lost much of its Greek character, as Demetrius of Scepsis affirmed. (Strab.
XIII. p. 610. Mel. I. 18.) The territory of Gargara, situated at the foot of mount Ida, is much
celebrated by the writers of antiquity for its great
richness and fertility, especially in corn.

> . . . nullo tantum se Mysia cultu
> Jactat, et ipsa suas mirantur Gargara messes.
>
> Virg. Georg. I. 102.

[b] Asia Minor, p. 128. The autonomous coins of Assus, with the epigraph ΑΣΣΙΟΝ, are rare. The imperial money ex-hibits a series from Augustus to Alexander Severus. Sestin. p. 72.

Hinc grata Cereri Gargara, et dives solum,
Quod Xanthus ambit nivibus Idæis tumens.

SENEC. PHŒN. Act. IV. v. 608.

(Cf. Steph. Byz. v. Γάργαρον. Plin. V. 32. Macrob. Saturn. V. 20. Etym. Magn. v. Γάργαρα.) Gargara must be sought for near the headland on which is now situated the village of *Iné* [c]. In the same vicinity stood Lamponia, or Lamponium, an Æo- Lamponia. lian city, named by Hecatæus and Hellanicus. (Ap. Steph. Byz. v. Λαμπώνεια.) Herodotus reports, that it was annexed to the Persian empire by the satrap Otanes, in the reign of Darius, son of Hystaspes. (V. 26.) Somewhat further from the coast were the towns of Andeira and Pionia. The territory of the Andeira. former was productive of a mineral substance, which, by different processes, became zinc, or the metal called orichalcum. (Strab. XIII. p. 610. Steph. Byz. v. Ἄνδειρα.) Pionia is mentioned by Pliny ; (V. 32.) Pionia. and the Ecclesiastical Notices name it as a bishopric of the Hellespontine province [d]. (Hierocl. Synecd. p. 663.) Near Andeira was to be seen a remarkable subterraneous passage, which was said to extend underground as far as Palæa, a village distant 130 stadia from Andeira. It was accidentally discovered by a goatherd, who found there one of his goats, which had strayed into the cavern. A temple was dedicated here to the goddess Cybele. (Strab. XIII. p. 614.)

Antandrus, the foundation of which seems to be Antandrus. ascribed by Herodotus to the Pelasgi, (VII. 42.) is

[c] Note to the French Strabo, tom. IV. p. 198. The coins of Gargara have the inscription ΓΑΡ. and ΓΑΡΓΑΡΕΩΝ. Sestini, p. 72.

[d] There are some few coins belonging to Pionia, with the legend ΠΙΟΝΙΤΩΝ. Sestini, p. 75.

mentioned as an Æolian colony by Thucydides.
(VIII. 108.) It seems also to have been occupied
at an early period by the Cimmerians and Edonian
Thracians, as appears from the epithets of Cimmeris
and Edonis applied to it by Pliny. (V. 32.) Aristotle, indeed, who is quoted by Steph. Byz., (v. Ἄν-
τανδρος, affirmed, that the Cimmerians retained possession of it for 100 years. Antandrus was advantageously situated on the coast, at the foot of mount
Alexandra, one of the summits of Ida; so called, as
it was said, from the judgment of Paris. The forests of this mountain supplied the Antandrians
with timber for building ships; they also exported
it in large quantities. The spot to which it was
carried down from Ida bore the name of Aspaneus.
(Strab. XIII. p. 607.)

.   .   .   .   classemque sub ipsa
Antandro et Phrygiæ molimur montibus Idæ.
VIRG. ÆN. III. 5.

In the eighth year of the Peloponnesian war, some
Lesbian exiles, aided by the Spartans, seized upon
Antandrus, and made war from thence upon the
Athenians and Mitylenians; (Thuc. IV. 52.) but
the former people, having defeated them in an engagement, retook the town. (IV. 75.) After the
Sicilian expedition, Antandrus fell into the hands of
the Persians, but the inhabitants, exasperated by
the conduct of Arsaces, the lieutenant of Tissaphernes, attacked his troops, and drove them from their
city. (VIII. 108. Cf. Herod. V. 26. Xen. Anab.
VIII. 4. Mel. I. 18. Scyl. Peripl. p. 36.)[e] The site
once occupied by this ancient city still retains the

[e] There are both autono-   Antandrus, but the former are
mous and imperial coins of   scarce. Sestini, p. 71.

name of *Antandro*. The Antonine Itinerary reckons
thirty-one miles from Antandrus to Adramyttium;
the Table, more correctly, only sixteen.   Strabo
places between Gargara and Antandrus a mountain
named Cillæum. (XIII. p. 612.)   Adramyttium, Adramyt-
which gave its name to the extensive bay on which ᵗⁱᵘᵐ˙
it stood, is said by Strabo to have been colonized
by the Athenians; (XIII. p. 606.) but the foundation of the city is ascribed by Aristotle to Adramys,
a brother of Crœsus. (Steph. Byz. v. ᾿Αδραμύττειον.)
Strabo also mentions, that several writers ascribed
its origin to the Lydians. (XIII. p. 613.)   But, if
we are to believe Eustathius, and other commentators, Adramyttium already existed before the Trojan
war.   Pliny indeed affirms, that it was no other
than the Pedasus of Homer. (V. 32.)   The writer
of the Not. Eccles. (p. 27.) identifies it with Lyrnessus.   However this may be, it is certain that
Adramyttium, from its advantageous situation, had
early become a flourishing city. (Herod. VII. 42.
Strab. loc. cit. Scyl. Peripl. p. 36.)   The Athenians
had settled there the inhabitants of Delos, whom
they had removed from their island when it was
purified; but these unfortunate exiles were afterwards cruelly massacred by Arsaces, the Persian general, who commanded under Tissaphernes. (Thuc.
VIII. 108. Pausan. Messen. c. 27.)   After the defeat of Antiochus, Adramyttium was ceded by the
Romans to the kings of Pergamus, under whom it
continued to prosper; but it suffered greatly during
the war with Mithridates, the whole senate, and
several of the principal inhabitants, having been
put to death by order of Diodorus, a partisan of
that monarch. (Strab. XIII. p. 614.)   Appian, on

the other hand, accuses the Adramytteni of having butchered many Roman citizens, to gratify Mithridates. (Bell. Mithrid. 23.) Xenocles, a celebrated orator of Adramyttium, was sent to Rome to plead the cause of his native city, and the whole province of Asia, suspected of having favoured the king of Pontus. (Strab. XIII. p. 614.) It was in a ship of Adramyttium that the apostle Paul commenced his voyage from Cæsarea to Italy, as a prisoner, to appear before the Roman emperor. (Acts xxvii. 2.) It is evident from Pliny's account, that Adramyttium was the most considerable of all the towns in this vicinity, since it was the seat of a conventus, in which all the causes of the neighbouring places were tried. (V. 32.) We find Adramyttium often mentioned by the Byzantine historians, and the ancient name is even now but little changed in that of *Adramiti* [f].

Astyra.

Between this city and Antandrus, Strabo places Astyra, a small town, with a celebrated temple and grove sacred to Diana. These belonged to the Antandrians. (XIII. p. 614. Scyl. Per. p. 36.) This Astyra must not be confounded with the place of the same name near Abydos. Not far from thence

Sapra lacus.

was a small lake, called Sapra, full of deep holes, and which communicated with the sea. (Strab. loc. cit.) Pausanias speaks of some warm baths at Astyra, the water of which was black. (IV. 35.) Pliny mentions several obscure streams which apparently discharged themselves in the gulf of Adra-

---

[f] The coins of Adramyttium have the legend ΑΔΡΑΜΥΤΤΗΝΩΝ; they attest the alliance of that town with several important cities, such as Mitylene, Ephesus, Laodicea. Sestini, p. 71.

myttium from Ida, such as the Astron, Cormalus, Eryannus, Alabastius, Hierus. (V. 32.)

The whole of the surrounding district, according to Homer, was once occupied by a colony of Cilicians, who were governed by Eetion, father of Andromache, at the time of the Greek invasion. His capital was Thebe, surnamed Hypoplacia, from being situated under a hill called Placos.

Thebe.

Placos
mons.

Ἤτοι γὰρ πατέρ' ἀμὸν ἀπέκτανε δῖος Ἀχιλλεὺς,
Ἐκ δὲ πόλιν πέρσεν Κιλίκων εὐναιετάωσαν,
Θήβην ὑψίπυλον· κατὰ δ' ἔκτανεν Ἠετίωνα,

. . . .

Μητέρα δ', ἣ βασίλευεν ὑπὸ Πλάκῳ ὑληέσσῃ,

Iʟ. Z. 414.

Ἠετίων, ὃς ἔναιεν ὑπὸ Πλάκῳ ὑληέσσῃ,
Θήβῃ Ὑποπλακίῃ Κιλίκεσσ' ἄνδρεσσιν ἀνάσσων.

Thebe, destroyed by Achilles, did not rise from its ruins; but the name remained throughout antiquity attached to the surrounding plains, famed for their fertility, and often ravaged and plundered by the different armies whom the events of war brought into this part of Asia. (Xen. Anab. VII. 8, 4. Polyb. XVI. 1, 7. XXI. 8, 13. Liv. XXXVII. 19. Pomp. Mel. I. 18.)

Thebes
campus.

Lyrnessus, another Homeric city, disappeared also with Thebe, and left no trace of its existence beyond the celebrity which the Iliad has conferred upon it. Pliny asserts that it stood on the banks of the little river Evenus, whence, as we learn from Strabo, the Adramytteni derived their supply of water. (XIII. p. 614. Plin. V. 32.) In Strabo's time, the vestiges of both Thebe and Lyrnessus were still pointed out to travellers; the one at a distance of sixty stadia to the north, the other, eighty stadia

Lyrnessus.

to the south of Adramyttium. (XIII. p. 612.) The
same geographer informs us, that Chrysa and Cilla,
both celebrated in the Iliad, were also situated in
the immediate vicinity of Adramyttium. Other
Chrysa. writers, however, identified Chrysa with the town
of that name, already noticed in the territory of
Alexandria Troas; but the geographer observes
that the latter had no port, and was besides too far
from Thebe, to which the city of Chryseis belonged,
as appears from Il. A. (366.): he however supposes
that the Alexandrian Chrysa was a colony of the
Cilla. Cilician town. Cilla stood on the side of Antandrus, and was still famed for the worship of Apollo
Cillæus.

Κλῦθί μευ 'Αγυρότοξ' ὃς Χρύσην ἀμφιβέβηκας,
Κίλλαν τε ζαθέην, Τενέδοιό τε ἶφι ἀνάσσεις.

IL. A. 37.

Cillæus flu-   There was also a small stream named Cillæus,
vius.
which descended from mount Ida, and flowed near
the sacred edifice. (XIII. p. 612.) The modern
name of this river is *Zikeli.* Chrysa was twenty
stadia from Astyra and fifty from Thebe, which was
consequently seventy from the latter. Andeira was
sixty stadia from Thebe. Before we leave the Trojan Cilicians, I would just observe that the name of
their chief city naturally induces a suspicion that
they were really Syro-Phœnicians, who had been
transplanted thither from the coast of Cilicia. The
form of the word Lyrnessus corresponds too with
the names of cities, which are so commonly met
with on the shores of the Lycian and Pamphylian
seas; such as Telmissus, Termessus, Pindenis-
sus, &c.

North of Adramyttium, Strabo points out a few

localities, of which we must not omit to speak.   He
seems to derive his information, with respect to
these points of detail, from the researches of Demetrius the Scepsian.   Speaking of the little river Hep- Heptapo-
taporus of Homer, but called also Polyporus, he   rus fluvius.
observes, that a traveller would cross it seven times
in journeying from the Beautiful pine to the little Pulchra
town of Celænæ and the temple of Æsculapius, Celænæ.
founded by Lysimachus.   He proceeds to report,
that this remarkable tree, from the account given of
it by king Attalus, was twenty-four feet in circumference, and that its stem, after rising to the height
of sixty-seven feet, was formed into three ramifications, which reunited near the summit.   The entire height was two plethra and fifteen cubits, or
about 220 feet.   It was 180 stadia from Adramyttium.   Sixty stadia further were two places named
Cleandria and Gordus, situated near the source of Cleandria.
the Rhodius, also mentioned by Homer ; but other Rhodius fl.
commentators of the poet, as we have seen [g], supposed this river to flow into the Hellespont, whereas
Demetrius asserted that it joined the Ænius, one of Ænius fl.
the tributary streams of the Æsepus. (Strab. XIII.
p. 603.)   In another passage, Strabo, still copying
from Demetrius, speaks of Corybissa, a small dis- Corybissa.
trict near Scepsis, and close to a rivulet called Eu- Eureis fl.
reis and a village of the same name, and the torrent et vicus.
Æthaloeis. (X. p. 473.)   The latter is perhaps the Æthaloeis
same which Pliny calls Etheleus. (V. 32.)   Strabo
names also Hippocorona as a spot near Adramyttium, and Corybantium in the vicinity of Hamaxitus. (loc. cit.)
    The promontory of Pyrrha closes the gulf of Pyrrha
                                                    promonto-
                  [g] P. 76.   rium.
                  K 2

Adramyttium, properly so called, to the south ; it answers to the cape called *Karatepe-bouroun* by the Turks, *S. Nicolo* by the Franks. Strabo reckons 120 stadia from this headland to the opposite cape of Gargara. A temple of Venus was seated on the summit. (XIII. p. 606.) Beyond this point the

Cisthene. same geographer places Cisthene, once a flourishing town and port, but deserted in his time; (XIII. p. 607. Pomp. Mel. I. 18. Plin. V. 32.) and somewhat inland some copper mines, and the towns of

Perperene. Perperene and Trarium. The former of these was
Trarium. the see of a bishop in the time of the Byzantine empire, (Eccles. Not. p. 43.) and appears also to have been called Theodosiopolis [h]. The line of coast which next follows was at one time known by

Acte, the name of Acte, or coast of the Mitylenians, be-
Mityle-
næorum. cause that people had founded there several small towns. (Strab. XIII. p. 605 and 607.) Thucydides alludes to them under the name of Ἀκταῖαι πόλεις.

Heraclea. (IV. 52.) Strabo names two of them, Heraclea and Coryphantis; (XIII. p. 607.) Pliny, " Heracleotes

Coryphas. " tractus, Coryphas oppidum." (V. 32.) The name of the latter place is corruptly written Corifanio in the Table Itinerary. Pliny points out in the same

Grylius fl. vicinity the two little rivers Grylius and Ollius,
Ollius fl.
Aphrodi- and the district of Aphrodisias. Next follows At-
sias regio.
Attæa. tæa, only known to Strabo, unless it is the same as

Atarneus. the Attalia of the Table. (Strab. loc. cit.) Atarneus is oftener mentioned by the classical writers. Herodotus says it was a town of Mysia, opposite to Lesbos, and that it was ceded to the Chians by the

---

[h] Several coins of the Roman empire from Nero downwards attest also the existence of this town. The epigraph is ΠΕΡΠΕΡΗΝΙΩΝ. Sestini, p.75.

Persians in the reign of Cyrus, for having delivered
into their hands the Lydian Pactyas. (I. 160.)   Scylax also says, Atarneus belonged to the Chians.
(p. 36. Cf. Pausan. IV. 35.)   The land around
Atarneus was rich, and productive in corn.   Histiæus was defeated and taken in an engagement
with the Persian forces at Malene, a spot not far Malene.
from this town. (Herod. VI. 28, 29.)   Xenophon
places it between Adramyttium and the Caïcus.
(Anab. VII. 8, 4.)   Strabo reports that Atarneus
was for some time the residence of Hermias, tyrant
of Assus. (XIII. p. 614. Cf. Pausan. VII. 2. Isocr.
Paneg. p. 70. Steph. Xen. Hell. III. 2, 9. Aristot.
Polit. II. 7. Plin. V. 32. Steph. Byz. v. Ἀτάρνα.)
The ruins of Atarneus are to be seen near the
modern village of *Dikheli* [i].

Herodotus names Carine as a town of Mysia in Carine.
the neighbourhood of Atarneus, through which the
army of Xerxes passed on its march to the Hellespont: it appears to have been situated between
Atarneus and Adramyttium. (VII. 42. Cf. Steph.
Byz. v. Καρήνη. Ephor. ap. eund. v. Βέννα. -Plin. V.
32.)   It is not improbable that in Xenophon (Anab.
VII. 8, 4.) we should read Καρίνης, instead of Κερτο- Certo-
νίου, as the situation of this latter place, mentioned   nium.
by no other author, agrees very well with that
assigned to Carine.   The MSS., however, it must be
confessed, do not favour such an alteration ; and it
may be further observed that Theopompus, quoted
by Steph. Byz., speaks of a Mysian town named
Cytonium. (v. Κυτώνιον.)   Carene may perhaps correspond with *Chirin-Kevi*, a small place near the

[i] There are some very scarce   Atarneus, with the legend ATA.
autonomous coins belonging to   and ATAP.

coast; and Cytonium, or Certonium, perhaps answers to *Kidonia*, a town somewhat to the south of it.

Pitane.   Pitane, an Æolian city of some note, possessed two harbours, and was situated near the mouth of Evenus fl. the Evenus, now called *Tchandeli :* an aqueduct carried water from this river, probably near its source, as far as Adramyttium. (Strab. XIII. p. 614. Cf. Scyl. Peripl. p. 37.)

Æoliam Pitanen a læva parte relinquit.
OVID. METAM. VII. 357.

Canaius fl.   Pliny places Pitane near the river Canaius, which no other writer notices. (V. 32.) This town was the birthplace of Arcesilas the philosopher, founder of the middle academy. (Strab. loc. cit. Diog. Laert. Vit. Arces. Cf. Steph. Byz. v. Πιτάνη. Hierocl. Synecd. p. 661.) Near Pitane was a spot called Atarneus Atarneus under Pitane, to distinguish it from the sub Pitane. town of the same name already mentioned. It was opposite the island of Elæussa. (Strab. XIII. p. 614.) The bricks made at Pitane were said to be so light as to float in the water. (Strab. ibid.) Pitane is supposed to occupy the site now called *Tchandeli.* The gulf of Adramyttium, taken in its widest extent, is closed here to the south-west by the pro-Cane pro- montory of Cane, now *C. Coloni.* Strabo says it montorium et was also called Ægan, and affirms that it was on mons. the south of the river Caicus, and 100 stadia from Eleæ, the port of Pergamus; (XIII. p. 615.) whereas Herodotus, speaking of the march of the Persian army under Xerxes, distinctly states, that having crossed the Caïcus they proceeded northwards, having the mountain of Cane on their left. (VII. 42.) Mela also places Cane north of the Caïcus, (I. 18.) as well

as Pliny. (V. 32.) Strabo, in another place, describes mount Cane as surrounded on the south and
west by the sea, on the east by the plain of the
Caïcus, on the north by the district of Elæa, which
sufficiently characterises *Cape Coloni.* There was
also a small town named Canæ, opposite to the
southernmost point of the isle of Lesbos. It was
founded by a colony of Locrians, who came from
Cynus. (Strab. XIII. p. 615. Steph. Byz. v. Κάναι.
Plin. V. 32.) The ruins of this town are to be
sought for near *Coloni* [k].

The Caïcus, the most considerable of the Mysian Caïcus fl.
streams, discharges its waters into a bay which took
its name from the port of Elæa, about thirty stadia
to the south-east of the town of Pitane. It rises
at the foot of the eastern extremity of that chain
which was known to the ancients by the name of
mount Temnus, and extends from mount Ida to the
borders of Phrygia and Bithynia. Another stream
named Mysius, rising in the same chain, but more to Mysius fl.
the west, mingled its waters with the Caïcus. (Æsch.
ap. Strab. XIII. p. 616.)

> Ἰὼ Κάϊκε Μύσιαί τ' ἐπιρροαί.

Saxosumque sonans Hypanis, Mysusque Caïcus.
>   GEORG. IV. 370.
Et Mysum capitisque sui ripæque prioris
Pœnituisse ferunt, alia nunc ire, Caicum.
>   OVID. METAM. XV. 277.

The plains watered by the Caïcus bore at a very Teuthra-
early period the name of Teuthrania, from Teu- nia regio
et urbs.

---

[k] D'Anville has erroneously
placed Canæ south of the Caïcus. Numismatic writers assign
to Canæ coins which bear the
epigraph KAMHNΩN, without

however accounting for the
change which it implies in the
name of the town. Sestini, p.
72.

thras, a king of Mysia, who is said to have adopted
Telephus, the son of Hercules and Auge. (Eurip.
ap. Strab. XIII. p. 615.) According to Strabo there
was a town as well as district named Teuthrania,
distant about seventy stadia from Elæa, Pitane, Atarneus, and Pergamus. (Cf. Xen. Anab. VII. 8, 10.
Hel. III. 1, 4.) The subjects of Eurypylus, son of Te-
Ceteii. lephus, are called Ceteii by Homer ; (Odyss. Λ. 520.)
a name which has much perplexed commentators,
though it is generally allowed that it must apply to
the Mysians. Strabo observes, that there was a
small river named Ceteius which fell into the Caïcus, and therefore tended to establish still further
the supposed connexion between the people mentioned by Homer and the Mysians. (XIII. p. 616.)
The Caïcus derives its modern name from *Ber-*
Perga- *gamo,* the ancient Pergamum. This celebrated city
mum. is mentioned for the first time, I believe, in the
Anabasis. (VII. 8, 4.) Xenophon remained here for
some time as the guest of Gorgion and Gongylus,
two brothers, who appear to have been the possessors of the place. (Cf. Hell. III. 1, 4.) Xenophon
made from thence a predatory excursion against a
Persian nobleman named Asidates, whom he captured, with all his family. (Anab. loc. cit.) It was
apparently a fortress of considerable natural strength,
being situated on the summit of a conical hill, and
was in consequence selected by Lysimachus, Alexander's general, as a place of security for the reception and preservation of his great wealth, said to
amount to the enormous sum of 9000 talents. The
care of this treasure was confided to Philetærus of
Tium in Bithynia, an eunuch from his earliest in-
fancy, and a person in whom he placed the greatest

confidence. Philetærus remained for a long time faithful to his charge ; but having been injuriously treated by Arsinoe, the wife of Lysimachus, who sought to prejudice the mind of her husband against him, he was induced to withdraw his allegiance from that prince, and declare himself independent. The misfortunes of Lysimachus prevented him from taking vengeance on the offender, and thus Philetærus remained in undisturbed possession of the town and treasure for twenty years, having contrived, by dexterous management and wise measures, to remain at peace with all the neighbouring powers. He transmitted the possession of his principality to Eumenes, his nephew, who added much to the territory he inherited from his uncle, and even gained a victory near Sardes over Antiochus, son of Seleucus. After a reign of twenty-two years, he was succeeded by his cousin Attalus, whose father Attalus was the younger brother of Philetærus. This prince was first proclaimed king of Pergamum, after a signal victory obtained by him over the Gallo-Græci, or Galatæ, and by his talents, and the soundness of his policy, deserves a distinguished place among the sovereigns of antiquity. (Polyb. XVIII. 24. Liv. XXXIII. 21. Strab. XIII. p. 624.) He early espoused the interests of Rome against Philip, king of Macedon, and, in conjunction with the Rhodian fleet, rendered important services to the former power. His wealth was so great as to become proverbial. (Hor. Od. I. 1, 12.) He had married Apollonias, a lady of Cyzicus, of obscure birth, but great merit and virtue : by her he had four sons, Eumenes, Attalus, Philetærus, and Athenæus. Eumenes ascended the throne on his father's death, which took place at an advanced age, after a prosperous reign of forty-three or forty-four years. (Polyb. Liv. et Strab. loc. cit.) The new sovereign, continuing to tread in his father's steps, and adhering to his policy, remained the firm friend of the Romans during all their wars against Antiochus and the kings of Macedonia, and received from them in recompense of his fidelity and valuable assistance all the territory conquered from Antiochus on this side of mount Taurus. Prior to this period, the territory of Pergamum did not extend beyond the gulfs of Elæa and Adramyttium. (Strabo loc. cit. Liv. XXXVIII. 39.) Waylaid by the hired assassins of Perseus, king of Macedon, he had nearly perished at Delphi ; (XLII. 14. et seq.) and yet he is represented by the Roman historian as subsequently favouring the cause of the man who sought to destroy him, and of having thereby incurred the ill-will and anger of the Roman people. (XLIV. 13. 20. XLVI. 1—9.) With that arrogant nation, past services were reckoned as nothing, if they were not accompanied by the most abject and slavish dependence ; and the uniform ingratitude with which they treated their allies who maintained some show of freedom, as in the case of the Ætolians, Rhodians, and Achæans, favours strongly the supposition that their conduct towards Eumenes was dictated by the same overbearing spirit. The king of Pergamum employed himself, during the leisure which a profound peace now afforded him, in embellishing his capital, and patronising the arts and sciences. He decorated the Nicephorium, a public building which Pergamum already owed to the munificence of Attalus, (Polyb. XVIII. 24. Liv. XXXIII. 21.) with walks and plantations, and built himself several other edifices. But the most lasting monument of his liberality, as well as his fame, was the great library which he founded, and which yielded only to that of Alexandria in extent and value. (Strab. XIII. p. 624. Athen. I. 3.) It was from their being first used for writing in this library that parchment skins were called " Pergamenæ chartæ." (Varr. ap. Plin. XIII. 11.) Plutarch informs us that this vast collection, which consisted of no less than 200,000 volumes, was given by Antony to Cleopatra. (Vit. Anton. p. 943.) Eumenes reigned forty-nine years, leaving an infant son under the care of his brother Attalus, who administered affairs as regent for twenty-one years with great success and renown. In conjunction with Alexander, son of Antiochus, he defeated Demetrius, son of Seleucus. Allied with the Romans, he assisted them in their war against the Pseudo-Philip. He likewise defeated Diegylis, king of the Thracian Cæni, and caused the overthrow and death of Prusias, king of Bithynia, by inducing his son Nicomedes to revolt against him. He was succeeded by his nephew Attalus, surnamed Philometor. This prince died after a reign of only five years, and left his dominions by will to the Romans. Aristonicus, a natural son of Eumenes, opposed this arrangement, and endeavoured to establish himself on the throne ; but was vanquished and taken prisoner; and the Romans finally took possession of the kingdom, which from henceforth became a province of the empire under the name of Asia. (Strab. XIII. p. 624. XIV. p. 646.) Pergamum continued to flourish and prosper as a Roman city, so that Pliny

does not scruple to style it " longe clarissimum
" Asiæ Pergamum." (V. 32.) To the Christian the
history of Pergamum affords an additional interest,
since it is one of the seven churches of Asia mentioned in the book of Revelations [1]. Though condem-
nation is passed upon it as one of the churches
infected by the Nicolaitan heresy, its faithful ser-
vants, more especially the martyr Antipas, are noticed as holding fast the name of Christ. (Rev. ii.
12. et seq.) The town was situated in a plain,
watered by two small rivers or torrents flowing

Pindasus mons.
Selinus fl.
Cetius fl.

from mount Pindasus, and named Selinus and Cetius ; these joined afterwards the Caïcus. The citadel was placed on the conical hill mentioned by
Strabo. (XIII. p. 623.) The modern town retains
the name of *Bergamah*, and yet presents to the eye
several extensive ruins, and other vestiges of its
former magnificence [m]. Dallaway, who has accurately described the ruins of Pergamum [n], mentions
" a wall, facing the south-east of the acropolis, of
" hewn granite, at least a hundred feet deep, en-
" grafted into the rock, and above that, a course of
" large substructions, forming a spacious area, upon
" which once rose a temple unrivalled in sublimity
" of situation, being visible from the vast plain, and

[1] Our translators of the New
Testament do not appear quite
accurate in rendering the name
of this city Pergamos; it should
be Pergamum: the Greek being
almost always τὸ Πέργαμον. It
is true, that Steph. Byz. writes
Πέργαμος, but he gives no authority for that form.

[m] The reader will find these
described in Smith's Account

of the Seven Churches of Asia,
and still more recently in Mr.
Arundell's Visit to the Seven
Churches of Asia. The coins
of Pergamum are very numerous, as may be seen from
Eckhel, Sestini, and other numismatical writers.

[n] Constantinople, Ancient
and Modern, &c. p. 303.

" the Ægean sea." He supposes it to have been
erected in honour of Trajan. The same antiquary
describes a great aqueduct, of one row of lofty
arches over the Selinus, and a massive pile of building which formed the front and grand entrance into
the Naumachia, which he considers as the most complete edifice of the kind in Asia Minor. At the
western extremity of the hill are the remains of a
theatre. Near the cemetery stood probably the celebrated temple and sanctuary of Æsculapius. (Appian. Bell. Mithr. c. 60. Tacit. Ann. III. 63.) Besides these, there are some massive remains of the
great church, dedicated to St. John the Evangelist.
The Selinus is called by the Turks *Tabaklar-tchay*,
the Cetius *Barmakpatras-tchay*, the Caïcus *Aksou*,
or *Bakir-tchay* [o]. In the plains watered by the
Caïcus, and in the vicinity of Pergamum, there yet
remain to be noticed some few towns, such as Alisarna, mentioned by Xenophon ; (Hell. III. 1, 4.
and Anab. VII. 8, 10.) in the latter passage it is
called Elisarne. Pliny writes it Haliserne. (V. 32. Alisarna.
Cf. Steph. Byz. v. 'Αλίσαρνα.) Comania, an obscure Comania.
town, noticed only by Xenophon. (Anab. VII. 8, 8.)
Parthenium, for the knowledge of which we are also Parthe-
indebted to the Anabasis, (loc. cit. and VII. 8, 12.) nium.
and Pliny. (V. 32.) Apollonia, which, according to Apollonia.
Strabo, was to the east of Pergamum on the way to
Sardes. (XIII. p. 625. Xen. Anab. loc. cit. Plin. V.
32. Steph. Byz. v. 'Απολλωνία.) Pliny names also
Cale, perhaps the same as the Calse of the Not. Cale.
Eccl. (Prov. As. p. 43.) Conisium, written Κονιοσίνη Conisium.
in the same document. Balcea, which Steph. Byz. Balcea.
places near the Propontis, (v. Βαλκεία) is perhaps

o Arundell's Visit, &c. p. 282. and 278.

Tegium.
Tiare.
Sarnaca.
Lycide.
Thymbre.
Oxyopum.
Lygda-
mum.
Hadriano-
theræ.

Bali-kesri. Tegium, Tiare, Sarnaca, Lycide, Thymbre, Oxyopum, Lygdamum, are unknown. Hadrianotheræ, a place so called from its having been a favourite hunting-seat of the emperor Hadrian, (Dio. Cass. LXIX. 10. Spart. Vit. Hadr. c. 20.) is placed in the Table Itinerary, where the name is corruptly written Hadreanuteba, at the distance of eight miles from Pergamum, and thirty-three from Miletopolis. We know from Aristides that it stood on the road from the latter town to Hadriani, his native city, situated in Bithynia. (I. 500.) It appears from its coins, which are numerous, to have been a place of some note, as it possessed a senate [p]. In the Ecclesiastical Notices it is enumerated among the sees of the Hellespontine province. (Hierocl. Synecd. p. 6.) Sestini is inclined to place Hadrianotheræ at *Trikala*, a village distant an hour and a half from *Soma*, which is eight hours from Pergamum : he obtained there a medal of Antinous, struck in that town [q]. In that case the distance from Pergamum marked in the Table must be wrong ; it is indeed certain that the distance between that town and Miletopolis is too small [r].

ÆOLIS.

In the course of the description which has just terminated of Mysia and Troas, we have had occasion to speak of several towns which undoubtedly lay just claim to an Æolian origin. It has been already indeed stated, in the introductory section,

---

[p] The epigraph is ΙΕΡΑ ΣΥΝΚΛΗΤΟΣ ΑΔΡΙΑΝΟΘΗΡΙ-ΤΩΝ. Sestini, p. 68. This antiquary, it should be observed, falsely ascribes Hadrianotheræ to Bithynia.

[q] Viaggi diversi, p. 135.

[r] Col. Leake's Asia Minor, p. 271.

that the Æolians, who were the first great body of
Grecian colonists that settled in Asia Minor, had
not long after the Trojan war founded several towns
on different points of the Asiatic coast, from Cyzicus to the river Hermus ; but it was more especially in Lesbos, which has a right to be considered
as the seat of their power, and along the neighbouring shores of the gulf of Elæa, that they finally con-
centrated their principal cities, and formed a federal
union, called the Æolian league, consisting of twelve
states, with several inferior towns to the number of
thirty. The description of Æolis will naturally connect itself with that of Mysia, though the latter terminates with the Caïcus, and will bring us from
that river along the shores of the Eleatic gulf to
the vicinity of the Hermus, where the Ionian confederacy, which will be more conveniently brought
under the head of Lydia, commences. Herodotus,
who ascribes to the Æolians a Pelasgic origin, informs us that they occupied at first the plains of
Thessaly, then called Æolis ; but being driven from
thence by the Thessali, who came from Thesprotia,
they migrated to Bœotia and Attica, and other parts
of Greece. (VII. 176. Cf. Pausan. X. 8.) The
Æolian name does not appear however to have been
in use before the Trojan war, at least it never occurs
in Homer, though he speaks of Æolus and his immediate descendants. The Æolian colonies, according to Strabo, were anterior to the Ionian migrations by four generations. He states that Orestes
had himself designed to head the first ; but his death
preventing the execution of the measure, it was prosecuted by his son Penthilus, who advanced with
his followers as far as Thrace. This movement was

contemporary with the return of the Heraclidæ into Peloponnesus, and most probably was occasioned by it[s]. After the decease of Penthilus, Archelaus, or Echelatus, his son, crossed over with the colonies into the territory of Cyzicus, and settled in the vicinity of Dascylium. Gras, his youngest son, subsequently advanced with a detachment as far as the Granicus, and not long after crossed over to the island of Lesbos, of which he took possession. Some years after these events, another body of adventurers crossed over from Locris, under the conduct of Clevas and Malaus, two chiefs descended from Agamemnon, and founded Cyme, and other towns on the gulf of Elæa : they also took possession of Smyrna, which became one of the twelve states of the league ; but this city having been wrested from them by the Ionians, the number was reduced to eleven in the time of Herodotus. These, according to that historian, were Cyme, Larissa, Neontichos, Temnus, Cilla, Notium, Ægiroessa, Pitane, Ægææ, Myrina, Grynea. (I. 149.) We learn from the same writer that the Æolians, in common with the other Greek colonists of Asia, had become subject to Crœsus ; but on the defeat of the Lydian monarch by Cyrus they submitted to the conqueror, and from thenceforth were annexed to the Persian empire. (I. 6, 28. II. 90.) They contributed sixty ships to the fleet of Xerxes. (VII. 95.) Herodotus observes of Æolis that its soil was more fertile than that of Ionia, but the climate inferior. (I. 149.) In the time of Xenophon, Æolis formed part of the Hellespontine satrapy held by Pharnabazus, and it appears to have comprised a considerable portion of

[s] See Larcher, Chronologie d'Hérodote, tom. VII. p. 417.

the country already described under the head of
Troas. (Hell. III. 1, 8.) Wrested by the Romans
from Antiochus, it was annexed to the dominions
of Eumenes. (Liv. XXXIII. 38. XXXVII. 8.
XXXVIII. 39.)

The first town which occurs on the coast after
crossing the Caïcus is Elæa, the port and naval Elæa.
arsenal of Pergamum. According to some traditions
it had been founded after the siege of Troy by the
Athenians under the command of Menestheus.
(Strab. XIII. p. 622.) Elæa was distant twelve stadia from the mouth of the Caïcus, and 120 from
Pergamum. (XIII. p. 615.) It gave the name of
Elæaticus to the bay in which it stood, and which Elæaticus
is also known by that of Cumæus sinus, now gulf sinus.
of *Tchandeli*. Strabo estimates the width of the
bay at eighty stadia between cape Harmatus, which Harmatus
terminates it to the north, and that of Hydra to the rium.
south. (XIII. p. 622.) Harmatus would seem from
thence to be a point of land between the mouth of
the Evenus and that of the Caïcus; but, according
to Thucydides, it was situated to the north of the
Arginusæ and opposite to Methymna, i. e. I conceive, the territory of that city. (VIII. 101.) The
earliest author who mentions Elæa is Scylax; (Per.
p. 37.) subsequently it is frequently alluded to in
the account of the wars between the kings of Pergamum and those of Macedonia and Syria. (Polyb.
XVI. 41, 5. XXI. 8. Liv. XXXVI. 43. XXXVII.
18.) It was besieged in vain by Prusias, king of
Bithynia. (Polyb. XXXII. 25, 9. Cf. Artemid. ap.
Strab. XIII. p. 622. Plin. V. 32. Ptol. p. 118.) Steph.
Byz. asserts that Elæa was formerly called Cidæ-
nis. (v. Ἐλαία.) The ruins of this town exist pro-

bably not far from the village of *Clisiakevi*, on the
road from Smyrna to *Bergamah*[a].   Next follows

Grynium
sive Gry-
nca.

Grynium, or Grynea, one of the twelve Æolian cities, (Herod. I. 149.) and celebrated for the worship
of Apollo, who derived from thence the surname of
Gryneus :

> His tibi Grynei nemoris dicatur origo :
> Ne quis sit lucus, quo se plus jactet Apollo.
>   VIRG. ECL. VI. 72.
>
> Sed nunc Italiam magnam Gryneus Apollo,
> Italiam Lyciæ jussere capessere sortes.
>   ÆN. IV. 345.

Strabo remarks, that the town belonged in his time
to the Myrinæans ; from whence we must infer that
it had much declined from its former prosperity and
fame.   The temple and oracle, however, still subsisted, at a distance of forty stadia from Myrina.
The edifice was remarkable for its size, and the
beauty of the white marble of which it was built.
(XIII. p. 622.) Grynium is noticed by Scylax, (Per.
p. 37.) Xenophon, (Hell. III. 1, 4.) Diodorus, who
reports that it was taken by Parmenio, (XVII. 7.)
Pliny, (V. 32.) and Steph. Byz. (v. Γρύνοι.) Beyond

Portus
Achivo-
rum.

was a haven, called the Port of the Greeks, where
was an altar erected in honour of the twelve gods.
(Strab. XIII. p. 622. Cf. Scyl. Per. p. 37.) Myrina,
according to Strabo, was a maritime city, distant
forty stadia from Grynium, and eighty from Elæa.
(XIII. p. 622.) The Table Itinerary reckons twelve

Myrina.

miles from the latter city. Myrina, reckoned by Herodotus among the twelve states of Æolis, (I. 149.)
is stated by Mela to have been founded by Myrinus
before the others. (I. 18.) We are informed by

[a] Smith's Account of the Seven Churches of Asia, p. 7.

Xenophon, that it was ceded, together with Grynea,
by Artaxerxes to Gongylus, an Eretrian, who had
been banished from his native city for favouring the
interests of Persia. (Hell. III. 1, 4.) Myrina, as we
find from Polybius and Livy, was occupied for some
time by Philip, son of Demetrius ; but being vanquished by the Romans, he was compelled by that
people to evacuate the place. (Polyb. XVIII. 27, 4.
Liv. XXXIII. 30.) Mention is made of this town
in Cicero's Letters ; (ad Fam. V. 20.) and we learn
from Tacitus, that it received a remission of im-
posts, in the reign of Tiberius, on account of the
damage it had sustained from an earthquake. (Ann.
II. 47.) It appears from Pliny to have subsequently
assumed the name of Sebastopolis. (V. 32.) Martial
pronounces the penultimate long : (IX. Ep. 42.) [b]

Campis dives Apollo sic Myrinis.

But the most considerable of the Æolian cities was
Cyme, surnamed Phriconis, because its first founders Cyr
had settled for some time around mount Phricium
in Locris, previous to crossing over into Asia. On
their arrival in Æolis, they found that country in
the possession of the Pelasgi ; but the latter, who had
sustained great losses during the Trojan war, were
unable to offer any resistance to the invaders, who
successively founded Neontichos, and afterwards
Cyme, though, according to some traditions, there
existed already a place of that name. so called from
Cyme, one of the Amazons. (Strab. XIII. p. 623.)
Mel. I. 18. Steph. Byz. v. Κύμη.) Cyme was one
among the many cities which laid claim to the honour of having given birth to Homer ; and if the

[b] The coins of this town
have the name written two

ways, MYPINA and MYPEINA.
Sestini, p. 78.

writer of the life of that poet, which some have
ascribed to Herodotus, is to be credited, the ancestors of the great bard were certainly natives of the
town to which our attention is now drawn. It is
also added, that he received the name of Ὅμηρος
during his residence there; that word in the Cy-
mæan dialect signifying " one blind." (c. 14.) Whatever may be thought of the pretensions of the Cymæans to be considered as the countrymen of Homer,
their right to another great Greek poet is indisput-
able; I mean Hesiod, whose father, by his own
account, was born in Cyme, though he quitted it to
reside at Ascra in Bœotia:

Ὅς ποτε καὶ τῇδ' ἦλθε, πολὺν διὰ πόντον ἀνύσσας
Κύμην Αἰολίδα προλιπὼν, ἐν νηΐ μελαίνῃ.

Op. et Di. 634.

Ephorus, one of the most distinguished historians of
Greece, but whose works are unfortunately lost to
us, was another illustrious native of Cyme. That
city, however, notwithstanding the celebrity it derived from the birth of such talented individuals,
was by no means generally famed for the genius
and wit of its citizens. On the contrary, they were
proverbially taxed with stupidity and slowness of
apprehension. (Strab. XIII. p. 622. Suid. Ὄνος εἰς
Κυμαίους. Plut. Vit. Cæs. §. 61.) Herodotus relates,
to the honour of the Cymæans, that when Pactyas
the Lydian had taken refuge in their city, to escape
from the vengeance of the Persians, they would not
surrender him up to the officer sent by Cyrus to
demand him, but allowed him to escape to Mitylene.
(I. 157 seq.) We learn from the same authority, that,
under the reign of Darius, the Cymæans, like most
of the Greek cities tributary to Persia, were go-

verned by a chief or tyrant possessed of absolute power. When the revolution excited by Aristagoras of Miletus broke out, the Cymæans, satisfied with obtaining their independence, deposed their prince without committing any act of violence against him. (IV. 138. V. 38.) They were, however, quickly reduced to subjection by the Persian forces commanded by Artaphernes, satrap of Lydia. (V. 123.) The remnant of Xerxes' fleet wintered in the harbour of Cyme, after the disastrous engagement off Salamis. (VIII. 130.) Successively held by the Persians, the kings of Syria, and of Pergamum, it was finally annexed to the latter empire by the Romans, at the same time that it was declared free from all taxes. (Corn. Nep. Alcib. c. 7. Polyb. V. 77, 4. XXII. 27, 4. XXXIII. 11, 8. Liv. XXXVII. 11. XXXVIII. 39.) In the reign of Tiberius, Cyme suffered, in common with other cities of Asia, from the terrible earthquake which desolated that province. (Tacit. Ann. II. 47. It still subsisted in the time of Pliny. (V. 32.) And ecclesiastical writings, much posterior to that author, attest its existence as the see of a bishop under the Byzantine emperors[c]. Cyme, according to the Itineraries, was nine miles from Myrina, but Strabo reckons only forty stadia. (XIII. p. 622.) Modern writers on comparative geography have generally placed its ruins near the Turkish village of *Sanderli*. "At the edge of the gulf " of *Sanderly*, on the right, are seen towers of a " wall or castle," says Dallaway, "nearly upon the " site of the ancient Cyme. In a large vineyard " we were shewn many marble columns of the Ionic

[c] Geogr. Sacr. Car. S. Paul. p. 238.

" order [d]."   Near the town was a small stream or
Xanthus fl. fountain called Xanthus [e].   The Hermus flowed a
little to the south-east of Cyme, and a mountain
which rose between that river and the city bore the
Sardene mons. name of Sardene, as we learn from the writer of
Homer's Life, who quotes these lines as from that
poet :

Αἰδεῖσθε ξενίων κεχρημένον ἠδὲ δόμοιο
οἳ πόλιν αἰπεινὴν Κύμην Ἐριώπιδα κούρην
ναίετε, Σαρδήνης πόδα νείατον ὑψικόμοιο·
ἀμβρόσιον πίνοντες ὕδωρ θείου ποταμοῖο
Ἕρμου δινήεντος, ὃν ἀθάνατος τέκετο Ζεύς.

Adæ.   Adæ, a place pointed out by Strabo, (XIII. p.622.)
on the authority of Artemidorus, between Cyme and
cape Hydra, at the distance of forty stadia from the
Larissa Phriconis. latter, is unknown to other writers.   Larissa, surnamed Phriconis, as well as Cyme, and for the same
cause, had been, as its name sufficiently attests, a
Pelasgic settlement, before the arrival of the Æolian
colony in this part of Asia ; and Strabo conceives,
with reason, that it is the city to which Homer
alludes when he says,

Ἵππόθοος δ' ἄγε φῦλα Πελασγῶν ἐγχεσιμώρων,
Τῶν οἳ Λάρισσαν ἐριβώλακα ναιετάασκον.   Il. B. 840.

When the Æolians had occupied the country, they
transferred the Pelasgi to their new city of Cyme :
Larissa, however, was not abandoned, since Hero-
dotus reckons it among the twelve cities of Æolis.
(I. 149. Strab. XIII. p. 621.) The author of Homer's
Life states, that the poet, in going from the Hermus

[d] Constantinople, p. 290.
Mannert, tom.VI.p.390. D'Anville assigns to it the site of
Nemourt, but this is more probably Myrina. Geogr. Anc. p.

102. fol.
   [e] As appears from the coins
of Cyme, which are numerous.
Sestini, p. 78.

to Cyme, passed by Neontichos and Larissa. (§. 11,
12.) In the Hellenics, Xenophon, to distinguish
this city from others of the same name, styles it the
Egyptian Larissa, because the elder Cyrus had established there a colony of Egyptian soldiers. (Hell.
III. 1, 5. Cyrop. VII. 1, 21.) Larissa appears from
the same historian to have been a place of great
strength, as it was besieged in vain by Thimbron.
(Hell. loc. cit.) Strabo remarks, that it was deserted
in his time. (XIII. loc. cit. Cf. Plin. V. 32. Steph.
Byz. v. Λάρισσα [f].)

Neontichos, founded by the Æolians as a tempo- Neonti-
rary fortress, on their first arrival in the country chos.
from Locris, was, according to Strabo, thirty stadia
from Larissa. Pliny leads us to suppose it was not
on the coast, but somewhat removed from it; and
we collect from a passage in the Life of Homer,
already quoted with reference to Larissa, that it
was situated between that town and the Hermus.
Herodotus names Neontichos among the leading
cities of Æolis. (I. 149.) In Homer's Life it is
stated, contrary to Strabo's authority, that Neontichos was founded eight years later than Cyme.
(§. 9. Cf. Steph. Byz. v. Νέον Τεῖχος.) The ruins of
this town should be sought for on the right bank of
the Hermus, and above *Giuzel-hissar*, on the road
from Smyrna to *Bergamah*.

Temnus, another Æolian town frequently men- Temnus.
tioned by Greek writers, was situated apparently on
the opposite bank of the river, in a commanding
situation overlooking the plains of Cyme, Phocæa,

---

[f] Sestini assigns doubtingly   brass medals, with the legend
to the Æolian Larissa some   ΛΛ and ΛΛΡΙ. p. 78.

and Smyrna. (Strab. XIII. p. 622.) I say apparently, because there is a passage in Pausanias
which would lead us to suppose it stood on the
northern side of the Hermus, opposed to mount
Sipylus. (Eliac. I. 13.) If, however, the Table Itinerary is correct in estimating the distance between
Cyme and Temnus at thirty-three miles, there could
be no doubt as to the southern situation of the latter
town with reference to the Hermus ; but this number of miles exceeds even the real distance from
Cyme to Smyrna, which, by the best maps, does
not appear to equal thirty. Most antiquaries are
inclined to place Temnus at *Menimen*, a large village to the north of Smyrna. Chandler states, that
" it is situated on a rising ground by the Hermus,
" and appears as a considerable place, with old cas-
" tles g." It seems, from the account of the same
traveller, that " the river has, during the lapse of
" ages, undergone great changes in its course. The
" mouth especially has been continually shifting and
" changing place, in consequence of the encroach-
" ments made on the sea." Pliny states that Temnus, which was once situated at the mouth of the
Hermus, no longer existed in his day. (V. 31.)
Xenophon speaks of it as a small town. (Hell. IV.
8, 5. Cf. Herod. I. 149.) Polybius states that the
town of Temnus, after being subject to Achæus,
surrendered to Attalus, when that prince invaded
Æolis. (V. 77, 4.) The same historian informs us,
that near the city there was a temple sacred to
Apollo Cynius, which was plundered and burnt by
Prusias, king of Bithynia. (XXII. 25, 12. Cf. Cic.

g Asia Minor, p. 93.

pro Flac. §. 18, 20, 21. Tacit. Ann. II. 47. Steph.
Byz. v. Τῆμνος [h].)

Ægæ was situated on the same range of hills as
Temnus, (Strab. loc. cit.) but more inland. (Scyl.
Peripl. p. 38. Plin. V. 32.) Herodotus calls it Αἰ-
γαῖαι, and the inhabitants Αἰγαιεῖς. (I. 149. V. 67.)
Xenophon, Αἰγεῖς [i]. (Hell. IV. 8, 5. Polyb. V. 77, 4.
Tacit. Ann. II. 47.) In Ptolemy, the name of this
town is corruptly written Ægara. The Ecclesiastical Notices enumerate it among the bishoprics of
the Hellespontine province. (Hierocl. Syn. p. 660 [k].)

Ægiroessa, one of the twelve Æolian cities, as
Herodotus reports, does not occur in any other historian or geographer; but it is not unlikely that
the name was subsequently changed; and, in the
absence of better information, we may conjecture
that the Attalia Agroira, which Stephanus assigns
to Lydia, (v. Ἀττάλεια,) but Pliny to Æolis, (V. 32.)
is no other than the town alluded to by the father
of history.

Posidea, mentioned by Pliny together with Attalia, has escaped the observation of other geographers.

Another Æolian town of uncertain position is
Parparon, called by some also Perine, where it is
reported that Thucydides ended his days. (Steph.
Byz. v. Παρπάρων.) The same geographer ascribes
to Æolis a river and island named Potamosacon.
(v. Ποταμοσάκων.) Pliny assigns to the "jurisdictio
"Pergamena," the Bregmenteni, Hieracometæ, Per-

(marginal notes) Ægæ. Ægiroessa. Attalia Agroira. Posidea. Parparon sive Perine. Potamosacon.

---

[h] The legend on the coins of
Temnos is ΤΗΜΝΟΣ and ΤΗΜ-
ΝΕΙΤΩΝ. Sestini, p. 78.
[i] The coins of Ægæ acknow-

ledge both forms, and also that
of Αἰγαιεῖς, which indeed is more
frequent. Sestini, p. 77.
[k] Geogr. Sacr. Car. S. Paul.

pereni, Tiareni, Hierolophienses, Attalenses, Panta-
enses, and others.

Having terminated the periplus of the Æolian
coast, we will conclude this section with some account of Lesbos, which, both from its position and
historical associations, naturally finds a place here
as one of the most celebrated and flourishing establishments formed by the Æolians.

Lesbos
insula.

According to Strabo, the circuit of the island was
1100 stadia, (XIII. p. 616.) in which number he
agrees with Agathemerus. (p. 17.) But Pliny
reckons 195, and Isidorus 168 miles; both of
which computations considerably exceed the number given by Strabo. It is probable that the latter
geographer measured his distances only from cape
to cape, and neglected the windings of the coast.
The same writer reckons 560 stadia from the promontory of Sigrium to that of Malea, the two extreme points of the island from north to south; this
is therefore to be considered as its greatest length:
its breadth was most considerable between cape Sigrium and the headland opposite to the little island
of Leuce, and not far from the town of Methymna,
distant, according to Strabo, 210 stadia from cape
Sigrium. The narrowest part of the island lay between Pyrrha and Ægireus, the former being situated in a bay deeply indenting the western coast.
(Strab. loc. cit.)

The earliest inhabitants of this large and fertile
isle appear to have been of Pelasgic origin, as may
be collected from the account of Strabo, and the appellation of Pelasgia given to it by Diodorus (V. 80.)
and Pliny. (V. 39. Cf. Steph. Byz. v. Μέταον.) It is
said to have derived from Lesbus, a grandson of

Æolus, (Diod. Sic. loc. cit.) the name by which it is best known in history, and which, according to Homer, was attached to it in the time of which his poem treats :

Δώσω δ' ἑπτὰ γυναῖκας ἀμύμονας, ἔργ' εἰδυίας,
Λεσβίδας· ἃς, ὅτε Λέσβον ἐϋκτιμένην ἕλεν αὐτὸς,
'Εξελόμην, αἳ κάλλει ἐνίκων φῦλα γυναικῶν.

Il. I. 128.

Καί σε, γέρον, τὸ πρὶν μὲν ἀκούομεν ὄλβιον εἶναι,
"Οσσον Λέσβος ἄνω, Μάκαρος ἕδος, ἐντὸς ἐέργει,
Καὶ Φρυγίη καθύπερθε, καὶ 'Ελλήσποντος ἀπείρων.

Il. Ω. 543.

Though the poet does not name any of the Lesbian cities, it is clear from the epithet of ἐϋκτιμένη that they were numerous and flourishing ; the last quotation is also calculated to give a very favourable idea of the fertility and commerce of the island in this early age. The first Greek colony, according to Strabo, was led into the island by Gras, son of Archelaus, and great grandson of Orestes, who had already formed settlements in Mysia and Troas. (XIII. p. 582. Cf. Pausan. III. 2. Hom. Vit. §. 38.) So prosperous was the condition of the Lesbians, that Strabo does not scruple to consider them as the head of the Æolian states. (XIII. p. 616.) This was especially the case after the cities of the continent had been subjugated by Crœsus and the Persians. For though they sustained a severe defeat by sea from the Samians under Polycrates, (Herod. III. 39.) they continued to hold a distinguished place among the maritime powers of Greece. Having taken an active part in the revolt of Aristagoras, (Herod. VI. 5, 8.) they became exposed to the vengeance of Darius, who sent a fleet against their island, after the defeat of Lade, and reduced all the male population to slavery. (VI. 31.) Delivered from the Persian yoke by the victories of Salamis and Mycale, the Lesbians readily joined the combined fleets, and contributed with zeal to the exigencies of the war. Athens having at this time acquired a marked ascendency over the confederate states, the Lesbians found themselves no longer in the same situation; for though the Athenians affected to treat them with deference as allies, it was apparent that they were in reality only dependents and subjects. (Thuc. III. 10.) Galled by the yoke, which began to press heavily upon them, and urged by the Bœotians, who were of kindred Æolian origin, the whole island, with the exception of Methymna, seized the opportunity offered by the Peloponnesian war for joining the Spartan alliance, and revolting from Athens. Unhappily for the Lesbians, the energy and promptitude of that power were met only by dilatoriness and indecision on the part of the Lacedæmonians, and the revolt was soon crushed by the capture of Mitylene, the capital of the island, and the chief seat of the rebellion. (Thuc. III. 50.) The Lesbians made another attempt to emancipate themselves from Athenian subjection after the disasters experienced by that people in Sicily; (VIII. 5.) but it was not till the siege and downfall of Athens ensued, that they succeeded in obtaining that freedom which they had so long wished for. So much of the history of this celebrated island is comprised in that of Mitylene, that it will be better to proceed at once to give some account of that city, and to commence from thence our circuit of the Lesbian coast.

Mitylene, or Mytilene, for the name is written
both ways, is said to have been so called from Mitylene, daughter of Macareus. (Steph. Byz. v. Mυ-
τιλήνη. Diod. Sic. V. 80.) Whoever was its founder,
we can have no doubt, from the superior advantage
of its maritime situation, that it was occupied in
preference to any other locality by the Æolian colonists, since it possessed two harbours; one, turned
towards the south, capable of being closed, and fit
for the reception of triremes, with docks for fifty
ships; the other, still more extensive and deep, and
defended by a mole. A small island, on which part
of the town was built, added still further to the security of the harbour off which it lay. (Strab. XIII.
p. 617. Pausan. VIII. 30.) Besides these natural
advantages, Mitylene was greatly adorned and beau-
tified by art; so that it not only became the seat of
commerce, but presented attractions which few other
spots could equal. It could boast of having given
birth to Sappho and Alcæus, and to the historians
Myrsilus and Hellanicus. Pittacus, one of the seven
sages of Greece, long presided over her counsels, and
directed her affairs; and though he was invested
with unlimited power, he only used it to put down
faction, and to favour the ends of benevolence and
justice. (Strab. XIII. p. 617. Plut. tom. IX. p. 265,
405. Diog. Laert. I. 75.) During his administration, Mitylene became engaged in a contest with
the Athenians, then governed by Pisistratus, for the
possession of Sigeum, on the coast of Troas. The
war was put an end to by the mediation of Periander of Corinth. (Herod. V. 94.) Mitylene was at
that time the most flourishing of the Æolian states;
it enjoyed a profitable trade with Egypt, (Herod.

II. 178.) and possessed several dependencies on the Asiatic coast. (Strab. XIII. p. 317.) In the reign of Darius, the Mitylenians were for a time subject to the authority of Coes, one of their citizens, who had obtained the sovereignty from the Persian monarch, in reward for an important service he had rendered that prince during the Scythian expedition, (V. 11.) but on the breaking out of the Ionian revolt they deposed Coes, and put him to death. (V. 38.)

In the beginning of the Peloponnesian war, we find the Mitylenians taking the lead in the formation of a plan for revolting from Athens, and sending deputies to the Peloponnesian assembly to demand immediate assistance. Had the Spartans displayed the same zeal and activity in supporting their new allies, which the latter did in resisting the Athenians, Lesbos must have been delivered, and all the dependencies of Athens probably wrested from her grasp. But on the first news of the revolt, a considerable squadron, under the command of Paches, was despatched to Lesbos, and the Mitylenians, after an unsuccessful action, were blockaded in their harbour; and the town was soon besieged by sea and land. The citizens, however, resolutely defended themselves, and had they been adequately supported, would ultimately have triumphed over the enemy. But the injudicious advice of Salæthus, the Spartan emissary, who recommended that arms should be given to the populace, proved fatal to their cause, since the people once armed, prevailed over the civic body, and opened the town to the Athenians. The folly of the Mitylenians in this respect is only surpassed by the cruelty of their enemies; and we shudder on reading Thucydides, to think how nearly a whole population had been swept away, to satisfy the vengeance of a mob, inflamed by the arts of a worthless demagogue. (Thuc. III. 2—50.) After this unsuccessful attempt to cast off their chains, the Mitylenians remained in passive subjection, till the losses experienced by Athens in Sicily once more induced them to revolt. The attempt was however feeble and premature, and was soon put down. (VIII. 22, 23.) Towards the close of the Peloponnesian war, we see Conon, the Athenian general, defeated off Mitylene by the Spartan Callicratidas, and blockaded in the harbour. He was soon however delivered, by the total defeat of the Peloponnesian fleet off the islands of Arginusæ. (Xen. Hell. I. 6, 10. et seq.) After these events, a long interval elapses before our attention is drawn to the affairs of Mitylene by any remarkable occurrence. The citizens of that town having favoured the cause of Mithridates against the Romans, were severely punished, first, by Lucullus, who slew a great number of them in an engagement, (Plut. Lucull.) and again, by M. Thermus, who besieged their city, and having taken it by assault, gave it up to be plundered and destroyed. (Liv. Epist. LXXXIX. 36.)

The friendship which Pompey felt for the historian Theophanes, a native of Mitylene, proved afterwards highly beneficial to his country; since by his influence it was not only raised from ruin, and restored to liberty, but rendered more prosperous and flourishing than before. The son of Theophanes, named Marcus Pompeius after his father's patron, succeeded also in conciliating the favour of Augustus and Tiberius for his countrymen. During their reigns, Mitylene held a distinguished rank among the first cities of the empire. (Strab. XIII. p. 617. Plut. Pomp. Vell. Paterc. II. 18.)

Laudabunt alii claram Rhodon, aut Mitylenen.

Hor. Od. I. 7.

Pliny styles it "libera Mitylene, annis MD potens." (V. 39[l].) The history of this city may be further illustrated by a reference to Polyb. XI. 5, 1. Cic. Ep. ad Fam. IV. 7. Senec. ad Helv. c. 9. Athenæus praises its shell-fish and wine, (III. 86. E. 92. D. I. 30. B.) *Metelin*, as it is now called, is still a considerable place, and gives its name to the whole island[m].

Methymna.   Next in importance to Mitylene was Methymna, an Æolian colony, (Herod. I. 151. Scyl. p. 36.) situated near the northernmost point of the island, and distant sixty stadia from the coast of Troas, lying between Polymedium and Assus. (Strab. XIII. p. 616.) It was the birthplace of Arion, the celebrated musician, whose adventure with the dolphin is related by Herodotus, (I. 23.) Strab. (loc. cit.) and of the historian Myrsilus, (Steph. Byz. v. Μήθυμνα.) The territory of this town was contiguous to that of Mitylene, a circumstance which appears to have created a considerable degree of rivalry between them, and probably induced the Methymnæans to adhere to the Athenians, while their neighbours were bent on detaching themselves from that power. (Thuc. III. 2, 18.) As a reward for their fidelity,

---

[l] The imperial coins of Mitylene exhibit an uninterrupted series, from Augustus to Valerian. The epigraph is invariably, I believe, ΜΥΤΙΛΗΝΑΙΩΝ, and not ΜΙΤΥΑΗΝΑΙΩΝ. Sestini, p. 79.

[m] For an account of its present state, see Tournefort, p. 149. and Le Bruyn, Voyage au Levant.

the Methymnæans were exempted from contributions in money, (VI. 85. VII. 57.) Towards the
close of the Peloponnesian war, Methymna fell into
the power of the Spartan commander, Callicratidas,
who, though urged to treat the citizens with severity, and to sell them as slaves, refused to comply
with the advice, declaring, that as long as he was
admiral, no Greek, as far as lay in his power, should
be enslaved. (Xen. Hell. I. 6, 8.) Theopompus, who
is quoted by Athenæus, (X. 442. F.) speaks of a
tyrant of Methymna, named Cleomenes, who was
at some pains to reform the licentious manners of
his subjects. The wine of Methymna was held in
great estimation;

Gargara quot segetes, quot habet Methymna racemos.

OVID. ART. AM. I. 57.

hence Bacchus was frequently called the god of
Methymna, (Athen. VIII. 363. B. Cf. Pausan. X.
19.) Further mention of this city is made in Polybius,
(XXXIII. 11.) Livy, (XLV. 31.) Diod. Sic. (XIII.
76.) Pliny, (V. 39.[n]) The remains of Methymna are
to be seen near the village of *Molivo*, at the northern
extremity of the island, where Ptolemy has placed
it. To the south of this place is a range of hills,
called *Leptimo*, which probably answers to the
Mons Lepetymnus of Pliny and others. (Antig. Lepetymnus mons.
Caryst. c. 17.) The same geographer names along
with it Ordymnus, Macistus, Creon, and Olympus,
(V. 39.) Mount Ordymnus is called Ordynus by
Theophrastus. (H. Pl. III. 18.) Ægireus was a Ægireus.
small place belonging to Methymna, and situated,

---

[n] In the autonomous and imperial coins of Methymna, the
inscription is both ΜΑΘΥΜΝΑΙ-
ΩΝ and ΜΕΘΥΜΝΑΙΩΝ; in the
more recent ones, only ΜΗ-
ΘΥΜΝΑΙΩΝ. Sestini, p. 79.

as Strabo reports, on the eastern coast of Lesbos, where that island is only twenty stadia broad. (XIII. p. 616.)

Sigrium prom.

Cape Sigrium forms the extreme point of the island to the north west. (Strab. loc. cit.) It retains the name of *Sigri*. Near this headland was situated

Antissa.

the ancient town of Antissa, (Herod. I. 151. Scyl. p. 36.) the birthplace of Terpander, the celebrated musician and poet, who is said to have first used the lyre with seven strings[o]. (Clem. Alex. Strom. I. p. 308. Strab. loc. cit. Steph. Byz. v. Ἄντισσα.) This place joined the Mitylenians in their revolt against Athens, and was in consequence attacked by the Methymnæans; but they were repulsed with loss by the inhabitants. (Thuc. III. 18.) On the reduction, however, of Mitylene, Antissa submitted to the Athenian forces. (III. 28.) Some centuries later, this town having sided with Antiochus against the Romans, was destroyed by the latter, and the lands were given up to Methymna. (Liv. XLV. 31. Plin. V. 39.) The ruins of this town were observed by Pococke, a little to the north of *Cape Sigri*, on the site called *Calas Limneonas*[p].

Eressus.

Eressus was situated on a hill, at a distance of twenty-eight stadia from C. Sigrium. It derives celebrity from having given birth to Theophrastus. The real name of this distinguished naturalist and philosopher was Tyrtamus; that of Theophrastus having been bestowed upon him by his master, Aristotle, on account of his superior eloquence. Phanias, another disciple of the great Stagirite, was likewise

[o] The head of a musician engraved on the coins of Antissa is that of Terpander, and not of Orpheus, as Sestini supposes,

p. 79.

[p] Travels in the East, tom. I. b. 3. c. 4.

a native of Eressus. (Strab. loc. cit. Steph. Byz. v. Ἔρεσσος.) Eressus revolted from Athens, together with Mitylene, but was reduced by Paches. (Thuc. III. 18. 35. It again revolted towards the end of the war, when it was besieged by an Athenian force, under Thrasybulus, but he was called away from thence, by the sailing of the Peloponnesian fleet into the Hellespont. (Thuc. VIII. 100. Diod. Sic. XIV. 94.) According to Archestratus, quoted by Athenæus, Eressus was famous for the excellence of its wheaten flour.

εὐκάρπου κριθῆς καθαρῶς ἠσκημένα πάντα
ἐν Λέσβῳ, κλεινῆς Ἐρέσου περικύμονι μαστῷ
λευκότερ' αἰθερίας χιόνος. θεοὶ εἴπερ ἔδουσιν
ἄλφιτ' ἐκεῖθεν ἰὼν Ἑρμῆς αὐτοῖς ἀγοράζει.

This town is mentioned by Herodotus, (I. 151.) Scylax, (p. 36.) Pliny, (V. 39.) P. Mela, (I. 18.) and Ptolemy. The site yet preserves the name of *Eresso*[q].

Pyrrha was situated in a deep bay, with a narrow Pyrrha. inlet, called from thence the Euripus of Pyrrha, (Aristot. ap. Athen. III. 88. C. Strab. XIII. p. 617.) and which answers to the Port *Caloni*. It sided with Mitylene in the Lesbian revolt, but was reconquered by Paches. (Thuc. III. 18, 25, 35. Cf. Scyl. p. 36. Steph. Byz. v. Πύρρα.) Strabo reports, that in his time the town no longer existed, but the suburbs and port were still inhabited; the latter was eighty stadia from Mitylene. (XIII. p. 618.) Pliny states that the town was destroyed by the sea. (V. 39.) Agamede, a place situated near Pyrrha, had like- Agamede. wise disappeared in that writer's day. (Cf. Steph.

[q] Pococke, Travels in the East, tom. I. b. 3. c. 4. Mannert, Geogr. tom. VI. p. 444. On its coins the name of this town is always written with one Σ. ΕΡΕ-ΣΙΩΝ. Sestini, p. 79.

Hiera. Byz. v. 'Αγαμήδη.) Hiera, though no longer existing when Pliny wrote, seems to have left its name to the gulf of *Jero*, called also *Olivieri* by the Franks[r]. (Plin. V. 39.) Our periplus of Lesbos closes with

Malea pro- Cape Malea, the extreme point of the island to the
montorium. south east, and nearly opposite to the promontory of Cane, in Æolis. Strabo states that it was seventy stadia from Mitylene, and 100 from Pyrrha. (XIII.

Malea lo- p. 617.) Mention is made of Malea in Thucydides,
cus. (III. 4.) where he seems to place it to the north of Mitylene; if there is no error in the text, this must apply to a place or station near the last mentioned town, where perhaps the temple of Apollo Maloeis, held in great veneration by the inhabitants, was situated. (Thuc. III. 3.) The cape also, it should be observed, would have been a bad station for the Athenian fleet and camp, nor could they have been joined there easily by the Methymnæan forces. (Thuc. III. 4.) Xenophon distinctly mentions Cape Malea as the station occupied by the fleet of Callicratidas, before the sea-fight off Arginusæ; but when he adds, that it is ἀντίον τῆς Μυτιλήνης, he means probably over against, and in a line with Mitylene. (Hell. I. 6, 19.) Its modern name is Cape *Maria*.

To complete our nomenclature of the Lesbian
Arisba. cities, we may add the names of Arisba, destroyed, as Pliny reports, by an earthquake. (V. 39.) Herodotus states, that it was conquered by the people of Methymna. (I. 151. Cf. Steph. Byz. v. 'Αρίσβη.
Geren. Strab. XIII. p. 590.) Geren, a town or village so called from Geren, the son of Neptune. (Steph. Byz.
Issa. v. Γέρην.) Issa, named also Himera. (Id. v. Ἴσσα.)

[r] Pocock, tom. I. b. 3. c. 4.

Metaum, founded by Metas, a Tyrrhenian chief. Metaum.
(Id. v. Μέταον.) Nape, a spot situated in the plain
country near Methymna. (Strab. IX. p. 426. Steph.
Byz. v. Νάπη.) Xanthus, a town of Lesbos. (Id. v.
Ξάνθος.) Penthile. (Id. v. Πενθίλη.) Polium, a spot
with a chapel (ἡρῷον) sacred to Tantalus. (Id. v. Πό-
λιον.) There was also a mountain of the same name
with that hero. (Id. v. Τάνταλος.) Brisa, a promon- Brisa.
tory where was a temple of Bacchus. (Id. v. Βρίσα.
Androt. ap. Etym. M.) Hyperdexion, a spot where
stood the shrines of Jupiter Hyperdexius and Mi- Hyper-
nerva Hyperdexia. (Id. v. Ὑπερδέξιον.) dexium.

Between Lesbos and the continent of Asia are
several islets noticed by ancient geographers. Strabo
reckons twenty, and observes that the name of Heca- Hecaton-
tonnesi was applied to the group, from Hecatus, or nesi.
Apollo, the deity most revered throughout the adjoining country. (XIII. p. 618.) Herodotus, however, writes the name Ἑκατὸν Νῆσοι, (I. 151.) as if it
was formed from the numerical adjective; and this
derivation is more simple and probable than that of
Strabo. (Cf. Steph. Byz. v. Ἑκατόννησοι.) The modern appellation of these islets is *Musco-nisi* [s]. The
largest of these contained a city of Æolian origin,
according to Herodotus, who does not however mention it by name. (I. 151.) But from other writers
we learn that it was called Pordoselene, or Porose- Pordoselene; the latter form being adopted, as Strabo con- Porose-
tends, by those who wished to avoid the indelicate lene.
allusion presented by the former [t]. Scylax writes
Pordoselene, (Peripl. p. 36.) as well as Steph. Byz.
and Hesychius. Pliny, who erroneously places it

[s] Note to the French Strabo.   πορδὴ, " crepitus ventris," tom.
[t] This being formed from   III. p. 277.

near Ephesus, (V. 38.) and Ptolemy, (p. 136.) Poroselene [u]. This town is known to us as a bishop's see in the seventh century. (Hierocl. p. 686.) Pliny names besides the following islets, Sandaleon, Leucæ, a group of five; Cydonea, one of them, was remarkable for a hot source. (V. 39.)

Sandaleon insula.
Leucæ insulæ.
Cydonea insula.
Arginusæ.

The Arginusæ, so celebrated in Grecian history for the naval victory gained by the ten Athenian generals over the Spartan fleet, but so barbarously and ungratefully turned against them by their own countrymen, are three small islands, situated close to the promontory of Cane, and about 120 stadia from Mitylene. Thucydides leads us to infer there was a spot of the same name on the neighbouring coast of Æolis. (VIII. 101. Diod. Sic. XIII. 98. Cf. Xen. Hell. I. 6, 19. seq. Plin. V. 39. Harpocr. v. Ἀργινοῦσαι.)

[u] The coins of this town invariably, I believe, exhibit the latter form, ΠΟΡΟΣΕΛΗΝΕΙΤΩΝ. Sestini, p. 75.

SECTION III.

BITHYNIA.

Origin and history of the Bithynians—Boundaries of the province under the Roman empire—Description of the coast on
the Propontis—Interior of the country around mount Olympus
and the lake Ascanius—Nicæa and Nicomedia, with the adjoining bays—Chalcedon and the Thracian Bosphorus—The
Euxine—Coast of that sea as far as the Sangarius—The Mariandyni and Caucones—Interior of eastern Bithynia.

THE early revolutions which Asia Minor seems to
have experienced in regard to its population, both
before the Trojan war and immediately after that
period, render it, as Strabo justly observes, a matter
of no small intricacy to assign to contiguous nations
their distinctive limits and proper territories. The
Greek geographer has felt this to be peculiarly the
case with the province of Bithynia, which appears
to have been successively occupied, with varying
boundaries, by the Phrygians, Mysians, and Bithynians. The latter people, as their name sufficiently
attests, became the permanent possessors of the country ; but this event cannot be considered as prior to
the siege of Troy, since Homer nowhere mentions
the Bithynians, but invariably designates the people
of that country by the name of Mysians and Phrygians. (Il. B. 862. N. 792. Strab. XII. p. 565.)
Strabo has also proved that the Mysians not only

occupied the shores of the lake Ascanius and the plains of Nicæa, but that they extended as far as Chalcedon and the Thracian Bosphorus. (XII. p. 566.) Though we cannot precisely fix the period at which the Bithyni settled in the fertile district to which they communicated their name, we can have no doubt as to the country from whence they came, since the testimony of antiquity is unanimous in ascribing to them a Thracian origin. Herodotus in particular asserts, that according to their own traditions they came from the banks of the Strymon, and having been driven from their country by the Teucri and Mysi, crossed over into Asia. (VII. 75.) Thucydides also and Xenophon expressly term them Bithynian Thracians. (Thuc. IV. 75. Xen. Hell. I. 3, 2. III. 2, 2.) The latter writer traversed their country on his return into Greece with the ten thousand, and had ample opportunities of knowing, both from their customs and language, that they were of the same great family with the Thracians of Europe. (Anab. VI. 4, 1.) Some geographers have noticed a distinction to be observed in regard to this people, namely, that the appellation of Bithyni was properly applicable to the inland population, while that of the coast took the name of Thyni. (Apoll. Rhod. II. 462. Eustath. ad Dionys. Perieg. 793. Plin. V. 32.) But historically speaking, it is of little value, and may therefore safely be neglected. The Bithynians, as Herodotus informs us, were first subjected by Crœsus. (I. 28.) On the dissolution of the Lydian empire they passed under that of Persia, and their country became the seat of a satrapy, sometimes known in history by the title of Dascylium, sometimes of the Hellespont, but more commonly of Bithynia. The people lived principally in villages ; the only considerable towns being situated on the coast, and inhabited by Greek colonists. This state of things lasted till the death of Alexander, who had taken military possession of the country after the defeat and expulsion of the Persian troops from the peninsula.

On the decease of the king of Macedon we find Botiras, the son of Dydalsus, a Thracian chief, seizing upon Astacus, a Greek town on the sea-coast, and after defeating Calantus, the officer who commanded the Macedonian forces in the country, establishing an independent principality which he transmitted, through his lineal descendants Bas and Xipœtes, to Nicomedes, son of the latter, who after the death of Lysimachus first assumed the title of king of Bithynia. (Memn. Exc. ap. Phot. p. 720. seq.) He gave his name to the city of Astacus, which from henceforth was called Nicomedia, and became the capital of the new kingdom. (Pausan. V. 12.) Nicomedes was succeeded by his son Prusias, surnamed Zeilas[a], (Polyb. XXXVII. 2, 1.) and he again by Prusias, the Hunter, who was long engaged in war with Attalus, king of Pergamum, and is well known in history for having abandoned Hannibal to his pursuers, when that great man sought refuge at his court from the animosity and vindictiveness of the Romans. (Liv. XXXIX. 46—51.) This sovereign had extended considerably the limits of the Bithynian empire by the accession of some important towns conceded to him by his ally, Philip of Macedon, (Strab. XII. p. 563. Liv. XXXII. 34.) and several advantages gained over the Byzantians and king

[a] See Schweighæuser's note to this fragment.

Attalus; but the latter was finally able to overcome his antagonist, by stirring up against him his own son Nicomedes, who, after drawing the troops from their allegiance to his father, caused him to be assassinated. (Liv. Epit. L. Justin. XXXIV. 4.) Nicomedes, after this unnatural crime, ascended the vacant throne, and reigned for several years. He was succeeded by his son Nicomedes Philopator, who found himself engaged not long after his accession in a war with Mithridates; and though he was supported by the Roman forces, he was compelled, after sustaining repeated defeats, to fly from his dominions, and abandon them to his victorious enemy. (Appian. Bell. Mithr. c. 7—20.) On his death, which occurred soon after these events, he bequeathed his kingdom to the Roman people, and, in pursuance of this arrangement, Bithynia, after the overthrow of Mithridates, was annexed to the empire. (Liv. Epit. XCIII. Plut. Cæs. §. 3.) Like other Asiatic sovereigns, the kings of Bithynia are said to have been sensual and effeminate. (Polyb. XXXVII. 2. Cic. Verr. V. 11.) The interior of the country was mountainous and woody; (Xen. Anab. VI. 5. Nicet. Chon. p. 128.) but near the sea it was covered with rich and fertile plains, thickly spread with towns and villages. The produce consisted in grain of every sort; wine, cheese, figs, and various kinds of wood. (Xen. Anab. VI. 4, 4. Strab. XII. p. 565. Plin. XI. 42.)

Bithynia, properly so called, is confined to the west by the Rhyndacus, which separates it from Mysia, and to the east by the river Sangarius; but if we include within its limits, as most geographers have done for the sake of convenience, the districts

of the Caucones and Mariandyni, we shall remove
the boundary on that side to the river Parthenius,
where Paphlagonia commences. On the north it is
bounded by the Propontis and the Euxine, and on
the south it is contiguous to the provinces of Phrygia and Galatia: the boundary on that side being
formed apparently by the chain of the Bithynian
Olympus, which runs nearly parallel with the
Euxine, and extends its ramifications beyond Paphlagonia as far as Pontus and the river Halys. The
western portion of Bithynia has received from the
Turks the name of *Khodavendkhiar;* and that
situated on the Euxine and around the Bosphorus
they call *Kodjaili.*

Commencing our survey of the Bithynian coast
from the Rhyndacus, where that of Mysia terminates, and travelling eastward, the first place which
we arrive at is Dascylium, which was once of suffi- Dascylium.
cient note to give its name to the Persian satrapy,
under which Mysia and Bithynia were comprehended. (Herod. III. 120, 126. VI. 33.) Alexander sent Parmenio to occupy this town after the
battle of the Granicus. (Arrian. I. 17.) Strabo informs us it gave its name to the Palus Dascylitis, Dascylitis
near which it stood; (XII. p. 575.) and Stephanus palus.
Byz. also acknowledges this lake; (v. Δασκύλιον,)
but Eustathius confounds it with the Aphnitis of
Strabo; (ad Il. B. 824.) and in this respect he seems
only to follow that geographer himself. (XII. p.
587.) Dionysius of Halicarnassus, on the other
hand, seems to suppose that the lake of Dascylium
is the same as the Palus Ascania; (Ant. Rom. I.)
but this is likewise an error; for modern researches
establish the existence of a large piece of water on

the right bank of the Rhyndacus, and not far from
the mouth of that river, in a tract of country to
which the name of *Diaskilo* is still attached [b].
P. Mela (I. 19.) and Pliny (V. 32.) write Dascylos.
A bishop of Dascylia in Bithynia is mentioned in
Ecclesiastical History. (Conc. Quin. p. 1194.) From
Xenophon we learn that Pharnabazus, the satrap
of Bithynia and the Hellespont, had his principal
seat and estate at Dascylium. He represents it as
situated in a rich and plentiful country, thickly
studded with large villages. The parks were beautifully laid out, and abounded in animals for the
chase. A river well stocked with fish ran through
the grounds, and the woods supplied every sort of
feathered game. This fine estate was completely
.ruined and devastated by the troops of Agesilaus,
during the war he carried on against Pharnabazus
in Asia. (Xen. Hell. IV. 1, 8, et seq.) The river
here mentioned by Xenophon is probably that stream
which flows from mount Olympus, near *Broussa*,
and, after forming the lake which took its name
from Dascylium, joins the Rhyndacus near its exit
into the Propontis. The Turks call this river *Ou-
fersou*, or *Niloufer*, and I imagine it answers to the
Odrysses fl. Odrysses of Hecatæus cited by Strabo. (XII. p. 551.)
Speaking of the Halizones, or Alazones, a people
mentioned by Homer, this ancient writer, in his
Periegesis, stated, " that Alazia, their principal town,
" was near the Odrysses, which flowed from the
" west, from the lake Dascylitis, and after travers-
" ing the Mygdonian plain joined the Rhyndacus.
" Alazia is now deserted, but there are several small
" towns inhabited by the Alazones, whose country

[b] Note to the French Strabo, tom. IV. b. xii. p. 115.

" is traversed by the Odrysses. Apollo is especially
" revered there, particularly in those parts which
" border on the territory of Cyzicus." This description, as may be seen from the map, agrees very
well with the *Niloufer*, except in one circumstance,
which, it must be confessed, is a very material one.
That river, instead of flowing, as the Odrysses of
Hecatæus, from west to east, runs in the opposite direction. The Macestus is the only river
which would fulfil the condition of falling into the
Rhyndacus from the west, but it comes from the
lake of Miletopolis, not the Dascylitis. Again, it
may be observed, that Menecrates of Elæa placed
the Halizones in the mountains above the coast of
Myrlæa, which agrees very well with the topography of Hecatæus and the course of the *Niloufer*.
(Strab. loc. cit.) Pliny also favours our supposition
by the mention of a river Horisius, which he connects with the Rhyndacus, and which can scarcely
be identified with any other stream than the Odrysses of Hecatæus, and the modern *Niloufer*. To
the east of Dascylium follows the Gebes, or Gelbes, Gebes, sive
an obscure river unknown to every geographer but Gelbes fl.
Pliny. (V. 32.) The same author places inland,
and on the banks of this river, the town of Helgas, Helgas,sive
or Booscœte, Βοὸς κοίτη, afterwards called Germani- Booscœte,
copolis. Mannert is inclined to identify this place postea Ger-
manicopo-
with the Cæsarea of Ptolemy (p. 118.) and Hiero- lis.
cles. (p. 693.) Dio Chrysostom also mentions a Cæsarea.
small town of that name very near Prusa. (Orat.
XLVII. p. 526.)

Myrlea, at some little distance from the coast, ac- Myrlea,
cording to Pliny, was a colony of Colophon. (Cf. postea
Apamea.
Mel. I. 19.) It flourished as an independent city

for several years, (Scyl. p. 35.) till it was taken and destroyed by Philip, son of Demetrius, king of Macedon, who ceded the territory to Prusias, sovereign of Bithynia, his ally. This prince rebuilt the town, and called it Apamea, after his queen. (Strab. XII. p. 563.) Stephanus Byz. is less correct in referring this to Nicomedes. (v. Μύρλεια.) From the latter geographer we collect, that the name of Myrleanus Sinus was sometimes applied to the gulf on which Myrlea stood, but which is more generally known by that of Cianus. Apamea received a Roman colony under the auspices of Julius Cæsar, as appears from the title of Colonia Julia Concordia Apamea on its coins[c]. It is mentioned as a flourishing town by Pliny the younger. (Epist. X. 56.) Asclepiades of .Myrlea is a grammarian frequently cited by Athenæus and the Scholiasts. The ruins of Apamea have been observed by various travellers near the site now called *Modania*, about six hours north of *Broussa*[d].

The deep bay whose southern shore we are now following took the name of Cianus from the ancient city of Cius, situated at the vertex of the angle made by its two sides. (Scyl. Per. p. 35.) It had been founded originally by a colony of Milesians, and was advantageously placed at the mouth of the river Ascanius, which discharged into the Propontis the waters of the Ascanian lake; and being navigable, rendered Cius the emporium of a large tract of surrounding country, and many inland towns of

Side notes:
Myrleanus Sinus.

Cianus Sinus. Cius.

[c] Sestini, p. 66. Some earlier coins exhibit the epigraph ΑΠΑΜΕΩΝ ΜΤΡΛΕΑΝΩΝ.

[d] Wheeler, tom. I. p. 209.

Pococke, tom. III. b. ii. c. 25. P. Lucas, Third Voyage, tom. I. p. 128.

Bithynia and Phrygia. (Plin. V. 32. Aristot. ap.
Schol. Apoll. Argon. I. 1177.) It was more particularly the port of Nicæa, the chief town of the
former province; and as late as towards the close
of the Byzantine empire, travellers coming from
Europe by sea landed at Cius, and having crossed
over land to the Ascanian lake, sailed to Nicæa.
(G. Pachym. p. 287.) Herodotus calls it a town of
Mysia. (V. 122.) Strabo informs us, that Philip,
son of Demetrius, having ruined Cius together with
Myrlea, in conjunction with Prusias, gave them up
to that sovereign, who founded a new town on the
site of the former, which he called Prusias. (XII. Prusias ad
p. 563.) This town appears to have been termed mare.
the maritime Prusias, to distinguish it from another
Bithynian town, named Prusias ad Hypium. (Memnon ap. Phot. Cod. CCXXIV.[e]) It is evident, however, that Cius either still subsisted as a separate
town from Prusias, or recovered its original appellation, since it is mentioned under that name by
several authors much posterior to the event alluded
to by Strabo. (P. M. I. 19. Plin. V. 32. Zosim. I.
35. Hierocl. Synecd. Anna Comn. p. 172, C. Nicet.
Chon. p. 233, C. and many others [f].) The site on
which it was built still retains the name of *Kio.*
The river Cius mentioned by Apollonius Rhodius Cius flu-
(I. 1178.) is probably that which has been already vius.
mentioned as flowing from the Ascanian lake into
the bay of Cius, though it must be admitted that

[e] This distinction is further
observable in the coins of Prusias; the inscription is ΠΡΟΥ-
CIEΩΝ ΤΩΝ ΠΡΟC ΘΑΛΑCCΑΝ.

[f] There are also coins, with
the epigraph KIANΩΝ, of the

reigns of Claudius, Hadrian,
and Severus. Sestin. p. 67.
There are, I believe, no imperial medals of Prusias on the
sea.

Pliny makes the Ascanius and Cius two different
Hylas flu- streams. (V. 32.)　The Hylas of the same geogra-
vius.
pher was supposed by mythological writers to be
the fountain where the youth of that name was
carried away by the Naiads. (Apoll. Arg. I. 1353.)
Strabo reports, that in his time the inhabitants of
Prusias celebrated a festival called Oribasia in commemoration of that event. (XII. p. 564.)　The little
Argantho- stream in question flowed probably from mount Ar-
nius mons. ganthonius, which tradition has connected with the
story of Hylas :

Τῆμος ἄρ᾽ οἵγ᾽ ἀφίκοντο Κιανίδος ἤθεα γαίης
᾿Αμφ᾽ ᾿Αργανθώνειον ὄρος προχοάς τε Κίοιο.

APOLL. RH. I. 1177.

Strabo says it rose above Prusias. (loc. cit.)　In the
Argonautics ascribed to Orpheus (v. 641.) it is called
Arganthus ; in Steph. Byz. ᾿Αργανθώνις.　This mountain terminates in a cape which forms the extreme
point of the northern shore of the Cianus Sinus.
Posidium Ptolemy names it Posidium promontorium ; the
promonto-
rium. modern appellation is *Bozburun*.　Near Cius was a
place called Bryllium, and a small tract of country
to which it gave the name of Bryllis. (Steph. Byz.
v. Βρύλλιον. Plin. V. 32.)

Before we quit the shores of the Propontis for
those of the Bosphorus, it will be proper to speak
of some few towns which are to be found in that
part of Bithynia which is situated between the coast
and the Mysian and Phrygian mountains.　The most
Prusa ad important of these is Prusa ad Olympum, so called
Olympum. from being placed at the foot of mount Olympus,
commonly termed the Mysian, to distinguish it from
the Thessalian chain.　Pliny asserts, without naming his authority, that this town was founded by

Hannibal. (V. 32.) By which expression we are probably to understand that it was built at the instigation of this great general, when he resided at the court of Prusias, from whom the name of the city seems evidently derived. But Strabo, following a still more remote tradition, affirms that it was founded by Prusias who made war against Crœsus. (XII. p. 564.) In Stephanus, who copies Strabo, the latter name is altered to Cyrus. (v. Προῦσα.) But it is probable that both readings are faulty, though it is not easy to see what substitution should be made g. Dio Chrysostom, who was a native of Prusa h, did not favour the tradition which ascribed to it so early an origin as that authorized by the reading in Strabo, since he says of it, (Orat. XLIII. p. 585.) Εὖ γὰρ ἴστε ὅτι οὐ μεγίστη τῶν πόλεων ἐστὶ, οὐδὲ πλεῖστον χρόνον οἰκουμένη. Stephanus Byz. remarks that Prusa was but a small town. Strabo, however, informs us that it enjoyed a good government. (loc. cit.) It continued to flourish under the Roman empire, as may be seen from Pliny the Younger; (Ep. X. 85.) but under the Greek emperors it suffered much from the wars carried on against the Turks. (Nicet. Chon. p. 186, D. p. 389, A.) It finally remained in the hands of the descendants of Osman, who made it the capital of their empire, under the corrupted name of *Brusa* or *Broussa*. It is still one of the most flourishing towns possessed by the Infidels in *Anatolia* [i].

g See the various emendations proposed in a note to the French Strabo, tom. IV. lib. xii. p. 82.

h There are autonomous and imperial coins of Prusa. The name of the people on these monuments is ΠΡΟΥΣΑΕΙΣ. Sestini, p. 70.

i For a good account of *Broussa* and its vicinity, see Browne's Travels in Walpole's Turkey, tom. II. p. 108.

The warm baths of Prusa, which are still held in great repute[k], were known to the ancients. Athenæus says they were commonly called the royal waters. (II. p. 43, A. Steph. Byz. v. Θερμά.) Mount Olympus, which rose above Prusa, was one of the highest summits of Asia Minor, being covered with snow during great part of the year[l]. The lower parts, and the plains at the foot, especially on the western side, had from the earliest period been occupied by the Mysians, whence it was generally denominated the Mysian Olympus. (Plin. V. 32.) Its sides were covered with vast forests, which afforded shelter to wild beasts, and not unfrequently to robbers, who erected castles there, and other strong holds. (Strab. XII. p. 574.) We read in Herodotus, that in the time of Crœsus an immense wild boar, issuing from the woods of Olympus, laid waste the Mysian lands, and became so formidable, that the inhabitants were obliged to send a deputation to the Lydian monarch, to request his aid for delivering their country from the monster. (I. 36.) The lower regions of this great mountain are still covered with extensive forests, but the summit is rocky, and destitute of vegetation[m]. The Turks call it *Anadoli dagh*. In the Byzantine historians mention is made of several fortresses which defended the passes of Olympus; such as Pytheca, (Nicet. Chon. p. 35, B. Cinnam. p. 21.) Acrunum, and Calogrœa, (Cinnam. ibid. Melangia Cedren. p. 553. Ann. Comn. p. 441.) More to the west, and near the sources of the Rhyndacus, a village now called

Olympus mons. [margin note]

---

[k] Browne describes them minutely, p. 109.
[l] Ibid. p. 112.

[m] Sestini Viaggio da Cizico a Broussa.

Edrenos naturally suggests the idea of its being on the site of Hadriani, a Bithynian town of some Hadriani. note, and the native place of Aristides the rhetorician, who often alludes to it in his Orations. We collect from his account that it was near a river, which is doubtless the Rhyndacus[n], and on the borders of Mysia, two days' journey from Cyzicus, 160 stadia from Pæmanenum, and more than one day's journey from Hadrianotheræ, on the road to Pergamum. (tom. I. p. 596.) Hadriani is known to the ecclesiastical writers as a bishopric in the Hellespontine province. (Socrat. Eccl. Hist. VII. 25. Hierocl. Synecd. p. 693.) Sestini observes that *Edrenos* is a large and flourishing village, about eight hours from *Broussa*, on the south side of mount Olympus[o]. Returning to Prusa, and advancing from thence to the north-east, we shall reach the banks of the Ascanian lake, already noticed under Ascanius the head of Cius. The country situated around this lacus. expanse of water is thought by Strabo to be the Ascania of Homer, though that poet places it in Ascania Phrygia : regio.

Φόρκυς αὖ Φρύγας ἦγε, καὶ Ἀσκάνιος θεοειδής,
Τῆλ' ἐξ Ἀσκανίης.   IL. B. 862.

Πάλμυν τ', Ἀσκάνιόν τε, Μόρυν θ' υἷ' Ἱπποτίωνος·
Οἵ ῥ' ἐξ Ἀσκανίης ἐριβώλακος ἦλθον ἀμοιβοί.
                                           IL. N. 792.

Subsequent writers, however, have assigned it to Mysia, as Euphorion, quoted by Strabo, (XII. p. 566.)

[n] The emblem of a river is also found on the coins of Hadriani, and sometimes allusion is made to the vicinity of Olympus, as in the epigraph ΑΔΡΙΑ-

ΝΕΩΝ ΠΡΟC ΟΛΥΜΠΟΝ. Sestini, Lettere Numism. tom. VIII. p. 16.
[o] Ibid. p. 14.

. . . Μυσοῖο παρ' ὕδασιν 'Ασκανίοιο :

and Alexander the Ætolian :

Οἱ καὶ ἐπ' 'Ασκανίων δωματ' ἔχουσι ῥοῶν
Λίμνης 'Ασκανίης ἐπὶ χείλεσιν· ἔνθα Δολίων
Υἱὸς Σιληνοῦ νάσσατο καὶ, Μελίης.

Ascania
pagus. According to Apollodorus, there was a place called Ascania on the shore of the lake. (Ap. Strab. XIV. p. 681.) Aristotle observes, that the waters of the Palus Ascania are so impregnated with nitre as to cleanse the clothes dipped in them. (Mirab. Ausc. c. 54. Cf. Plin. XXXI. 10.) Col. Leake describes the Ascanian lake as " about ten miles long, and " four wide, surrounded on three sides by steep " woody slopes, behind which rise the snowy sum- Nicæa. " mits of the Olympus range ᴾ." Nicæa, the capital of Bithynia, according to Strabo, was situated on the eastern shore, in a wide and fertile plain, though somewhat unhealthy in summer. Stephanus states that it was first colonized by the Bottiæi, and was called Anchore. (v. Νίκαια.) Strabo mentions neither of these circumstances, but states that it was founded by Antigonus, son of Philip, who called it Antigonia; it subsequently received that of Nicæa from Lysimachus, in honour of his wife, daughter of Antipater. The circumference of the town, which was built in the form of a square, measured sixteen stadia, and the streets were drawn at right angles to each other, so that from a monument which stood near the gymnasium it was possible to see the four gates. (XII. p. 565.) Pliny the Younger, in his Letters, makes frequent mention of Nicæa and its public buildings, which he had undertaken to restore, being at that time governor of Bithynia. (X. 40, 48,

ᴾ Asia Minor, p. 7.

et seq.) It was the birthplace of Hipparchus the astronomer, (Suid. v. "Ἵππαρχος.) and Dio Cassius. Nicæa is also spoken of by Cicero, (pro Dejot. §. 9. Epist. Fam. XIII. 61.) Dio Chrys. (Or. XXXVIII.) Memnon, (ap. Phot. Cod. CCXXIV. p. 383.) and others. Under the Byzantine emperors it was often taken and retaken during their wars with the Turks. Nicetas states, that at this time the walls were built of brick. (p. 181.) The present town of *Isnik*, as it is called by the Turks, has taken the place of the Bithynian city, but " the ancient walls, towers, " and gates are in tolerably good preservation. In " most places they are formed of alternate courses " of Roman tiles and of large square stones, joined " by a cement of great thickness. The Turkish " town never was so large as the Grecian Nicæa, " and it seems to have been almost entirely con- " structed of the remains of that city ꝗ." Nicæa is celebrated in the ecclesiastical annals for the council held there against the Arian heresy, A. D. 325; whence the creed drawn up by the prelates assembled on that occasion is called Nicene.

Pliny reckons twenty-five miles from Prusa to Nicæa. (V. 32.) On the Ascanian lake, and 120 stadia from Cius, was a place rendered remarkable by some springs which were observed to fail in winter, but to overflow in summer. In Antigonus of Carystus (c. 188.) this spot is named Mythopolis, and in the treatise de Mir. Ausc. (c. 55.) Mythepo- Mythepolis lis; but I should apprehend that the real name of sive potius Pythopolis.

ꝗ Leake's Asia Minor, p. 10, 11. Walpole's Turkey, tom. II. p. 146. from Browne's Memoir. The coins of Nicæa, both under the Bithynian sovereigns and the Roman emperors, from Augustus to Gallienus, abound in collections; the epigraph is ΝΕΙΚΑΙΕΩΝ. Sestini, p. 69.

the place is Pythopolis, as we find it written in
Pliny (V. 32.) and Steph. Byz., who assigns it to
Mysia, (v. Πυθόπολις.) Plutarch quotes a story related by Menecrates, in his account of Nicæa, to
prove that this town had been founded by Theseus.

Soloon fl. The neighbouring brook received the name of Soloon from one of the hero's companions. (Thes.
p. 12.) Stephanus places near the bay of Astacus
a spot called Pythium; (vv. Πύθιον, Θερμά.) and Procopius speaks of some baths, and a church of St.
Michael, repaired by the emperor Justinian. These
possibly may all be referred to Pythopolis. (Procop.
de Ædif. V. 1.) The Byzantine historians notice
several small towns or fortresses in the district of
Nicæa, which serve at least to shew how populous

Basilea it was then. Basilea, a place forty stadia distant
sive Basi-
lionopolis. from Nicæa, (Niceph. Bryen. II. p. 52.) is probably
to be identified with the Basilionopolis of Hierocles,
and the councils, and the Basinopolis of Synesius.
(Epist. 66.) G. Pachymeres speaks of Belocome, a
place of great strength, (p. 288.) also Angelocome,
Anagurdes, Platanea, Melangea, (p. 286.) Crulla,
Catœcia, (Κατοικία,) Heracleum, and Nemicome : (p.
287.) he observes, that the road from these two last
places to Cius passed through a woody country.

Heracle- Heracleum answers doubtless to the village of *Era-
um.
kli* observed by Lucas on his way from Nicomedia
to Nicæa [r]. Frequent mention is also made of
Georgii Castellum : (Ann. Comn. p. 313, B.) near
it were Rhodomerus, Monastra, and Azala. (p. 315,
B.) South of Nicæa, *Lefke* is easily identified with

Leucæ. Leucæ, noticed by Anna Comnena on the road from
that city to Dorylæum : (p. 469.) near it was a

[r] Second Voyage, tom. I. c. 21.

place called Armeno Castrum. *Lefke* is situated
in a valley watered by a river named the *Sakaria;*
but Col. Leake justly observes, that this river is not
the Sangarius, but that branch of it known anciently
by the name of Gallus. Strabo states that this Gallus fl.
stream had its source at a place called Modra, in
Phrygia Epictetus, and joined the Sangarius about
300 stadia from Nicomedia. (XII. p. 543.) It was
from this river that the priests of Cybele were
named Galli. (Steph. Byz. v. Γάλλος. Plin. V. 32.)
Ammianus Marcellinus describes its course as very
winding. (XXVI. 8.) Beyond Leucæ was Agrilium, Agrilium.
noticed by Ptolemy, (p. 118.) and the Table Itinerary,
which fixes its situation between Nicæa and Dorylæum, of Phrygia, twenty-four miles from the
former, and thirty-five from the latter. Col. Leake
is inclined to identify it with *Vizirkhan*, about four
hours from *Lefke*. Strabo seems to place in this
direction also a small town named Otrea, as it was Otrea.
said, from Otreus, a Phrygian prince, mentioned in
the Iliad, (Γ. 186. Cf. Hymn. Ven. 111. and 147.) it
may perhaps answer to *Ortakevi*, a Turkish village
which Browne traversed on his road from *Broussa*
to *Kutaieh*[s].

Returning to the shores of the Propontis, and advancing eastward of Cape Posidium, we have to
speak of a nameless promontory, near which, ac- Megaricum
cording to Pliny, stood a small town, founded by oppidum.
some Megarians. (V. 32. Cf. Steph. v. Μεγαρικόν.)
Prænetus, a town often mentioned by the Byzantine Prænetus.
historians and ecclesiastical writers, is known to
have been situated on the coast. The Table Itinerary places it under the corrupt name of Pronetios,

[s] In Walpole's Turkey, tom. II. p. 113.

N 4

on the sea, and twenty-eight miles from Nicæa, (Steph. Byz.) who calls it Pronectus, reports, that it was founded by the Phœnicians. (v. Πρόνεκτος.) According to Cedrenus, it was destroyed by an earthquake. (p. 457. Cf. Socr. Eccl. Hist. VI. 16. Hierocl. Synecd. p. 690.) The site seems to answer to that of *Debrende*. Drepane, a place also on the coast, is mentioned by more than one writer. (Steph. Byz. v. Δρεπάνη. Etym. M. v. Δρέπανον.) The name of this town was afterwards changed to that of Helenopolis, by Constantine, in honour of his mother. (Niceph. Callist. VII. 49.) Frequent reference to the city under its new denomination is made in the Byzantine history. (Philost. II. p. 483. Socr. H. Eccl. I. 4, 18. Procop. de Æd. V. 1. Ann. Comn. p. 462.) Col. Leake is of opinion that Helenopolis was near the modern *Ersek*[t]. A small river, now called the *Dil*, which empties itself into the Propontis, is doubtless the Draco of Procopius. That historian remarks, that it was necessary to cross the Draco more than twenty times in going from Helenopolis to Nicæa; the course of this stream was altered by Justinian, to facilitate communication. (Ædif. V. 1.) Col. Leake states, that he crossed the *Dil* as many times on the same road[u]. The Draco is also mentioned by Anna Comn. (p. 286.) Pliny names several other small rivers which discharge themselves into this part of the Propontis. They are the Æsius, Bryazon, Plataneus, Areus, Æsyros, and Gendos; this last was also called Chrysorrhoas. Elsewhere the same geographer speaks of a river of Bithynia, named Olachas, which flowed near Bryazon, and whose water could not be endured by those

Drepane postea.

Helenopolis.

Draco fl.

Bryazon sive Olachas fl.

[t] Asia Minor, p. 10. [u] P. 10.

who had sworn falsely. (XXXI. 18.) The Plataneus recalls to mind Platanea, a place in the vicinity mentioned by G. Pachymeres, (p. 286.) And it
is not improbable that Brunga and Pontamus, two
stations placed in the Jerusalem Itinerary, between
Chalcedon and Nicomedia, are corruptions of Bryazon
and Plataneus.

The gulf, along whose southern shore we are Astacenus
now advancing, was anciently termed Astacenus, or nus Sinus.
Olbianus Sinus, from Astacus and Olbia, two Greek
cities of note, situated on the coast; if indeed they
are not the same city under two different names. It
is certain that Scylax, in describing the Mysian
coast, speaks of the Sinus Olbianus, and places there
Olbia and its port, without naming Astacus. (p. 35.) Olbia.
On the other hand, Strabo speaks only of Astacus, Astacus.
which, he says, was founded by the Megarians and
Athenians. This is confirmed by Memnon, cited by
Photius. (p. 722.) He says, the Megarians settled
here in the 17th Olympiad, and it was not till some
years after that the Athenian colony joined them.
Astacus was afterwards seized by Dædalsus, a native chief, who became the founder of the Bithynian
monarchy. In the war waged by his successor Xipœtes, with Lysimachus, Astacus was ruined; but
Nicomedes, the son of the former, transferred the
inhabitants to the city which he founded, and
named Nicomedia, after himself. (Strab. XII. p.
563.) Hence it appears that Pliny is greatly mistaken in stating that Nicæa had previously been
called Olbia. (V. 43.) Astacus seems to have been
still extant in the time of Arrian, who is cited by
Steph. Byz. (v. Ἄστακος. Μεγαρικόν. Cf. P. Mela.
I. 19. Steph. Byz. v. Ὀλβία.)

Nicomedia being the chief residence of the Bithy- Nicomedia.

nian kings, soon became a large and flourishing city,
and it continued to prosper under the Roman emperors, as may be collected from the letters of Pliny
to Trajan, in which he speaks of several public
buildings belonging to this city, such as a senate
house, an aqueduct, a forum, a temple of Cybele, &c.
He mentions also its having suffered much from a
great fire. (Ep. X. 42, 46.)

In still later times, Nicomedia was often the residence of the Roman emperors, when engaged in
carrying on war with the Parthians or Persians.
(Niceph. Callist. VII. ad fin.) It was however
nearly destroyed by an invasion of the Scythians
(Amm. Marcell. XXII. 9, 12.) and an earthquake.
(Philost. IV. p. 506.) The orator Libanius, in
his lament over the fortunes of Nicomedia, μονῳδία
ἐπὶ Νικομηδίᾳ, mourns the loss of its Thermæ, Basi-
licæ, temples, Gymnasia, schools, public gardens, &c.
Some of these were restored by Justinian. (Procop.
Æd. V. 1.) It was however finally conquered by
the Turks, who call it *Ismid.* Nicomedia gave birth
to Arrian, the historian of Alexander, (Steph. Byz.
v. Νικομηδεία.) and Constantine the Great breathed
his last at his villa Ancyron, near the city. (Cassiod.
Chron. Const. Philost. II. p. 484.) Scylax (p. 35.)
names with Olbia, and in the same bay, the Greek
Callipolis. city Callipolis, with a harbour. This is unknown
to other geographers, but it may have been the
Megaric colony, mentioned by Pliny, on the edge of
Craspedites the bay, hence sometimes called Craspedites Sinus.
Sinus. (V. 43.) On the other side of the gulf, the same
Leucatas Latin geographer notices the promontory of Leuca-
sive Acri- tas, thirty-seven miles from Nicomedia. This is
tas pro-
montori- probably the same as the Acritas of Artemidorus
um. (ap. Steph. Byz. v. Χαλκίτης.) and Ptolemy. (p. 118.)

Cibotus appears to have been a name given to the Cibotus.
narrow passage across the bay of Nicomedia, by the
Byzantine historians. (Ann. Comn. p. 309. A.) Col.
Leake, however, seems to place it in the gulf of
Cius[x]. Ægyllus was a spot near Cibotus. (Ann.
Comn. p. 438. D.) Eribolum, according to the Table Eribolum
Itinerary, stood on the bay, a little to the south of sive Eribœa.
Nicomedia. Xiphilinus also speaks of it as a landing place on the gulf, near that city. Ptolemy
likewise mentions it, under the name of Eribœa,
(p. 118.) and the Jerusalem Itinerary calls it Hyribo-
lum. (p. 573[y].) The site answers to that of *Kara-
musal.* Libum, a station of the Jerusalem Itine- Liba.
rary, on the same road between Eribolum and
Nicæa, and twenty-one miles from Nicomedia, is
called Liba by Cedrenus. (p. 451.) On the north
side of the gulf we have to notice *Ghebse,* or
Dchebse, which doubtless answers to the Dacibyza Dacibyza.
of the Byzantines. (Sozom. Hist. Eccl. VI. 14. G.
Pachym. Andr. Palæol. I. p. 64. Zonar. XIII. 16[z].)
Not far from thence stood Libyssa, a spot celebrated Libyssa.
in antiquity as the deposit of Hannibal's remains.
Plutarch, in the life of Flamininus, describes it as a
small village on the coast of Bithynia, and we know
from Ammianus (XXII. 9.) and the Itineraries,
that it stood on the road from Chalcedon to Nicomedia. These documents reckon twenty-three miles
from the latter city to Libyssa, and thirty-seven
from the former. (Cf. Plin. V. 43. Steph. Byz. v.
Λίβυσσα.) Appian speaks of a river Libyssus, and Libyssus fl.

---

[x] Asia Minor, notes p. 316.
[y] If Sestini is correct in his
reading of EPIBOIEΩN in a medal he assigns to this town, the

true name of the town is that
used by Ptolemy.
[z] Leake's Asia Minor, p. 9.

the plain Libyssa. (Syr. c. 11.) Some writers have identified Libyssa with *Ghebse*[a], but col. Leake, from a more accurate computation of distances, is inclined to fix this interesting site at *Maldysem*, or *Malsum*, a few miles to the south of *Ghebse*[b].

Pantichium.

Pantichium, situated according to the Itineraries, twenty-two miles from Libyssa, and fifteen from Chalcedon, retains the name of *Pantichi*[c]. (Itiner. Hieros. p. 571. Itiner. Anton. p. 140.) This place is likewise noticed by the ecclesiastical writers, Philostorgius (XI. p. 541.) and Sozomenus. (VII. 21.) Artemidorus, in his account of this coast, (ap. Steph. Byz. v. Χαλκίτης.) places, after Cape Acritas, 120 stadia further, another headland, named Hyris,

Trarium sive Trallium.

and near it the island Pityodes. Trarium, which Ptolemy places in this direction, is probably the same town which Steph. Byz. calls Trallium, near the bay of Astacus. To the south-east of Nicomedia is an extensive lake, and a chain of mountains, which encloses it to the west and south. These are frequently mentioned by the historians of the lower

Sophon lacus et mons.

empire by the name of Sophon. (Cedren. p. 451.) G. Pachymeres calls the former Siphones. (Andr. Pal. p. 228.) This I imagine to be the lake alluded to by Pliny the Younger, in his letter to Trajan, (X. 50.) and from which he was desirous of cutting a canal to the sea, to convey thither more easily the produce of the interior, consisting in marble, timber, provisions. He states that there were vestiges of a cut made under the Bithynian kings. Trajan, in his reply, desires him to have the levels of the lake and sea examined. In Ammianus, the same lake

[a] Mannert, tom. VI. p. 586. [b] Asia Minor, p. 9. [c] Leake, p. 8.

seems alluded to by the name of Sunonensis, or Su-
monensis. (XXVI. 8.) Evagrius also mentions a
lake called Boane, near Nicomedia. (Hist. Eccl. II.
14.) This piece of water now takes its name from
the village of *Shabanja,* which is probably a corruption of Sophon. Telemæa and Petræa were
places in the vicinity, according to Cedrenus. (p. 801.)
Petræa stood towards Nicæa, and about fifteen stadia from it. Metabole was a fortress on mount
Sophon, and near it was another mountain called
Maroscus, and a place named Trisca. (Niceph.
Bryenn. II. p. 56.)

We must now speak of Chalcedon, a celebrated Chalcedon.
Grecian city, situated at the southern extremity of the
Bosphorus. It was founded by a colony of Megarians,
on the site previously called Procerastes and Col-
pusa. (Plin. V. 43. P. Mela I. 19.) The inhabitants
were often taunted with the appellation of blind
men, because, having the choice of so magnificent a
site as that of Byzantium to build their city on,
they had preferred one so avowedly inferior. Herodotus says, this observation was first made by Me-
gabyzus, the Persian general; and he informs us, by
the way, that Chalcedon was prior to Byzantium
by seventeen years. (IV. 144. Cf. Tacit. Ann. XII.
63.) It was not merely with respect to the beauty
of situation that Chalcedon was inferior to its opposite neighbour, but, what was of much greater consequence, it laboured under great disadvantage in a
commercial point of view; since the current which
set in strongly from the Euxine carried vessels directly into the harbour of Byzantium, but prevented
their approach to Chalcedon in a straight course.
(Polyb. IV. 43.) Notwithstanding these disadvan-

tages, the Chalcedonians were sufficiently favoured, both in regard to climate, the fertility of the surrounding country, and opportunities for carrying on trade, to become a prosperous and wealthy people. They appear to have preserved their independence till the reign of Darius, to whose arms they were forced to submit. (Herod. V. 26.) They recovered their liberty, however, after the repeated defeats of the Persians, under Xerxes, and became the allies, or rather the tributaries, of the Athenians, to whom the ports of the Bosphorus were an object of the highest commercial and financial importance. (Thuc. IV. 75. Xen. Hell. I. 1, 14.) The disasters of Sicily gave them an opportunity of throwing off their chains, and they consequently joined the Peloponnesian alliance, and received a Spartan harmost. But Alcibiades, after his success off Cyzicus, blockaded Chalcedon by sea and land, and the Spartan general being slain in a sortie, the citizens were forced to comply with the terms offered by the victor; they once more, therefore, were obliged to pay the accustomed tribute, besides all the arrears which were due. (Hell. I. 3, 7.) This state of things lasted however only till the battle of Ægospotami; Chalcedon then opened its gates to Lysander, whose first object seems to have been to secure the entrance of the Bosphorus, by the possession of this city and Byzantium. (Hell. II. 2, 1.) Theopompus, who is quoted by Athenæus, observes, that the Chalcedonians at first possessed good institutions, but having been tainted by the democratical principles of their neighbours, the Byzantines, they became luxurious and debauched. (XII. 526. F.) Chalcedon afforded a refuge to the Roman troops under Cotta, from the pursuit of Mithridates. (Appian. Bell. Mithr. c. 71. Eutrop. VI. 5.)

Chalcedon is further celebrated in ecclesiastical history for the council held there against the Eutychian heresy. (A. D. 451.) Hierocles assigns to it the first rank among the cities of the province, then called Pontica prima. (p. 690.) It is to be observed, that in writing the name of this town, ancient writers have not been uniform, some writing it Καλκη-δών, others Χαλκηδών. The former mode is however much more frequent, and it is confirmed by the existing coins, the epigraph of which is invariably ΚΑΛΧΑΔΟΝΙΩΝ, according to the Doric form[d]. The town was situated on a rising ground, near the mouth of a rivulet of the same name. It had two ports separated by an isthmus, one looking west, the other east. There were many beautiful public buildings and monuments, but the most remarkable was a temple of Apollo. (Dionys. Byzant. p. 23.) The site of this ancient city is now occupied by the Turkish village *Kadikevi*, but the Greeks still preserve the classical name. *Scutari*, a well-known town and harbour, opposite Constantinople, is thought to represent Chrysopolis, a port of Chalcedon, often Chrysopolis. mentioned in history. The Athenians established there a toll, towards the close of the Peloponnesian war, to be paid by all ships coming from the Euxine. (Xen. Hell. I. 1, 14. Polyb. IV. 44, 3.) The 10,000 Greeks were encamped there for some days prior to crossing over into Thrace. (Xen. Anab. VI. 6, 22.) It is mentioned by Strabo as a small town, (XII. p. 563.) and Pliny says, " Fuit Chrysopolis." (V. 32.)

---

[d] Eckhel Doctr. Num. Vet. P. i. vol. I. p. 410. Sestini, p. 67.

Several writers of a later date, however, continue to speak of it. (Zosim. II. 30. Socrat. Hist. Eccl. I. 4. Amm. Marcell. XXII. 12.) Steph. Byz. (v. Χρυσόπολις) gives various etymological derivations of the name. Opposite to the coast of Chalcedon are ranged some islets, the nearest of which to the entrance of the Bosphorus still retains its ancient name of Prote. The next is Chalcitis, (Artemid. ap. Steph. Byz. v. Χαλκίτης.) now *Karkia*. The last, which is also the most considerable, called *Prinkipo*, or Princes' island, is often mentioned under that name in the Byzantine annals. (Ann. Comn. p. 462, 463.) And a monastery was built there by Justinian, the ruins of which may still be seen[e]. But the more ancient name of this island was Pityodes, -or Pityusa, as we learn from Artemidorus. (ap. Steph. Byz. v. Χαλκίτης. Cf. Plin. V. 32.) The two latter isles were also called Demonesi, and they appear to have been celebrated for the brass which they contained. (Hesych. v. Δημονήσιος χαλκός. Poll. V. 39. Aristot. Mirab. Ausc. p. 877.) Pliny names with these, other obscure islets, such as Elæa, Rhodussæ, Erebinthodes, and Megale. (V. 44.)

The ancients gave the name of Thracian Bosphorus to the narrow channel which establishes a communication between the waters of the Euxine and those of the Propontis. Tradition asserted that it was derived from the passage of Io, who during her metamorphosis had crossed this arm of the sea, and the names of Βοῦς and Δάμαλις were applied to the spot where the fabled heifer had landed in Asia. (Polyb. IV. 44. Eust. ad Dion. Perieg. 140.) Other writers, however, asserted, that Damalis was the name

Marginal notes:
Prote insula.
Chalcitis insula.
Pityodes insula.
Bosphorus Thracius.

e P. Gyllius Bosph. Thrac. III. 12.

of a lady, wife of the Athenian general, Chares.
(Dionys. Anapl. Bosph. ap. P. Gyll. III. 9.) The
breadth of this celebrated channel is variously estimated by different writers. Strabo seems to say,
the narrowest part, which he calls τὸ Βυζαντιακὸν
στόμα, (II. p. 86.) is four stadia broad ; but Polybius
says, the narrowest part is about the Hermæan promontory, somewhere midway between the two extremities, and he does not compute the breadth at
less than five stadia ; he adds, that it was at this
point that Darius built his bridge when he made
his Scythian expedition. (IV. 44.) Herodotus agrees
with Strabo, and appears to place the bridge of Darius where Polybius does. (IV. 87.) The same historian estimates the length of the channel at 120
stadia. Polybius has described at some length the
action and direction of the currents setting in from
the Euxine. (IV. 43.) But of all ancient writers,
no one has been so minute in his account of the
Bosphorus as Dionysius of Byzantium, who composed a work expressly on this subject. Of this,
some considerable fragments have been preserved to
us, of which P. Gythius has availed himself in his
description of the strait, but the originals have disappeared[f]. On the side of Chalcedon, the Byzantine topographer notices north of that city the
fountain Hermagora, and the heroon of Eurostus.
Strabo places above Chalcedon the fountain Azari-
tia, which contained small crocodiles. (XII. p. 563.
Cf. Steph. Byz. v. Ζάρητα.) Then follows the promontory Bos, so called from the monument raised
to the wife of Chares, as appears from the epigram
inscribed on it, and quoted by Dionysius. Beyond,

[f] See the preface to the Geogr. Minores, tom. III.

is the wide and beautiful harbour of Chrysopolis;
then succeed two points of land called Discus and
Ῥοιζοῦσαι ἄκραι, or bluffs, against which the waters
beat; the spot named Ciconium; Nausimachium, so
called from a sea fight; the bay of Lycadium, or
Cycladium; the promontory Perirrhous; the spots
called Echæa Nausicleia, where the Chalcedonians
gained a naval victory; Potamonion, the point
Lembus, and the island Blabe, so termed from the
shipwrecks it occasioned. After Lembus, comes
Phiela, a natural circular mound, having the appearance of a theatre; then the port of Phrixus;
the promontory Oxyrrhoum; the basin called Κα-
τάγγειον, which abounded with fish; the plain

Portus named Gronychia, and the bay of Amycus. Pliny
Amyci.
calls it the port of Amycus, and places near it the

Nicopolis. town of Nicopolis. (V. 43.) Steph. Byz. acknowledges also a Nicopolis in Bithynia; beyond, we
have the promontory called Aetorynchus, or the
Eagle's beak[g]; the bay of Mucaporis, with a very
good haven, so called from a certain king of Bithynia. Then the spot named Δάφνη μαινομένη, from
a laurel which grew there after the death of Amycus, killed by Pollux, and whose branches were said
to cause insanity in those that wore them. Arrian
says this place was eighty stadia from Byzantium,
and forty from the temple of Jupiter Urius. (Peripl.
Eux. p. 25.) Beyond were the Nymphæum, the
couch (Κλίνη) of Hercules, the Argyronium, (Cf.
Procop. Æd. I. 9.) and the low land called Anaplus.

Hieron   Immediately above this was a high point of land,
sive tem-
plum Jovis with a temple built by Phrixus in honour of Jupi-
Urii.

[g] In the Geogr. Min. p. 20.   ly a corruption or false print
the word is Ἀετόρχηχον, evident-   for Ἀετίρυγχον.

ter Urius, others say of Neptune. This, being a situation commanding the strait and surrounding country, had been fortified, and was often contested by the Byzantines and Chalcedonians. The former finally prevailed, as they were more powerful, and also because they consented to pay a sum of money for it to Callimedes, a general of Seleucus. This Hieron, as it is often simply called, was for some time in the hands of the Gauls, who had crossed over into Asia. (Dionys. Byz. p. 19.) Polybius says that Jason, on his return from Colchis, sacrificed here to the twelve gods; (IV. 39, 6.) and elsewhere he states, that it was wrested from the Byzantines by Prusias, who carried away all the most valuable materials. On making peace, however, he was obliged to replace them. (IV. 50—52.)

The promontory seems to be called Estia by Pliny. (V. 43 h.) Beyond is the spot called Chelæ; and Pantichium, so named from its being surrounded by trenches; the promontory Coracium; a low island, with some reefs and rocks about it, named Cyaneæ; an elevated mound surmounted by a round rock called Medea's tower; Ancyreum, a promontory so called because the Argonauts took from thence a rock to serve in the place of an anchor. This promontory is described by Dionysius as nearly opposite to the Cyanean or Symplegades rocks off the European coast; and here the Bosphorus may be said to terminate, and the Euxine to begin. This Pontus sea is said, from its stormy nature, or the wildness Euxinus. of its coasts, to have been formerly called Ἄξενος, or "the inhospitable." (Plin. IV. 24. VI. 1. Mel. I. 19.)

h We should read, " deinde Naulochum : promontorium Estiæ ;
" templum Neptuni."

The Grecian navigators, however, had explored its coasts at a very early period, if we are to credit the celebrated expedition of the Argonauts; and long before the time of Herodotus, the colonies which they had established on various points of the Asiatic and European coasts must have familiarized the mariners of the mother country with this once dreaded sea. Herodotus, who probably took his accounts from Hecatæus and Scylax, and other geographers of that period, appears to have had no very accurate notion of the shape of the Euxine, at least of the northern side; but he had taken pains to ascertain the measurement of its greatest length and breadth. The former he reckoned at nine days and eight nights' sail, which, allowing 70,000 orgyæ for a day, and 60,000 for a night, make the sum of 1,110,000 orgyæ, or 11,100 stadia. The breadth he found to be three days and one night's sail, or 3300 stadia. The former direction was measured from the mouth of the Phasis to the straits of the Bosphorus; the latter from Themiscyra in Pontus to Sindice, a country near the Palus Mæotis. (IV. 86.) Strabo allows only 8000 stadia from the Bosphorus to the Phasis, (XII. p. 548.) which agrees with Agrippa's measurement, given by Pliny. (VI. 1.) The latter geographer gives also several estimates of the whole circuit of this sea, which furnish a mean of about 2500 miles. The whole shape of this great bason was considered to be curved in the manner of a bow, made after the Scythian fashion; the middle bend being formed by the Palus Mæotis, the chord by the coast of Asia Minor. (Plin. loc. cit. Strab. II. p. 125. Agathem. II. c. 14.) Of this last, with which we are at present more immediately concerned, we have a very detailed periplus or survey set down from actual observation by Arrian, the historian of Alexander's expedition, and author also of a history of Bithynia, a country which he was qualified for describing, since it was his native land. We have also another periplus, apparently of a more recent date, and compiled in great measure from Arrian, Marcian of Heraclea, and others [i]. Menippus of Pergamum, an earlier geographer, had written a work on the same subject, but we have now only a few fragments of it occasionally cited by Stephanus Byz. [k]

There exists also a fragment of a third periplus, by an anonymous writer, who is evidently posterior to Arrian, and has compiled from his work and other sources. It is by the help of these documents, and the Itineraries, that we shall endeavour to trace the remainder of the Bithynian coast, as well as that of Paphlagonia and Pontus. After passing the temple of Jupiter Urius, and proceeding ninety stadia, or twelve miles, we reach the mouth of the little river Rhebas, mentioned by several poets, and nearly all the geographers.

Rhebas fluvius.

> . . . . . . αἶψα δὲ τοίγε
> Ῥήβαν, ὠκυρόην ποταμὸν, σκόπελόν τε Κολώνης.

APOLL. ARG. II. 652.

> Ἀγχὶ δὲ Βιθυνοὶ λιπαρὴν χθόνα ναιετάουσι,
> Ῥήβας ἐνθ᾽, ἐρατεινὸν ἐπιπροΐησι ῥέεθρον,
> Ῥήβας, ὃς Πόντοιο παρὰ στομάτεσσιν ὁδεύει,
> Ῥήβας, οὗ κάλλιστον ἐπὶ χθονὶ σύρεται ὕδωρ.

DIONYS. PERIEG. v. 793.

---

[i] The two surveys have been published in the Geogr. Min. tom. I. and tom. II.

[k] These fragments are also given in the Geogr. Min. The Scholiast to Apollonius mentions likewise several other peripli.

(Orph. Argon. 711. Fest. Avien. 974.)   Pliny observes that some writers have called it Rhesus. (VI. 1. Cf. Scyl. Peripl. p. 34. Arrian. Peripl. Eux. p. 13.) In the Table Itinerary, the name of this stream is disguised under that of Ad Herbas. Tournefort in-

Melæna promontorium. forms us it is now called *Riwa*[1]. Cape Melæna was 150 stadia further to the east. It had a small haven formed by an inland. (Marcian. Peripl. p. 69. in Geogr. Min. tom. I.)

"Ακρην δ' ού μετά δηθά παρέξ ένέοντο Μέλαιναν.

APOLL. ARG. II. 653.

Artanes fluvius. (Cf. Arrian Peripl. p. 13.) The little river Artanes, with a haven, and a temple of Venus at its mouth, is placed by Arrian (p. 13.) 150 stadia from Melæna. (Cf. Marcian. Peripl. p. 69.) From the Ar-

Psillis fluvius. tanes to the Psilis, or Psillis, another little river, with a port for small craft, protected by a rock, we have again 150 stadia. (Arrian. p. 13. Marcian. p. 69. Strab. XII. p. 543.) This river is also called Psillus (Steph. Byz. Ψίλλον.) and Phyllis:

Τῇδ' ἄρ' ἔπι προχοὰς Φυλληΐδας, ἔνθα πάροιθε
Διψακὸς υἷ' Ἀθάμαντος ἐοῖς ὑπέδεκτο δόμοισιν.

APOLL. ARGON. II. 654.

Calpe portus et fluvius. From this river to the river and port of Calpe the ancients reckoned 210 stadia. (Arrian. Peripl. p. 13.) Xenophon, who halted here for some time with his fellow-soldiers, describes Calpe as an excellent port, about half way between Byzantium and Heraclea. It was formed by a rocky hill advancing into the sea, and enclosing on the land side a considerable tract of excellent land. The port lay beneath the rock, and was supplied with an abundant source of fresh water. The surrounding hills afforded also beautiful timber for building ships, and other pur-

[1] Lettre 16.

poses; and the soil yielded every kind of grain, and wine and fruit, in the greatest plenty. (Anab. VI. 4. Cf. Arrian. Peripl. p. 13.)

Τοῦ μέν θ' ἱερὸν αἶψα καὶ εὐρείας ποταμοῖο
Ἡϊόνας, πεδίον τε, βαθυῤῥείοντά τε Κάλπην
Δερκόμενοι παράμειβον.   APOLL. ARG. II. 660.

Strabo calls the river Calpas. (XII. p. 543. Cf. Steph. Byz. v. Κάλπη. Plin. VI. 1.) The modern name of the promontory and harbour of Calpe is *Kirpe.* Advancing eastward twenty stadia, we have to notice the little haven of Rhoe; and twenty sta- Rhoe por-dia further, the small island of Apollonia, having a ^{tus.} port, and situated close to the land. (Arrian. p. 13.) Its more ancient name was Thynias, which was Thynias afterwards changed for that of the deity worshipped ^{quæ et} Apollonia there. insula.

Τῆμος ἐρημαίης νήσου λιμέν' εἰσελάσαντες
Θυνιάδος, καμάτῳ πολυπήμονι βαῖνον ἔραζε.
                          APOLL. ARG. II. 674.

Εἰ δ' ἄγε δὴ νῆσον μὲν ἑῷου Ἀπόλλωνος
Τήνδ' ἱερὴν κλείωμεν.   IDEM, 688.

(Cf. Plin. VI. 12. Scyl. p. 34. Strab. XII. p. 543. Mela. II. 7. Steph. Byz. v. Θυνίας.) It is situated near the promontory of *Kirpe.* Chelæ was a spot Chelæ. twenty stadia beyond. (Arrian. Peripl. p. 13.) The Table Itinerary reckons twenty-seven miles from the river Psilis to this place, which nearly agrees with the maritime surveys. The Sangarius flows Sangarius fluvius. into the sea about 180 stadia further to the east. This is one of the largest and most celebrated of the rivers of Asia Minor, being mentioned by Homer, and several other poets and historians:

Ἤδη καὶ Φρυγίην εἰσήλυθον ἀμπελόεσσαν,
Ἔνθα ἴδον πλείστους Φρύγας, ἀνέρας αἰολοπώλους,

O 4

Λαοὺς 'Οτρῆος καὶ Μύγδονος ἀντιθέοιο,
Οἵ ῥα τότ' ἐστρατόωντο παρ' ὄχθας Σαγγαρίοιο.

IL. Γ. 184.

'Ασίῳ, ὃς μήτρως ἦν "Εκτορος ἱπποδάμοιο,
Αὐτοκασίγνητος 'Εκάβης, υἱὸς δὲ Δύμαντος,
Ὃς Φρυγίην ναίεσκε ῥοῆς ἔπι Σαγγαρίοιο.   IL. Π. 717.

.   .   .   .   .   Dindyma fundunt
Sangarium, vitrei qui puro gurgite Galli
Auctus, Amazonii defertur ad æquora ponti.

CLAUDIAN. IN EUTROP. II. v. 263.

Strabo says, " it takes its source in Upper Phrygia,
" near a place called Sangia, about 150 stadia from
" Pessinus. It then traverses a great part of Galatia
" and Phrygia and Bithynia, receiving in its course
" the waters of the Thymbres and Gallus, and other
" streams; and becoming navigable near its mouth,
" falls into the Euxine." (XII. p. 543. Plin. VI. 1.
Scyl. p. 34. Liv. XXXVIII. 18.) The modern name
is *Sakaria*.   The Sangarius in ancient times separated the Bithynians from the Mariandyni, a people
of uncertain origin, but who, differing neither in
language nor in customs materially from the Bithynians, might justly be considered as part of the
same great Thracian stock. (Strab. XII. p. 542.)
That they were barbarians is allowed by all; and
Theopompus, whose authority is referred to by
Strabo, reported, that when the Megarians founded
Heraclea in their territory, they easily subjected the
Mariandyni, and reduced them to a state of abject
slavery, similar to that of the Mnotæ in Crete, and
the Penestæ in Thessaly. (Ap. Strab. XII. p. 542.
Cf. Pausan. Eliac. I. 26. Posidon. ap. Athen. VI.
263.)   They formed part of the third division or
satrapy of the Persian empire, with the Bithynians

Marian-
dyni.

and Paphlagonians. (Herod. III. 90. Cf. VII. 72.) Some further particulars respecting this people will be found in Athenæus, (XIV. p. 620.) Steph. Byz., (v. Μαριανδυνία.) and Eustathius on Dionys. Perieg. (v. 788.)

Ἔνθεν δ' ἀντιπέρην ποταμοῦ στόμα Σαγγαρίοιο,
Καὶ Μαριανδυνῶν ἀνδρῶν ἐριθηλέα γαῖαν.

APOLL. ARG. II. 724.

Leaving the Sangarius, we shall reach, after a course of 180 stadia, a river named Hypius, men- Hypius tioned by Apollonius, Scylax, Arrian, and several ^fluvius. other writers.

Ἀλλά με νῦν Βέβρυκες ὑπερβασίῃ τ' Ἀμύκοιο
Τηλόθι ναιετάοντος ἐνόσφισαν Ἡρακλῆος,
Δὴν ἀποτεμνόμενοι γαίης ἅλις, ὄφρ' ἐβάλοντο
Οὖρα βαθυρρείοντος ὑφ' εἰαμεναῖς Ὑπίοιο.

APOLL. ARG. II. 794.

(Scyl. Peripl. p. 34. Arrian. Peripl. p. 13. Marcian. Peripl. p. 70.) In an extract made from the historian Memnon by Photius, (c. 44.) we are told, that this river once afforded shelter to a large portion of Mithridates' fleet during a violent storm. It is now called *Mitan.* The town of Prusias, situated inland, Prusias ad and on its banks, acquired from that circumstance ^Hypium. the characteristic denomination of ad Hypium, to distinguish it from another Bithynian city of the same name, situated near the sea, in the bay Cius. Both probably were equally founded by king Prusias ; but the maritime Prusias is much oftener men- ˑ tioned in history, and its situation is much more precisely ascertained, than the one of which we are now speaking. Pliny is singular in mentioning the latter, not with reference to a river, but a mountain called Hypius. That there was a chain of this name cannot indeed be doubted, since the scholiast to Apollonius affirms, that the river had its source in the Hypian mountains. (Arg. II. 797.) And if Pliny is correct in his topography, we must look for the ruins of the Hypian Prusias not far from the source of the river. The site is generally supposed to exist near the modern *Uskub.* This town is noticed by Ptolemy, and in the Latin Acts of the Nicene Council. (p. 54.) One of the subscribing prelates is Hesychius of Prusias, near the river Hypius[m]. A lake of some extent, formed by the waters of the Hypius, above *Uskub,* answers probably

Daphnusis palus. to the Daphnusis palus, which Steph. Byz. places near the Bithynian Olympus. (v. Δαφνοῦς.) The modern name is *Efnanly.* The Episcopal Notices record also a see named Daphnusia in Bithynia.

Dia. .Dia was a town and small harbour sixty stadia from the mouth of the Hypius. (Marcian. Peripl. p. 70.) It was known to Ptolemy (p. 117.) and Steph. Byz., who calls it Dia of Bithynia on the Pontus. (v. Δία.)[n]

Lilium emporium. Lilium was an emporium forty stadia further to the east, according to Arrian. (Peripl. p. 13.) Pliny

Lilæus fluvius. mentions the Lilæus among the rivers of Bithynia; (V. 43.) and the Table Itinerary calls it Bylæus.

Elæum emporium. Elæum was another haven, sixty stadia from Lilium. (Arrian. loc. cit.) According to Marcian,

Elæus fluvius. there was also a river Elæus, (Peripl. p. 70.) and it is thought to be the same which Ptolemy calls Elatas.

Cales fluvius et emporium. From thence to Cales, another emporium, Arrian and Marcian agree in reckoning 120 stadia.

---

[m] It is clear from the coins of this town that its real name was Prusias, since the epigraph is ΠΡΟΥCΙΕΩΝ ΠΡΟCΤΠΙΩ; whereas in those of Prusa it is ΠΡΟΥCΑΕΩΝ. Sestini, p. 70. Ptolemy and Pliny, therefore, are less accurate when they call it Prusa.

[n] Sestini ascribes to this town some very scarce coins, with the inscription ΔΙΑΣ.

But the latter notices, besides the haven, a river of
the same name, which is doubtless the Calex of
Thucydides. That historian speaks of an Athenian
squadron, commanded by Lamachus, having been
wrecked, whilst at anchor in this river, from the
effect of a violent land-storm and flood. The Athenians, having lost their ships, were forced to march
through Bithynia, as far as Chalcedon. (IV. 75.)
In Memnon the name is written Calles; (ap. Phot.
c. 23.) in Pliny it is distorted to that of Alces.
(V. 43.) Forty stadia from the Cales we find the
Lycus, a river mentioned by Xenophon and several Lycus flu-
other writers with reference to the city of Heraclea, vius.
whose territory it watered. The maritime surveys
reckon twenty stadia from the river to the city, and
Xenophon says distinctly that it flowed through the
plain of Heraclea. (Anab. VI. 2.) Pliny, less accurately, states that the town was on the river. (VI. 1.)

Καὶ Μαριανδυνῶν ἀνδρῶν ἐριθηλέα γαῖαν,
Ἧε Λύκοιο ῥέεθρα.   APOLL. ARG. II. 725.

Huc Lycus, huc Sagaris, Peniusque, Hypanisque, Calesque,
  Influit et crebro vortice tortus Halys.

OVID. ELEG. PONT. X. 47.

Xenophon says its breadth was two plethra. (Anab.
loc. cit.) The plain through which it flowed was
named Campus Lycæus. (Memnon. ap. Phot. c. 51.)

Heraclea, surnamed Pontica, from its situation on Heraclea
the Euxine, was founded, according to the general Pontica.
testimony of antiquity by the Megarians[o], who had
already formed extensive establishments on the Bos-

---

[o] In Strabo it is called a colony of the Milesians; but this
doubtless is an error of the
transcribers; and Casaubon has
altered the reading to Megarians, in which he has been
followed by subsequent editors,
XII. p. 542.

phorus, and who, on this occasion, were joined by
some Bœotians from Tanagra. (Pausan. Eliac. I.
26.) This Grecian colony appears to have early
attained to a considerable degree of wealth and prosperity, since its citizens are said to have subjected
the neighbouring people of Mariandyni, and their
success and enterprise in commerce is attested by
the foundation of Chersonnesus and Callatis in
Thrace. (Theopomp. ap. Strab. loc. cit.) The Heracleotæ adopted wise laws and institutions, and
maintained their independence for several years,
subject probably, however, to a tribute paid to the
Persian monarch.   On the arrival of the 10,000
Greeks before their city, the Heracleots, alarmed at
the appearance of so great a body of troops, and
doubtful of their intentions, collected all their property and provisions within the walls, and closed
their gates. But they afterwards supplied the army
with vessels, in order to get rid of them sooner.
(Anab. VI. 2.)   It was about this period that Cle-
archus, one of the principal citizens of the place,
and who had been educated at Athens, in the schools
of Plato and Isocrates, usurped the sovereign authority, and overthrew the republican constitution
of his native city.   He was succeeded by his son
Dionysius, who, though addicted to pleasure, was
of a mild and gentle disposition, and, unlike his
Sicilian namesake, seemed to reign solely for the
good of his subjects, and by their desire assumed
the title of king.   He had married Amastris, a niece
of Darius, the last king of Persia; and at his death
left her the sole guardian of his sons, and regent of
the principality of Heraclea.   Amastris afterwards
married Lysimachus, one of Alexander's successors;

but being divorced by him, she returned to Heraclea, where she was put to death by her unnatural sons. Lysimachus, however, not long after, seized these monsters, and by a signal punishment made them atone for their crime. These details and incidents relative to the history of Heraclea are preserved to us in the Fragments of Memnon, collected by Photius. (Cod. CCXIV. p. 703—758.) Memnon had composed a history of the tyrants who reigned at Heraclea during a space of eighty-four years; but we have only now the abridgment of Photius [P], which is confirmed by incidental notices contained in Aristotle, (Polit. V. 5.) Strabo, (XII. p. 542—544.) and Athenæus. (III. 85, B. XIII. 549, A.) The Heracleots, after remaining eighty-four years under kingly authority, recovered for a short season their independence; they then successively passed under the dominion of Mithridates, and afterwards under that of Rome. The town was defended for nearly two years by the troops of the former against the Roman general Cotta, who having finally taken the city by assault, tarnished the glory of his success by the cruel and avaricious use he made of victory; since he put to death many of the inhabitants, plundered the city of its most valuable images and statues, among others, one of Hercules, the supposed founder of the town, which was of the most costly description; and finally set fire to the principal buildings. (Memnon. ap. Phot. Justin. XVI. 3.) Before the battle of Actium, Heraclea was occupied for a short time by Adiatorix, tetrarch of Galatia,

[P] Memnon probably collected much of his information from Nymphis, whose history of Heraclea is cited by Athenæus and others.

who had espoused the cause of Marc Antony. But
he was finally conquered by Augustus, after the defeat of Antony, and put to death at Rome. (Strab.
XII. p. 543.) Other particulars relative to Heraclea may be collected from Athenæus. (VIII. 531, C.
351, C. D.) It was celebrated for its wine, almonds,
and nuts. (I. 32, B. II. 53, D. 54, B.) Heraclea
continued to flourish under the Roman emperors,
being dignified with the titles of Metropolis and
Augusta in the coins of Trajan and Severus [q]. We
find it also mentioned as a city of note by Arrian,
(Peripl. p. 14.) Pliny, (VI. 1.) Marcian, (Peripl.
p. 70.) and the Itineraries. And from the incidental
references made to it in the Byzantine annals we
find it retained some degree of prosperity as late as
the reign of Manuel Comnenus. (Nicet. Ann. p. 158,
B.) And even now some traces of the ancient name
are still apparent in that of *Erekli.* Near Heraclea

Aconæ.   was a spot called Aconæ, either from its abounding
with whetstones, or the aconite plant. (Steph. Byz.
v. Ἀκόναι. Athen. III. 85, B. Strab. XII. p. 543.
Eustath. ad Dionys. Perieg. v. 792.) Pliny calls it
a port. (VI. 1.) Beyond it the same writer places

Acherusia   the Acherusian cave, where Hercules is said to have
chersone-
sus.   dragged forth the hell-hound Cerberus to light.

Καὶ Μαριανδυνῶν ἱερὸν πέδον· ἔνθ’ ἐνέπουσιν
Οὐδαίου Κρονίδαο μέγαν κύνα, χαλκεόφωνον
Χερσὶν ἀνελκόμενον μεγαλόφρονος Ἡρακλῆος;
Δεινὸν ἀπὸ στομάτων βαλέειν σιαλώδεα χυλόν.

                        DIONYS. PERIEG. v. 788.

Xenophon, who terms it the Acherusian peninsula,
says, that Hercules descended there to the shades in

---

[q] Sestini, p. 68. There are   of Heraclea, and his queen A-
also medals of Dionysius, king   mastris.

quest of Cerberus ; and he affirms, that traces of his
descent, for upwards of two stadia in depth, were
shewn in his day. (Anab. VI. 2. Cf. Diod. Sic.
XIV. 261. Mel. I. 19.)

Arrian names beyond Heraclea, at a distance of
eighty stadia, Metroum ; and forty stadia further, Metroum.
cape Posidium. Marcian reduces the whole space Posidium
promonto-
to 100 stadia. (p. 70.) Mannert says this promon- rium.
tory is now called *Tchantsche-Aggisi* [r]. Next is a
spot named Tyndaridæ, forty-five stadia from cape Tyndaridæ.
Posidium ; (Arrian. p. 14.) and fifteen stadia further, Nymphæum. From thence to the river Oxi- Nymphæum.
nas, noticed by both geographers, are fifteen stadia. Oxinas
fluvius.
Mannert supposes this stream to be the Soonautes Soonautes
fluvius.
of Apollonius. (Arg. II. 748. et Schol. Cf. Plin.
VI. 1.[s]) But, besides this, we have two others named
by Pliny, the Pædopides and Callichorus ; the latter Pædopides
fluvius.
of which is also mentioned by Scylax. (Peripl. p. 34.) Callichorus
fluvius.
After the Oxinas appears the haven of Sandaraca, Sandaraca
portus.
at a distance of ninety stadia. Then Crenidæ, sixty Crenidæ.
stadia ; Marcian says only twenty. Psyllum was a Psyllum.
port thirty stadia from Crenidæ. (Arrian. p. 14.
Marcian. Peripl. p. 70. Cf. Steph. Byz. vv. Κρανίδες,
Ψύλλα. Ptol. p. 117.)

Tium, which next follows, was a Greek town of Tium.
some note, founded by the Milesians, in a district
belonging to the Paphlagonians, but annexed by
Prusias to Bithynia. (Memnon. c. 17—19. Arrian.
Peripl. p. 14.) In Strabo's time it was but a small
place, remarkable only as the birthplace of Philetærus, founder of the Attalic dynasty. (XII. p. 543.
Plin. VI. 1. Steph. Byz. v. Τίος.[t]) The town ap-

---

[r] Geogr. tom. VI. part i.   [s] Ibid. p. 615.
p. 614.   [t] There are medals of Tium

pears to have been advantageously situated on a peninsula, at the mouth of the river Billæus. The
site is called *Filios*, or *Filbas*, which is also the
modern name of the river. The Billæus is a considerable stream which rises on the confines of ancient Phrygia and Galatia, and was accounted by
some geographers the limit of Bithynia and Paphlagonia. (Marcian. Peripl. p. 71.) But it is more
usual to extend the confines of the former province
to the Parthenius, a few miles further to the east.
(Arrian. Peripl. p. 14.)

Παφλαγόνες τ' ἐπὶ τοῖς Πελοπήϊοι εἴκαθον αὔτως,
Ὅσσους Βιλλαίοιο μέλαν περιάγνυται ὕδωρ.

APOLL. ARG. II. 792.

The Mariandyni did not occupy the whole space
between the Sangarius and Parthenius; for Tium
and the adjacent coast were attributed by several

writers to the Caucones, a people apparently of great
antiquity, and once widely diffused, since they had
wandered as far as the western coast of the Peloponnese [u]. Some authors assigned to this people a
Scythian origin; others looked upon them as a Pelasgic tribe; while some again maintained that they
came originally from Macedonia; which three opinions, it may be observed by the way, might all be
perfectly consistent. Callisthenes, a commentator on
Homer, even affirmed, that the Caucones of Pontus
were mentioned by the poet in conjunction with
the Paphlagonians, and produced two lines to that
effect in the catalogue of ships, which however were
not found usually in the MSS. (Ap. Strab. XII.
p. 542.)

as late as the reign of Gallie- Sestini, p. 71.
nus. The ethnic is TIANΩN. [u] Anc. Greece, t. III. p. 77.

Καύκωνας αὖτ' ἦγε Πολυκλέος υἱὸς ἀμύμων
Οἳ περὶ Παρθένιον ποταμὸν κλυτὰ δώματ' ἔναιον.

Strabo reports, that in his time there was a remnant of this people near the Parthenius, named Cauconites : and Ptolemy also ranges them next to the Mariandyni.

The interior of Bithynia is much less known to us than the coast; and though the Itineraries give us the details of the principal roads which traversed the province, the names of places which occur there are for the most part obscure and unknown. The country indeed, being very woody and mountainous, could never have been thickly peopled; and it is for this reason that so few towns of note present themselves in the interior. The principal of these was Bithynium, which probably was a considerable place in ancient times, and perhaps gave its name to the whole province. Mannert is inclined to suppose that it was first founded by Zipœtes, king of Bithynia, who called it by his name; but this is only a conjecture, resting on no solid foundation [x]. Respecting the position of Bithynium, we learn from Strabo, that it was situated above Tium, in a district named Salone, celebrated for its excellent pastures, and a cheese much esteemed at Rome. (XII. p. 565. Plin. XI. 42. Steph. Byz. v. Σαλώνεια.) And we collect from the Itinerary of Antoninus, that there was a road leading from it to Ancyra. Pausanias further leads us to suppose it was on the banks of the Sangarius, or near it. (Arcad. 9.) It appears from Ptolemy, and other authorities, that Bithynium afterwards changed its name to Claudiopolis, which it retained till the downfall of the east-

(marginal notes:) Bithynium postea Claudiopolis.

(marginal note:) Salone.

[x] Geogr. tom. VI. part i. p. 618.

ern empire. This change probably occurred in the reign of Tiberius, for the name first presents itself in a medal struck under his auspices. Claudiopolis, as the birthplace of Antinous, the favourite of Hadrian, received several privileges from that emperor [y]. (Dio Cass. LXIX. 11. Pausan. loc. cit. Xiphil. p. 262.) Under the emperor Theodosius it was made the capital of the province Honorias. Many years after, we learn from Anna Comnena (p. 967.) and Leo Diaconus, (IV. 9.) who describe it as the most wealthy and flourishing city of Galatia, that it was almost totally destroyed by an earthquake, attended with vast loss of lives.

Hadrianopolis.

Hadrianopolis of Bithynia is not to be confounded with Hadriani in the same province, near mount .Olympus and the Rhyndacus. The former of these towns is known to us from Hierocles, (Synecd. p. 695.) who places it in the province Honorias, the Notitiæ Imperii, and its coins [z]. Most antiquarians agree in fixing the site of this ancient town at *Boli*, a Turkish city of some size, near the *Filbas*, or Billæus [a]. Ptolemy places in the interior of Bithynia, Flaviopolis, called also Cratia. Besides the

Cratia quæ et Flaviopolis.

fact of its having borne these two names, little is known respecting this town, except that the Itineraries place it between Claudiopolis and Ancyra, twenty-four miles from the former. It was an episcopal see, (Hierocl. Synecd. p. 695.) and coined its own money [b]. The Table Itinerary lays down a

---

[y] Some coins of that emperor, struck at Claudiopolis, are inscribed with the name of Antinous. Sestini, p. 67.

[z] These begin with Hadrian, and end with Philip. Sest. p. 68.

[a] Leake's Asia Minor, p. 309.

[b] Sestini adduces one autonomous coin, with the epitaph KPH, for Cratia ; and several of imperial die, from Antoninus Pius to Gallienus. p. 67.

road leading from Nicomedia, through the interior
of Bithynia, into Galatia, Paphlagonia, and Pontus.
The three first stations are Lateas, Demetrium,
Dusepro Solympum.   Of these, Lateas, which is
twenty-four miles from Nicomedia, is most probably the Latania of Ptolemy.   In Col. Leake's map Latania.
this site is made to correspond with *Kondek*, but
from the distance it should be on the left bank of
the Sangarius.   Demetrium, thirteen miles further, Demetri-
is unknown.   Dusepro Solympum is evidently a corruption of the Greek Δύσις πρὸς ῎Ολυμπον, implying a Dusis pros
station at the foot of mount Olympus, i. e. a continuation of the mountain properly so called.   Modern travellers have pointed out in this direction a
Turkish village, whose name, *Dustchè* [c], bears considerable analogy to the station of the Itinerary,
which is placed at a distance of thirty miles from a
considerable town, without a name, on the left bank
of the Sangarius.   The latter circumstance should
agree with Claudiopolis, but Col. Leake is inclined
to think Hadrianopolis is meant [d].

Another road led from Nicæa to Ancyra, passing
to the south of the former, and along the valley of
the Sangarius.   The Bithynian stations on this road
are, Tateabio, a corruption of Tattæum, or Tottæum, Tattæum,
(Itin. Anton. p. 141. Itiner. Hieros. p. 573.) forty tæum.
miles from Nicæa ; Dablæ, twenty-eight or twenty- Dablæ.
nine miles from Tottæum, which Ptolemy calls Dables ; Dadastana, which next follows, at a distance Dadastana.
of forty or forty-five miles from the preceding station, is noticed in history as the place where the
emperor Jovian died on his return from Syria to

---

[c] Otter, Voyage en Turquie, c. 48. Tavernier, tom. I. c. 2.
[d] Asia Minor, p. 309.

Constantinople. (Socrat. Hist. Eccl. III. in fin. Sozom. VI. 6. Ammian. Marcell. XXV. in fin. Philo-
storg. VIII. 8.) These writers state it to have been
on the borders of Galatia and Bithynia. Ptolemy
Juliopolis, prius Gordium. assigns it to the latter province, as well as Juliopolis, which next follows, at a distance of twenty-six
miles from Dadastana. This town could boast of
considerable antiquity, having been formerly under
the name of Gordium, the residence of the ancient
Phrygian kings Gordius and Midas. (Strab. XII.
p. 568.) It is also celebrated in history as the scene
of Alexander's exploit in cutting the famous Gor-
dian knot. Arrian, who relates the circumstances of
this adventure at length, says it took place in the
citadel of Gordium, which had been the palace of
.Gordius. The historian remarks also, that the town
was near the Sangarius, and in Hellespontine Phrygia. Alexander appears to have remained some time
at Gordium, being joined there by some fresh troops
and the deputations sent by different towns. (Arrian. I. 29, 7. II. 3. Quint. Curt. III. 1, 12. Justin.
XI. 7.) In the time of Strabo the original town
had sunk into the condition of a mere village, but
Cleon again raised it to the rank of a city. This
person had rendered himself famous by his robberies
and marauding warfare in the fastnesses of Olympus; and having conciliated first the favour of Marc
Antony, by thwarting the measures of Labienus his
enemy, who commanded in Asia Minor, and afterwards that of Augustus, by deserting his former
patron, obtained several concessions and grants from
the emperor. He was at the same time priest of
Jupiter Abrettenus in Mysia, of Comana in Pontus,
and possessed besides the Mysian districts of Morene

and Abrettene : but he did not long enjoy this accumulation of dignities, being seized, soon after his
arrival at Comana, with an acute disorder, which in
a short time carried him off. (Strab. XII. p. 574.)
Gordium is mentioned by Polybius as a small place
of Galatia, in his account of the operations of Cn.
Manlius against the Gauls of Asia Minor. (XXII.
20, 8.) Livy, who alludes to the same event, and
exhibits at length the account of Polybius, of which
the above citation is only a fragment, adds, that
Gordium was a small town in itself, but a place of
much traffick, from its central situation, being nearly
equidistant from the Hellespont, the Euxine, and
the sea of Cilicia. (XXXVIII. 18.) It continued
to flourish, under the name of Juliopolis, from the
reign of Augustus for several centuries, being mentioned by Pliny, (V. 43.) Ptolemy, and the Itineraries. Procopius leads us to suppose, however, that
in the time of Justinian it had suffered from the inundations of a neighbouring river, and was therefore repaired by that emperor. (Ædip. V. 4.) This
stream, as we learn from the coins of the town, was
called Scopas [e]. It is the Scopius of Pliny. (V. 43.) Scopas
fluvius.
The Jerusalem Itinerary mentions another river,
called Hieros, which it was necessary to cross in Hieros
going from Juliopolis to Ancyra, thirteen miles to fluvius.
the east of the former. Pliny also names it, and
remarks besides, that it separated Bithynia from
Galatia. (loc. cit.) When Procopius says Justinian
made a bridge over a river, Siberis in Galatia, about
ten miles to the east of Juliopolis, and close to a
spot called Sycei, there is very little doubt that he
is speaking of the same stream. (Ædip. V. 4.[f]) In

[e] Sestini, p. 68.   [f] Leake's Asia Minor, p. 79.

P 3

the Itinerary of Antoninus we have a road leading from Claudiopolis to Ancyra in Galatia, by Cratia, or Flaviopolis, Carum vicum, and Legna. Of Carus nothing is known, unless it should be the Caue of Xenophon, which is mentioned as a large village of Phrygia, on the road to Paphlagonia. (Hell. IV. 1, 10.) Legna is no doubt the Laginia of Stephanus Byz., which belonged to Bithynia. (v. Λαγίνια.) The same Itinerary furnishes another road from Nicæa to Ancyra in Galatia, by Juliopolis. The first station is called Oriens Medio, sixteen miles from Nicæa. The meaning of the name, as well as the position, are quite unknown. Beyond, the road passes, as in the Table, through Tottiæum and Dables. The next station to that is Cœnon Gallicanon, known also from Ammianus Marcellinus, who reports that the sister of the emperor Constantius was there seized with a sudden fever, and carried off. (XIV. 11.)

Besides the towns hitherto mentioned, and of which something is known, we have now to add a few with which we are acquainted in name only. These are, in Ptolemy, Callica, near Nicomedia; Patavium, to the south of the Ascanian lake[g]; Protomacra, between Nicæa and Dadastana, written Protunica in the Jerusalem Itinerary; (p. 573.) Timæa, more to the east; Dadaucana, between Prusa, on the Hypius and Bithynium; Clitæ, near the Parthenius; and a mountain named Orminius.

In Pliny we find mention made of the Agrippenses, among the towns of Bithynia, and Parthenopolis and Coryphanta; the two last no longer existed

Marginal notes: Callica. Patavium. Protomacra. Timæa. Dadaucana. Clitæ. Orminius mons. Agrippenses. Parthenopolis. Coryphanta.

g Wesseling thinks this name should be altered to Tattæum. (Itin. Anton. p. 141.)

in his day. (IV. 43.)   He names also the rivers
Syrius, Lapsias, Pharmacias, Crynis.   Of these, the Syrius fl.
Pharmacias, or Pharmicas, is perhaps the river cor- Pharma-
ruptly named Pharnutis in Suidas, and which, he Crynis fl.
says, flowed near Nicæa.

Stephanus Byz. names, in Bithynia, Alyatta, per- Alyatta.
haps the same which Livy calls Alyattus, (XXXVIII.
18.) though that should seem rather to belong to
Galatia.   Mazæum, a place mentioned by Arrian, Mazæum.
in his Bithyniaca. (v. ʼΑμαζόνειον.)   Amaxa, cited Amaxa.
from Eratosthenes. (v. ʺΑμαξα.)   Bysnæi, a tribe of Bysnæi
the Bebryces, the aboriginal inhabitants of Bithy- gens.
nia. (v. Βυσναῖοι.)   Epiphanea, (v. ʼΕπιφάνεια.)   Zipœ- Zipœtius.
tium, founded by king Zipœtes, near mount Lype- Lyperus
rus. (v. Ζιπώτιον.)   The latter fact is stated by the mons.
historian Memnon. (Ap. Phot.)   Corone. (v. Κορώνη.) Corone.
Cossus, a mountain mentioned by the poet Demos- Cossus.
thenes, in his Bithyniaca. (v. Κοσσός.)   Ladepsi and Ladepsi,
Tranipsi, Bithynian tribes, cited from the Hellenics Tranipsi,
of Theopompus. (v. Λαδειψοί.)   Hodiopolis and Mo- Mocata.
cata, mentioned by Domitius Callistratus, in his
work on Heraclea. (vv. ʻΟδιούπολις, Μόκατα.)   Nico- Nicome-
medium, an emporiumī, according to Arrian, whose dium.
Bithyniaca are referred to.   Sete, or Seti. (v. Σητία.) Sete.
Simana, a town situated between two rivers. (v. Σί- Simana.
μανα.)   Tarantus, where Jupiter was worshipped Tarantus.
under the name of Tarantæus.   It was also called
Darandus by some writers; from the Bithyniaca of
Demosthenes. (v. Τάρας.)   Tarsus and Tarseia, from Tarsus.
the same poet. (v. Ταρσός.)   Charax, a considerable Charax.
emporium in the bay of Nicomedia: this must be
said of a very late period in the Byzantine empire.
(v. Χάραξ.)

SECTION IV.

PAPHLAGONIA.

THE antiquity of the Paphlagonian nation is sufficiently established by the fact of its being enumerated by Homer among the Asiatic defenders of Troy. (Il. B. 851.) The Heneti also, whom the poet mentions as one of their tribes, have given rise to much discussion on the part of his commentators and scholiasts in connexion with the well-known people of the same name, who occupied the head of the Adriatic, and were said to have been transplanted thither by the Trojan Antenor. Whatever may be thought of this tradition, which was certainly ancient, and accredited by many writers, as appears from Strabo's account, (XII. p. 544. XIII. p. 608.) it is plain that no change had taken place in the great body of the nation, from the period alluded to by Homer to that of the above mentioned geographer; since the places mentioned by the poet as belonging to the Paphlagonians still subsisted in the latter's time, and are assigned by him to that people. Strabo himself hazards no remark respecting the origin of the Paphlagones ; but he incidentally introduces an observation, which proves that in his opinion there was a considerable similarity between their language and that of the Cappadocians. Now these last are allowed on all hands to have been Syrians, and therefore if the Paphlagonians spoke the same language, they must have had a common origin. It must be confessed, however, that this argument is not conclusive, for the Cappadocians may have once occupied the country of the Paphlagonians, and this may have produced that uniformity of tongue, which Strabo notices. (XII. p. 553.) And this, in fact, seems to be made out by a circumstance recorded by Herodotus ; namely, that the Cappadocians, whom he calls Syrians, once extended on the left bank of the Halys, as far as the Parthenius ; (II. 104.) that is, they occupied the whole length of coast usually assigned by ancient geographers to Paphlagonia. The probability therefore is, that the Paphlagonians coming from the west, drove the Leuco-Syri from the country, and finally compelled them to retire beyond the Halys. If I am right in reasoning thus, it will follow, that the Paphlagonians are to be looked upon as being of the same race with the Bithyni, Mysi, and Phryges, that is, they were a Thracian people. Theopompus, indeed, as we learn from Strabo, classed them with the Mariandyni and Bithyni. (XII. p. 541.) Another circumstance which seems further to confirm this opinion is the name of Cotys, which is given by Xenophon to one of their chiefs, (Hell. IV. 1.) and which is so frequently found to occur in the nomenclature of Thracian sovereigns. We may add also from Herodotus, that their arms and accoutrements were very similar to those of the Phrygians. Paphlagonia appears to

have been governed by native princes, from the
earliest period till its conquest by the Romans; and
even at that epoch we find there were chiefs who
boasted of their descent from Pylæmenes, the leader
of the Paphlagonian Heneti in the Trojan war, and
whose claims were admitted by Pompey. (Strab.
XII. p. 541.) When the Lydian monarchy had become so powerful as to bring into subjection the
whole Asiatic peninsula within the Halys, Paphlagonia formed the extreme portion of the empire of
Crœsus to the east, being separated from the Leuco-
Syri or Cappadocians, by the channel of that river.
(Herod. I. 72.) On the dissolution of the Lydian
empire by the defeat and capture of Crœsus, Paphlagonia submitted, with the rest of Asia Minor, to
.the Persian arms, and in the reign of Darius formed,
with the cities on the Hellespont, the Bithynians,
Phrygians, and Cappadocians, the third division or
satrapy of the empire. (III. 90.) The Paphlagonians furnished a numerous and well appointed body
of troops for the great armament of Xerxes. And
about a century later we find the whole force which
the country could supply estimated by Xenophon
at no less than 120,000 men, horse and foot. The
cavalry, indeed, was esteemed by the Persians to be
superior to any they possessed; and the whole territory presented great advantages for a defensive warfare. (Anab. V. 6.) Under these circumstances, the
Paphlagonian chiefs, knowing their strength, considered themselves almost independent of the Persian satraps, and were ready to join any power at
war with those governors which held out sufficient
inducement for them to take the field on its side.
Thus when Agesilaus had invaded the Persian do-

minions, and was carrying on a destructive war in
the plains of Caria and Phrygia, one of his first
objects seems to have been to engage the Paphlagonian chief, Cotys, to join the Lacedæmonian army.
For this purpose, he himself proceeded into Paphlagonia, and easily secured the alliance of its sovereign, through the intervention of Spithridates, a
Persian nobleman, who had attached himself to
Agesilaus out of enmity to Pharnabazus. A mar-
riage was afterwards brought about between Cotys
and the daughter of Spithridates, at the desire of
the Spartan king. Not long after, however, the
unjust treatment they met with at the hands of
Herippidas, a Lacedæmonian officer, induced the
Paphlagonian prince and Spithridates to quit the
camp with all their troops ; an event which, as Xenophon observes, was more felt by Agesilaus than
any other which occurred in the course of the war.
(Hell. IV. 1, 1—13.) Paphlagonia submitted to Alexander after the battle of the Granicus, (Arrian. II.
4, 1.) and on the death of that prince it fell to the
share of Eumenes, one of his most distinguished
generals. (Plut. Eum. Quint. Curt. X. 10.) But the
constant wars in which Eumenes was engaged against
Antigonus and others, prevented him from securing
the possessions allotted to him. During the agita-
tion which pervaded the whole of Asia and Greece,
from these contests between Alexander's successors,
the kings of Pontus, who possessed a small sovereignty on the shore of the Euxine, and between
Paphlagonia and Colchis, gradually emerged from
the obscurity in which they had hitherto remained
concealed, and began to prove formidable neighbours to the Greek colonies on the Euxine, and the

native chiefs of Paphlagonia. Mithridates, of Persian extraction, one of these sovereigns, extended his dominions to the river Halys, and even proceeded to attack Sinope, a flourishing Greek colony on the coast beyond that river. (Appian. Mithr. c. 9. Polyb. IV. 56.) Sinope resisted his attack with success, through the assistance of the Rhodians; but it was afterwards compelled to yield to his son Pharnaces, (Polyb. XXIV. 10, 1.) who even engaged in war with the kings of Pergamum and Cappadocia, and was only stopped in his career of conquest by the intervention of the Romans. (Polyb. III. 3, 6. XXV. 2. seq.) His grandson, the celebrated Mithridates, surnamed Eupator, not only made war against Nicomedes, king of Bithynia, with such success that he stripped him of his dominions, but even defeated the Romans in several engagements, and for a time was left in possession of nearly the whole peninsula of Asia, except the towns of Chalcedon and Cyzicus. Checked, however, by the exertions of Sylla in Greece, and of Lucullus in Asia Minor, Mithridates saw the fruits of his victories rapidly snatched from him, till he was left solely in the possession of his hereditary dominions. Of these, too, he was finally stripped by Pompey, who annexing the greatest part of Paphlagonia to the province of Bithynia, allotted the remainder to certain native chiefs, who boasted of being descended from Pylæmenes, king of the nation, in the Trojan war. (Strab. XII. p. 541.) The last of these Paphlagonian sovereigns was Dejotarus, son of Castor, and tetrarch of Galatia. (Strab. XII. 562. Cic. pro Dejot.) We find that in the time of the younger Pliny, the whole of Paphlagonia, as far as the Halys, acknowledged his authority as prætor of Bithynia. But the province was commonly known by the name of Pontica[a].

We shall consider Paphlagonia under its more ancient limits; which were, the Parthenius on the side of Bithynia, and the Halys on that of Pontus and Cappadocia. On the north it was bounded by the Euxine, and on the south it was separated from Galatia by a lofty chain of mountains connected on one side with the Bithynian Olympus, on the other with the Cappadocian and Pontic ridges. This range of mountains was covered with forests, which supplied abundance of excellent timber for ship-building, and various kinds of wood for making tables, and other ornamental works. They contained also salt mines, and a rich supply of the mineral called sandarach. Eudoxus reported that fossil fish were likewise to be found in some parts of the country. (Strab. XII. p. 561—563.) The plains afforded rich pastures for horses and cattle, and the mules of the Paphlagonian Heneti were celebrated as early as the days of Homer.

Ἐξ Ἐνετῶν, ὅθεν ἡμιόνων γένος ἀγροτεράων.

Il. B. 852.

The sheep of the county adjoining the Halys furnished wool much esteemed for the fineness of its quality. (Strab. XII. p. 546.) And the Euxine along the whole extent of coast supplied great quantities of excellent fish; especially the kind of tunny called pelamys. (Strab. XII. p. 545. Athen. VII. p. 307.)

The Parthenius, with which we shall commence Parthenius fl. our description of maritime Paphlagonia, is a considerable river according to Xenophon, and not

[a] Inscr. ap. Cellar. Geogr. Ant. t. II. p. 206.

fordable. (Anab. V. 6, 3.) It was supposed to derive its name from the gentleness of its stream, or because Diana loved to bathe in its waters.

Καὶ δὴ Παρθενίοιο ῥοὰς ἁλιμυρήεντος
Πρηΰτάτου ποταμοῦ παρεμέτρεον· ᾧ ἔνι κούρη
Λητωὶς ἄγρηθεν ὅτ' οὐρανὸν εἰσαναβαίνει,
Ὃν δέμας ἱμερτοῖσιν ἀναψύχει ὑδάτεσσιν.

APOLL. ARG. II. 938.

(Cf. Schol. ad loc. Steph. Byz. v. Παρθένιος.) It is mentioned for the first time by Homer, in his Catalogue of ships. (Il. B. 854.)

Ἀμφί τε Παρθένιον ποταμὸν κλυτὰ δώματ' ἔναιον.

Herodotus also mentions the Parthenius. (II. 104.) And Strabo affirms that it was so called from the beauty of the country which it traversed. (XII. p. 543.) Its source was in Mount Pœmen, a Paphlagonian mountain, situated in the interior of the province, (Steph. Byz. v. Ποιμήν.) and after a winding course it fell into the Euxine, not far from the town of Amastris. (Id. v. Παρθένιος.) The modern name is *Bartan*.

The first town to be noticed on the right bank of Sesamus postea Amastris. this river is Sesamus, a Greek colony from Miletus probably, and of great antiquity, since it is alluded to in the Iliad. (B. 853.)

Οἵ ῥα Κύτωρον ἔχον, καὶ Σήσαμον ἀμφενέμοντο.

Scylax has also mentioned it in his Periplus. (p. 34.) From Strabo we learn that it was afterwards colonized by Amastris, niece of Darius Codomanus, and wife of Dionysius, tyrant of Heraclea, who transmitted her name to the new settlement. Cromna and Cytorum, two neighbouring towns, contributed also to the foundation of Amastris, but Sesamus was the acropolis and seat of royalty. (XII. p. 544. Cf.

Plin. VI. 2. Steph. Byz. v. Σήσαμον. Schol. Apoll.
Arg. II. 945.) According to Arrian, Amastris was
ninety stadia from the Parthenius, (Peripl. p. 15.)
which measurement is confirmed by Marcian. (Peripl. p. 70.) We learn from Pliny the Younger that
in his time Amastris was a handsome town, adorned
with squares and public buildings; in one of his
letters to Trajan, he recommends that a common
sewer which was open, and was a great public nui-
sance and disfigurement to the town, should be
covered. This was allowed by the emperor. (X. 99.)
Ecclesiastical writers speak of Amastris as a flourishing town and episcopal see, in the seventh century. (Hierocl. p. 696. Nicet. Paphlag. Orat. in
S. Hyacinth. XVII.) The Table Itinerary calls it
Mastrum. Abulfeda, the Arabian geographer, *Sam-
sari.* The modern name is *Amasera*[b].

Sixty stadia further east we find Erythini, (Ar- Erythini.
rian. Peripl. p. 15.) which, according to the Scholiast
of Apollonius, were cliffs or hills.

> Νυκτί τ᾽ ἔπειτ᾽ ἄλληκτον ἐπιπροτέρωσε θέοντες,
> Σήσαμον, αἰπεινούς τε παρεξενέοντ᾽ Ἐρυθίνους.
>
> ARG. II. 942.
>
> Κρῶμνάν τ᾽, Αἰγίαλόν τε, καὶ ὑψηλοὺς Ἐρυθίνους.
>
> IL. B. 855.

Strabo reports that there were two rocks called
Erythini, in his time, from their colour. (XII.
p. 545.) Stephanus says there was a town so named.
(v. Ἐρυθίνοι.) Cromna, another place mentioned by Cromna.
Homer, was sixty stadia from thence. (Arrian. loc.
cit. Apoll. loc. cit. Plin. VI. 2. Strab. XII. p. 544.)

[b] There are coins extant, the epigraph ΑΜΑΣΤΡΙΑΝΩΝ.
both of queen Amastris and the Sestini, p. 64.
city she founded, the latter have

It belonged to Amastris. (Steph. Byz. v. Κρῶμνα.)

Cytorum. The site retains the name of *Cromena*[c]. Cytorum was ninety stadia further. It was a Greek town of great antiquity, since Homer alludes to it :

Οἵ ῥα Κύτωρον ἔχον, καὶ Σήσαμον ἀμφενέμοντο.

It is also mentioned in the Periplus of Scylax. (p. 34.) According to Ephorus, cited by Strabo, it took its name from Cytorus, son of Phrixus, and belonged to the Sinopians. This place derived further cele-

Cytorus mons. brity from mount Cytorus, which rose above it, and was covered with boxwood.

Et juvat undantem buxo spectare Cytorum.

VIRG. GEORG. II. 437.

Κρωβίαλον, Κρώμναντε, καὶ ὑλήεντα Κύτωρον.

APOLL. ARG. II. 944.

Mox etiam Cromnam atque jugo pallente Cytoron.

VAL. FLACC. V. 106.

(Cf. Plin. VI. 2.) The modern name is *Sagra*. In the Table Itinerary, as Col. Leake has well observed, the road which followed the coast to Sinope has by an error of the transcriber been moved out of its proper direction along the sea, into the interior. This is evident from the names of Cromea, Cytherum, and Carambus, for Cromna, Cytorum, and Carambis[d]. The vestiges of Cytorum have been observed by travellers near the present *Kidros*, which is evidently a corruption of the ancient name[e].

Ægialus. The ancient geographers applied the name of Ægia-

---

[c] Sestini notices some autonomous coins belonging to Cromna.

[d] Col. Leake has in my opinion most satisfactorily accounted for this mistake, by shewing that the similarity of name between Amastris and Amasia induced the transcriber to substitute the coast road from Amastris to Sinope, for that leading from Amasia to Sinope. Asia Minor, p. 307.

[e] Tavernier, Voyage, tom. III. c. 6.

lus to a portion of the Paphlagonian coast in the
immediate vicinity of Cytorus, and which extended
for a hundred stadia towards cape Carambis. There
seems also to have been a small town of this name
sixty stadia from Cytorus. (Arrian. Peripl. p. 15.)
Strabo observes, that some commentators of Homer
read Cobialus in that poet for Ægialus. (XII. p.545.)
And it is worth while to remark, that in Apollonius
we find the place called Crobialus, (Arg. II. 944.) Crobialus.
which is imitated by Valerius Flaccus. (Arg. V.102.)

> Altius in ventos recipit ratis; ac fugit omne
> Crobiali latus, et fatis tibi, Tiphy negatum
> Parthenium.

The Homeric appellation prevailed however in the
time of Arrian; and still later we find in the Table
Itinerary the corrupt word Egilan for Ægialus.
From thence to a spot called Climax, Marcian in Climax.
his Periplus reckons fifty stadia. (p. 71.) It is acknowledged also by Ptolemy. Timolæum, according Timolæum.
to Marcian, (Peripl. p. 71.) was sixty stadia from
Climax. Thymena, called also Teuthrania by the Thymena.
last geographer, was forty stadia further, or ninety
from Ægialus, as Arrian reports. (p. 15.) Cape Ca- Carambis.
rambis, which next follows, forms an important promontorium.
feature on this coast, since it advanced so far as to
divide as it were the Euxine into two distinct seas,
with the opposite cape of Criumetopon. (Strab. XII.
p. 545. Plin. VI. 2.)

> Ἐιθάδε αὖτε Κάραμβιν ἄμ' ἠελίοιο βολῆσι
> Γνάμψαντες, παρὰ πουλὺν ἔπειτ' ἤλαυνον ἐρετμοῖς
> Αἰγιαλόν.
>
> APOLL.-ARG. II. 945.
>
> Καραμβίδος ἔγγυθεν ἄκρης.
>
> DIONYS. PERIEG. 785.

This headland is not however the most northern point of Asia Minor, since its latitude falls somewhat short of that attained by the promontory of *Inje* to the north-west of Sinope. The ancient name is easily recognised in that of *Kerempe*, which it

Carambis urbs.

bears at present. Scylax speaks of a Greek town which bore the same appellation as the Cape; (Peripl. p. 34.) a fact which is confirmed by Pliny. (VI. 2.) Marcian places next to Carambis the little town of

Callistratia.

Callistratia, twenty stadia distant. (Peripl. p. 73.) This place, according to the anonymous author of the Periplus, was also called Marsilla; (p. 6.) then

Zephyrium.

follows the Zephyrium of Arrian, (Peripl. p. 15.) sixty stadia from Carambis, consequently forty from

Garium.

Callistratia. Garium was eighty stadia further, ac-

Abonitichos.

cording to Marcian's computation. Aboni-tichos, a small town and harbour noticed by Strabo (XII. p. 545.) and Arrian, (Peripl. p. 15.) was the birthplace of an impostor named Alexander, who assumed the character of Æsculapius. Lucian, who exposes the fraud in his Pseudopropheta, affirms that this man had the boldness to petition the emperor—it is not stated who he was—to allow his native town to take the name of Ionopolis for that of Aboni-tichos[f], a request which seems to have been granted, since Marcian affirms that the later name prevailed in his time. And it is evident that the modern *Ineboli* is only a corruption of Ionopolis. (Lucian. Pseudoproph. II. p. 262. Marcian. Peripl. p. 72. Hierocl. p. 695. Steph. Byz. v. Ἀβώνου Τεῖχος.)

Æginetes.

Arrian places Æginetes, a small town and har-

---

[f] There are coins of Antoninus and L. Verus, with the legend ΑΒΩΝΟΤΕΙΧΙΤΩΝ and ΙΩΝΟΠΟΛΙΤΩΝ. Sestini, p. 64.

bour, 160 stadia to the east of Abonitichos. (Peripl.
p. 15.) Marcian (p. 72.) reckons 160. Stephanus
mentions also a river of the same name. (v. Αἰγινή- Æginetes
της.) Cinolis, or Cimolis, next follows, at a distance fluvius.
of sixty stadia; this is a naval station, and is men- Cinolis.
tioned by Scylax, (p. 34.) Strabo, (XII. p. 544.) Arrian, (p. 15.) Marcian, (p. 72.) Mela, (I. 19.) and
Pliny. (VI. 2.) Abulfeda, the Arabian geographer,
calls it Kinuli, and the site yet retains the name of
Kinla. Anticinolis was another small haven, proba- Anticino-
bly on the opposite side of the bay, and sixty stadia lis.
distant. (Strab. loc. cit. Marc. loc. cit.) Stephane lay Stephane.
150 stadia more to the east. (Arrian. p. 15. Marc.
p. 72. Scyl. p. 34. Steph. Byz. v. Στεφανίς. Plin. VI. 2.)
The site, according to Tournefort, preserves the name
of *Stephanio,* or *Estifan.* Scylax seems to place between Stephane and Cinolis a Greek town named
Colussa, which no other writer has noticed. (p. 34.) Colussa.
Potami, a station probably situated at the mouth of Potami.
some small river, follows, after an interval of 150
stadia from Stephane. (Arrian. p. 15. Marc. p. 72.)
Cape Inje, the most northern point on this coast,
appears under two different names in the ancient
maritime surveys, which constitute our principal
authorities. Arrian calls it Lepte, (p. 15.) but Mar- Syrias sive
cian and the anonymous Periplus, Syrias. (Marcian. Lepte pro-
p. 72. Anonym. Peripl. p. 7.) In both cases the montori-
distance of 120 stadia from Potami is specified. um.
From this cape the shore bends gradually to the
south-east in the form of a crescent, at the extremity
of which stands *Sinub,* the representative of the
ancient Sinope. But before we speak of that celebrated city, we have to point out the situation of
Armene, a small town and port belonging to the Armene.

Sinopians. It was a place of so little traffick or note, that it gave rise to the proverb,

῞Ος ἔργον οὐκ εἶχε 'Αρμένην ἐτείχισεν.

(Strab. XII. p. 545.) Scylax says it was a Grecian colony, (p. 33,) and places after it, towards the west, another town named Tetracis, which is unknown to all other geographers. Xenophon states that the ten thousand, after obtaining vessels to convey them home, were stationary for some days in the port of Armene. (Anab. VI. 1, 9. Cf. Arrian. p. 15. Marcian. p. 72. Steph. Byz. v. 'Αρμένη. P. Mel. I. 19. Plin. VI. 2.) A small river which flowed into the sea close to this place is called Ochosbanes by Marcian; (p. 72.) Ochthomanes, by the anonymous writer of the Periplus; (p. 7.) and Ocheraenus, by Scylax. (p. 33.) The modern name is not known to me, but Armene corresponds with the site of *Aklimen.*

Sinope.

Sinope was a town of great antiquity, since its origin was referred by some writers to the Argonauts, by others to the Amazons. Mythologists derive the name from the nymph Sinope, daughter of the Asopus.

Αὐτίκα δ' Ασσυρίης ἐπέβαν χθονός· ἔνθα Σινώπην
Θυγατέρ' 'Ασωποῖο καθίσσατο, καί οἱ ὄπασσε
Παρθενίην Ζεὺς αὐτὸς ὑποσχεσίῃσι δολωθείς.

APOLL. ARG. II. 947.

. . . . alta Carambis
Raditur, et magnae pelago tremit umbra Sinopes.
Assyrios complexa sinus stat opima Sinope;
Nympha prius, blandosque Jovis quae luserat ignes,
Coelicolis immota procis.

VAL. FLACC. V. 108.

The Sinopians themselves assigned the foundation

of their city to Autolycus, a companion of Hercules, and one of the Argonauts. They erected statues to him, and even paid him divine honours. (Strab. XII. p. 546.) But the original town was of small extent and power, till the accession it received from a colony of Milesians. This people, as we learn from Scymnus of Chios, were in their turn dispossessed by the Cimmerians, to whom Herodotus seems to assign the foundation of the city. But when they had been driven away by the Scythians, and overran Asia, the Milesians returned, and regained possession of their colony. (Scymn. Ch. Frag. v. 204—215. Anonym. Peripl. Eux. p. 8.) Towards the commencement of the Peloponnesian war, the Sinopians, who had fallen under the government of a tyrant named Timesileon, received assistance from the Athenian people; and after the tyrant had been expelled, Pericles, who was then at the head of affairs, proposed that 600 colonists should be sent to Sinope, which was agreed to, and carried into execution. (Plut. Pericl. c. 20.) At the time of the retreat of the ten thousand, we collect from Xenophon that Sinope was a rich and flourishing city, holding many of the neighbouring towns in its dependence, and possessing considerable influence over the barbarian tribes of Paphlagonia and Cappadocia. Among its colonies were Cerasus, Cotyora, and Trapezus, all situated on the Euxine, and flourishing settlements. It was principally through the assistance of the Sinopians, that the Greeks were enabled to procure ships to convey them to Heraclea. (Anab. V. 5. Diod. Sic. XIV. c. 32.) Strabo also reports, that the navy of Sinope held a distinguished rank amongst the maritime powers of Greece. It was

mistress of the Euxine as far as the Cyanean rocks, and divided with Byzantium the lucrative fishery of the pelamys, a kind of tunny. It appears, from a curious passage in Tacitus, that in the time of Ptolemy Soter, who sent an embassy to Sinope, that city was governed by a prince named Scydrothemis, who was doubtless a Paphlagonian. (Hist. IV. 82—84. Cf. Plut. II. 361.) Its great wealth, and the peculiar advantages of its situation, rendered it however in later times a most desirable acquisition to the neighbouring sovereigns of Pontus, a state almost unknown in history before the time of Alexander. It was assailed for the first time by Mithridates IV. great grandfather of the celebrated king of that name, in the year 220, B. C.[h] Polybius, who is our chief authority for this event, thus describes the situation of Sinope : (IV. 56.) " Sinope is situ-
" ated in that part of the Pontus which lies to the
" right in sailing along towards the Phasis. It is
" built on a certain peninsula, which advances out
" into the sea. The isthmus, which connects this
" peninsula with the continent of Asia, is not more
" than two stadia in breadth, and is entirely barred
" by the city which comes up close to it ; but the
" remainder of the Chersonnese stretches out to-
" wards the sea. It is quite flat, and of easy access
" from the town, but on the side of the sea it is
" precipitous all round, and dangerous for vessels,
" and offers very few spots for effecting a landing.
" The Sinopians, therefore, fearing lest Mithridates
" should erect works on the side of Asia, and at the
" same time by making a descent from the sea, and
" advancing to the level part of the peninsula, and

[h] Clinton, Fast. Hell. Append. P. II. p. 425.

" those points which overhang the town, should
" blockade them, set about fortifying the peninsula
" with trenches and pallisades on every point which
" was accessible from the sea: they also placed
" engines of war and soldiers in the most favourable
" stations, which they were easily enabled to defend,
" as the ground was naturally strong, and of no
" great extent." Strabo, describing the Sinopian
peninsula, says, " It is girt all round with rocks
" hollowed out in the form of basons, thence called
" Chœnicides. At high water these troughs are
" filled, and render the shore inaccessible, especially
" as the rocks are every where so pointed, that it is
" impossible to walk on them with bare feet." The
Sinopians, though severely pressed by the king of
Pontus, defended themselves with great vigour and
courage, and finally, through the timely support
and assistance they derived from the Rhodians, compelled Mithridates to raise the siege. They were
not so successful in resisting the attack of Pharnaces, his son and successor. This prince having
assaulted the town unexpectedly, found the citizens
unprepared to resist, and easily overpowered them.
(183. B. C.[i]) Sinope from that time became the chief
town and residence of the kings of Pontus. (Strab.
XII. p. 545—546. Polyb. XXIV. 10, 2.) Pharnaces
was succeeded by Mithridates, surnamed Euergetes,
who was an ally of the Romans, and obtained Phrygia in return for his services. (Justin. XXXVIII. 5.)
This prince having been assassinated at Sinope,
(120 B. C. Strab. X. p. 477.) left the crown to his
son, the famous Mithridates Eupator, who was born
and brought up in the city which we are now no-

[i] Clinton, Fast. Hell. Append. P. II. p. 425.

ticing. When at the height of his power, Mithridates, owing to this circumstance, employed himself in embellishing the place of his birth, and adding the contrivances of art to its local advantages. He formed a harbour on each side of the isthmus, erected naval arsenals, and constructed admirable reservoirs for the tunny fishery.

When the king of Pontus, after the disasters of Cyzicus, found himself forced to retreat before the victorious Lucullus, he left a strong force in Sinope, under the command of Bacchides, with orders to defend the town to the last extremity. This officer, suspecting the fidelity of the citizens, treated them with great cruelty and oppression, which precluded him from deriving any aid from their exertions; so that the Roman general easily overpowered the garrison, which consisted chiefly of Cilician troops, and put them to the sword[k]. (Plut. Lucull. c. 18. Appian. Bell. Mithr. c. 83.) Lucullus treated the Sinopians with kindness, and left them in possession of all the works of art which embellished their city, with the exception of the sphere of Billarus and the statue of Autolycus. (Strab. XII. p. 546. Cic. pro Leg. Manil. 8. Plut. loc. cit. Appian. loc. cit.) Pharnaces, the son of Mithridates, for a short time regained possession of Sinope; but after the rout of that prince at Zela, it opened its gates to Cæsar, who took the city under his protection, and sent a Roman colony there[1]. Strabo informs us, that in his time Sinope

[k] Sestini is inclined to ascribe to these Cilicians a coin of Sinope, with Phœnician characters, which he reads SINUP-KERT. Lettere Numismat. t. VII. p. 37. Class. Gen. p. 63. I should be inclined to refer it rather to a much earlier period, when the Leuco-Syri occupied Paphlagonia as far as the Parthenius.

[1] This appears from a coin of

was in a flourishing state. He describes it as surrounded by strong walls, and adorned within with
fine porticoes, squares, gymnasia, and other edifices.
It possessed also extensive suburbs, and numerous
villas in the immediate vicinity. (XII. p. 546. Cf.
Plin. VI. 2. Steph. Byz. v. Σινώπη.) It appears from
Pliny's Letters, that the Sinopians suffered some
inconvenience from the want of a good supply of
water. This Pliny appears to have endeavoured to
obviate by obtaining a grant from Trajan to erect
an aqueduct, for the purpose of conveying water
from a distance of sixteen miles. (X. 91.) Sinope
was yet a flourishing town in the time of Arrian
and that of Marcian. In the middle ages it formed
part of the small empire of Trebizond, and fell into
the hands of the Turks in the reign of Mahomet II,
about 1470. Sinope is further remarkable for having given birth to the Cynic Diogenes; Baton, an
historian, whose works are cited by Athenæus and
Plutarch; and Diphilus, a much esteemed writer of
the middle comedy. (Strab. XII. p. 546.) Near Si-
nope was a small island, named Scopelus, which Scopelus
insula.
larger vessels were obliged to circumnavigate before
they could enter the harbour; but small craft could
pass between it and the land, by which means a
circuit of forty stadia was avoided. (Marcian. Peripl. p. 72, 73.) Sinope, according to Strabo, was
3500 stadia from the Hieron of Jupiter Urius; 2000
from Heraclea; and 700 from cape Carambis. (XII.
p. 546.) As these distances agree with those of
Marcian, it is probable that they are both derived

Sinope, with the letters C. I. C.
F. S. for Colonia Julia Cæsarea Felix Sinope. The imperial
series extends from Augustus
to Gallienus. Sestini, p. 63.

from Artemidorus, whom Marcian professes to follow. Eighty stadia beyond Sinope, the geographers
Evarchus fl. notice the river Evarchus, (Marcian. Peripl. p. 73.
Anonym. Peripl. p. 9.) which was once the boundary of Paphlagonia and Cappadocia. The anonymous geographer says it was commonly called Evechus in his time. (Cf. Menipp. ap. Steph. Byz. v. Καππαδο-κία. Plin. VI. 2.) Near this river was the station called Cyptasia by Ptolemy, Cloptasa by the Table,
Carusa. which reckons seven miles from Sinope. Carusa was seventy stadia further, or 150 from Sinope, according to Arrian, who observes its port was very insecure. (p. 15. Marcian. p. 73.) Scylax also notices Carusa, and dignifies it with the title of Greek town. It answers to the station now called *Kerze*, ·unless this should be thought to represent the Gurzubanthon of the anonymous geographer, sixty sta-
Gazorum. dia from Carusa. Gazorum of the same geogra-
Zagora. pher is probably the Zagora of Arrian and Marcian, though they do not agree precisely in the distance; Arrian assigning 150 stadia from Carusa, Marcian 120, and the Anonymous Periplus 150 from Gurzubanthon. The latter writer states, that Gazorum was afterwards called Calippi. (p. 9.) In Ptolemy it is evident we should read Gazorum, instead of Galorum. I conceive the Orgibate of the Table to be the Gurzubanthon of the anonymous geographer.
Zalecus fluvius. From Zagora to the little river Zalecus, Marcian reckons 120 stadia; the anonymous geographer only ninety from Gazorum; which makes it still more doubtful whether we ought to identify those two places. Ptolemy writes the name of the river here spoken of, Zaliscus. It is, I imagine, the Helega of the Table. From thence to the great river

Halys, which forms the boundary of Paphlagonia,
Marcian reckons 150 stadia, the Anonymous Periplus only 110. The course of the Halys will be
described when we have to speak of Pontus and
Cappadocia; we shall therefore now leave the coast,
and proceed to describe the remaining part of Paphlagonia.

The interior of Paphlagonia was divided, as appears from Strabo, into a number of small districts,
some of which he names, but without defining accurately their positions or their extent. On the side
of Bithynia he places the region called Timonitis, Timonitis
and in succession the territory of Gezatorix and the regio.
districts called Marmolitis, Sanisene, and Potamia.
But the principal feature in the internal geography
of the province is an elevated chain, now called
Ulgaz, and anciently Olgasys, which extends from Olgasys
the Parthenius to the Halys. Strabo describes it as mons.
a lofty chain, and of difficult access, and adds, that
the surrounding country was filled with temples
erected by the Paphlagonians. Modern travellers
speak of this mountain as being in some parts covered with snow nearly all the year. At the foot
of Olgasys, and on the side of Sinope, was an ancient fortress, named Cimiata, which had been the Cimiata.
strong hold of Mithridates Ctistes, the first sovereign of his line who effected the conquest of Pontus, as his surname indicates. Cimiata, according
to Strabo, was the capital of a small district called
from thence Cimiatene. (XII. p. 562.) More to Cimiatene
the north, and nearer the sea, the country was less regio.
mountainous, and consequently more productive,
and better peopled. It was principally watered by
the river Amnias, celebrated for a great battle Amnias
fluvius.

fought on its banks between Nicomedes, king of
Bithynia, and Mithridates Eupator, in which the
former was defeated with great loss. This decisive
victory was followed by the conquest of Bithynia,
and nearly the whole of Asia Minor. (Strab. XII.
p. 562. Appian. Mithr. c. 18.) The Amnias is the
river of *Castamouni*, which rises in the northern
chain of hills, running parallel with the coast, and
at no great distance from it. After a course of
nearly 120 miles, from N. W. to S. E., it falls into
the Halys, about thirty miles south of Sinope.
The country which this river traverses was an-
Blæne
regio.
ciently known by the names of Blæne and Doma-
Domanitis nitis. Strabo (XII. p. 562.) places in this part of
regio.
Paphlagonia, but apparently nearer the Halys, a
Pompeio- town which, from its name of Pompeiopolis, would
polis.
appear to have been founded by Pompey the Great.
The Table Itinerary reckons twenty-seven miles from
Sinope to Pompeiopolis, which would fix the site of
the latter in the valley of the Amnias, not far from
the modern *Tash-Kupri*[1]. Pompeiopolis is often
referred to, as an episcopal see of Paphlagonia, by
the ecclesiastical writers. (Socrat. II. 39—41. Sozom. 22. Hierocl. Synecd. p. 695. Justinian. Novell.
XXIX. 1. Steph. Byz. v. Πομπηϊούπολις [m].) In the
vicinity of this town Strabo places the great mine
Sandara- of sandarach, already noticed when speaking of the
curgium.
productions of this province. The mineral was extracted from a mountain, which was pierced in several directions to a considerable depth. The works
were carried on at the public expense; and such

[1] Capt. Kinneir observed some
ruins at *Tash-Kupri*. p. 286.
[m] There are some imperial
medals belonging to this town,
but not earlier than the reign
of M. Aurelius. Sestini, p. 64.

was the unwholesome nature of the service, that it was found necessary to employ slaves, and even malefactors. Owing to the little profit derived from the mine, the works were frequently suspended. When Strabo wrote, about 200 slaves were in employment. (XII. p. 562.) The particular district in which this mine was situated is called Pimolisene Pimolisene. by Strabo; a name derived from Pimolisa, a royal Pimolisa. fortress near the Halys, but in ruins at the time of which the geographer was speaking.

To the south of mount Olgasys, and at a distance of thirty-five miles from Pompeiopolis, according to the Table, stood Gangra, a city of some note, and Gangra. the royal residence of Morezus, or Morzus, a Paphlagonian prince mentioned by Livy. (XXXVIII. 26.) It was afterwards held by Dejotarus, the last sovereign of the country. (Strab. XII. p. 563. Cf. Plin. VI. 2. Ptol. p. 117.) Alexander Polyhistor, in his account of Paphlagonia, ascribed the foundation of this town to a goatherd, who had found one of his goats straying there: the word Gangra in the Paphlagonian language being significative of that animal. (Ap. Steph. Byz. v. Γάγγρα.) Frequent mention of this town occurs in the ecclesiastical writers, as the metropolitan see of Paphlagonia. A provincial synod assembled there in the fifth century. (Socrat. II. 43. Sozom. III. 14. Hierocl. Synecd.) This town was much exposed to the attacks of the Persians under the Byzantine emperors, and the historians of that period mention its having been often taken and retaken. (Nicet. Chon. Ann. p. 14, 15. Cinnam. p. 8. Cedren. p. 347, 361.) Some traces of the ancient name are yet perceptible in that of *Kiengareh*, or *Kangreh*, a Turkish town of some size, which occupies the same site [n]. Before we quit Gangra, it may be worth while to mention, from Athenæus, that its orchards produced apples, which were much esteemed by the Romans. (III. 82.)

Germani-
copolis.   Near Gangra was the town of Germanicopolis, as we collect from the Novellæ of Justinian. (XXIX. 1.°) The period of its foundation is uncertain, but it was probably built in honour of Germanicus. Its coins, however, are not of a higher date than the reign of M. Aurelius [p]. The mention of the Halys on these monuments proves that it was situated near that river. Germanicopolis is named by Ptolemy in his list of Paphlagonian towns. The same

Audrapa,
sive Neo-
claudiopo-
lis.   geographer mentions also Neoclaudiopolis, which, before it received that name, was called Andrapa. The latter appellation appears, however, to have been still used as the title of the see attached to the town. (Hierocl. p. 705. Justinian. Novell. XXIII.) The coins of Neoclaudiopolis bear the dates and effigies of M. Aurelius, Sept. Severus, and Caracalla [q]. Ptolemy seems to place this town to the south-east of mount Olgasys. In the same direction we have

Conica.   Conica, which is perhaps the Ciniata of Strabo.

Sacorsa.
Moson.
Zagira.
Plegra.
Secora.
Elvia.
Tobata.
Xoana.
Sora.   More to the west, Sacorsa and Moson. Further north Ptolemy has Zagira, Plegra, and Secora : in the central region, Elvia, Tobata, and Xoana : all obscure places, which occur nowhere else. Sora, or Zora, is mentioned by Hierocles (Synecd. p. 695.) and Constantine Porphyrogenetes (Them. I. 7.) as

Dadybra.   an episcopal town of Paphlagonia ; also Dadybra,

---

[n] Tavernier, Voyages, I. 2. Pococke, Travels, tom. III. p. 136.

[o] See Wesseling's note on Hierocles, p. 695.

[p] Sestini, p. 64.   [q] Ibid.

or Dadibra, which is besides known to the Byzantine historians. It was taken by the Turks in 1196.
(Nicet. Ann. p. 305, C.) Mastya, which Pliny styles Mastya.
a Milesian colony, is thought to correspond with
the Mastrum of the Table Itinerary, if that name is
not there intended to designate Amastris [r].

Mantinium, mentioned by Socrates, the ecclesias- Mantini-
tical historian, as a town of Paphlagonia, is un- um.
known. (II. 38.)

We have also some obscure stations in the Table
Itinerary, which stand much in need of illustration
by a comparison with the accounts of modern travellers. In the road which stands in the Table
along the coast from Tium to Sinope, but which, as
Col. Leake observes, is certainly misplaced, we have
the following stations. From Tium to Mastrum,
XII. M. P. ; to Tycæ, XX ; to Cereæ, XV ; to Mi-
letum, XV ; to Sinope, XVIII. The only stations
on this road which are well known are those of
Tium and Sinope ; the rest are all open to conjecture. It is certain that the distances are much too
short ; for the real distance from Tium to Sinope,
in a straight line, cannot be less than 180 miles,
whereas the Itinerary only furnishes for the sum
total of its stages eighty miles. I may observe
here, that *Tosia,* a town situated on the *Derek,* a
river which falls into the Halys, represents the Do- Docea.
cea of the Byzantine historians. (Nic. Ann. p. 336.
Curopal. p. 843.)

Castamouni, another Turkish town of some population and extent, is evidently the Castamon so Castamon.
often mentioned by the same writers. (Nicet. Ann.

[r] Sestini adduces a coin with   he ascribes doubtingly to this
the epigraph ΜΑΣΤΙΕΩΝ, which   town. p. 64.

p. 14, 15. Niceph. Bryenn. p. 63, 64.) Near it was an extensive plain, called Gunaria. Capt. Kinneir says, " Castamouni stands in a hollow, in the cen- " tre of which rises a lofty and perpendicular rock, " crowned with a ruined fortress, formerly possessed " by the noble house of Comneni." The same tra- veller estimates its population at more than 12,000 souls[s].

Another road is indicated in the Table, as leading from a large town without a name, but which there is good reason to suppose is Hadrianopolis, to Gangra: the intermediate stations are, Manoris, XX; Poto- mia Cepora, XXXII; Antoniopolis, XV; Anady- nata, XXVIII; Gangaris, XXXVI. Manoris is quite unknown. Potomia Cepora is a corruption *Seporas fluvius.* probably for Potamos Seporas, a river which is not mentioned by any other writer, but which seems to be the *Beinder sou,* a branch of the Parthenius[t]. *Antonio- polis.* Antoniopolis, which Col. Leake imagines to be An- tinoopolis [u], may be placed at *Tchirkis.* Perhaps we should read Antoninopolis; in which case it would indicate a town founded by the emperor An- toninus. On the Bithynian frontier we must place, *Scorobas mons.* with Appian, a mountain named Scorobas, which is perhaps the *Beinder dagh* of modern travellers[x]. *Protopa- chium.* Near it was a fortress called Protopachium, where the generals of Mithridates defeated the Romans commanded by Manius (Appian. Mithr. c. 19.)

Daridna. Stephanus of Byzantium enables us to add to our list of Paphlagonian towns, Daridna, from Alexan-

---

[s] Travels in the East, p. 281.
[t] Kinnier's Travels, p. 278. At present there seems to be no road leading from *Boli* to *Giengareh* directly, but through *Angorah.*
[u] Map of Asia Minor.
[x] Kinneir's Travels, p. 278.

der Polyhistor. (v. Δάριδνα.) Candara, which was Candara.
about three schœni, or twelve miles, from Gangra,
and possessed a temple sacred to Juno Candarena.
(v. Κάνδαρα.) Thariba was another small place in Thariba.
the same vicinity, (Steph. Byz. ead. v.) perhaps the
same as Dadibra. Coryleum, a place so called from Coryleum.
Corylas, a king of Paphlagonia, mentioned by Xenophon. (Anab. VI. 1, 1. Steph. Byz. v. Κορύλειον.)
Cressa, founded by Meriones, after the siege of Cressa.
Troy; but afterwards occupied by Zeilas, son of
Nicomedes. (Steph. Byz. v. Κρῆσσα.) It was probably on the sea coast, and perhaps should be identified with Carussa. Papitium. (v. Παπίτιον.) Timo- Papitium.
nium, a fortress which gave its name apparently to
the district called Timonitis by Strabo. (v. Τιμώνιον.)
Tiriza, the inhabitants of which are named Tirizi- Tiriza.
bani by Ctesias. (v. Τίριζα.)

SECTION V.

PONTUS.

———

Dynasty of Pontus from its foundation as a kingdom till its conquest by the Roman arms—Boundaries and geographical features—Course of the river Halys—Description of the coast—Interior.

THE name of Pontus implies a political rather than a geographical division of territory: having been applied in the first instance to the coast of the Euxine situated between the Colchian country and the Halys, it was in process of time extended to the mountainous districts which lie towards Cappadocia and Armenia; and it even, at one time, included Paphlagonia and part of Bithynia. The denomination itself was unknown to Herodotus, who always designates this part of Asia by referring to the particular tribes who inhabited it, and who then enjoyed a separate political existence, though tributary to the Persian empire. Xenophon also appears to have been ignorant of it, since he adheres always to the same local distinctions of nations and tribes used by Herodotus; such as the Chalybes, Tibareni, Mosynœci, &c. It was not indeed till after the death of Alexander, that the Pontic dynasty makes any figure in history; and I think it probable, that the first sovereign of his line who assumed the title of king of Pontus was Mithridates, surnamed Ctistes, or the founder. This prince, by the common consent of ancient authorities, was descended from one of the seven Persian nobles who conspired against the false Smerdis and his brother; and his ancestors, during three generations, had held a small principality in Cappadocia and Paphlagonia[a]. Having assisted Eumenes, the general of Alexander, in his wars against Antigonus, Mithridates became naturally exposed to the vengeance of the latter, and after the death of Eumenes was forced to abandon his principality, and seek refuge in the fastnesses of Paphlagonia. It was here, as we learn from Strabo, that he maintained himself in the fortress of Cimiata, amongst the passes of mount Olgassys; and not only resisted the attacks of his enemy, but when his attention had been withdrawn to more formidable adversaries, was enabled gradually to extend the frontiers of his little territory, till it had acquired a form and power worthy of the title of kingdom. (Appian. Mithr. c. 9. Plut. Demetr. c. 4. Strab. XII. p. 562.) According to Diodorus, he reigned thirty-six years, and was slain by order of Antigonus at Cius, who suspected him of forming designs against his power, in conjunction with Cassander. (Diod. Sic. XX. 111.) Lucian reports, that he lived to the advanced age of eighty-four years, on the authority of Hieronymus of Cardia, and other historians. (Macrob. III. c. xiii. p. 217.) His death happened in 302. B. C.[b] He was succeeded

[a] These, according to Mr. Clinton, were, Ariobarzanes I, Mithridates I, Ariobarzanes II, Mithridates II, or Ctistes : for the proofs of this lineal arrangement, the reader will consult with advantage his very learned and valuable work, Fast. Hellen. part II. Append. Kings of Pontus, p. 421.

[b] Clinton, Fasti Hellen. part II. Append. p. 422.

by Mithridates his son, of whom it is only known
that he reigned thirty-six years, leaving the crown
to his successor Ariobarzanes. (Diod. Sic. XX. 111.)
This prince, as we learn from Memnon, conquered
Amastris, (ap. Phot. p. 720.) and drove from the
country, in conjunction with the Gallo-Græci, or
Galatæ, lately arrived in Asia Minor, an Egyptian
force sent by Ptolemy. (Apollod. ap. Steph. Byz.
v. Ἄγκυρα.) He was succeeded by his son Mithridates IV. who was a minor when his father died. This
sovereign makes a more conspicuous figure in history. He made war upon the Sinopians; (Polyb.
IV. 56.) married two of his daughters to Antiochus
Theus, king of Syria, and Achæus, who was then
master of a considerable part of Asia Minor; (Polyb. V. 43. VIII. 22.) and made several munificent
donations to the Rhodians, whose city had been
overwhelmed by the shock of an earthquake. (Polyb. V. 89, 90.) Mithridates IV. reigned nearly fifty
years, and left the kingdom to his son Pharnaces,
who conquered Sinope and Tium, (Strab. XII. p.
545. Diod. Sic. Frag.) and was engaged in a war
with Eumenes, king of Pergamum, which lasted for
some years, and was put an end to chiefly through
the interference of Rome. (Polyb. Exc. XXIV. 4.
et seq.) Polybius records of Pharnaces, that he
was the most wicked of all the kings who had preceded him. (XXVII. 15, 1. XXV. 2, 7.) Mithridates his son, the fifth of that name, ascended the
throne about the year 150 B. C., and took the surname of Evergetes, probably from the services he
rendered to the Romans. He assisted that people
in the conquest of Pergamum, and furnished them
with a few ships against Carthage in the third Punic

war; (Appian. Mithr. c. 10.) and received from them in return the province of Phrygia Major. (Justin. XXXVII. 1.) On his death, which took place at Sinope, by the hand of an assassin, he was succeeded, after a reign of nearly thirty years, by his son, the celebrated Mithridates Eupator. This great sovereign, who, by the splendour of his reign, and the brilliancy of his talents, throws all the other princes of his dynasty in the shade, ascended the throne in the year 120 B. C. The first war in which he distinguished himself was against Nicomedes, king of Bithynia, whom he engaged in Paphlagonia, on the banks of the Amnias, and totally routed. He was equally successful against the Roman generals Cassius, Manius, and Oppius, who had moved forward to support their Bithynian allies. These rapid and brilliant victories rendered him master of Bithynia, Mysia, and Phrygia ; and he soon after added Ionia, Lydia, and Pamphylia to his conquests; so that the whole of Asia Minor might be said to have fallen under his arms. (Appian. Mithr. c. 17 —22.) Not content, however, with this success, and feeling that his conquests could never be secure as long as so many Roman citizens remained in the country, he formed the bold, but atrocious design of cutting off in one day many thousand families, living in peace and security throughout the different provinces. This horrid design was but too well executed. Secret letters having been despatched to all the governors and commanders in the several towns and districts under his authority, on an appointed day a general massacre of the Romans and Italians took place, in which neither age nor sex was spared, but all were slain indiscriminately, and

even their bodies were denied the rites of burial,
and their goods were declared forfeited to the king.
The readiness with which the people of Asia executed this sanguinary decree proves, as Appian observes, that the Romans had already made themselves odious throughout the different countries in
which they resided rather as masters than allies.
No less than 80,000 souls are said to have perished
in this barbarous manner. (Appian. Mithr. c. 22—
24. Cic. pro Leg. Manil. 3—5. Vell. Paterc. 11,
18. Liv. Epit. LXXVIII. Val. Max. IX. 2.) Mithridates, feeling now secure in Asia Minor, despatched his general Archelaus with a large army
into Greece, in the hope of wresting that country
also from the Roman dominion; while he himself
was engaged in reducing such places as yet with-
stood his power. The determined resistance of the
Rhodians baffled however all his efforts to obtain
possession of their city in a long and vigorous siege,
so that, despairing of success, he gave up the attempt,
and employed himself in the prosecution of his enterprise in Greece and other countries. (Appian.
Mithr. c. 24—28.) His empire was indeed now the
most formidable which the Romans had had to contend with; since, in addition to the great resources
which the possession of Asia Minor placed in his
hands, he was master also of Colchis and the different warlike tribes inhabiting round the Euxine
and Palus Mæotis, as far as Thrace and the country
of the Bastarnæ. He was besides allied to Tigranes,
king of Armenia, and Arsaces, king of the Parthians. His infantry, at the commencement of the
war, amounted to 250,000, his cavalry to 40,000
soldiers. His fleet consisted of 300 galleys, the

whole admirably appointed, and commanded by able and experienced officers. (Appian. Mithr. c. 15—17.) Had Mithridates himself led his forces into Greece, and carried on the war there with vigour, before the Romans had assembled their forces, his success in that quarter would probably have been no less decisive. But his love for Monimia, a young lady of Stratonicea in Caria, is said to have detained him in Asia, and prevented him from prosecuting his designs against the Romans with his usual energy. Archelaus, though an able general, was no match for the great commander whom the Romans opposed to him in Greece. Sylla commenced his operations by the siege of Athens; and though it was vigorously and obstinately defended by Archelaus in person, he succeeded at length in overpowering all resistance, and taking the place by assault. (Appian. Mithr. c. 30—40. Plut. Syll.) Archelaus withdrew into Bœotia, where he was joined by large reinforcements sent by Mithridates; and he soon found himself at the head of 120,000 troops. Sylla, though unable to bring into the field a force amounting to one third of so great an army, marched also without hesitation into Bœotia, and, after a series of able manœuvres, compelled the enemy to fight near Chæronea, under great disadvantages, and succeeded in gaining a complete victory. (Appian. Mithr. c. 41—45. Plut. Syll.) Such was the activity, however, with which Mithridates collected and sent reinforcements to his general, that Archelaus was soon enabled to encounter his adversary once more in the plains of Orchomenus. He was nevertheless again defeated, and his camp forced; himself escaping with difficulty to Chalcis

in Eubœa. (Appian. Mithr. c. 49, 50. Plut. Syll.)
Whilst Sylla was thus successfully carrying on
the war in Greece, Cinna, and his other enemies
at Rome, had caused him to be superseded in his
command, and had sent out Flaccus with troops to
carry on operations in Asia Minor against the king
of Pontus. Flaccus, a man of no experience in military affairs, and hated by the soldiers for his ava-
rice and cruelty, was soon deprived of the command
through the intrigues of Fimbria, a Roman, who
had been sent by the senate to assist him with his
counsels, and not long after was put to death at Nicomedia. Fimbria then assumed the command, and
proceeded to carry on the war with vigour against
Mithridates. He defeated his son, and compelled the
king of Pontus himself to seek refuge within the walls
of Pergamum. From thence, however, he escaped
to Pitane, and finally sailed to Mitylene. Meanwhile, negotiations were carried on between Sylla
and Archelaus in Greece; and these being happily
concluded, Sylla was enabled to march his army
through Macedonia and Thrace, and to cross into
Asia Minor, with the view of taking vengeance on
Fimbria and his party, and compelling Mithridates
to ratify the conditions agreed upon with his general
Archelaus. Sylla had an interview with that monarch near Abydos, and it was finally settled that
Mithridates should give up all his ships of war;
restore all the prisoners he had taken; withdraw
his garrisons from the places he had occupied
since the beginning of hostilities; pay all the expenses of the war; restore Bithynia to Nicomedes,
Cappadocia to Ariobarzanes; and retire within his
hereditary dominions. (Appian. Mithr. c. 54—58.

Plut. Syll.) Thus ended the first Mithridatic war. The peace which ensued was not, however, of long duration, being broken, in the first instance, by Murena, whom Sylla had left as commander in Asia, while he himself returned to oppose Cinna and his faction in Italy. Murena, without any apparent motive but that of a vain desire to distinguish himself, crossed the Halys, and ravaged the territory of Mithridates, who, finding expostulation vain, and perhaps secretly desirous of renewing the war under advantageous circumstances, since Sylla was no longer opposed to him, collected a large force, and suddenly attacked the Roman general near the Halys, drove him from his position with great slaughter, and compelled him to retreat hastily, and with considerable difficulty, into Phrygia. Sylla and the Roman senate, conscious that hostilities had been unjustly commenced on the part of their officer, sent Aulus Gabinius to forbid Murena from prosecuting the war, and to renew the treaty made with Mithridates. This, according to Appian, was the conclusion of the second Mithridatic war. (c. 64—66.)

Mithridates now employed himself in conquering the Cimmerian Bosphorus, which he assigned to one of his sons: he made also war upon some Sarmatian nations, and formed a still closer alliance with Tigranes, king of Armenia. At this period he received overtures from the Roman general Sertorius, who was at the head of a formidable party in Spain, which were too inviting to be easily rejected, and which induced him to take up arms once more against the Romans; since Sertorius promised to cede to him the whole province of Asia, with Bithynia, Paphlagonia, Cappadocia, and Galatia. Mithridates, once resolved on undertaking a war which he saw would be implacable and final, applied his whole energies to this one object, and collected all the resources of his empire, and those of the numerous barbarous and warlike nations contiguous to his dominions, both in Asia and in Europe. Having thus assembled a well-appointed force of 140,000 infantry, and 16,000 horse, besides a vast number of irregular troops, in the year 680 of Rome, or 74 B. C., he invaded Bithynia, which had just been bequeathed to the Romans by the last will of Nicomedes. Cotta, the Roman governor, fled on his approach to Chalcedon; and thus the whole province, with the exception of that city, fell without a blow into the hands of the king of Pontus. Mithridates, after reducing Chalcedon, proceeded to invest the important city of Cyzicus, which had refused to surrender: but though he employed every resource which art could suggest, and the powerful means he possessed rendered available, he was unable to overcome the gallant resistance of the Cyzicenes. Meantime Lucullus, who had been appointed to the command in Asia, arrived in that province; and though unable, with an army greatly inferior in numbers, to give battle to the enemy, he took up an advantageous position in the vicinity of Cyzicus, and by continually harassing the besiegers, cutting off their supplies, and intercepting communications, and routing some detached corps, he finally compelled Mithridates to raise the siege, and to withdraw his forces hastily to Parium, which he did not effect without considerable loss. And finally, after encountering fresh disasters both by sea and land,

he retreated to Sinope, abandoning the whole of Bithynia, and his other conquests, to the victor. From
Sinope he proceeded to Amisus, and finally into Armenia, where he was received by Tigranes, his son-
in-law, and with his assistance prepared to renew
the war with fresh vigour. He sent likewise to his
son Machares, who commanded in Bosphorus, to
collect all the reinforcements that he was able. Lucullus, after settling the affairs of Bithynia, crossed
the Halys, and commenced the sieges of Amisus,
Eupatoria, and Themiscyra, important cities of Pontus. To relieve these, Mithridates moved forward
from Armenia, and fixed his quarters at Cabira, a
strong fortress on the borders of Armenia and Pontus, and at no great distance from the besieged
places. He was now at the head of 40,000 foot,
and 4000 horse ; and as he received daily reinforcements, it became necessary to dislodge him from his
position, or bring him to an action. In the campaign which now ensued among the mountains of
Pontus and Cappadocia, it appears that Mithridates
made such skilful movements, that in several actions
he had a decided advantage over the Romans, and
finally reduced Lucullus to such distress, by cutting
off his supplies, that he was on the point of commencing his retreat. An unsuccessful attack on the
part of Mithridates' cavalry had the effect, however,
of deranging all the plans of that monarch, and
finally deciding the fate of the war ; since the defeat
of this corps threw such a sudden panic into the
whole camp, that the soldiers abandoned their en-
trenchments and baggage, and fled in the greatest
confusion, pursued by the Roman legions. Mithridates and a few followers escaped with difficulty to

Comana, and thence once more joined Tigranes. Despairing now of success, he despatched the eunuch Bacchus to his palace at Sinope, with orders to put to death his sisters, wives, and concubines. The execution of this barbarous decree was the signal for a general defection on the part of the governors and other officers who held situations of trust throughout Pontus. They now joined, with few exceptions, the Roman general, who soon reduced Heraclea and Amastris, and proceeded to besiege Sinope by sea and land, which, after a vigorous defence on the part of the governor Bacchus, or Bacchides, and his garrison, was taken by assault. Amisus likewise surrendered; and Lucullus, having received the submission of Machares, son of Mithridates, who commanded in Bosphorus, and sent an embassy to Tigranes, to demand that Mithridates should be delivered up to him, returned into the province of Asia, which required his presence.

In the spring of the ensuing year, finding that the king of Armenia not only refused to give up his ally, but seemed disposed to support him with his forces, Lucullus moved forward with a small but chosen army, and having crossed the Euphrates, invaded Armenia. Such was the celerity and secresy of his movements, that Tigranes had only time to throw some troops into Tigranocerta, his capital, and to withdraw hastily into the interior of his dominions. Lucullus now commenced the siege of Tigranocerta, which was a place of great strength ; he had already made some progress, when the approach of Tigranes, at the head of a large army, amounting, according to Appian's statement, to 250,000 foot, and 5,000 cavalry, compelled him to desist, in order to meet the enemy. Mithridates in vain urged his ally to avoid an engagement, but to harass the Romans by protracted operations and petty assaults; Tigranes, relying on the vast numerical superiority of his forces, marched to the attack. His positions, however, were so ill chosen, and the movements of his troops so confused and disorderly, that Lucullus, seizing a favourable opportunity, made a combined attack of infantry and cavalry on his columns, and routed them with immense slaughter. Tigranocerta now fell into the power of the Romans, and the war seemed at an end; but such was the vigour and perseverance of Mithridates, who was now intrusted by Tigranes with the whole of the military operations, that he was again ready to take the field in the ensuing year with an army of 70,000 foot and 35,000 horse, chiefly disciplined after the Italian manner. The campaign was chiefly employed in marches and countermarches, and skirmishes, without any decisive action being fought; and on the approach of winter, both parties retired into their quarters. Mithridates now proceeded into Pontus, whither he was followed by Lucullus: here different partial engagements took place, in several of which Mithridates was victorious; especially in one, which was fought when Triarius the lieutenant of Lucullus commanded in that general's absence. The king of Pontus defeated him with considerable loss, and would have gained a complete victory, if a severe wound he received had not spread alarm among his soldiers, and caused them to desist from the pursuit. When the king was sufficiently recovered from his wound, he moved his quarters into the lesser Armenia; thither he was followed by

Lucullus, but the campaign ended without any decisive advantage being gained on either side; and the Romans being now pressed at home by the Italic war, and the injuries done to their commerce and revenue by the pirates of Cilicia, were forced to desist from carrying on operations in Pontus, till they could remedy the evils which were more sensibly felt by them. (Appian. Mithr. c. 66—91. Plut. Lucull.) When Italy had been reduced, and the pirates had been destroyed by Pompey, the Mithridatic war was intrusted to that general. (A. U. 687.) After an unsuccessful attempt to form negotiations for peace on the part of Mithridates, the Roman commander opened the campaign with 30,000 foot and 3,000 horse, of the choicest troops. He commenced his operations by endeavouring to blockade Mithridates within his lines, and cutting off his supplies, in which project, through the unaccountable supineness of his enemy, he succeeded so well, that after enduring every privation for several days, Mithridates was forced to abandon his camp, and escape at night by bad and difficult roads. Though closely pursued by the Romans, he succeeded in making good his retreat to a very strong position among the mountains, which was only accessible on one point. The next day both sides prepared for battle; but before the army of Mithridates was ready, the action commenced on the part of the Roman horse with such vigour, that the enemy were thrown into confusion, and the disorder increasing throughout the camp, a complete rout ensued; Mithridates lost ten thousand men, and his camp, with all his stores and baggage. Escorted by a few troops, he proceeded first to Sinorega, a strong fortress, where he kept his treasures. Having drawn from thence 6000 talents, he advanced to the sources of the Euphrates, and traversing Chotene, a district of Armenia, he entered Colchis, and the territory of the Iberians ; and wintered at Dioscurias, a port on the Euxine, near the mouth of the Phasis. (Appian. Mithr. c. 97—101. Plut. Pomp.) Though vanquished, the mind of this extraordinary man remained unbroken and unsubdued, and shewed itself yet greater in adversity than before. He now formed the daring project of collecting another army on the Cimmerian Bosphorus, and opposing a new front to his antagonists. Thither therefore he proceeded ; and as he received every where on his passage through the Sarmatian and Scythian hordes, demonstrations of respect and admiration, and promises of support, he felt his hopes raised to the highest pitch; and he now conceived the gigantic design of penetrating through Thrace and Pæonia into Macedonia and Illyria ; and from thence crossing the Alps, and carrying the war into Italy itself. (Appian. Mithr. 101—103.) Whilst he was forming these plans, and raising troops throughout the Bosphorus, treachery began to shew itself in his own family, and among his own subjects: the Phanagoreans revolted, and their example was followed by several other towns: still Mithridates persisted in his design of advancing towards Italy, and crossing the Alps, as Hannibal had done before him ; and he had already concerted measures with the Gauls for that enterprise, when the treachery of Pharnaces, his favourite son, who incited the army to open rebellion, disconcerted all his plans, and brought him to the grave. Abandoned by his followers, and

dreading lest he should be betrayed into the hands
of the Romans, to grace the triumph of Pompey, he
swallowed poison, which he always carried about
his person; but the effect of the deadly potion being
counteracted by the frequent use of antidotes, to
which he had had recourse to guard against the
designs of others, he hastened death by the sword
of a Gaul, who remained faithful to the last. Thus
died Mithridates, in the 68th year of his age, after
a reign of fifty-seven years, the last and perhaps the
most formidable antagonist which the colossal power
of Rome had to contend with ; and whose life, if it
had not been tarnished by vices and deeds of cruelty,
which are to be charged in great measure perhaps
to eastern habits of despotism, would call forth
the highest degree of admiration and praise. It
should be remembered, too, that these dark crimes
have been handed down to us by historians who are
not altogether free from the suspicion of partiality ;
and it is much to be regretted, that we have no
good ancient life of this extraordinary man. The
body of Mithridates was sent by the traitor Pharnaces to Pompey, who caused it to be deposited with
kingly honours in the royal tombs at Sinope. Pharnaces, as a reward for his perfidy, was proclaimed
king of Bosphorus, and styled the ally and friend of
the Roman nation. (Appian. Mithr. c. 103—114.)
Pompey annexed the greatest part of Pontus to
Bithynia, and the rest he assigned to Dejotarus,
tetrarch of Galatia, and a zealous ally of Rome ; a
small portion of Paphlagonia, as we have before
said, being reserved for some native chiefs of that
country. (Strab. XII. p. 541—547. Appian. Mithr.
c. 114.) During the civil wars waged by Cæsar

and Pompey, Pharnaces made an attempt to recover his hereditary dominions, and succeeded in taking Sinope, Amisus, and some other towns of Pontus. But Julius Cæsar, after the defeat and death of Pompey, marched into Pontus, and encountering his army near the city of Zela, gained a complete victory; the facility with which it was gained being expressed by the victor in those celebrated words, " Veni, Vidi, Vici." (Hirt. Bell. Alex. c. 72. Plut. Cæs. p. 731. E. Suet. Cæs. c. 37. Dio Cass. XLII. 47.) After his defeat, Pharnaces retired to the Bosphorus, where he was slain by some of his own followers. (Appian. Mithr. c. 120. Dio Cass. XLII. 47.) He left a son named Darius, who was made king of Pontus for a short time, by Antony; (Appian. Bell. Civ. V. 75.) but he was soon deposed, and Polemo, son of Zeno of Apamea, was appointed in his stead. This person, who had the art to ingratiate himself alike with Antony, Augustus, and Agrippa, was made king of that eastern portion of Pontus, named Polemoniacus from him, and which will be more particularly described in the course of this section. Polemo was killed in an expedition against some barbarians of Sindice, near the Palus Mæotis; but his widow, Pythodoris, was reigning in his stead at the time that Strabo wrote his Geography. (XII. p. 556. 578. Dio Cass. LIII. 25. LIV. 24.) Ptolemy divides Pontus into three districts, which he terms Galaticus, Cappadocius, and Polemoniacus; and under the Byzantine emperors the two former were included under the name of Helenopontus, derived from the mother of Constantine, as they had been usually comprehended before by the Romans themselves under that of Pontica Prima.

(Dio Cass. LI. 2. Sueton. Ner. 18. Ptol. p. 125. Justin. Novell. XXVIII. 1. Not. Imp. c. 1. Hierocl. Synecd. p. 701, 702.)

We shall consider Pontus as extending along the coast of the Euxine from the Halys to the river Acampsis, which separated it from Colchis, though some geographers have been disposed to remove this eastern boundary as far as the Phasis[c]; (Ptol. p. 125.) but Strabo does not carry it beyond Trapezus, (XII. p. 548.) and Pliny only as far as the Apsarus. (VI. 4.) On the south, Pontus is separated from Cappadocia by a lofty range of mountains, which connects itself towards the west with the Paphlagonian chain, and in a southerly direction with the central ridge of Taurus. On the side of Armenia and Colchis, the same chain, under the various names of Paryadres, Scydisces, and generally the Moschic mountains, extends as far as the Phasis, and unites with the different ramifications of Caucasus and Ararat. It will be seen from this outline that Pontus is chiefly mountainous; especially towards the north-east frontier. Here we have some of the highest table land in Asia, from whence flow the great streams of the Euphrates and Tigris, the Araxes, and the Phasis. The climate was consequently extremely bleak and severe, the soil rugged and barren, and the different tribes scattered over its surface wild and savage to the last degree. (Xen. Anab. V. 4. Strab. XII. p. 548, 549.) But the western portion of the country around the Halys, and the valleys of the Thermodon and Iris,

[c] This arrangement has been adopted by Mannert, tom. VI. p. 358. Cellarius does not extend the limit of Pontus on this side beyond Trapezus. Geogr. Ant. tom. II. p. 197. I have adhered to that of D'Anville. Geogr. Anc. p. 98. ed. fol.

were rich and fertile, and abounded in produce of
every kind, and furnished the finest flocks and herds.
There were also mines of salt, iron, and rock crystal; and the coast exhibited some large and flourishing Greek cities, possessed of good harbours, and
having an extensive traffick with the other parts of
the Euxine, the Hellespont, and the Ægean.

The Halys, which divides Pontus from Paphlago- Halys flu-
nia, is by much the largest river of Asia Minor, vius.
since, as Herodotus observed, it nearly divides the
peninsula in two. According to that historian, it
had its rise in the mountains of Armenia, and after
flowing through part of Cilicia, separated first the
Matieni from the Phrygians, and next the Syrians
of Cappadocia from the Paphlagonians. (I. 72.)
Strabo reports that it took its source in Great Cappadocia, but towards Pontica, and the particular
district called Camisene. He adds, that it flowed
for a considerable space from east to west, but afterwards taking a turn towards the north, traversed
the country of the Galatæ, and divided the Paphlagonians from the Leucosyri. (XII. p. 546.)

This description agrees very little with that of
Herodotus, who says nothing about the long course
from east to west, but rather makes it flow from
south to north. Arrian, however, in his Periplus,
(p. 16.) criticises the geography of Herodotus on
this point, and observes, that it does not flow as he
states from the south, but from the east, and falls
into the Euxine between Sinope and Amisus. Pliny,
on the other hand, seems to adhere rather to the
description of the father of history, since he makes it
rise in mount Taurus, and flow through Cataonia
and Cappadocia, (VI. 2.) Cataonia being that south-

eastern portion of Cappadocia which was contiguous to Cilicia, and the valley of the Euphrates.

These apparent discrepancies are however cleared up, when we find that the Halys, now called *Kizil-Ermak*, has two main branches, which rise at a considerable distance from each other. The one, according to the best modern maps, has its source towards the south, in that part of Taurus which supplies the Sarus and Pyramus, Cilician rivers which flow into the Mediterranean. This seems to answer to the account of Herodotus and Pliny. The other is laid down in the same maps as flowing from the mountains of lesser Armenia, considerably to the northeast of the former branch. This runs in a westerly direction for a considerable space, as Strabo and Arrian report, and joining the other near *Manjour*, they flow in one stream towards the north, and discharge their waters into the Euxine near *Bafra*, and between *Samsoun* and *Sinoub*[d].

Strabo reports that the Halys took its name from some salt mines near which it flowed. (XII. p. 546, 561.) This great river formed the boundary of the Median and Lydian empires, when they were swayed by Cyrus and Croesus ; (Herod. I. 72.) and it is fur-

[d] In the best maps hitherto published of Turkey in Asia, the eastern branch of the *Kizil-Ermak* is made to come from the mountains a little to the east of *Siwas*, the ancient Sebaste ; but a recent traveller is disposed, from personal observation, confirmed by the reports of the natives, to remove its source as far back as *Sunnur*, in the vicinity of *Baibout*, a town of Armenia. I do not think, however, that the evidence adduced by Mon. Fontanier, the writer in question, is conclusive on the subject ; and though I am disposed to think with him that this branch of the *Kizil-Ermak* ought to be removed more to the east of *Siwas*, I do not imagine it will be found to rise so far back as *Sunnur*. Fontanier, Voyages en Orient. Paris, 1829, 8vo. p. 41 and p. 140—146.

ther connected with the history of the latter monarch, by the ambiguous oracle which might have been construed into a warning, but which ambition led him to interpret in a manner most congenial to his wishes. (Herod. I. 53. Aristot. Rhet. III. 5. Cic. de Divin. II. 56.) Xenophon reports that the Halys was not less than two stadia, or nearly a quarter of a mile in breadth, towards its mouth ; (Anab. V. 6, 3.) and Mr. Kinneir, who crossed it in a ferry near *Bafra*, describes it as a wide and powerful river.

On the right bank of the Halys were once established the Syrians of Cappadocia, whom the Greeks termed Leuco-Syri, or white Syrians, to distinguish them from their more swarthy countrymen who occupied Syria Proper on the shores of the Mediterranean. (Strab. XII. p. 544.) The poets not unfrequently call the district which they occupied, Assyria.

Τοῖσι δ' ὁμοῦ μετέπειτα θοῇ πεφορημένοι αὔρη
Λεῖπον Ἅλυν ποταμὸν, λεῖπον δ' ἀγχίρροον Ἶριν,
Ἠδὲ καὶ Ἀσσυρίης πρόχυσιν χθονός.

APOLL. ARG. II. 964.

And a little before he had said, v. 948,

Αὐτίκα δ' Ἀσσυρίης ἐπέβαν χθονός· ἔνθα Σινώπην
Θυγατέρ' Ἀσωποῖο καθίσσατο.

Assyrios complexa sinus stat opima Sinope.

VAL. FLACC. V. 110.

Τοῖς δὲ μετ' Ἀσσυρίης πρόχυσις χθονὸς ἐκτετάνυσται.

DIONYS. PERIEG. 784.

Scylax also calls the district of which we are speaking, Assyria. (p. 33.) Herodotus never uses the appellation of Leuco-Syri, but calls them Syrians, and says that the Medes, whose subjects they had been before the time of Cyrus, gave them the name

of Cappadocians. (I. 72. V. 49. VII. 72.) Pindar
also, in a passage quoted by Strabo, applied the
denomination of Syrians to this people. (XII. p.544.)
Herodotus mentions likewise another curious particular respecting these Syrians, which strongly connects them with the Phœnicians and Syrians of
Palestine. It is, that they practised the rite of circumcision; and though he pretends that they derived it from the Colchians, who themselves borrowed it from the Egyptians, it appears in fact
much more rational to suppose it had been transmitted to them by the mother country. It is true,
that the facts stated by Herodotus have been much
controverted, and in particular it has been denied
that the Syrians of Palestine used the rite of circumcision, unless he meant indeed to call the Jews
by that name, which was the opinion of Josephus.
(Ant. Jud. VIII. 10.) But though it certainly appears from the incontrovertible testimony of scrip-
ture, that the Philistines did not use circumcision
in the time of Saul and David, it does not follow
that in the time of Herodotus the practice had not
prevailed among them also, especially when the
Jews had become settled in these towns, and so
many of the neighbouring nations had learned to
use it. (Herod. II. 104. where see the observations
of Wesseling, and the list of authors whom he
quotes.) We have already seen from the same historian that the Leuco-Syri once extended on the left
bank of the Halys as far as the Parthenius, a fact
which is confirmed by other writers of authority;
(Eustath. ad Dion. Perieg. 772.) and though we
have no positive account of their migration from
the east or south, it is not improbable that they

owed their position on this coast to some remote event under the great Assyrian empire, of which no certain record has reached us. Ctesias, indeed, who is quoted by Diodorus, reported that the Assyrians had penetrated into these parts as early as the reign of Ninus, (II. 2.) and if the Syrians of Cappadocia had formed a part of the Assyrian empire, it would be easy to account, from that circumstance, for their having afterwards become subject to the Medes.

After the mouth of the Halys, Arrian (p. 16.) notices a marsh and station called Naustathmus, distant ninety stadia; Marcian says 120 : (p. 74.) then another marsh named Conopeium, fifty stadia further ; Marcian writes 120, but his numbers are certainly not correct. It seems to answer to the site of *Coumjougaz*. From thence to Eusene, Arrian reckons 120 stadia. Ptolemy places this station inland, but the Table on the coast twenty miles from Naustathmus, and eight from Amisus. *[marginal: Naustathmus. Conopeium. Eusene.]*

It appears from Herodotus that the country on this side the Halys was in his time known by the name of Pteria ; since he states, that Crœsus having crossed the Halys, marched into that part of Cappadocia which is opposite to the Sinopian territory, and is called Pteria. After wasting the country, and taking the principal town and others in the neighbourhood, he was encountered by Cyrus, and a great battle was fought in Pteria, but without any decisive result. (I. 76.) Stephanus Byz. is the only other author who speaks of Pteria, and it is probable he merely copied Herodotus. (v. Πτερία.) This district, which Herodotus describes as the best and most important part of the Leuco-Syrian territory, is noticed by Strabo under the names of Gadilonitis *[marginal: Pteria regio et urbs. Gadilonitis vel Gaze-lonitis regio.]*

and Saramene. The former he places immediately after the mouth of the Halys, and he reports that it was a rich champaign country, producing every sort of fruit and grain, and a breed of sheep whose wool was so fine, that it was found necessary to protect their fleeces with skins. (XII. p. 546.) There was also to be found in this country a particular sort of goats (ζόρκες) which are rare elsewhere. Some commentators have supposed that these were the famous goats of *Angora*, which are now so much esteemed for the fine quality of their hair[f]. Gadilonitis, or Gazelonitis, appears to have taken its name from Gadilon, or Gazelon, a town situated in this vicinity. (Plin. VI. 2.) After Gazelonitis follows the canton Saramene, and the city of Amisus, situated on the coast at a distance of 900 stadia from Sinope. It was founded, as we learn from Theopompus, quoted by Strabo, (XII. p. 547.) by the Milesians, but was subject for a time to the authority of a Cappadocian chief; afterwards it received an Athenian colony, led by Athenocles, and took the name of Piræus[g]. Amisus subsequently fell under the dominion of the kings of Pontus. Mithridates enlarged the town, and adorned it with several temples and palaces. (Cic. pro Leg. Manil. §. 8. Strab. loc. cit.) In the wars waged by that sovereign against the Romans, it was besieged and taken by Lucullus. Some years after, it was again occupied by Pharnaces, on which occasion

Marginal notes: Gadilon sive Gazelon. Amisus.

[f] Note to the French edition of Strabo, t. III. and XIII. p. 35.

[g] The date of this event is not ascertained. Amisus does not appear to have existed in the time of Scylax; nor is it mentioned by Herodotus or Xenophon. The Athenian colony was therefore certainly posterior to the time of the Anabasis. There are some coins with the legend ΠΕΙΡΑ, which are assigned to Amisus, and which appear to be more ancient than those with the epigraph ΑΜΙΣΟΥ. Sestin. p. 58.

the inhabitants were treated with the greatest cruelty. (Appian. Bell. Civ. II. c. 91. Strab. loc. cit.) Cæsar, after defeating Pharnaces, restored them to liberty. Antony annexed their town to the kingdom erected by him in favour of Polemo; but they were oppressed for a time by a tyrant named Strato: finally, however, Augustus took Amisus under his protection, and made it a free city. It possessed, as we learn from Strabo, an ample and fertile territory, (XII. p. 547.) and enjoyed laws and privileges of its own. (Plin. Epist. X. 93.) The chief magistrate was named Ecdicus, and there were, besides, a senate and a popular assembly. (Epist. X. 111. Cf. Plin. Hist. Nat. VI. 2. Plut. Lucull. p. 514. Polyæn. Strat. VII. 21. Arrian. Peripl. p. 16. Marcian. Heracl. p. 74. Steph. Byz. v. Ἀμισός. Ptol. p. 116.) Amisus still continued to flourish under the Greek emperors of Byzantium and Trebizond, but the name was corrupted to that of *Samsoun*, which it retains at the present day. (Georg. Acrop. p. 6. D. Abulfed. Tab. XIX. p. 318.) In Constantine Porphyrog. the name is written Aminsus; (Them. I. 2.) in the Table Itinerary, Missos. After Amisus, we find the town and river of Lycastus mentioned by Lycastus urbs et Scylax (Peripl. p. 33.) and Marcian from Artemido- fluvius. rus and Menippus. (P. 74. Cf. Menip. ap. Steph. Byz. v. Χαδίσια. Anonym. Peripl. p. 10.) Arrian omits them. The former geographers reckon twenty stadia from Amisus to Lycastus, and forty stadia to an- other river called Chadisius, which Arrian again Chadisius fl. passes over in silence. From thence to the port Ancon, so called from a bend made here by the Ancon portus. land, Marcian reckons 100 stadia; Arrian gives 160 from Amisus to the same place. Ancon is mentioned also by Apollonius Rhodius, (II. 369.) but rather as a headland.

Κεῖθεν δὲ προτέρωσε μέγας καὶ ὑπείροχος ἀγκὼν
Ἐξανέχει γαίης.

Iris fl.   It was close to the mouth of the Iris, a considerable river of Pontus, which flowed from the mountains on the frontier of Cappadocia, and after receiving the Lycus, and other smaller streams, fell into the bay of Amisus. We shall have occasion to speak more particularly of its course in the interior when we come to Amasia, the native city of Strabo, near which it flows. The Iris, according to Xenophon, was three plethra, or half a stadium, in breadth. (Anab. V. 6, 3.)

Ἀκτῇ ἐπὶ προβλῆτι ῥοαὶ ʺΑλυος ποταμοῖο
Δεινὸν ἐρεύγονται. μετὰ τόνδ' ἀγχίῤῥοος ʼΙρις
Μειότερος λευκῇσιν ἐλίσσεται εἰς ἅλα δίναις.

APOLL. ARG. II. 366.

ʼΙρις δ' ἐξείης καθαρὸν ῥόον εἰς ἅλα βάλλει
Τῷ δ' ἐπιμορμύρουσι ῥοαὶ ʺΑλυος ποταμοῖο.

DIONYS. PERIEG. 783.

(Cf. Eustath. ad loc.) This river is now called *To-katlu*.

After the mouth of the Iris, we come to the cape
Heracleum and port Heracleum, distant, according to Arrian,
promont. 360 stadia; (p. 16.) but the anonymous Periplus
et portus. reckons only 106, which is much nearer the truth. Apollonius alludes to this cape when he says,

.... ἤματι δ' αὐτῷ
Γνάμψαν Ἀμαζονίδων ἕκαθεν λιμενήοχον ἄκρην·
ʺΕνθα ποτὲ προμολοῦσαν Ἀρητιάδα Μελανίππην
ʺΗρως Ἡρακλέης ἐλοχήσατο· καί οἱ ἄποινα
Ἱππολύτη ζωστῆρα παναίολον ἐγγυάλιξεν.

APOLL. ARG. II. 966.

The Scholiast informs us from Artemidorus that there was a temple sacred to Hercules on this headland, which in modern charts is named *Thermeh.* From Heracleum to the mouth of the Thermodon the ancients reckon 100 stadia. This river is celebrated by the poets of antiquity as the fabled seat of the Amazons. It would exceed the limits I have proposed to myself in the execution of the present work, to enter into a discussion of the origin and groundwork of a tale which seems to have obtained so much credit in former ages. I shall confine myself at present to those authorities which prove their existence in Asia Minor. Homer certainly recognises them in this part of the peninsula, when he speaks of their wars with the kings of Phrygia.

Thermodon fluvii

Ἤδη καὶ Φρυγίην εἰσήλυθον ἀμπελόεσσαν,
Ἔνθα ἴδον πλείστους Φρύγας, ἀνέρας αἰολοπώλους,
Λαοὺς Ὀτρῆος καὶ Μύγδονος ἀντιθέοιο,
Οἵ ῥα τότ' ἐστρατόωντο παρ' ὄχθας Σαγγαρίοιο.
Καὶ γὰρ ἐγὼν ἐπίκουρος ἐὼν μετὰ τοῖσιν ἐλέχθην
Ἤματι τῷ, ὅτε ἦλθον Ἀμαζόνες ἀντιάνειραι·

Iʟ. Γ. 184.

In another passage the poet alludes to their defeat by Bellerophon. (Il. Z. 186.)

Τὸ τρίτον αὖ, κατέπεφνεν Ἀμαζόνας ἀντιανείρας.

Several grammarians and commentators pretended also that the Halizones, whom he elsewhere mentions as the allies of the Trojans, were the same as the Amazons; and some critics contended that the word Amazones ought to be substituted for Halizones; but Strabo, who seems to have examined every thing connected with the Homeric geography with great care and attention, rejects this opinion

as destitute of foundation. He seems to allow, however, that the traditions which established the Amazons on the Ionian coast in the vicinity of Smyrna,
Ephesus, and Cyma, were better supported, especially since they were advocated by Ephorus, who
was a native of the latter city. (Strab. XII. p. 550—
552.) Herodotus places also the Amazons on the
Thermodon, and affirms that it was from thence
they advanced into Greece, and invaded Attica. (IX.
27.) He likewise speaks of an expedition undertaken
by the Greeks against these warlike females, in which
the latter were defeated near the Thermodon, and
led away captive. A part of them however escaped
to Scythia, and became the mothers of the Sauro-
matæ. (IV. 110.) The same historian adds, that
the Scythian term which answered to the Greek
word Ἀμάζων was Oirpata, i. e. the manslayer; corresponding, it should seem, with the Homeric expression ἀντιάνειραι. Other traditions relative to the wars
of the Amazons with Hercules and Theseus, and
still more anciently with Bacchus, are noticed by
Pausanias. (Attic. 15. Ach. 2. Plut. Thes. et Quæst.
Gr. p. 541. Diod. Sic. IV. 16. II. 44. Justin. II. 4.)
Apollodorus states that the Amazons cut off their
right breast, in order that they might use the bow
with greater effect, but preserved the left, to be able
to suckle their offspring. (II. 5, 9[h].) The poets with
one consent recognise the shores of the Euxine and
the banks of the Thermodon as the principal seat
of this singular people.

---

[h] See the observations of
Heyne on this passage, who
justly remarks, that this circumstance is not generally adhered to by the sculptors of
antiquity. Obss. p. 153, 154.

. . ἔνθ' Ἀμαζόνων στρατὸν
Ἵξει στυγάνορ', αἳ Θεμίσκυράν ποτε
Κατοικιοῦσιν ἀμφὶ Θερμώδονθ'—

ÆSCHYL. PROM. VINCT. 748.

Quales Threïciæ cum flumina Thermodontis
Pulsant et pictis bellantur Amazones armis.

VIRG. ÆN. XI. 659.

Qualis Amazonidum nudatis bellica mammis
Thermodontæis turba lavatur aquis.

PROPERT. III. 14.

The district which they occupied is sometimes called
by Apollonius Rhodius the Dœantian plain, from a Dœantius chief named Dœas, as we are told by the Scholiast. campus.
The same poet adds, that the community of the
Amazons was divided into three separate cantons,
though acknowledging the authority of the same
queen.

. . ἐπὶ δὲ στόμα Θερμώδοντος
Κόλπῳ εὐδιόωντι Θεμισκύρειον ὑπ' ἄκρην
Μύρεται, εὐρείης διαειμένος ἠπείροιο,
Ἔνθα δὲ Δοίαντος πεδίον· σχεδόθεν δὲ πόληες
Τρισσαὶ Ἀμαζονίδων—   ARG. II. 370.

Οὐ γὰρ Ἀμαζονίδες μάλ' ἐπητέες, οὐδὲ θέμισσας
Τίουσαι πεδίον Δοιάντιον ἀμφενέμοντο·
Ἀλλ' ὕβρις στονόεσσα καὶ Ἄρεος ἔργα μέμηλε.

. . . .

Ἔνθα Θεμισκύριαι Ἀμαζόνες ὡπλίζοντο.
Οὐ γὰρ ὁμηγερέες μίαν ἀμπόλιν, ἀλλ' ἀνὰ γαῖαν
Κεκριμέναι κατὰ φῦλα διάτριχα ναιετάεσκον.
Νόσφι μὲν αἵδ' αὐταὶ, τῇσιν τότε κοιρανέεσκεν
Ἱππολύτη, νόσφιν δὲ Λυκάστιαι ἀμφενέμοντο,
Νόσφι δ' ἀκοντόβολοι Χαδήσιαι—

IB. V. 989—1002.

The Thermodon, according to Strabo, is a large
river, formed by the junction of several minor

streams which watered the fertile plain of Themiscyra. (XII. p. 548.) Apollonius affirmed that these
rivulets were not less than ninety-six in number.

Τῆς οἵγ' ἐν κόλπῳ προχοαῖς ἐπὶ Θερμώδοντος
Κέλσαν· ἐπεὶ καὶ πόντος ὀρίνετο νισσομένοισιν.
Τῷ δ' οὔτις ποταμῶν ἐναλίγκιος· οὐδὲ ῥέεθρα
Τόσσ' ἐπὶ γαῖαν ἵησι παρὲξ ἔθεν ἄνδιχα βάλλων.
Τέτρακις εἰς ἑκατὸν δεύοιτό κεν, εἴτις ἕκαστα
Πεμπάζοι· μία δ' οἴη ἐτήτυμος ἔπλετο πηγή.
Ἡ μέν τ' ἐξ ὀρέων κατανίσσεται ἠπειρόνδε
Ὑψηλῶν, ἅτε φασὶν Ἀμαζόνια κλείεσθαι.
Ἔνθεν δ' αἰπυτέρην ἐπικίδναται ἔνδοθι γαῖαν
Αντικρύ· τῷ καὶ οἱ ἐπίστροφοι εἰσὶ κέλευθοι.
Αἰεὶ δ' ἄλλυδις ἄλλη, ὅπη κύρσειε μάλιστα
Ἠπείρου χθαμαλῆς εἰλίσσεται· ἡ μὲν, ἄπωθεν,
Ἡ δὲ, πέλας· πόλεες δὲ πόροι νώνυμνοι ἔασιν,
Ὅππη ὑπεξαφύονται· ὁ δ' ἀμφαδὸν ἄμμιγα παύροις
Πόντον ἐς Ἄξεινον κυρτὴν ὑπερεύγεται ἄκρην.

ARG. II. 972.

Xenophon also describes the Thermodon as a considerable river, not less than three plethra, or half
a furlong, in width, and not easy for an army to
cross. (Anab. V. 6, 3.) Dionysius Periegetes affirms, that crystal and jasper were found on its
banks. (v. 773—182.)

Ἔνθ' Ἀμαζονίδεσσιν ἀπ' οὔρεος Ἀρμενίοιο
Λευκὸν ὕδωρ προΐησιν Ἐνυάλιος Θερμώδων.
. . . .
Κείνου δ' ἀν ποταμοῖο περὶ κρυμώδεας ὄχθας
Τέμνοις κρυστάλλου καθαρὸν λίθον, οἷά τε πάχνην
Χειμερίην· ὄψεις δὲ καὶ ὑδατόεσσαν ἴασπιν.

(Cf. Eustath. ad loc. et Plut. de Fluv. Val. Flacc.
Arg. IV. 600. IV. 122. Plin. VI. 2.) This river,
which retains the name of *Thermeh*, rises in the

mountains to the north-east of *Niksar*, which separate its course from that of the *Carahissar* river,
the ancient Lycus. The plain of Themiscyra,
watered by the Iris and Thermodon, is described by
Strabo as a most rich and .beautiful district, ever
verdant, and able to supply food for innumerable
herds of oxen and horses. The principal kinds of
grain cultivated there were panic and millet; and
these, from the constant supply of water, were always produced in great abundance ; so that scarcity
was never known in the country. Towards the
mountains, the soil furnished a great variety of
fruits, such as grapes, apples, pears, and nuts in
such quantities, that they were suffered to waste on
the trees, or drop off without being gathered. This
great supply of vegetable food naturally caused a
great quantity of game of every sort to resort thither. (XII. p. 548.)   Scylax mentions a town of
the name of Themiscyra which he terms a Greek Themis-
city ; (p. 33.) Herodotus also speaks of it ; (IV. 86.) cyra urbs.
and Appian reports that it was besieged by Lucul-
lus after the retreat of Mithridates from Cyzicus.
The Themiscyrians defended themselves with vigour, and when their walls were undermined, they
sent bears, and other wild beasts, and even swarms
of bees, against the workmen of the enemy. (Mithr.
c. 78. Steph. Byz. v. Θεμίσκυρα. Hecat. ap. eund. v.
Χαδισία.) The plain of Themiscyra belonged to
Amisus in Strabo's time, as well as that of Sidene, Sidene re-
situated next to it towards the east. It derived gio.
its name from Side, a town seated on the coast ;
and was likewise fertile and well watered. This district consists also of a valley, through which flows
the river *Sidin*, which recalls the ancient name.

Pliny, indeed, calls it Sidenus. (VI. 4.) Arrian does not speak of Side, or Sidene, but he names after *Beris sive Bires fluvius.* the Thermodon the river Beris, distant ninety stadia. (p. 16.) The anonymous geographer, who calls it Bires, says sixty stadia. (p. 10.) From thence to *Thoaris fluvius.* the river Thoaris, Arrian measures sixty stadia, the anonymous Periplus ninety. Thirty stadia fur-*Œnoe.* ther we find Œnoe. (Arrian. p. 16.) This was a town, and not a river, as the anonymous writer calls it, and it still retains the name of *Unieh*. It was a place of some consequence in the middle ages, being often mentioned by the Byzantine writers, who call it Œnæum. (Nicet. Ann. p. 410. D. Cinnam. p. 102.) In the Table Itinerary it is probable that we ought to read Œnoe for Cœna, which is . placed at a distance of thirty miles from Heracleum. *Phigamus fluvius.* From Œnoe to the river Phigamus, Arrian reckons forty stadia, in which he agrees with the anonymous geographer. After the Phigamus the anonymous *Ameletum. Phadisana.* Periplus names Ameletum, twenty stadia, and Phadisana, or Phadissa, which Arrian also recognises, 150 stadia [k]. This place probably answers to the Phauda of Strabo, (loc. cit.) and is now called *Polemonium.* *Fatsah*. Ten stadia further bring us to Polemonium, which evidently derives its name from Polemo, the favourite of Antony and Augustus, and king of that portion of Pontus named Polemoniacus from him. Polemonium is not named by Strabo, and therefore was probably founded after his time ; but it is noticed by Ptolemy; and in the Table Itinerary it is marked as a place of consequence. The same document names between it and Cœna, which

---

[k] Geogr. tom. VI. p. 439.

I take to be Œnoe, Camisa, which is probably
Phigamus, eight miles from Cœna, and beyond it
Pytane, twenty from Polemonium ; this last place is
doubtless the Phadisana of Arrian, but the distances
are incorrect. Pliny reckons 120 miles from Amisus to Polemonium[1]. (VI. 4.) Mannert is inclined
to think that the latter place usurped the name and
situation of Side, which is mentioned by no writer
posterior to Strabo[m]. From Polemonium to the
promontorium Jasonium, Arrian and the other Peri- Jasonium
plus reckon 130 stadia. This cape was so called promont.
from the ship Argo having anchored in its vicinity.
(Xen. Anab. VI. 2, 1.) It is also mentioned by
Strabo, (XII. p. 548.) and it preserves evident vestiges of the ancient appellation in that of *Iasoun*.
From thence to the isle of the Cilicians the mari- Cilicum in-
time surveys reckon fifteen stadia. This islet is sula.
not laid down in modern charts. The whole of this
coast from the Jasonian cape to the vicinity of the
Thermodon was once inhabited by the Chalybes, Chalybes
a barbarous people, celebrated in antiquity for the sive Chal-
great iron mines and forges which existed in their dæi gens.
country.

$$. . . . . \text{῞Ηματι δ' ἄλλῳ}$$
Νυκτί τ' ἐπιπλομένῃ Χαλύβων παρὰ γαῖαν ἵκοντο·
Τοῖσι μὲν οὔτε βοῶν ἄροτος μέλει, οὔτε τις ἄλλη
Φυταλιὴ καρποῖο μελίφρονος· οὐδὲ μὲν οἵγε
Ποίμνας ἐρσήεντι νομῷ ἔνι ποιμαίνουσιν·
Ἀλλὰ σιδηροφόρον στυφελὴν χθόνα γατομέοντες,
Ὦνον ἀμείβονται βιοτήσιον· οὐδέ ποτέ σφιν
Ἠὼς ἀντέλλει καμάτων ἄτερ, ἀλλὰ κελαινῇ
Λιγνύϊ καὶ καπνῷ κάματον βαρὺν ὀτλεύουσι.

APOLL. ARG. II. 1002—10.

[1] This distance is much too great.   [m] Geogr. tom. VI. p. 439.

. . μετὰ δὲ σμυγερώτατοι ἀνδρῶν
Τρηχείην Χάλυβες καὶ ἀτειρέα γαῖαν ἔχουσιν
Ἐργατίναι· τοὶ δ' ἀμφὶ σιδήρεα ἔργα μέλονται.

APOLL. ARG. v. 374.

. . . . . . sævissima quamquam
Gens Chalybum ; duris patiens cui cultus in arvis,
Et tonat adflicta semper domus ignea massa.

VAL. FLACC. ARG. IV. 610.

At Chalybes nudi ferrum, virosaque Pontus
Castorea— VIRG. GEORG. I. 58.

Τοῖς δ' ἔπι καὶ Χάλυβες στυφελὴν καὶ ἀπηνέα γαῖαν
Ναίουσιν, μογεροῦ δεδαηκότες ἔργα σιδήρου
Οἲ ῥα βαρυγδούποισιν ἐπ' ἄκμοσιν ἑστηῶτες
Οὔποτε παύονται καμάτου καὶ ὀϊζύος αἰνῆς.

DIONYS. PERIEG. v. 768.

(Cf. Eustath. ad loc.) We are ignorant of the grounds on which the ancients attributed this active employment in the manufacture of iron to the Chalybes, for it does not appear at present that this part of Asia is at all productive of that most useful metal ; perhaps, however, if the mountainous district was examined accurately, there would be found traces of the ancient works. It is clear, however, that they had not ceased to furnish a good supply of metallic ore in Strabo's time, for he observes, that the two great articles of produce in the land of the Chalybes, who were then commonly called Chaldæi, or Chaldi, where the fisheries of the pelamys, and the iron works ; the latter kept in constant employment a great number of men. (XII. p. 549.) Strabo observes also, that these mines formerly produced a quantity of silver ; and this circumstance, together with some affinity in the names, led some commen-

tators of Homer to identify the Alybe of that poet
with the Chalybes of Pontus.

Αὐτὰρ ʿΑλιζώνων ʿΟδίος καὶ ʾΕπίστροφος ἦρχον,
Τηλόθεν ἐξ ʾΑλύβης, ὅθεν ἀργύρου ἐστὶ γενέθλη.

Il. B. 856.

Strabo himself strongly contends for this interpreta-
tion, though he has against him Hecatæus of Miletus, Menecrates of Elæa, and Palæphatus, who placed
the Halizones, or Alazones, in Mysia ; (XII. p. 550.)
but the geographer justly observes that the word
τηλόθεν cannot be applicable to a people situated so
near Troy, and besides, it does not appear that the
northern part of Mysia, in which those writers
placed the Halizones, was ever rich in silver. Upon
the whole, then, I am inclined to adhere to the geography of Strabo ; and the Halizones, as Mannert
ingeniously observes, may have derived their name
from the river Halys, on whose banks their country
was situated [m]. It is remarkable that Herodotus
names the Chalybes among the nations of Asia
Minor which were conquered by Crœsus, (I. 28.)
and yet they certainly are found afterwards considerably beyond the Halys, which separated his dominions from those of Cyrus : either therefore they
must have shifted their position, or Crœsus subsequently lost what he had gained on the right bank
of the Halys. In the enumeration of the armament of Xerxes the Chalybes are not mentioned,
though Wesseling has supposed that there is an
omission of a people immediately after the Asiatic
Thracians, (VII. 76.) and proposes to insert there
the name of the Chalybes, chiefly on account of
the oracle of Mars, which is said to have existed

[m] Geogr. tom. VI. p. i. p. 455.

T 2

among this nameless people. But if Herodotus had named the Chalybes, he would surely have classed them with the Macrones, Tibareni, Mosynœci, and other Pontic nations contiguous to them. (VII. 78.) The nameless people, considering that they are classed with the Cabelees, Lasonii, and Milyæ, who were certainly in the northwest and north-east of Lycia, should be rather sought for in Pisidia and Isauria. It is not improbable that the Chalybes, whose business it was to furnish a great supply of iron for the use of the army, would be exempted from military service. Xenophon, who traversed the country of the Chalybes with his fellow-soldiers, speaks of them as being few in number, and subject to the Mosynœci; he adds, that their chief employment was forging iron. But it is worthy of remark, that he places these Chalybes more to the east than other writers. (Anab. V. 5, 2.) Zeunius therefore is of opinion that this people must have lived a wandering sort of life, and have often changed their territory [n]. Xenophon, however, speaks elsewhere of some other Chalybes who were situated apparently on the borders of Armenia, and were much more numerous and warlike. (Anab. IV. 7, 10.) Strabo reports, that the Chalybes in his time had changed their name to that of Chaldæi; (XII. p. 549.) and it is remarked, that Xenophon speaks of an Armenian tribe of Chaldees, who encountered the Greeks near the river Centrites. (Anab. IV. 3, 4. Cf. Eustath. ad Dion. Perieg. v. 768.) but Menippus in his Periplus calls

[n] Dissert. Geogr. ad Anabas. p. xxvii. ed. Oxon. 1809. This would also appear from Ephorus, quoted by Strabo. (XIV. p. 678, 679.

the Pontic tribe Chaldi, and their canton Chaldia. (ap. Steph. Byz. v. Χαλδία.) Contiguous to the Chalybes, towards the east, were the Tibareni, or Ti- Tibareni. bari, who are named by Scylax, Herodotus, Hecataeus, Strabo, and other geographers. The form Tibareni is the more usual, but the other occurs also in Menippus (ap. Steph. Byz. Χαλδία Hecataeus ap. eund. v. Χοιράδες) and Euseb. Praep. Ev. (I. p. 11. C.) They occupied a small extent of coast from cape Genetes to the extremity of the bay of Cerasus. Xenophon describes their country as consisting of fertile plains, and possessing some fortified places along the coast. (Anab. V. 5, 3.) Other accounts speak of the Tibareni as possessed of numerous flocks, and they are said also to have been a most laughter-loving people. (Ephor. ap. Steph. Byz. v. Τιβαρηνία P. Mel· I. 19.) Eusebius, on the other hand, affirmed, that they destroyed their old men by casting them down precipices. (Praep. Ev. I. p. 11.[o]) A more harmless and ridiculous custom was that of causing the married women to attend upon their husbands after parturition, as if they had undergone the labour of childbirth.

Τοὺς δὲ μέτ' αὐτίκ' ἔπειτα Γενηταίου Διὸς ἄκρην
Γνάμψαντες, σώοντο πάρεξ Τιβαρηνίδα γαῖαν.
῎Ενθ' ἐπεὶ ἄρ κε τέκωνται ὑπ' ἀνδράσι τέκνα γυναῖκες,
Αὐτοὶ μὲν στενάχουσιν ἐνὶ λεχέεσσι πεσόντες,
Κράατα δησάμενοι· ταὶ δ' εὐχομέουσιν ἐδωδῇ
᾿Ανέρας, ἠδὲ λοετρὰ λεχώϊα τοῖσι πένονται.

APOLL. ARG. II. 1011.

(Cf. Nymphodor. ap. Schol. ad loc.) The same poet elsewhere says,

[o] Possibly some other name should be substituted for that of the Tibari, or Tibareni ; perhaps that of the Tapyri.

Ἄγχι δὲ ναιετάουσι πολύρρηνες Τιβαρηνοὶ,
Ζηνὸς ἐϋξείνοιο Γενηταίην ὑπὲρ ἄκρην.

APOLL. ARG. II. 377.

(Cf. Dionys. Perieg. v. 767. and Eustath. ad loc.)

Genetes prom. et fluvius. The Genetæan promontory, which formed the commencement of the Tibarenian district, took its name from a small river and port named Genetes, which is noticed by Scylax, (Peripl. p. 33.) and the Scholiast to Apollonius, who observes that there was a temple of Jupiter on the promontory. (Cf. Steph. Byz. v. Γενήτης.) Strabo also calls the cape Genetes, but in Arrian's time this appellation appears to have been lost, since he mentions directly after the cape Jasonium and the island of the Cilicians a place called

Boona. Boona, which is easily recognised in that of *Vona*, which it now bears ; and cape *Vona* can be no other than the Genetes of Strabo, and others. (XII. p. 548.) The ancient surveys reckon fifty-five stadia from the isle of the Cilicians to the river Genetes,

Cotyora. and twenty from thence to Boona. Cotyora, which next follows at a distance of ninety stadia, was a place of note, as appears from Xenophon, who reports that it was a colony of Sinope, and able to furnish supplies for the ten thousand Greeks who were quartered in its vicinity forty-eight days. (Anab. V. 5, 4. Diod. Sic. XIV. p. 261.) In Arrian's time it was scarcely more than a village ; a circumstance accounted for by Strabo, who states that the population had been removed to the more modern town of Pharnacia. (XII. p. 548. Arrian. Peripl. p. 17. Steph. Byz. v. Κοτύωρα Mel. I. 19. Plin. VI. 4. Ptol. p. 125.) The situation of Cotyora would seem to answer to the modern *Buzuk-*

kalé, about ten miles to the south-east of cape *Vona*[p].
It must have possessed a port, since the 10,000 embarked there for Heraclea.   After crossing the river
Melanthius, we enter upon the territory of the Mo- Melanthius
synœci, who were divided apparently by that stream Mosynœci
from the Tibareni.   Cotyora, according to Xeno- gens.
phon, belonging to the latter. (Anab. V. 5, 4.)   The
Maritime Itineraries give sixty stadia from that town
to the Melanthius. (Arrian. Peripl. p. 17. Anonym.
p. 12.)   That little river, according to modern maps,
still serves to separate the district of *Djanik* on its
left bank from that of *Heldir* on the right.   The
Mosynœci were so called by the Greeks from their
dwelling in small wooden turrets, termed μόσυνοι.
They are described as a savage race, subsisting
chiefly on the flesh of wild animals and roots; and
addicted to robbery, and other lawless habits. (Strab.
(XII. p. 549.)   They were said to keep their chief
a close prisoner in one of their wooden huts ; and if
he ordered any thing contrary to law, they deprived
him of food. (Anonym. Peripl. p. 12, 13. Scymn.
Ch. v. 162. Nic. Damasc. Excerpt. Mel. I. 19.)

Τῇ δ' ἐπὶ Μοσσύνοικοι ὁμούριοι ὑλήεσσαν
Ἑξείης ἤπειρον ὑπωρείας τε νέμονται,
Δουρατέοις πύργοισιν ἐν οἰκία τεκτήναντες
Κάλλινα, καὶ πύργους εὐπηγέας, οὓς καλέουσι
Μόσσυνας· καὶ δ' αὐτοὶ ἐπώνυμοι ἔνθεν ἔασιν.

APOLL. ARG. II. 379.

Ἱερὸν δ' αὖτ' ἐπὶ τοῖσιν ὄρος καὶ γαῖαν ἄμειβον,
Ἧι ἔνι Μοσσύνοικοι ἀν' οὔρεα ναιετάουσι
Μόσσυνας· καὶ δ' αὐτοὶ ἐπώνυμοι ἔνθεν ἔασιν.
Ἀλλοίη δὲ δίκη καὶ θέσμια τοῖσι τέτυκται.
Ὅσσα μὲν ἀμφαδίην ῥέζειν θέμις, ἢ ἐνὶ δήμῳ,

p Mr. Kinneir places it at   the east, and may perhaps agree
Ordou, which is a little more to   better in point of distance.

T 4

*Ἡ ἀγορῇ, τάδε πάντα δόμοις ἔνι μηχανόωνται·
῎Οσσα δ' ἐνὶ μεγάροις πεπονήμεθα, κεῖνα θύραζε
᾽Αψεγέως μέσσῃσιν ἐνὶ ῥέζουσιν ἀγυιαῖς.

. . . .

Αὐτὰρ ἐν ὑψίστῳ βασιλεὺς μόσσυνι θαάσσων
᾽Ιθείας πολέεσσι δίκας λαοῖσι δικάζει,
Σχέτλιος· ἢν γάρ που τὶ θεμιστεύων ἀλίτηται,
Λιμῷ μιν κεῖν' ἦμαρ ἐνικλείσαντες ἔχουσιν.

APOLL. ARG. II. 1017.

Xenophon, who passed through their country, enters
into great detail respecting their habits and manner
of life. He found them, on his arrival with the
Greek army, in a state of dissension, and by siding
with one party obtained the victory over the other
faction, who were determined to oppose his progress,
and thus secured a safe passage for the army. It
·appears from his narrative, that the Mosynœci had
several villages, all built of wood, and a chief town,
or metropolis, which was taken, and set on fire.
On which occasion the king of the Mosynœci, re-
fusing to quit his tower, was burnt, together with
his attendants. In this town were found great
stores of bread and corn ; also pickled fish, chestnuts,
and wine. Their villages were generally not more
than eighty stadia apart, and being situated on the
heights, it was easy to shout from one to the other,
by which means they assembled their forces. They
had also a great number of canoes, made of one
single tree, and able to contain three men. (Anab.
V. 4.) The tract of country which this people inhabited is now called *Heldir*. Following the coast,
we have to notice with the Itineraries the river
Pharmate- Pharmatenus, (Arrian. p. 17.) or Pharmantus,
nus fluvius.
(Anonym. p. 12.) 150 stadia from the Melanthius.
Pharnacia. After which we find, 120 stadia further, Pharnacia,

as Arrian reports, more anciently called Cerasus, Cerasus. a town of some celebrity, colonized by the Sinopians. Xenophon and the Greeks rested there for ten days, having been three days on their march from Trapezus. (Anab. V. 3, 5. Diod. Sic. XIV. c. 31.) Cerasus is named by Scylax, but not in its proper place, for it occurs in the text as it stands at present after Sinope. This is probably an interpolation, and it remains uncertain whether the town existed at the time he wrote his Periplus. (p. 33.) Ammianus Marcell. affirms, that the cherry derives its name from Cerasus, having been brought from thence by Lucullus. (XXII. 13.) Arrian is the only writer who affirms that Pharnacia had usurped the place of Cerasus, for though he is copied in this instance by the anonymous geographer, yet that writer afterwards places Cerasus 530 stadia further to the east. (p. 13.) It should be observed also that Strabo says that Cotyorum, and not Cerasus, had contributed to the foundation of Pharnacia; (XII. p. 548.) and he afterwards names Cerasus as a small place distinct from that town and nearer Trapezus. Pliny moreover distinguishes Pharnacia and Cerasus, and he besides informs us that the former was 100 miles from Trapezus, (VI. 4.) a distance much too great to be accomplished by an army in three days, especially over a difficult country. It is apparent, therefore, that the Cerasus of Xenophon is not to be identified with Pharnacia[p], though it might be thought so in Arrian's time; and it is remarkable that this opinion should have prevailed so strongly, as to leave the name of *Keresoun* to the site occupied by the ancient Pharnacia. With respect to

[p] This is also the opinion of Mannert, Geogr. t. VI. p. ii. p. 386.

this town, it appears to have been founded by Pharnaces, grandfather of Mithridates Eupator, though
we have no positive authority for the fact[q]. We know
only that it existed in the time of Mithridates Eupator, being mentioned by Plutarch in the life of Lucullus. (p. 502.) Mannert is inclined to think that
Pharnacia was founded on the site of a Greek settlement named Chærades, which Scylax places in this
vicinity: (p. 33.) it is also noticed by Steph. Byz.
as a town of the Mosynœci on the authority of
Hecatæus. (v. Χοιράδες.) From Pharnacia, Arrian
Aretias in- reckons thirty stadia to the islet called Aretias, or
sula.
Mars' island, and this distance agrees nearly with
that of the little islet to the east of *Keresoon*. This
rock is celebrated in the Argonautic mythology as
. the spot occupied by the two Amazon queens, Otrere
and Antiope, who erected there a temple sacred to
Mars.

Τοὺς παραμειβόμενοι, λισσῇ ἐπικέλσετε νήσῳ,
Μήτι παντοίη μέγ' ἀναιδέας ἐξελάσαντες
Οἰωνοὺς, οἳ δῆθεν ἀπειρέσιοι ἐφέπουσι
Νῆσον ἐρημαίην· τῇ μέν τ' ἐνὶ νηὸν Ἄρηος
Λάϊνεον ποίησαν Ἀμαζονίδων βασίλειαι
Ὀτρηρή τε καὶ Ἀντιόπη, ὁπότε στρατόωντο.

APOLL. ARG. II. 384.

Zephy-   (Cf. Arg. II. 1032—1234.) Pliny calls it Chalceri-
rium.
tis. (VI. 12.) From the island of Mars to Zephyrium the surveys measure 120 stadia.   Here was a
small port (Cf. Scyl. p. 33.) which doubtless answers
Tripolis. to the *Zefré* of modern charts.   From thence to
Tripolis ninety stadia.   Pliny also mentions this
place as a fortress seated on a river; (VI. 4.) and

q There are some autono-   the epigraph ΦΑΡΝΑΚΕΙΑΣ, and
mous coins of Pharnacia with   ΦΑΡΝΑΚΕΩΝ. Sestini, p. 60.

there is no doubt of its answering to the present *Tireboli* at the mouth of the river of *Gumeh-kaneh*. Strabo places in this neighbourhood a town named *Ischopolis*, which seems to have been in ruins when he wrote; this possibly may have been replaced by Tripolis. Beyond Tripolis we find Argyria, or Argyra, twenty stadia distant. (Arrian. Peripl. p. 17. Anonym. p. 13.) Thence to Philocalea, ninety stadia. This place is noticed by Pliny, who leads us to suppose it was situated on a river. (VI. 4.) From this circumstance, I should be disposed to fix the site of Philocalea at *Helehou*, about half way between *Keresoun* and *Trebizond*. In Ptolemy, the name of Philocalia is corruptly written Cocalia. (p. 125.) Apollonius Rhodius places on this coast, after the Mosynœci, the Philyres, who were supposed to be the offspring of Philyra and Saturn.

Ischopolis.

Argyria.

Philocalea.

Philyres gens.

Νήσου δὲ προτέρωσε καὶ ἠπείροιο περαίης
Φέρβονται Φίλυρες· Φιλύρων δ' ἐρύπερθεν ἔασι
Μάκρωνες. ARG. II. 394.

Elsewhere the same poet mentions the island of the Philyres, which the Argonauts passed soon after leaving that of Mars.

Νυκτί δ' ἐπιπλομένῃ Φιλυρηΐδα νῆσον ἄμειβον,
"Ενθα μὲν Οὐρανίδης Φιλύρῃ Κρόνος, εὖτ' ἐν 'Ολύμπῳ
Τιτήνων ἤνασσεν, ὃ δὲ Κρηταῖον ὑπ' ἄντρον
Ζεὺς ἔτι Κουρήτεσσι μετετρέφετ' 'Ιδαίοισιν.

ARG. II. 1235.

Philyreis insula.

In captain Gauttier's chart, I find two small islands laid down close to *Tireboli*, one of which answers doubtless to the isle of Philyra. From Philocalia the Itineraries reckon 100 stadia to Coralla, the name of which is preserved in that of *cape Kourélih*. The anonymous geographer then proceeds to Cera-

Coralla.

Cerasus.

sus, which he places on a river of the same name
sixty stadia from Coralla, (p. 13.) while Arrian,
passing over this intermediate station, goes on to
Hieron Oros, or the sacred mountain, which, according to his reckoning, is 150 stadia from Coralla.
The anonymous writer also places Hieron Oros immediately after Cerasus, at the distance of ninety
stadia from that town, or 150 from Coralla, so that
they both agree exactly in the whole distance. The
difference between the two geographers, with regard
to the mention of Cerasus, is however important,
and, from what has been said above, there can be
little doubt that the authority of the anonymous
geographer is here superior to that of Arrian; for
though he was certainly much posterior to that historian, he appears to have followed older authors,
especially Scymnus of Chios, in whose time Cerasus
still existed as a place of note[r]. It seems therefore
probable, that the original Cerasus, where Xenophon
and the Greeks remained for ten days, was situated
near the site called *Skefié* in modern charts, between capes *Kourelih* and *Ioroz*, the latter being
the Hieron Oros of the ancients. From the coins of
Cerasus, we know that it existed in the reigns of
Antoninus Pius and M. Aurelius, and as late as
Alex. Severus. The Byzantine writers also, (Nic.
Ann. p. 340. D.) and the ecclesiastical councils, attest
its existence under the Greek emperors[s]; but I ima-

[r] In the fragments of Scymnus, I observe that Cerasus is
certainly placed in the vicinity
of the isle of Mars, but the
passage is very mutilated, and
affords no decisive evidence on
the point in question. Geogr.
Min. tom. II. p. 53. v. 173.

I understand the expression Κε-
ρασοῦς κτισθεῖσ᾽ ὑπ᾽ αὐτὸ, to refer to the proximity of the town
to the Hieron Oros, which must
have been mentioned previously.

[s] Geogr. Sacr. a Car. S.
Paul, p. 257.

gine all these notices refer to the Pharnacian Cerasus of Arrian, or *Keresoun*. The Hieron Oros is
alluded to by Apollonius Rhodius, and he places it
on the coast of the Mosynœci;

'Ιερὸν δ' αὐτ' ἐπὶ τοῖσιν ὄρος καὶ γαῖαν ἄμειβον,
'Ἡι, ἐνὶ Μοσσύιοικοι ἀν' οὔρεα ναιετάουσι.

ARG. II. 1017.

but Suidas the historian, as the Scholiast reports,
placed it in the country of the Macrones; and Aga-
thon, in his Periplus of the Pontus, fixed its position
still more precisely at the distance of 100 stadia
from Trapezus. From this point commences the
bay of *Trebizond*, and as all writers agree in assigning this part of the coast to the Macrones, it is probable they were separated from the Mosynœci by
the headland above mentioned. The Macrones are
called Macrocephali by Scylax, (p. 33.) but Pliny
seems to distinguish them as two different people.
(VI. 4.) The more usual appellation is however
Macrones.

. . . . . . Φιλύρων δ' ἐφύπερθεν ἔασι
Μάκρωνες.   APOLL. ARG. II. 395.

Μάκρωνες, Φίλυρές τε καὶ οἳ μόσσυνας ἔχουσι
Δουρατέους.   DIONYS. PERIEG. 766.

(Cf. Schol. Apoll. et Eust. ad loc.) Herodotus mentions the Macrones on more than one occasion; they
formed, with the Tibareni and Mosynœci, the nineteenth section of the Persian empire under Darius,
and contributed 300 talents to the royal treasury. All
these people likewise served in the army of Xerxes,
and were equipped alike. (Herod. III. 94. VII. 78.)
Elsewhere the same historian affirms that the Macrones used circumcision, having, as they themselves

reported, lately derived the practice from the Colchians. (II. 104.) The natural inference to be drawn from this passage is, that the Macrones were of Colchian origin. According to Xenophon, who with the ten thousand journeyed through their country, the Macrones occupied the mountains contiguous to the Colchians, and above Trapezus. They were separated by a river from another people called Scythini, and whose name bears some affinity to the mount Scydisces of Strabo, (XII. p. 548.) and the Scotius of Appian. (Mithr. c. 100.) It is to be observed, however, that Xenophon extends the Colchians as far as Trapezus, (Anab. IV. 8, 17.) whereas other writers assign that town to the Macrones. Strabo affirms that this people were in his time no longer called by their ancient appellation, but were named Sanni, (XII. p. 548.) and Eustathius, who confirms this statement, writes the word Tzani, according to the more modern Greek orthography. (ad Dionys. Perieg. v. 766.) I am of opinion that the modern name of *Djanik* is a corruption of Sannice. (Cf. Menipp. ap. Steph. Byz. v. Χαλδία.) Arrian, however, identifies the Sanni with the Drilæ, whom Xenophon places in the mountains above Trapezus, and describes as the most warlike people of that district. (Anab. loc. cit.) Arrian says that they were once tributary to the Romans, but that confiding in their fastnesses they disclaimed all subjection. He promises, however, the emperor Hadrian, that he would compel them to pay tribute for the future. (Peripl. p. II. Steph. Byz. v. Δρυλαὶ leg. Δριλαί.) After the Sacred Mountain, where, according to the anonymous Periplus, was a town and port, we have Cordyle, another maritime sta-

Sanni gens.

Drilæ gens.

Cordyle portus.

tion, forty stadia; then Hermonassa, forty-five sta- Hermo-
dia further. (Arrian. p. 17.) In the anonymous nassa.
geographer the name is corruptly written Ermyse.
Hermonassa is mentioned as a small town on this
coast between Cerasus and Trapezus; (XII. p. 548.)
and Menippus, who is cited by Steph. Byz. (v. Ἑρ-
μάνασσα) affirmed that it belonged to the latter city.
It was also known to Hecatæus and Theopompus.
Pliny does not mention Hermonassa; but he places
next to Trapezus an unknown town named Livio- Liviopolis.
polis. (VI. 4.) The situation of Hermonassa answers
nearly to that marked in captain Gauttier's chart
under the name of *Platana*. Trapezus was sixty Trapezus.
stadia further. This city, which under the modern
name of *Trebizond* is still a considerable and flourishing sea-port, is acknowledged by all ancient
authorities to have been colonized by the Sinopians,
who, as we have seen, formed extensive establishments on this coast. (Xen. Anab. V. 8. Arrian, p. 1.
Scyl. p. 33.) It was pretended indeed by the Arcadian Trapezuntii, that they were the ancestors of
the Pontic colony; but this was probably an opinion
grounded only on the similarity of name; and it
was perhaps only a piece of policy in the Sinopians,
who wished to strengthen the infant colony, to re-
ceive these Arcadian refugees as friends and kinsmen.
(Pausan. Arcad. c. 27.) Trapezus was already a
flourishing town, when Xenophon and his fellow-
soldiers reached it in the course of their memorable
retreat. They remained in its vicinity for thirty
days, during which they were treated in the most
friendly and hospitable manner by the citizens, and
received every assistance for the prosecution of their
journey home. The abundant supplies which were

furnished to them for subsistence, and votive offerings, prove that the town was opulent, and the
country fertile and populous. (Anab. V. 8, 17.) Trapezus at that time was situated in the Colchic territory, but later writers remove the Colchians considerably further to the east, and include it within
the district occupied by the Macrones. Ancient
geographers reckoned about 6600 stadia from the
temple of Jupiter Urius, at the entrance of the Bosphorus, to Trapezus, and 1400 stadia from that city
to the mouth of the Phasis. (Strab. XII. p. 548.)
We learn from Arrian, that Trapezus was the most
considerable place on their coast when he visited it,
as governor of Pontus, under Hadrian. He commences his letter, which contains the Periplus, and
is addressed to the emperor, from thence. He reminds Hadrian of the spot he had once visited,
from whence it was supposed that Xenophon and
the ten thousand first beheld the sea, and where
altars had been erected, with inscriptions comme-
morative of that event. Arrian signifies his in-
tention of erecting altars of white marble, instead
of the rude monuments then existing, and he re-
quests the emperor to send his statue, to add further
to the decoration of the spot; the effigy which stood
there being a coarse and inelegant representation of
him. (Peripl. p. 1—3.) The spot alluded to by
Arrian seems to have been above Trapezus, and at
no great distance from the town; but it appears
from Xenophon, that the mountain from which he
and the army beheld the sea, and which he calls
Thekes, or the Sacred Mount, was in the country of
the Scythini, above the Macrones, and at least five
days' journey from Trapezus. (Anab. IV. 7.) But

we will reserve the discussion of this interesting question on ancient topography for a future opportunity, in order to conclude what we have to say respecting Trapezus, and the remaining coast of Pontus. That town is noticed by Tacitus as an ancient and important seaport on the Euxine. (Annal. XIII. 39. Hist. III. 47.) Pliny styles it a free town. (VI. 4. Cf. Mel. I. 19. Steph. Byz. v. Τραπεζοῦς.) In the reign of Gallienus it was sacked and burnt by the Goths, who were spreading devastation along the shores of the Euxine. (Zosim. I. p. 30.) Some centuries later we find it becoming the seat of a small empire, under the government of a branch of the princely house of the Comneni. Its sovereigns assumed the pompous title of emperors of Trebizond, and declared themselves independent of the Greek empire.

This principality even stood for some time after the taking of Constantinople; but, too feeble to resist the overwhelming power of the Turks, it finally yielded by capitulation in 1460 to Mahomet II; and Trebizond from that time became a Turkish city. (Chalcond. IX. p. 263—266. Duc. c. 45ᵗ.) Modern travellers describe it as situated on an elevated terrace above the sea, whence the name of Trapezus was doubtless derived, and surrounded by hills which are succeeded at a greater distance by loftier mountains. (Cf. Plin. VI. 4.) The citadel is built on a rock, which advances out into the sea, and forms the port anciently called Daphni. (Anon. Daphni portus.

ᵗ For a further account of the empire of Trebizond, see the Fam. Byzant. of Du Cange, quoted by Gibbon in the Decline and Fall of the Roman Empire, tom. XI. p. 249.

Peripl. p. 13.) This port is by no means protected against the north winds, which blow with violence during the winter season. There are no ruins of any size or interest, as they chiefly belong to the lower Greek empire. The modern town has a population of about 60,000 or 70,000 souls, and keeps up an active trade with different ports on the Black Sea. It is the chief town of a Turkish pashalik, to which it gives its name [u].

Hyssus portus.

From Trapezus the Itineraries lead us to Hyssus, a port afterwards called Susarmia, and distant 180 stadia; (Arrian. p. 3. Anonym. p. 14.) perhaps this

Psoron portus.

is the same haven which Scylax calls Psoron; (p.33.) at all events the name of Susarmia agrees with that of the little river called *Sourmenah*. The port Hyssus was probably therefore situated at the mouth of it.

Ophius fl.

From thence to the river Ophius, where was a naval station, the anonymous geographer reckons ninety stadia: he states also that this river separated the Colchi from the district of Thianitice; (Peripl. p.14.) perhaps we should read Sannice. Various barbarous tribes are noticed on this coast by ancient writers.

Μάκρωνες· μετὰ δ' αὖ περιώσια φῦλα Βεχείρων.
'Εξείης δὲ Σάπειρες ἐπὶ σφίσι ναιετάουσι·
Βύζηρες δ' ἐπὶ τοῖσιν ὁμώλακες, ὧν ὕπερ ἤδη
Αὐτοὶ Κόλχοι ἔχονται ἀρήιοι.

APOLL. ARG. II. 396.

Κεῖθεν δ' αὖ Μάκρωνας, ἀπειρεσίην τε Βεχείρων
Γαῖαν, ὑπερφιάλους τε πάρεξ ἐνέοντο Σάπειρας,
Βυζηράς τ' ἐπὶ τοῖσιν.   IBID. 1246.

[u] Tournefort, Voyage au Levant. Kinneir's Travels, p. 340. Fontanier, Voyages dans l'Orient, p. 17—23. There are only imperial coins of Trapezus from Trajan to Philip: the epigraph is ΤΡΑΠΕΖΟΥΝΤΙΩΝ. Sestini, p. 60.

Φράζεο δ' ἐκ Κόλχων καὶ Φάσιδος ἐς δύσιν ἤδη
Εὐξείνου παρὰ χεῖλος, ἐπιλαδὸν ἔθνεα Πόντου
Ἄχρι Θρηϊκίου στόματος, τόθι Χαλκὶς ἄρουρα
Βύζηρές τοι πρῶτα καὶ ἄγχοθι φῦλα Βεχείρων.
Μάκρωνες Φίλυρές τε.   DIONYS. PERIEG. 762.

Scylax, after the Phasis and the Colchi, proceeding from east to west, names the Byzeres, Ecechiries, Bechires, and Macrocephali, who are the same as the Macrones. (p. 32, 33.) The Bechires then appear to follow the Macrones, and after them the Ecechiries, whom the anonymous Periplus places between the Ophius and Archabis. (p. 16.) The Byzeres, according to Strabo, were afterwards called Hepta-Cometæ. They were a wild and savage race who inhabited mount Scydisces, and cut to pieces three cohorts of Pompey's army by placing on their way a quantity of honey, which had the effect of intoxicating them, and depriving them of the power of resistance. (XII. p. 549.) This singular circumstance recalls to mind the description given in Xenophon of a similar effect produced by honey on the Greeks in the country of the Colchians, near Trapezus. (IV. 8.) Pliny affirmed that this honey was chiefly extracted from the flower of the rhododendron, and he states that it was found in the country of the Sanni. (XXI. 13.) Aristotle also noticed it as peculiar to the neighbourhood of Trapezus. (ap. Steph. Byz. v. Τραπεζοῦς.) The Ophius, or Orphis, as Arrian (p. 6.) writes the name, is probably the river *Caouchi*. After an interval of thirty stadia we find another small stream called Psychrus, or the *Cold* river ; and at an equal distance the Calos, or *Beautiful* stream, where was a station named Cale Parembole. (Anon. p. 14. Ar-

Bechires gens.

Ecechiries gens.

Byzeres qui et Hepta-Cometæ gens.

Psychrus fluvius.

Calos fluvius.

Cale Parembole.

u 2

rian, p. 7.) It must have been situated a little to the west of *Cape Foudgi*. Rhizius, a port and river 120 stadia from thence, is easily recognised in the present *Rizieh*, a commercial town of some size near the eastern extremity of the Black Sea[x]. It is probably the Bechireus portus of Scylax. (p. 33.) Rhizæum is also mentioned by Ptolemy, (p. 125.) and Procopius. (Bell. Got. IV. 2.) The port was improved by Justinian. (Procop. Æd. III. 7.) From thence to the mouth of the Ascurus, Arrian reckons thirty stadia. (Per. p. 7.) The anonymous Periplus calls this river Ascurnas. (p. 14.) From thence to the Adienus we have sixty stadia. (Arrian. p. 7. Anonym. p. 14.) It is probably the river *Mapourah*. Then follows, after an interval of 100 stadia, a place called Cordyle, (Anonym. p. 14. Ptol. p. 125.) and eighty stadia further a small port, which derived the name of Athenæ from a temple of Minerva erected there. (Arrian, p. 6, 7. Anonym. p. 14. Steph. Byz. v. Ἀθῆναι.) It is probably the same place which Scylax calls Ordinius, and styles a Greek town. (Per. p. 32.) Procopius also mentions Athenæ in the history of the Gothic wars. (IV. 2.) The site is now called *Ordouna*. Beyond Athenæ was the river Zagatis, seven stadia; and thirty-three stadia further the Prytanis, with a spot called the palace of Anchialus. (Arrian. p. 7. Anon. Per. p. 15.) Scylax names the river Pordanis, and places it near a town called Limne. (Per. p. 32.) After the Prytanis we have the Pyxites, ninety stadia distant; (Cf. Plin. VI. 4.) then the Archabis at an equal distance. (Arrian. p. 7. Anonym. p. 15.) Scylax calls the latter Arabis. (p. 32.) The modern

Marginal notes:
Rhizius fluvius et portus.
Ascurus fluvius.
Adienus fluvius.
Cordyle.
Athenæ portus.
Zagatis fluvius.
Prytanis fluvius.
Anchialij regia.
Armene Limne.
Pyxites fluvius.
Archabis fluvius.

[x] Peyssonel, Commerce de la Mère Noire.

name is *Arkava*. The anonymous Periplus places between the Prytanis and the Pyxites a spot called Armene, twenty-four stadia from the former and sixty-six from the latter. From the Archabis to Apsarus sixty stadia were reckoned. The name of this last place, it was said, had been originally called Apsyrtus, from the brother of Medea, but the barbarians had corrupted it to its present form. Arrian reports that it was a town, and military station for five cohorts. (Peripl. p. 7. Anon. p. 15.) Pliny writes, " flumen Absarum cum castello cognomine " in faucibus a Trapezunte CXL. mill. passuum." (VI. 4.) Procopius speaks of it as a more consequential place, since it possessed a theatre, an hippodromus, and other public buildings. The tomb of Absyrtus was shewn in the vicinity. (Bell. Got. IV. 2. Cf. Arrian. p. 6.) Absarum was probably not far from the modern town of *Gonieh*. Arrian after this place names the river Acampsis, which he describes as a navigable river, from the mouth of which a fresh breeze set in toward the sea about sun-rise. It was fifteen stadia from Absarum [y]. Now there is no river of any size in this part of the coast but the *Tchorok*, or river of *Batoun*, which flows from the south, having its source in the mountains of *Baibont* and *Sunnur*, not far to the west of *Erzeroum*. This is evidently therefore the Acampsis of Arrian ; but other geographers have named the same river Apsarus, probably from the town situated near its mouth. Thus Scylax seems to identify the Apsarus and Acampsis, as he only

Apsarus portus.

Absarus, qui et Acampsis fluvius.

[y] Arrian nowhere speaks of Apsarus as a river, but as a military station ; this has not been sufficiently attended to by Mannert, and other geographers.

names the former.   He mentions besides the Daraa-
non and Arion, which no other geographer recognises. (Perp. p. 32.)   Pliny says the Absarus flowed
from mount Paryadres, and separated the greater
from the lesser Armenia. (VI. 9.)   Ptolemy, who
writes the name Apsorrus, says also that it rose in
the Armenian mountains, and was formed by the
junction of two principal streams which he names
Glaucus   Glaucus and Lycus. (p. 125.)   Of these the Glau-
fluvius.
cus appears to come from the south-west, and is the
real *Tchoroksou*.   Fontanier says it has two distinct sources, one rising in mount *Agh-Dagh*, the
other more to the west : they meet about two leagues
below *Baibout*, and fall into the Euxine near *Batouni*.   But there is another main branch of the
·*Tchoroksou*, which rises in the mountains to the
north of *Erzeroum*, and joins the former near *Ar-
tavani*; it is called *Gorgoro* in modern maps, and
Lycus flu- answers to the Lycus of Ptolemy.   Procopius, speak-
vius.
ing of the same river, says it was called Acampsis
Boas flu-   near its mouth, but Boas in the upper part of its
vius.
course. (Bell. Got. IV. 2. Cf. Pers. II. 17.)   It appears therefore from all that has been said, that
the Acampsis of Arrian, and the Absarus of other
writers, are the same river, namely, the *Tchoroksou*
of modern geography[z].   It should be observed also
that the latter name of the two is more generally
used, and better attested.   Before we quit this extremity of Pontus, it may be proper to say a few
words respecting Ptolemy's account of it.   This

[z] D'Anville, in his map of
Asia Minor, has confounded the
Acampsis and Bathys, a stream
which flowed to the north of
Batouni, and has made the Ap-
sarus a distinct river from the
Acampsis.

geographer places in succession on this coast after Trapezus, the river Ophius, the port Rhizus, the promontory Athenæ, Chordyle, a place called Mar- Marthyla. thyla, the river Arcadis, (the Arcabis of Arrian,) a town named Xyline, and the rivers Cissus and Apsorrus. Now with respect to the former of these rivers it may be observed, that its name corresponds with that of the Cissii, a people to whom Ptolemy Cissii. assigns this part of the coast. The Table Itinerary names also Cissa as a station on this line of coast, Cissa. and I am inclined to think that this people are the same as the Zygi of Strabo, (XI. p. 492.) and Dionysius Perieg. (v. 687.) and Pliny. (VI. 7.) Arrian, it should be remarked, calls them Zichi, and certainly places them north of the Phasis; (Per. p. 19.) but continual changes seem to have taken place in the situation of these small tribes, for we find the Heniochi, who were also near the Mœotis at one Heniochi time, and the Machelones, taking the places of the Machelones gens. Bechires and Ecechiries; (Anonym. Peripl. p. 15.) lones gens. and most probably a portion of the Zygi, or Zichi, Zygi gens. were shifted at the same time. It is certain that Strabo places a town called Zygopolis on this coast, Zygopolis. (XII. p. 548.) and the Zagatis, or Zygatis, of the Anonymous Periplus may be referred to the same people. (Cf. Steph. Byz. v. Ζυγοί.) Another people who are noticed in this part of Pontus, but rather more inland and among the mountains, are the Cer- Cercetæ cetæ, (Κερκεταὶ,) who are placed by Strabo in this Apaïtæ. direction, and also with the Zygi and Heniochi near Sindice and the Palus Mœotis; the Armenian Cercetæ had in his time exchanged their name for that of Apaïtæ, but there seems to be some trace of the ancient appellation in Xenophon, who calls them

U 4

Cœti, (Κοῖτοι.) He does not mention them in the course of his narrative, but at the end of the work, where he sums up the different nations they had met with in the whole of the retreat; he there names the Cœti as an independent people, together with the Macrones, Mosynœci, and Tibareni; but as the Scythini, who are named in the narrative more than once, do not appear in this summary, perhaps the Cœti are no others than this people, who are also, I think, the Cercetæ of Strabo. The Scythini of Xenophon I certainly think are connected with the mountain called Scydisces by Strabo, and Scotius by Appian, (Mithr. c. 100.) as we know besides that they were contiguous to the Macrones. The position of this people is of consider-
.able importance with respect to the geography of the Anabasis, as it will enable us to fix the point where the ten thousand entered Pontus from Armenia, and, generally speaking, the line of march which brought them from the river called Harpasus by Xenophon to Trapezus and the sea. According to the historian, it seems that the Harpasus was a river of Armenia, apparently separating the country of the Armenian Chalybes from that of the Scythini, and four plethra in width, which shews that it was a considerable stream. Now there is no river in Armenia of this size but the Araxes, and one of its branches called *Harpasou*, which in all probability is the Harpasus of Xenophon[a]. At the same time, in order to bring the Greeks to the *Harpasou*, which flows through the district of *Kars*, we must suppose with Rennell that they wandered for several

[a] See Rennell's Illustration of the Retreat of the Ten Thousand, p. 225.

days without a guide, and were obliged to retrace
their steps when they came to that river, of which
circumstance, it must be confessed, there is no apparent indication in the Anabasis [b]. From the Harpasus they proceeded through the country of the
Scythini, which appears to have consisted of plains,
for four days, and having rested three days in some
villages, they marched on again for four days, till
they came to a large, opulent, and populous town
called Gymnias. The governor of this place on
their approach sent a person to the Greeks offering
them a guide who should conduct them, on pain of
forfeiting his life, in five days to a place whence they
should see the sea. The position of this town is
very uncertain : Rennell places it at *Coumbase,* or
Kumakie, on the northern bank of the Araxes [c],
about ninety-one geographical miles from the *Harpasou,* and 110 from Trebisond [d]. A more recent
writer is inclined to suppose Gymnias may be *Ip-
sera* on the *Tchorok* [e], but it is not easy to see how
the Greeks could get there ; and besides, that town
is so much nearer the sea, that it would not require
five days to bring them in sight of it.

However, the situation of this place is not of so
much importance, perhaps, as that of the Scythini,
who certainly were contiguous to the Macrones, whose
position is well ascertained. They were divided
from the Macrones by a river, which from the map
could hardly be any other than the western branch
of the Apsarus, or *Tchorok,* which flows near the

[b] Illustrations of the Retreat
of the Ten Thousand, p. 224.

[c] In Lapie's map of the
Turkish empire *Coumbase* stands
on the southern shore of the

Araxes.

[d] P. 236.

[e] An Essay on the Geography of the Anabasis, p. 309.

town of *Baibout*. Appian, in the history of the Mithridatic war, (c. 101.) speaks of a part of Armenia situated on the borders of Pontus, and near the sources of the Euphrates : he calls it Chotene, a name which bears some analogy to that of the Scythini, or Cœti, of Xenophon. Chotene, besides, was contiguous to Iberia and the river Apsarus ; all which circumstances concur in fixing the march of the ten thousand in the line of *Erzeroum* and *Baibout*. It was before, however, they arrived on the borders of the Macrones that they beheld the sea. (Anab. IV. 7.) The Sacred Mountain, or Thekes, could not therefore be *Tekeh* near *Gumiskend*, as major Rennell supposes [f] ; but it must have been situated between *Erzeroum* and *Baibout*, where the road crosses some of the highest table land in Asia. On crossing the river of *Baibout* the Greeks would enter the territory of the Macrones, which they traversed in three days, till they came to another high range occupied by the Colchi. These were no doubt the Sanni of Strabo and Pliny, who came afterwards to be identified with the Macrones, and to absorb that name within their own. Having driven the Colchians from the heights, and passed through the mountainous defiles, the Greeks descended, and after resting some time in the villages of the enemy, where they found the honey which had so singular an effect upon them, they marched for two days more, and reached Trapezus. The only obstacle to the

[f] " Tekes, or the Sacred " Mountain, is the great chain " lying between *Erzeroum* and " *Trebisond*. Here is a summit, with a castle called *Teke*, " one day's journey from *Gu-* " *miskend*, the noted silver " mine." Major Rennell estimates the distance from Teke to the sea to be about thirty English miles.

line of march here marked out for the Greek army, is the distance at which they must have been from the sea at the point where I have supposed them to come in sight of it, being not less than fifty miles in a straight line. But there is no impossibility in their seeing the sea from that, or a still greater distance, if they had attained to a sufficient elevation, and their view was not intercepted by other mountains. This question, in fact, can only be decided by actual observation [g]; but it should be borne in mind that, according to Xenophon's account, the Greeks were certainly not less than six days' march from the sea when they beheld it. I am not aware of any other route by which they could have come down upon Trapezus, except the one I have traced. It is that which nature seems to have pointed out from the earliest time for establishing a communication between Pontus and Armenia; and it is clearly laid down in the Table Itinerary as leading from Trapezus into the latter country. The first station on leaving Trapezus was Magnana, distant twenty miles from that city. It is probably the site called *Machka* by modern travellers [h]. The next stage, according to the Itinerary, was Gihenenica, ten miles from Magnana. The analogy of names points out the site of *Ghemiskhana* as likely to answer to this second station. It would appear, however, from Kin-

[g] The view from the summit of mount *Cop Dagh*, the ancient Sydisces, according to Kinneir, is most magnificent; and though he does not state that he beheld the sea from thence, I see no reason why it might not be visible on a clear day. The guides said they could discern mount Ararat from thence. Mr. Kinneir observes, that he had been ascending all the way from Trebisond to this mountain, p. 357.

[h] Fontanier, Voyages en Orient, p. 37.

neir's account, to be more than thirty miles from
Trebisond [i]. Fontanier, however, reckons only ten
leagues [k]. Bylæ, which next follows in the Table
at a distance of eighteen miles, has been thought by
some travellers to be *Bayboot*, but the distance of
that town from Trebisond seems to allow this. I
should imagine Bylæ, which ought perhaps to be
written Pylæ, is the *Boos Kela* of Kinneir [l]. Fri-
gidarium, six miles further, would be the station on
the summit of the mountains beyond, and Patara,
which is eight miles beyond it, is probably *Bala-
kare* [m]. Medocia, twelve miles further, must be
looked for near *Bayboot*. It is not necessary to follow this Itinerary further; enough has been traced
to shew its agreement with the present route from
Trebisond to *Erzeroum*, which I conceive also to
have been that of the Ten Thousand.

Having now sufficiently surveyed the coast of
Pontus, and likewise discussed the ancient geography of the eastern extremity of that province in
connexion with the Anabasis, we must once more
return to the river Halys, for the purpose of ex-
ploring those districts in the interior of Pontus
situated along that river and the upper valleys of
the Iris, Lycus, and Thermodon. We have already
said that Strabo gave the name of Gazelonitis, or
Gadilonitis, to the district on the right bank of the
Halys, at no great distance from the sea. It de-

Gazelon
sive Gadi-
lon.

rived its name apparently from Gazelon, or Gadilon, the principal town, but noticed only by Strabo

---

[i] Fontanier, Voyages en
Orient, p. 348.
[k] Ibid. p. 39.
[l] The village of *Booskela*

stands at the foot of a stupen-
dous rock, crowned by an ancient castle, p. 350, 351.
[m] P. 351.

(XII. p. 547.) and Pliny. (VI. 2.) It was probably situated in the vicinity of *Vizir-Kupri*, not far from the Halys, and between *Bafra* and *Osmanjik*. Contiguous to Gazelonitis, on the south-east, was Pha-zemonitis, a district so called from Phazemon, a small town, in the vicinity of which Pompey founded a colony named Neapolis. Hence the same district appears to have been sometimes termed Neapolitis [n]. (Strab. XII. p. 560.) Steph. Byz., who, copies Strabo, writes the name Phamizon. (v. Φαμιζῶν.) Phazemon is generally supposed to correspond in situation with the modern town of *Mazifun*. On the north-eastern side of Phazemonitis apparently, and towards the Iris, was an extensive lake named Stiphane : it abounded in fish, and its shores were surrounded by excellent pastures [o]. Above this lake was a hill, with a deserted and ruinous fortress, named Cizari. This had once been a royal residence. (Strab. XII. p. 560.) Towards the south-west, and in the direction of Amasia, were some warm medicinal springs, accounted very efficacious in the cure of various disorders. Mr. Kinneir ob-

Marginal notes: Phazemonitis. Phazemon. Neapolis. Stiphane palus. Cizari castellum. Thermæ Phazemonitarum.

---

[n] The text of Strabo is here supposed to be corrupt. The reader may consult an elaborate note on the passage in the French translation of that author, vol. IV. p. ii. p. 71. See also Mannert, tom. VI. p. ii. p. 465.

[o] No mention is made of this great lake by modern travellers, nor is there any appearance of it in the maps. Could this be the same which is spoken of in the Life of Gregory Thaumaturgus, and which is said to have been dried up at his prayer, p. 277 : ἤπειρον ἐποίησε, τῷ ὄρθρῳ τὴν λιμνὴν ξηράν τε καὶ ἄνικμον. ὡς μηδὲ ἐν τοῖς κοίλοις ἔχειν τί τοῦ ὕδατος λείψανον, τὴν πρὸ τῆς εὐχῆς πελαγίζουσαν. It is remarkable, that the last word in the quotation agrees so nearly with the expression in Strabo, λίμνη πελαγία τὸ μέγεθος. The biographer of Gregory says again, p. 279, καὶ πᾶς ἡ ἀντὶ θαλάσσης οὖσα τῷ τόπῳ τὸ πρότερον, νῦν πρὸς καρπῶν ἄνεισι φοράν.

serves, that on the road from *Vizir Kupri* to *Marziwan* there is a place called *Gouzu*, famous for its mineral baths. The springs are very abundant, and there are also to be seen some ancient ruins of considerable magnificence [p]. Here was also a fort

Sagylium castellum.

named Sagylium, placed on a lofty conical hill. This castle, being a place of great strength and well provided with water, had been of great service to the kings of Pontus; but Pompey rendered it useless by filling up the wells with great stones. Strabo reports, that in consequence of this, Arsaces, a rebel chief, who was guardian of the sons of Pharnaces, and had retired to this fortress, was forced to surrender to Polemon, king of Pontus, and Lycomedes, priest of Comana, who besieged him [p]. (Strab. XII. p. 560.) Contiguous to Phazemonitis to the east, was the city and territory of Amasia, the birthplace of Strabo; a circumstance which accounts for his dwelling on its topography with so much feeling and evident graphic accuracy of detail.

Amasia.

" My native town," says the geographer, (XII. p. 560.) " is situated in a deep and large valley, " through which flows the river Iris. It has been " provided in a surprising manner, by art and

---

[p] Travels, p. 298.

[p] The passage in Strabo, as it stands at present, is evidently corrupt. 'Ενταῦθα δὲ ἑάλω, καὶ διεφθάρη ὑπὸ τῶν Φαρνάκου τοῦ βασιλέως παιδων 'Αρσάκης (var. lect. 'Αρσάνης) βασιλεύων (MSS. δυναστεύων) καὶ νεωτερίζων, ἐπιτρέψαντος οὐδενὸς τῶν ἡγεμόνων. ἑάλω δὲ οὐ βίᾳ τοῦ ἐρύματος ληφθέντος ὑπὸ Πολέμωνος, καὶ Λυκομήδους βασιλέων ἀμφοῖν ἀλλὰ λιμῷ. Here it is said that this Arsaces, or Arsanes,

was taken and destroyed by the sons of king Pharnaces; and from the sequel it follows that Polemo and Lycomedes were those princes, which is absurdly false. It is evident that we ought to read, 'Ενταῦθα δὲ ἑάλω καὶ διεφθάρη, ἐπὶ τῶν Φαρνάκου τοῦ βασιλέως παιδων 'Αρσάκης δυναστεύων. " Arsaces, who was at " the head of affairs in behalf, " or as guardian of the sons of " Pharnaces."

" nature, for answering the purpose both of a city
" and fortress. For there is a lofty and perpendicu-
" lar rock which overhangs the river, having on
" one side a wall built close to the bank of the
" river where the town has been built; while on
" the other, it runs up on either hand to the summits
" of the hill. These are two, connected with each
" other, and excellently provided with towers. With-
" in this peribolus are the royal residence, and the
" tombs of the kings. But the heights have on each
" side a very narrow neck of land, about five or six
" stadia in height, as you ascend from the river and
" the suburbs. From this ridge to the summits,
" there remains another sharp ascent, about a sta-
" dium in length, which it would be impossible to
" force. In this direction, too, water is carried up,
" by means of two channels cut in the rock, one
" towards the river, the other towards the ridge.
" Two bridges are thrown over the river; the one
" from the town to the suburb, the other from the
" suburb to the outer country: for the mountain
" which overhangs the rock, terminates at the point
" where this bridge is placed." (XII. p. 561.) Modern travellers have borne witness to the accuracy
of this description, though time has produced some
change in the position of the town. Busbequius,
who visited Amasia· in the sixteenth century, found
it situated on both banks of the river, and rising in
the form of an amphitheatre on either side. Tavernier says, it is placed on the hollow slope of a mountain, and that on the south the view extends over a
fine plain. Towards the west he observed the ruins
of the citadel, which stood on an elevated summit.
The same traveller noticed also some remains of the

conduits mentioned by Strabo[r]. That geographer tells us nothing of the origin and history of his native city : we collect only from his account, that it was a place of considerable importance and antiquity, from the mention of the king's palace and the royal tombs. The sovereigns here alluded to, were most probably some of the early kings of Pontus. When Strabo wrote, Amasia formed part of the Roman province ; (XII. p. 561.) and we learn from its coins that it bore the title of Metropolis of Pontus[s]. (Cf. Plin. VI. 3. Ptol. p. 125. Steph. Byz. v. Ἀμάσεια. Herocl. p. 701. Procop. Hist. Arc. c. 18.) Some of its public buildings were restored by Justinian. (Procop. Æd. III. 7. Cf. Nicet. Ann. p. 331. Leo Diacon. VI. 3. p. 59.) *Amazieh*, as it is now called by the Turks, preserves still its ancient site, and many vestiges of its former state. A recent traveller reports, that there are considerable portions of the walls leading up to the citadel remaining. In the upper town are to be seen the ruins of a temple, a fountain, and the aqueducts mentioned by Strabo ; these remains are in a good state of preservation, and it is supposed that excavations would be attended with success. Outside the town are some curious caverns, which the traveller in question supposes may have been the royal tombs ; but Strabo positively states that they were within the walls. The country about *Amasieh* is beautiful, and the valley of the *Tokatlou* highly picturesque, and richly cultivated[t].

---

[r] Voyages, I. c. i. p. 9.

[s] These coins are of the reigns of Trajan, Hadrian, and Antoninus ; the epigraph is AMACIAC ΜΗΤΡΟΠΟΛΕΩC or ΠΡΩTHC ΠΟΝΤΟΥ. Sestini, p. 58.

[t] Fontanier, Voyages en Orient, ch. 17. p. 233.

The territory of Amasia, as Strabo informs us, was extensive and very productive; though it had suffered greatly from the wars waged by Mithridates against the Romans, many towns being destroyed, and several tracts of land depopulated. Towards the north, the valley of the Iris widened to an extensive plain named Chiliocomon, and contiguous to this were the two fertile districts, Diacopene and Pimolisene, which reached to the Halys. (XII. p. 561.) The valley of the Iris is called Gazacena by Pliny, (VI. 3.) and Strabo himself incidentally recognises the appellation. (XII. p. 553.) Towards the south-east, and still keeping on the right bank of the Halys, Amasia included within its jurisdiction the cantons of Babanomus[t] and Ximene. The latter contained some salt mines, from which the Halys was supposed to derive its name. (Strab. XII. p. 561.)

Chiliocomon campus.
Diacopene regio.
Pimolisene regio.
Gazacena regio.

Babanomus regio.
Ximene regio.

The Iris, according to the same geographer, rose in the mountains of Pontus, passed the town of Comana, and watered the fertile plains of Daximonitis from east to west. On reaching Gazioura, it turned towards the north, and then again to the east; after which, having received the Scylax, and several other rivers, it flowed under the walls of Amasia; and being then joined by the Lycus in the plains of Phanarœa, it traversed the rich lands of Themiscyra, and finally reached the Euxine. The Scylax seems to be the river of *Gulkiras*, which joins the *Tokatlou*, or Iris, about ten miles above Amasia, coming from the south-west. Gazioura was once a place of note, and a royal residence, but it was de-

Scylax fluvius.

Gazioura.

t This is probably the same district which Strabo elsewhere calls Bamonitis. XII. p. 553.

serted when Strabo wrote his description of the country. (loc. cit.) It is also noticed by Dio Cassius, as a place where Mithridates took up a position to oppose the Roman general Triarius. (XXXV. p. 5. Cf. Plin. VI.3.) Gaziura is said to retain the name of *Azurnis*[u].

Daximoni- Daximonitis must be sought for in the upper valley
tis regio. of the Iris, near the modern town of *Tokat.* The
Zela. town of Zela and its territory, was situated on the left bank of the Iris, towards the frontier of Galatia: (Strab. XII. p. 561.) it appears to have been a place of great antiquity, since Strabo reports that it was erected on the mound of Semiramis. It was at first apparently a spot consecrated to the worship of the goddess Anaïtis, a deity highly revered by the Persians, Armenians, and Cappadocians. (XII. p. 559.) The same writer elsewhere relates, that the temple of Zela had been raised by the Persians in commemoration of a signal victory obtained by their arms over the Sacæ, who had penetrated into Pontus and Cappadocia. They raised a mound on a rocky foundation, and having surrounded it with walls, erected two temples, one to the goddess Anaïtis, the other to the Persian deities Omanus and Anandates : a festival, named Sacæa, was likewise instituted to commemorate the same event. The priest of the temple was considered as sovereign of the district of Zela ; he was possessed of great wealth, and was surrounded with much pomp and state. (XI. p. 511, 512. XII. p. 559.) Zela remained however a small town, till Pompey, after the defeat of Mithridates, increased its population and extent, and raised it to the rank of a city. (XII. p. 560.)

[u] Sestini, p. 69, who ascribes to it some scarce coins with the epigraph ΓΑΖΙΟΥΡΩΝ.

Zela is further rendered remarkable in history, by a
victory obtained over the Roman forces under Triarius, by Mithridates, and still more by the defeat and
discomfiture of Pharnaces, son of the latter, which
Cæsar expressed in the laconic sentence—" Veni,
" Vidi, Vici." (Plin. VI. 3. Appian. Mithr. c. 89.
Plut. Cæs. p. 731. Hist. Bell. Alex. c. 72. Dio Cass.
XLII. p. 207.) This town is noticed also by Ptolemy, (p. 125.) Hierocles, (p. 701.) and Steph. Byz.
(v. Ζῆλα.) We learn from the Itineraries, that Zela
stood on the road leading from Tavium, in Galatia,
to Neocæsarea. The name of *Zeleh* sufficiently
marks the site about thirty miles to the south-west
of *Tokat*.

The town of Comana, (surnamed Pontica, to dis- Comana
tinguish it from a Cappadocian city of the same Pontica.
name,) was apparently situated to the north-east of
Zela, and not far from the source of the Iris. (Strab.
XII. p. 547.) It was celebrated for the worship of
the goddess Ma, supposed to answer to the Bellona
of the Greeks, and likewise revered with equal honours in the Cappadocian town. The priesthood
attached to the temple was an office of the highest
emolument and dignity, and was sought after by
kings and princes. Strabo mentions that it had been
conferred on Dorylaus, one of his maternal ancestors, by Mithridates Eupator; afterwards Pompey
bestowed it on Archelaus, and added to the sacred
territory a district of sixty stadia. Archelaus was
succeeded by Lycomedes, but he having been deposed, the priesthood was bestowed on Cleon, the
Olympian robber, who founded Juliopolis, (XII.
p. 575.) but he died soon after his appointment, and
Augustus then conferred it on Dyteutus, son of

Adiatorix, a Galatian chief, whom he had put to death for having zealously espoused the cause of Antony. Dyteutus, his eldest son, was to have been executed with him, but he was saved by the generous devotion of his younger brother, who perished in his stead. Augustus, on learning too late this heroic trait, restored Dyteutus to his favour, and gave him the priesthood of Comana. This city was large and populous, and kept up a considerable traffick with Armenia. The festivals of Bellona, which were held twice a year, drew thither an immense concourse from the surrounding countries and towns, as well as more distant parts. There were no less than 6000 slaves attached to the service of the temple, and most of these were courtesans. Hence it was remarked that the citizens were generally addicted to pleasure, and the town itself was styled by some, the little Corinth. The chief produce of the country was wine. (Strab. XII. p. 559. Cf. Appian. Mithr. c. 82. Hist. Bell. Alex. c. 34, 35.) When the Romans, under Lucullus, invaded Pontus, a report was spread, probably by Mithridates, that they were come for the express purpose of plundering the shrine of Comana. (Cic. Leg. Manil. §. 9.) In Pliny's time the town appears to have fallen into decay, the oracle alone subsisted; since he says, " Comana nunc Manteium." (VI. 3. Ptol. p. 125.) The Table Itinerary places Comana of Pontus on a road leading from Tavium in Galatia, and which appears to be partly the same as that from Tavium to Zela, but the names of some stations are omitted, and others are very corrupt, so that it is difficult to decide any thing on this point. We know, however, from Strabo, that Comana was seated in the upper valley of the Iris, and some remains which exist not far from *Tokat*, under the name of *Komanak*, sufficiently point out the ancient site[x].

The Lycus, which has been already mentioned as joining the Iris below Amasia, is a considerable river, now called *Carahissar*. It rises on the eastern border of Pontus, in the high mountains to the south of *Ghemizkhan*, which belong to the chain of Paryadres and Scydisces. Pliny informs us that the Lycus separated Pontus from Armenia Minor, near the town of Neocæsarea, now *Niksar*. Below that town it traversed the rich and fertile district of Phanarœa, accounted the most productive of Pontus, and joined the Iris in the plains between Amasia and Themiscyra. Precisely at the confluence of these two rivers, Mithridates had founded a town named Eupatoria, which was not yet completed, when he was forced to fly from Pontus by the Roman armies. Pompey, after the conquest of the country, completed the town, added to its territory, and called it after himself, Magnopolis. (Strab. XII. p. 556.) Appian says, Eupatoria was near Amisus, and that it was besieged by Lucullus; (Mithr. c. 78.) he also speaks of its second foundation by Pompey, under the name of Magnopolis. (c. 115.) Strabo has elsewhere bestowed on this town the appellation of Megalopolis, (XII. p. 560.) and Mannert has been led by that circumstance, to suppose these were two distinct places[y]; but this is very improbable, when we consider that the geographer places them together

Lycus fluvius.

Eupatoria postea Magnopolis.

---

[x] There are some few autonomous and imperial coins belonging to Comana. The legend is KOMANΩN and KOMA-NEΩN. Sestini, p. 59.

[y] Geogr. tom. VI. p. ii. p. 480.

in the vicinity of Zela and Comana, and assigns both to Pythodoris, widow of Polemon, and queen of Pontus. (XII. p. 559, 560. Cf. Plin. VI. 3.) The vestiges of Magnopolis are to be seen near *Tchenikeh*, a little below the junction of the Iris and Lycus[z].

Pythodoris, besides the above-mentioned towns Phanarœa and territories, possessed the whole of Phanarœa, which Strabo describes as a broad and extensive valley, watered by the Iris and Lycus, and confined between the chain of Paryadres to the east, and mounts Lithrus and Ophlimus to the west. The soil was the best in Pontus, and yielded excellent wine and oil, and other produce in abundance. (XII. p. 556.) This tract of country now takes its name from the modern town of *Niksar*. The mountains Lithrus and Ophlimus are unknown to other geographers. I should imagine, from Strabo's account, that they must be sought for on the right bank of the Iris, in the neighbourhood of *Tokat*. The same writer places, apparently in the Phanarœa, 150 stadia to the south of Magnopolis, and at the foot of Paryadres, the town of Cabira, which had once been the favourite residence of Mithridates. His palace, and park, and preserves were still in existence when Strabo wrote, as well as a water-mill, ($\dot{v}\delta\rho\alpha\lambda\acute{\epsilon}\tau\eta\varsigma$,) erected by him, probably for the use of the mines which were in this vicinity. (XII. p. 556.) It was here that Mithridates posted himself with his army in the campaign which followed the disastrous retreat from Cyzicus, in order that he might afford succours to the neighbouring towns of Amisus and

Marginal notes: Phanarœa regio. Lithrus et Ophlimus montes. Cabira.

---

[z] Note of Monsieur Gosselin. French Strabo, tom. IV. p. ii. p. 69.

Eupatoria, besieged by Lucullus. (Appian. Mithr. c. 78.) On his second defeat, however, it fell into the hands of that general, with several other places. (Plut. Lucull. p. 502. Eutrop. VI. 7.) Pompey afterwards enlarged the place, and changed its name to Diopolis. Pythodoris subsequently made further improvements in this town, and having finally fixed her residence there, bestowed on it the appellation of Sebaste. (Strab. loc. cit.) Sebaste, or Sebastia, is mentioned also by Pliny and the Itineraries, but there is also a Sebastopolis in this part of Asia Minor, which causes some difficulty in regard to the site of Cabira. The Antonine Itinerary places both on a route leading from Tavium, through Pontus, into Armenia; the stations are from Tavium to

	M. P.
Mogaron	XXX.
Doranon	XXIIII.
Sebastopolis	XL.
Virisa	XXIIII.
Phiarasi	XII.
Sebastia	XXXVI.

from which it appears that Sebastia was seventy-two Roman miles from Sebastopolis. Pliny, however, in his usual hurried manner, collocates them in the district of Colopene : " In Colopena vero Sebastiam " et Sebastopolim; hæc parva, sed paria supra dictis." (VII. 3.) The Table Itinerary places Sebastia on a route leading from Cæsarea in Cappadocia, into Armenia; and there can be little doubt that the direction of this road, leading up the Halys to *Siwas,* points out, together with the strong analogy of the name, that site as the representative of Sebastia. But was this Sebastia the Cabira of Mithridates, and the Se-

baste of Pythodoris? I conceive not. For in the
first place, *Siwas* is at least 120 miles from the site
of Magnopolis, whereas, according to Strabo, Cabira
was only 150 stadia from that town. Nor, in the
second place, would so distant a place have answered
Mithridates' purpose of relieving the towns near the
coast, besieged by Lucullus. Again, Sebastia is
spoken of in the Martyrologium as a town of Armenia, which agrees rather with the position of
Siwas, than that which, from the Itineraries, ought
to belong to Sebastopolis; that town, according to
these documents, being seventy miles nearer Tavium. Ptolemy also places Sebastopolis to the south-
west of Neocæsarea, which is known to be *Niksar*,
and near the Iris. Sebastopolis, and not Sebastia, or
Siwas, was therefore the successor of Cabira, and
the capital of Pythodoris, who would of course fix
her residence in the Phanaroea, the best part of her
principality, and also the most central. Gregory of
Nyssa, in his Life of Saint Macrina, quoted by Wesseling, (Itin. Anton. p. 205.) speaks of Sebastopolis
as a small town of Pontus; and this was already the
case in Pliny's time, Neocæsarea having doubtless
attracted many of the neighbouring inhabitants to
resort thither under the auspices of the Roman
emperor, who had taken the new city under his
protection. But it is impossible to admit, with Mannert[z], that Cabira, or Sebaste, and Neocæsarea, are
one and the same town, since Pliny and the Itineraries, together with other authorities, forbid our
entertaining such a supposition. It appears then,
that we should look for the ruins of Cabira, or Sebastopolis, on the right bank of the Lycus, and between

[z] Geogr. tom. VI. p. ii. p. 473.

Niksar and *Tchenikeh,* or Magnopolis. Some antiquaries place it at *Turkal,* to the north of *Tokat,*
but[a] this site is on the Iris, a circumstance which
would not have been omitted by Strabo, if it had belonged to the topography of Cabira, or the river[b].

At a distance of somewhat less than 200 stadia
from Cabira, stood once the fortress of Cænoncho- Cænonchorion, one of the strongest holds of Mithridates. It rion.
had been erected, as Strabo reports, on a precipitous
rock, which rose to a very great elevation ; a situation which rendered it impregnable. A plentiful
source gushed out from the rock near the summit,
and a river flowed in a deep valley at the foot of
the fortress. The surrounding country was thickly
covered with wood, and so hilly and barren, that,
from want of subsistence, no army could encamp
nearer than 120 stadia. When Pompey took possession of this castle, after the defeat and flight of
Mithridates, he found there all the most precious
jewels and other articles belonging to that monarch,
together with his secret correspondence and papers.
Pompey caused all these valuable curiosities to be
removed to Rome, and deposited them after his
triumph in the Capitol. (Strab. XII. p. 556. Plut.
Pomp. §. 36, 37.) Appian does not speak of Cænonchorion, but says Mithridates kept his most precious
effects in the town of Talauri, where Pompey found
them[c]. The historian enumerates in particular

a Marginal note of the edit.
of the French Strabo, tom. IV.
p. ii. p. 61.

b There are some few autonomous coins of Cabira, with
the epigraph KABHPΩN. Sestini, p. 59 ; and some also of Sebastopolis struck under Antoni-

nus Pius, ΣΕΒΑΣΤΟΠΟΛΙΤΩΝ.
Sestini, p. 60.

c As no historian or geographer speaks of this place, I
should imagine the name is
corrupt, and for ἐν Ταλαύροις, I
would propose reading ἐν Γαζιού-
ροις or ἐν Καβείροις.

" 2000 goblets of onyx stone, set in gold; many
" cups also, and wine-coolers, chalices, couches, and
" richly ornamented seats ; likewise bridles and
" trappings ; all equally adorned with jewels and
" goldwork. Some of these costly articles had be-
" longed to Darius Hystaspes, others had come from
" the court of the Ptolemies, having been presented
" to the people of Cos by Cleopatra, and by them to
" Mithridates. But the greater number had been
" collected by that monarch, who was fond of what
" was ornamental and splendid." (Mithr. c. 115.)

Cænonchorion must be sought for in the mountainous district, to the north of *Niksar*, and on the
right bank of the Lycus. The whole of this country, as we have already learned from Strabo, belonged in his time to Pythodoris. She held besides

Templum Men Pharnacis. the temple of Men Pharnaces, who was supposed to
be the deity of the moon, and was worshipped by
the Phrygians, Pisidians, and Albanians[d]. This
edifice was held in the greatest veneration by the
kings of Pontus, and the most solemn oath which
they pronounced was, " By the Fortune of the King
" and Men Pharnaces !" It was situated in or near

Ameria. a place named Ameria ; Strabo styles it κωμόπολιν,
or a village which might almost be called a town ;
and from the number of dependents attached to the
temple, and the ample revenues annexed to the pon-
tifical office, it must have had a considerable population ; so that it is somewhat surprising that no
mention is made of this place in any other writer.

[d] The worship of the god Men appears to have its principal seat in Asia Minor; but it was doubtless introduced by
the Phœnicians, or Assyrians. Isaiah seems to allude to it under
the name of Meni. LXV. 11. Cf. Biel. Nov. Thes. Phil. tom.
III. p. 479.

(XII. p. 557.) If however, as I am inclined to think, Ameria is to be identified with Neocæsarea, which must have been in the immediate vicinity, this silence of all subsequent writers to Strabo respecting the former, is readily accounted for. Now we have nowhere any positive information of the foundation of Neocæsarea; but we are pretty certain on the one hand, that it did not exist in Strabo's time, or he would have noticed it; and on the other, we know that it existed less than a century after, since it is named by Pliny. But the coins of Neocæsarea enable us to fix the æra of its foundation with still greater precision. The earliest we have, bear the effigy of Tiberius, and were doubtless struck in his reign. It is therefore highly probable, that Neocæsarea was founded, or received a new name and existence in the time of that emperor, and after Strabo had composed his work[e]. Its rise and progress must have been very rapid, since in the time of Gregory Thaumaturgus, who was a native of the place, it is stated to have been the most considerable town of Pontus[f], and he flourished in the middle of the third century. (Greg. Neoc. Vit. p. 577. Cf. Ammian. Marc. XXVII.) It appears also from the Life of the same saint, that Neocæsarea was the principal seat of pagan idolatry and superstitions, which affords another presumption that it had risen on the foundation of Ameria and the worship of Men Pharnaces. We know from Pliny that

[margin: Neocæsarea.]

[e] Sestini mentions one earlier coin, which he calls " au- " tonomus unicus." Epigraphe ΝΕΟΚΑΙΣΑΡΕΙΑΣ. But there is a great reason for doubting its authenticity; for how could a town be autonomous in the time of the Cæsars?

[f] On the coins of Valerian we find it styled the metropolis of the province. Sest. p. 60.

Neocæsarea was situated near the Lycus, and frequent mention of that river is made in the Life of Gregory. The Itineraries and ecclesiastical writers also often name the town. From Steph. Byz., who quotes Phlegon Trallianus, it would seem that it was once called by the name of Hadrianopolis. (v. Νεοκαισάρεια.) *Niksar*, the modern representative of Neocæsarea, is a town of some size, and the capital of a district of the same name in the pashalick of *Siwas*, or *Roum*.

Beyond Neocæsarea, the upper valley of the Lycus constituted a separate district from Phanarœa, Colopene. known to the ancients by the name of Colopene, or Couloupene. Strabo places this small canton in Pontus, but on the borders of Armenia Minor. (XII. p. 560.) Pliny likewise speaks of it as a portion of Pontus Cappadocius; and since he states that the Lycus, to the east of Neocæsarea, separated that province from Armenia Minor, it is plain that Colopene must have been situated on the right or northern bank of the river. On the other hand, by including in this district the towns of Sebastopolis and Sebastia, the latter of which is certainly *Siwas*, it would seem that he gives to it a much greater extent than Strabo contemplated. (Plin. VI. 3.) The name was probably derived from a place called Colope, or Couloupe, but not recorded by any geographer. Some vestige of this appellation, however, exists in that of *Koulei hissar*, which is at once the name of a small town on the right bank of the Lycus, and of the adjacent country.

Sebastia. The origin of Sebastia, which Pliny places in Camisene Colopene, is uncertain. Camisene, another district regio. Camisa. near it, we know took its name from Camisa, an

ancient fortress, according to Strabo, near which
were some salt mines; and the Itinerary of Antoninus informs us, that it was twenty-four miles beyond Sebastia, on the road to Nicopolis. Strabo
besides has elsewhere reported, that the Halys had
its source in the district of Camisene, on the borders
of Pontus and Cappadocia; (XII. p. 546.) and as
we know, from the report of modern travellers, that
the *Kizil-Ermak* rises some miles to the east of
Siwas, we can have no doubt as to the situation of
Camisa and its territory. With respect to Caranitis, Caranitis.
another small district of Pontus, Strabo says it had
belonged to Ateporix, a Galatian prince; but on his
death it devolved to the Roman empire, and was
kept under the jurisdiction of a separate governor
from the other petty principalities of Pontus. (XII.
p. 560.) Carana, the capital of this small government, is mentioned by no writer subsequent to
Strabo; I think it therefore extremely probable,
that it afterwards changed its name to Sebastia, the
latter being unknown to that geographer, but known
to Pliny. The latter however, it must be allowed,
speaks of Caranitis as a *præfectura* of Armenia Major, in which the Euphrates had its source; (V. 24.)
and this would carry us as far to the east as *Erzeroum;* but Strabo's statement allows us at the most
to include it within the boundaries of the Lesser
Armenia; and it is observable, that Sebastia is often
attributed to the latter province by the ecclesiastical
writers. The identity of Sebastia with the modern
Siwas is fully established by the resemblance of
names, and still more by the agreement of the latter
site with the description of Gregory of Nyssa. That
father states Sebastia to have been situated in the

valley of the Halys. A small river flowed through
the town, and fell into a neighbouring lake, which
communicated with the Halys. (Orat. I. in 40 Martyr. p. 501. Orat. II. p. 510. Cf. Basil. M. Epist.
VIII. Hierocl. Synecd. p. 703.) Under the Byzantine emperors, Sebastia is spoken of as a large and
flourishing town of Cappadocia. (Nicet. Ann. p. 76,
C. Cf. Duc. p. 31.) Steph. Byz. assigned it to Armenia. (v. Σεβαστή. Cf. Sozom. Hist. Eccl. IV. 24.
Theodor. Hist. Eccl. II. 24.) Other documents style
it the metropolitan see of Armenia Prima [g]. In the
Table Itinerary the name appears already corrupted
to that of Sevastia, and in Abulfeda it is actually
Siwas. (Tab. XVII. p. 303.) This town is still
large and populous, and the capital of an extensive
pashalick, to which it gives its name. A modern
traveller noticed there the remains of a citadel, but
which appeared to him to belong to the Byzantine
empire ; some fragments of columns, and several
coins, but no inscriptions. He adds, that it is entirely built in the plain ; from which circumstance
he justly doubts whether it can be the representative of Cabira. Some extensive ruins were reported
to exist about six leagues to the south of *Siwas*,
which he conceives might be referred to Sebaste ;
but the Itineraries will not allow us to admit this
hypothesis [h].

Between Sebastopolis and Sebastia the Antonine
Itinerary places two stations, Virisa and Phiarasi.
The former is supposed, with great probability, by
Wesseling to be Berissa, an episcopal see of Arme-

Berissa,
forsan quæ

[g] Geogr. Sacr. Car. S. Paul.
p. 255.
[h] Fontanier, Voyages en Orient, p. 179. This gentleman
constantly misquotes Xenophon
for Strabo. p. 149.

nia Prima, according to the Ecclesiastical Notices[i].
(Itin. Ant. p. 205. not.) We ought perhaps also to
identify it with the Boryza of Steph. Byz., (v. Bó-
ρυζα,) and Borissus, a small town of Cappadocia 2da,
mentioned by Philostorgius. (Hist. Eccl. IX. p. 529.)
This place, according to the above-mentioned Itinerary, was twenty-four miles from Sebastopolis. Phiarasi was thirty-six miles nearer Sebastia, or *Siwas*.
Wesseling, with equal judgment, traces this station
to the Phiara of Ptolemy. (p. 126.) The latter geo- Phiara.
grapher names several other obscure sites, of which
a few only can be made to agree with other authorities. In Pontus Galaticus he places Bænasa, Tebenda, Choloe, Piala, Pida, Sermuta. Tebenda, or
Tebenna, as Anna Comnena writes the name, is
stated to have been a town of Pontus, in the vicinity of Trapezus. (p. 364, B.) I imagine also, that
the name of this place is disguised in the Table Itinerary under that of Tomba, a station on the road
from Tavium to Comana, and sixteen miles from
the former. The same Itinerary exhibits the three
next towns named by Ptolemy, on the road from
Amasia to Neocæsarea, in the following order : Palalce, (Piala[k],) fifteen miles from Amasia ; Coloe, Piala.
twelve from Palalce ; Pida, (Pidis in the Table,)
ten from Coloe. Sermuta, or, as it should probably
be written, Seramusa, appears in the same Itinerary Seramusa.
on a road leading from Tavium to Neocæsarea by
Zela, fifty-four miles from the last-mentioned town,
and sixteen from Neocæsarea. There is, however,

---

[i] Geogr. Sacr. Car. S. Paul.
p. 256.

[k] Palalce is a corruption of
Pialasus, as Phiarasi of Phiara-

sus. The Cappadocian and Armenian names of places very
generally end in *sus*.

another Sermusa in the Table, between Tavium and Cæsarea in Cappadocia. Itonia, which Ptolemy places between Choloe and Piala, is probably the same town with the Ægonne, or Eugone, of the Table ; in which case we should correct the former by the Itinerary. But, *vice versa*, the station which the latter places on the same road from Tavium to Neocæsarea, by Zela, immediately after Ægonea, under the corrupt name of Pterami, must be restored by the help of the Alexandrine geographer, who writes it Pleumaris. In the interior of Pontus Polemoniacus, Ptolemy has a great many obscure names, of which the following seem confirmed by other authorities. (p. 126.) Gazalina is probably the Gazacena, or Gazelonitis, of Strabo. (XII. p. 553.) Carvanis should be referred to the Carana of the same geographer. (XII. p. 560.) Sarbanissa is known from its coins to have been once dependent on Sinope [1]. Danaë, or Danati, seems to have some affinity with the Daranon of Antonine. (Itin. p. 205.) Metorome, or Mesorome, answers probably to the Rogmon of the Table, on the road from Tavium to Neocæsarea, by Zela. Metadula, or Megaluda, I am inclined to refer to the Mesyla of the same Itinerary, on the road from Tavium to Comana Pontica. Sabalia seems to correspond with the station ad Stabulum, on the same route. Metalassus, or Megalossus, should perhaps be connected with Mogaron, a station in the Antonine Itinerary, on the road from Tavium to Sebastopolis, (p. 205.) and which Wesseling, with great probability, identifies with

Ægonea, vel Eugonea.

Pleumaris.

[1] On one side is the head of king Polemo ; on the reverse a figure of Fortune, with the legend ΣΑΡΒΑΝΙΣΣΕΩΝ ΤΩΝ ΣΙΝΩ. Sestini, p. 60.

Mogarissus, a village of Cappadocia, mentioned in the Life of St. Theodosius Abbas. (c. 1.) Eudiphus, Ablata, and Saurania, are not recognised by other authorities, unless the former name should be read Euliphus; in which case it may be identified with Eulepa, a station placed by the Antonine Itinerary on the road from Cæsarea to Satala. (p. 206.) In the interior of Pontus Cappadocius, Ptolemy places, in addition to certain sites which have been already noticed in the description of the sea-coast, Aza, Asiba, Mardara, and Camuresarbum. Asiba is also known from its coins [m]. Mardara is evidently the Marandara of the Antonine Itinerary, between Cæsarea and Sebastia. (p. 206.) Camuresarbum I should imagine to be corrupt, and we ought perhaps to read Camisa, Zara, as in the Itinerary just referred to. (p. 207.) I should here present the reader with a list of the several roads which traversed Pontus in various directions, but I have thought it better to defer this part of our inquiry till we could connect it with the topography of Galatia, on which it materially depends. I shall conclude this section with a list of names of places and tribes classed under the head of Pontus by Stephanus Byz. Abrinatæ, a people. (v. Ἀβρινάται.) Arazus, a town. (v. Ἄραζος.) Arbanium, a town apparently on the coast. (v. Ἀρβάνιον.) Diobulium, a small place near Pontus. (v. Διοβούλιον.) Thiba, a spot so called from an Amazon slain by Hercules. The inhabitants, called Thibii, were said to be enchanters, whose breath was poisonous, and eye malignantly fascinating. (v. Θίβα.) Other authors,

[m] Sestini, p. 59. Imperatorius unicus Gordiani. Epigraphe ΑCΙΒΑΙΩΝ.

who have mentioned the Thibii, asserted that they could not perish by water, but would float on the surface. (Plut. Symp. V. 7. Phylarch. ap. Plin. VII. 2.) Creme, a town mentioned by Phlegon. (v. Κρέμη.) Crossa, noticed by Hecatæus. (v. Κρόσσα.) Mares, a people near the Mossynœci. (v. Μάρες.) They are also named by Herodotus in conjunction with that people; (III. 94.) and elsewhere he states that they furnished a body of troops for the expedition of Xerxes. (VII. 79.) Patrasys, a town noticed by Hecatæus. (v. Πατρασύς.) Sionia. (v. Σιωνία.) Charimatæ, a people placed next to the Moschi and Cercetæi by Palæphatus and Hellanicus. (v. Χαριμάται.)

SECTION VI.

IONIA AND LYDIA.

General history of the Ionian colonies and their confederacy—
Description of the twelve states of Ionia and the adjacent
islands—Origin of the Meonians and Lydians—Dynasties of
Lydia—Boundaries and topography of that country.

THE beautiful country which received the name
of Ionia from the Greek colonists who settled on its
shores, had, previous to that event, been peopled by
a race of barbarians, so often alluded to by the ancients under the indefinite appellations of Leleges
and Carians. These, unable to resist their more
powerful invaders, withdrew from the coast, and
retired across the Mæander, to that portion of Asia
Minor which, from the latter people, obtained the
name of Caria. (Pherecyd. ap. Strab. XIV. p. 632.
Herod. I. 146. Paus. Ach. 2.) The causes which
led to the Ionian migration are well known. The
chief of these, according to Thucydides, was the
crowded state of Attica; a poor and barren country,
unable to support the great influx of population
which the disturbed state of Greece had drawn thither. The greatest number of these refugees were
Ionians, who had been expelled from the Ægialus
of Peloponnese by the Achæans, and had retired to
Attica, the mother country of the Ionian race. At
this time a dissension arose between Medon and

Neleus, the descendants of Codrus, respecting the succession to the throne of Athens; and when the oracle of Delphi had decided in favour of the former, Neleus determined, in conjunction with the other sons of Codrus, to abandon Attica, and form settlements in Asia Minor, already colonized for many years by the Æolians. The Ionians gladly listened to the proposals made to them, of joining the expedition, and their numbers were soon swelled by a mixed multitude collected from almost every part of Greece. Herodotus names in particular the Abantes of Euboea, who migrated in great numbers; the Minyæ of Orchomenus; the Cadmei, headed, as Pausanias reports, by Philotas, grandson of Peneleus; (Ach. 2.) the Dryopes; a body of Phocians; some Molossians, Arcadians, and Dorians of Epidaurus; besides several other tribes. (Herod. I. 146. Cf. Pausan. loc. cit.) On the arrival of the emigrants on the coast of Asia, they proceeded to found several towns, under the conduct of different leaders. The followers of Androclus, the legitimate son of Codrus, colonized Ephesus, which, from that circumstance, was always denominated the royal city of Ionia. (Pherecyd. ap. Strab. XIV. p. 633.) Another party, under the command of Neleus, settled at Miletus, the foundation of which, however, was much more ancient. Cydrelus, a third son of Codrus[a], occupied Myus: Andropompus, Lebedos. Andræmon, likewise a descendant of Codrus, built Colophon. Priene was founded by Æpytus, son of Neleus[b], in conjunction with Philotas, a Boeotian leader. Teos owed its first origin to Athamas; but,

[a] Pausanias calls him Cyaretus. Ach. 2.

[b] He is named Ægyptus by Pausanias.

on the arrival of the Ionians, it was recolonized by Nauclus, a natural son of Codrus, together with Apœcus and Damasus of Athens, and Geres the Bœotian. Cnopus, another son of Codrus, was the founder of Erythræ. Philogenes, at the head of a body of Athenians, colonized Phocæa: Paralus [c], Clazomenæ. The island of Chios received different settlers, collected from various nations, under the command of Egertius, or Egertilus. Samos, finally, was occupied by two successive colonies, under Timbrion and Procles of Epidaurus. (Strab. loc. cit. Pausan. loc. cit.) These were the twelve states, which, not long after their foundation, united themselves into one political body, called the Ionian confederacy. Herodotus accounts for this particular number, from the circumstance of its having been previously adopted by the Ionians, when they occupied the northern coast of Peloponnese, under the name of Pelasgi Ægialees. He reports, that even at that early period they had formed a confederacy of twelve cities, and probably carried with them the same political system into Asia [d]. (I. 146.) The Ionians then formed a federal body, whose solemn meetings and festivals were held in a temple called Panionium, dedicated to the Heliconian Neptune, and erected on the promontory of Mycale, opposite to Samos. But the government in each state or city appears to have been decidedly monarchical, and in many instances this subsequently degene-

---

[c] Pausanias writes the name Parphorus, which sounds corrupt, and ought probably to be corrected from Strabo.

[d] The Tyrrhenian Pelasgi appear to have introduced the same confederate form in Etruria.

Y 3

rated into absolute power. Some of these Ionian princes, as Herodotus informs us, were descended from the Lycian Glaucus ; others claimed a Pylian origin through Codrus, the son of Melanthus, and some again could trace their pedigree to both sources. (I. 147.) The country occupied by these Grecian colonists surpassed, in the opinion of the same historian, all other lands in beauty and mildness of temperature. To this were added several other important local and physical advantages : great richness and fertility of soil ; large and abundant rivers intersecting wide and beautiful valleys ; spacious and commodious harbours, admirably calculated for commercial enterprise and connexion with every part of the Mediterranean sea. All these combined tended to render the Ionians a most opulent and flourishing people, and had their spirit and energy been equal to the means which nature had placed within their reach, they might have become the founders of a powerful empire ; but the softness of the climate, and the great facility afforded by so rich a country for procuring the necessaries of life, rendered them an indolent and voluptuous nation, so that they not only ceased to aspire to extend their power and influence by conquest, but were content to live in subjection, first to the effeminate Lydians, and afterwards under the more powerful, but equally mild sway of the Persians. Some resistance, indeed, was offered by individual cities to the arms of both Crœsus and Cyrus, and rare instances of patriotic devotion and love of liberty, more especially in the case of the latter, were manifested by the citizens of Phocæa and Teos. But the general conduct of the Ionians on that occasion, and their appeal to Sparta, proves them as a nation to have been weak and contemptible. (Herod. I. 152.)

A more determined and noble effort to recover their liberty and independence was made by the Ionians in the revolt against the Persians, to which they were instigated by Histiæus and Aristagoras. But though quickly roused, their zeal and ardour in the cause of freedom was not equal to endure an arduous and protracted conflict against so formidable a power as that of Persia. The capture and burning of Sardis was but a short-lived triumph, followed by some signal defeats which broke the courage of the revolters, and speedily exhausted their means of resistance by land. (Herod. V. 99—124.) The contest was still, however, carried on by sea, and with some hopes of success, since the Persians were not equally formidable on that element. But here again the national indolence, together with disunion, and the treachery of some of their princes, paralysed the efforts of the brave and well-intentioned, and speedily terminated the struggle in favour of the Persian monarch. (Herod. VI. 7—22.) After the glorious victory achieved by the Greeks, Ionia for a time regained her freedom ; but the respite was of short duration, and the battle of Mycale seemed only to have caused a change from one state of subjection to another, and to have merely transferred the wealth of the country from the royal treasury at Susa, to that of the Acropolis at Athens. (Thuc. I. 95.) During the greater part of the Peloponnesian war, the latter power drew considerable resources from the tribute imposed on the Ionians, and the fear of losing so rich a portion of

their dominions induced the Athenians to make the
greatest efforts, after their overthrow in Sicily, to
preserve it from the united attacks of Sparta and
the Persian Tissaphernes.   Destined to be the prize
of one or the other of the belligerent parties, the
Ionians remained, except in the affair of Miletus,
(Thuc. VIII. 25.) passive spectators of the contest.
They were sure to pay contributions, and they cared
but little whether it was enforced by the Athenian
galleys, the Spartan harmosts, or the Persian satrap.
Agesilaus, indeed, during the war he carried on in
Asia against Pharnabazus, succeeded in exciting
among-the Ionians a warlike spirit, and a degree of
enthusiasm, of which the nation hitherto had exhibited so little indication. (Xen. Hell. III. 4.)   But
on the departure of that great prince, the excite-
ment died away, and the disgraceful treaty of Antalcidas resigned the Ionians once more to their wonted
condition of slaves to the Persian monarch. (V. 1,
28.)   Unworthy of liberty, they beheld with indiffer-
ence the exploits of Alexander, and the subsequent
contentions of his captains.   The victory of Magnesia wrested them from the feeble sway of Antiochus, and gave them to the Romans ; but if we may
judge from the readiness with which they obeyed
the mandate of Mithridates to massacre his enemies, they had less reason to be satisfied with the
prætorial or proconsular administration than that of
the lieutenant of Persia or Syria.   But if the political and moral history of the Ionian colonies offers
but little on which the admirer of national virtue
and the lover of liberty may wish to dwell, this de-
fect is in part redeemed and supplied by interest of
another kind.   If Ionia is inferior to its mother coun-

try in the patriotism, moral feeling, and energy
of its inhabitants, yet in the arts and sciences, in
the polish and refinement of life, it equals all that
we are accustomed to admire in Grecian genius,
elegance and purity of taste. Æolis and Ionia
were the nurses of Grecian poetry and literature of
almost every kind, if we except the drama. Ionia
exclusively led the way to those contemplations and
studies which were subsequently improved by the
philosophers of Greece. She had schools also of
painting and sculpture, and in grandeur of design
and beauty of proportions her temples were accounted, by no incompetent judge in this branch of
architecture, to have surpassed those of the mother,
or any other country. (Pausan. Ach. 5.) In navi-
gation also and commercial enterprise we find the
names of Samos, Phocæa, and Miletus, already famous, when scarcely any city of the parent state,
with the exception perhaps of Corinth, possessed
vessels of burden calculated for a distant voyage.
Whatever Ionia therefore had originally received
from Greece, just emerging from barbarism, she improved in a tenfold degree ; through her channel the
arts and language of the mother state attained to a
state of cultivation and polish hitherto unknown,
and were disseminated and established in distant
countries, cut off apparently from civilized society
and the means of intercourse[e].

The length of coast occupied by the Ionian settlements is estimated by Strabo at 3430 stadia, including all the sinuosities of the different bays by

[e] This is remarkably the
case with respect to Marseilles,
founded by the Phocæans, and
the Milesian colonies on the
Borysthenes.

which it is indented. The distance by land in a
straight line is much smaller. The two extreme
points between which it lies, are, to the north, the
cape, near which stood the city of Phocæa, close to
the mouth of the river Hermus, and between it and
the bay of Cyme; to the south, the promontory of
Posidium in the Milesian territory, and on the left
bank of the Mæander. (Strab. XIV. p. 632.) The
extent of territory possessed by the Ionian states on
the land side was narrowly circumscribed by a chain
of mountains extending from the Hermus to the
Caystrus. This ridge, known to the ancients under
the celebrated names of Sipylus and Tmolus, formed
the natural separation between them and the plains
of Lydia. Beyond the Caystrus another mountain,
named Messogis, ranged along the remainder of the
Ionian coast till it terminated in the promontory of
Mycale: then follows the mouth of the Mæander
and the territory of Miletus, circumscribed by that
Phocæa. river, and the bay and mountain of Latmos. Phocæa, the most northern of the Ionian cities, was
founded, as Pausanias reports, by some emigrants of
Phocis under the guidance of two Athenian chiefs
named Philogenes and Damon. The town was
built, with the consent of the Cumæans, on part of
their territory; nor was it included in the Ionian
confederacy till its citizens had consented to place
at the head of the government princes of the line
of Codrus. Phocæa, from the excellence of its harbours, and the enterprising spirit of its inhabitants,
soon obtained a distinguished name among the early
maritime states of the world. Herodotus has given
us some very interesting particulars on this head.
He states that the Phocæans were the first Greeks

who undertook distant voyages, and made their
countrymen acquainted with the Adriatic, and the
coasts of Tyrrhenia and Spain. Tartessus, in the
latter country, was the spot which they most frequented; and they so conciliated the favour of Ar-
ganthonius, sovereign of the country, that he sought
to induce them to leave Ionia, and settle in his dominions. On their declining this offer he munifi-
cently presented them with a large sum of money,
for the purpose of raising a strong line of fortifications round their city, a precaution which the growing power of the Median empire seemed to render
necessary. The historian observes, that the liberality of this Iberian sovereign was attested by the
circuit of the walls, which were several stadia in
length, and by the size and solid construction of
the stones employed. Phocæa was one of the first
Ionian towns besieged by the army of Cyrus under
the command of Harpagus. Having invested the
place, he summoned the inhabitants to surrender, declaring that it would be a sufficient token of submission, if they would pull down one battlement of
their wall, and consecrate one dwelling in the city.
The Phocæans, aware that to comply with this demand was to forfeit their independence, but conscious also of their inability to resist the overwhelming power of Cyrus, determined to abandon their
native soil, and seek their fortune in another clime.
Having formed this resolution, and obtained from
the Persian general a truce of one day, under the
pretence of a wish to deliberate on his proposal,
they launched their ships, and embarking with their
wives and children, and their most valuable effects,
sailed to Chios. On their arrival in that island

they sought to purchase the Œnussæ, a neighbouring group of islands belonging to the Chians ; but
as they refused to comply with their wishes, they
resolved to sail for Corsica, where, twenty years
prior to these events, they had founded a town named
Alalia.   On their way thither they touched at Phocæa, and having surprised the Persian garrison left
there by Harpagus, put it to the sword.   They then
bound themselves by a solemn oath to continue
the voyage on which they had determined : nevertheless one half of their number, overcome by the
feelings which the sight of their native city recalled
to their minds, could not be prevailed upon to for-
sake it a second time.   The rest continued their
voyage to Corsica, and were well received by their
countrymen already settled in the island.   During
the five years in which they remained there, they
rendered themselves formidable to the surrounding
nations by their piracies and depredations, so that
at length the Tuscans and Carthaginians united
their forces to check these aggressions and destroy
their power.   The hostile fleets met in the Sardi-
nian sea, and, after a most obstinate engagement, the
Phocæans succeeded in beating off the enemy.   They
sustained however so great a loss in the conflict,
and their ships were so crippled, that, despairing of
being able to continue the contest against their
powerful foes, they resolved to abandon Corsica and
proceed to Rhegium in Italy.   Soon after their arrival at that port, they were persuaded to settle at
Velia, or Elæa, in Lucania, by a citizen of Posido-
nia.   This new colony became in process of time a
considerable and flourishing town. (Herod. I. 163—
168.)   It is remarkable that Herodotus, in this de-

tailed account of the settlements made at different
times by the Phocæans, should have made no mention of the most important and celebrated of their
foundations ; I mean Marseilles, which he only notices once, and that incidentally, and not as a Pho-
cæan colony. (V. 9.)   Thucydides, however, distinctly ascribes the origin of that city to the Phocæans, (I. 13.) as also Strabo, who enters very
fully into the history of that event. (IV. p. 179—
180. XIV. p. 647. Cf. Liv. V. 34. Athen. XIII. p.
576. A. Harpocr. et Steph. Byz. v. Μασσαλία.)   I
think it probable that Marseilles had been already
founded by the Phocæans before they were forced
to abandon Ionia by the Persians ; and that the
Corsican settlement was but an off-set of the principal colony.   Phocæa still continued to exist under
the Persian dominion, but greatly reduced in its population and commerce.   This is apparent from the
fact of its having been able to contribute only three
ships to the combined fleet of the revolted Ionians
assembled at Lade.   Dionysius, the commander of
this small force, was evidently however a man of
genius and courage, and if the confederates had followed implicitly his directions, affairs might have
taken a very different turn. (VI. 11.)   Herodotus
relates that in the sea-fight, fought soon after, Dionysius took three ships of the enemy ; but finding
that success was hopeless, he first of all sailed to
Phœnicia, where he destroyed many merchant-
vessels, and collected much valuable booty ; after
which he retired to Sicily, and committed various
acts of piracy on the ships of the Carthaginians and
Tuscans. (VI. 17.)   Little mention is made of Phocæa subsequent to these events ; (Thuc. VIII. 31.)

but some centuries later it is described by Livy as a
town of some size and consequence, on occasion of
its being besieged by a Roman naval force in the
war against Antiochus. (XXXVII. 31.) "The town,"
says the historian, " is placed in the inmost recess
" of a bay.   Its shape is oblong, and the walls en-
" close a space of 2500 paces : they unite afterwards
" so as to form a narrower wedge.   This they call
" Lampter [f], and it is about 1200 paces in breadth.
" A tongue of land, advancing out towards the sea
" for the space of 1000 paces, nearly divides the
" bay into two equal portions, and forms on either
" side of the narrow isthmus a very secure port.
" The one towards the south was called Naustath-
" mus, from the circumstance of its being able to
" contain a great number of vessels.   The other was
" situated close to the Lampter."   The town was
taken by the Romans after an obstinate resistance,
and given up to plunder, though the inhabitants had
submitted, and voluntarily opened their gates : but
the prætor was unable to restrain the fury and ra-
pacity of his soldiers.   The town, with its territory, was however restored to the inhabitants by
that officer. (XXXVII. 32. Polyb. XXII. 27, 7. Cf.
V. 77, 4. XXI. 4. Liv. XXXVIII. 39.)   Subsequently the Phocæans incurred the anger of the
Roman senate, from having espoused the cause of
Aristonicus, who pretended to the throne of Pergamum : and they would have been severely punished,
if the inhabitants of Marseilles had not strongly in-
terceded in their behalf. (Justin. XXXVII. 1. XLIII.
3. Strab. XIV. p. 646.)   We can trace the existence
of Phocæa through the Cæsars by means of its

---

[f] In Greek Λαμπτήρ, i. e. the light-house.

coins[g], and Pliny, (V. 31.) and even down to the
latest period of the Byzantine empire, with the help
of its annalists and the ecclesiastical writers. (Hierocl. Synecd. p. 661. Act. Concil. Eph. et Concil.
Chalced.) We learn from Mich. Ducas, that a new
town was built not far from the ancient site, which
still retains the name of *Palæo-Phoggia*, by some
Genoese, in the reign of Amurath, A. D. 1421. (Ann.
p. 89.) This, as Chandler informs us, is situated on
the isthmus, mentioned above in Livy's description[h].

A little to the south of Phocæa was a small town Leucæ
named Leucæ, (Scyl. Peripl. p. 37.) which Aristonicus, a descendant of the kings of Pergamum, occupied, in his attempt to recover the throne of his
ancestors. He was however defeated, and put to
death by the Romans; but Marcus Peperna, his
conqueror, and Publius Crassus before him, both
died at Leucæ. (Strab. XIV. p. 646. Tit. Liv. Epist.
LIX. Justin. XXXVI. 4. Vell. Paterc. II. 4.)
Leucæ, as we are informed by Diodorus, had in
former times been a subject of contention between
the Clazomenians and Cymæans, but it had been
awarded to the former by the oracle of Delphi. It
was at that time an island, and deserted, but Ta-
chos, a Persian, who had revolted from Artaxerxes,
built a town on it. (IV. 18. Cf. Plin. V. 31.) According to Chandler, it would seem to be now joined
to the main land, " having a small mountain or hill
" with a smooth top; and a long spit now runs from

---

[g] Sestini mentions some gold
staters, coined at Phocæa, without any epigraph. The imperial
series reaches from Claudius to
the Philips. The legends are

ΦΩ. ΦΩΚΑΙ. ΦΩΚΑΕΩΝ and ΦΩ-
ΚΑΙΕΩΝ, p. 83.

[h] Travels in Asia Minor, p.
96. Le Brun, p. 166.

" it out into the sea[i]."   Near this are several rocks,
which were anciently called Myrmeces.   In Pliny's
time they stood at the mouth of the Hermus, but
that river appears to have undergone great changes
since then, and at present it discharges its waters

Hermus
fluvius.

into the sea much nearer Smyrna[k].   The Hermus,
according to Strabo, had its source in mount Dindymene, on the borders of Mysia; or, as Pliny reports,
near Dorylæum in Phrygia. (V. 31.)   It received
the waters of the Pactolus, Hyllus, called also Phrygius, and other less celebrated streams, and discharged itself into the sea between Phocæa and
Smyrna. (Strab. XIII. p. 626. Herod. I. 80. V.
101. Arrian. Exp. Alex. V. 5, 6.)   The Hermus was
reported to contain gold among its sand; a circumstance for which it was probably indebted to the
Pactolus.

> Sed neque Medorum silvæ, ditissima terra,
> Nec pulcher Ganges, atque auro turbidus Hermus,
> Laudibus Italiæ certent.   GEORG. II. 136.

Servius thinks it was a figurative allusion to the
fertility of its plains.

> Vel quum sole novo densæ torrentur aristæ,
> Aut Hermi campo, aut Lyciæ flaventibus arvis.
> ÆN. VII. 720.

Homer applies to this river the epithet δινήεις; (Il.
Υ. 392.)

> Ὕλλῳ ἐπ' ἰχθυόεντι καὶ Ἕρμῳ δινήεντι.

and again, in the poet's Life, ascribed to Herodotus.
(c. 9.)

[i] Travels in Asia Minor, p.
95.

[k] Chandler expatiates on the
probable alterations which will
in time be effected on this coast

by the Hermus; but his imagi-
nation seems to outstrip the
course of time and the powers
of the river, p. 96.

'Αμβρόσιον πίνοντες ὕδωρ θείου ποταμοῖο,
'Ερμοῦ δινήεντος, ὃν ἀθάνατος τέκετο Ζεύς.

This fine river is known to the Turks by the name
of *Sarabat*.

Smyrna, situated in a gulf which lies nearly east Smyrna.
of the mouth of the Hermus, was said to derive its
name from an Amazon so called, who, having conquered Ephesus, had in the first instance transmitted her appellation to that city. The Ephesians
afterwards founded the town, to which it has ever
since been appropriated; and Strabo, who dwells at
length on this point, cites several poets, to prove
that the name of Smyrna was once applied speci-
fically to a spot near Ephesus, and afterwards generally to the whole of its precincts. The same writer
affirms, that the Ephesian colonists were afterwards
expelled from Smyrna by the Æolians; but being
aided by the Colophonians, who had received them
into their city, they once more returned to Smyrna,
and retook it. He cites the following fragment of
Mimnermus, in confirmation of this fact:

'Ημεῖς δ' αἰπὺ Πύλον Νηλήιον ἄστυ λιπόντες
Ἱμερτὴν 'Ασίην νηυσὶν ἀφικόμεθα.
'Ες δ' ἐρατὴν Κολοφῶνα βίην ὑπέροπλον ἔχοντες
'Εζόμεθ' ἀργαλέης ὕβριος ἡγεμόνες.
Κεῖθεν δ' 'Αστήεντος ἀπορνύμενοι ποταμοῖο
Θεῶν βουλῇ Σμυρνην εἵλομεν Αἰολίδα[1].

Herodotus differs from Strabo in some particulars:
(ap. Strab. XIV. p. 634.) he states that Smyrna originally belonged to the Æolians, who received into

[1] I have given this passage
according to Brunck, who has
been followed by Prof. Gais-
ford. Poet. Min. vol. I. p. 424.
The French translators of Strabo
have taken unwarrantable liber-
ties with some of the lines in
their version, tom. IV. p. ii.
p. 271.

the city some Colophonian exiles. These afterwards, taking advantage of a festival held without the town, to which the Smyrnæans resorted in great numbers, shut the gates, and became masters of the place. From that time Smyrna ceased to be an Æolian city, but was received into the Ionian confederacy. (I. 150. Pausan. Ach. 5.) Of all the different cities which laid claim to the birth of Homer, Smyrna seems to assert her pretensions to that honour with the greatest zeal and plausibility ; and if we are to credit the author of his Life, commonly supposed to be Herodotus, we can have no hesitation in adhering to the accounts which he has collected on this very interesting point of history, supported as they are by other traditions and testimonies of antiquity. The Smyrnæans, as we learn from Strabo, were so convinced that the great poet was their country-man, that they had erected and dedicated to him a temple containing his statue. This edifice was called Homerium, a name also given to a brass coin struck at Smyrna, in commemoration of the same event. (Strab. XIV. p. 646. Cic. pro Arch. c. 8.)

They also shewed a cave, where it was said that Homer composed his verses[m]. (Pausan. Ach. 5.) It was objec ed, by those who sought to weaken the claims of Smyrna, that the poet had never once mentioned the name of that town, nor the river Meles which ran through it; but Strabo does not consider the objection to have any weight, (XII.

[m] Chandler informs us that he had searched for this cavern, and succeeded in discovering it above the aqueduct of the Meles. It is about four feet wide, the roof of a huge rock, cracked and slanting, the sides and bottom sandy. Beyond it is a passage cut, leading into a kind of well, &c. Travels in Asia Minor, p. 91.

p. 554.) and besides, as Smyrna was not in existence during the Trojan war, it could only have
been alluded to by anticipation. The author of the
Poet's Life introduces the following verses, said to
be written by him, and which speak of Smyrna as
his native city. (c. 14.)

Οἵη μ' αἴσῃ δῶκε πατὴρ Ζεὺς κύρμα γενέσθαι
Νήπιον αἰδοίης ἐπὶ γούνασι μητρὸς ἀτάλλων,
Ἥν ποτ' ἐπύργωσαν βουλῇ Διὸς αἰγιόχοιο
Λαοὶ Φρίκωνος, μάργων ἐπιβήτορες ἵππων,
Ὁπλότεροι μαλεροῖο πυρὸς κρίνοντες Ἄρηα,
Αἰολίδα Σμύρνην ἁλιγείτονα ποτνιάνακτον
Ἥν τε δι' ἀγλαὸν εἶσιν ὕδωρ ἱεροῖο Μέλητος.

Smyrna was attacked by Gyges, king of Lydia, but
resisted with success. (Herod. I. 14. Mimner. ap.
Pausan. Bœot. 29.) It was compelled to yield however to his descendant Alyattes, and in consequence
of this event it sunk into decay, and became deserted
for the space of 400 years. (Herod. I. 16. Strab.
XIV. p. 646.) Alexander is said to have formed the
project of rebuilding the town; in consequence of a
vision he had on mount Pagus, a hill above the
river Meles. Whilst he slept near the temple of
Nemesis, the goddess appeared to him, and ordered
him to found a city for the Smyrnæans on the site
where he then lay. (Pausan. Ach. 5.) The Macedonian king did not live to execute the design, but
it was commenced by Antigonus, and finally completed by Lysimachus, in compliance with the oracle
delivered by the Clarian Apollo.

Τρισμάκαρτες κεῖνοι καὶ τετράκις ἄνδρες ἔσονται,
Οἳ Πάγον οἰκήσουσι πέρην ἱεροῖο Μέλητος.

(Paus. loc. cit. Strab. XIV. p. 646.) The new town
was built at a distance of twenty stadia from the

ancient site, partly on the side of the hill, but chiefly
in the plain, and extending to the sea-coast, on which
stood the harbour, the temple of Cybele, and the
gymnasium. The streets were remarkably handsome, well paved, and drawn at right angles. There
were several fine square porticos, a public library,
the temple of Homer, and other buildings, which
rendered it one of the most beautiful cities of Ionia.
(Strab. loc. cit.) In an inscription preserved amongst
the Marmor. Oxon. it is styled πρώτη τῆς Ἀσίας κάλλει καὶ μεγέθει, καὶ λαμπροτάτη, καὶ μητρόπολις τῆς Ἀσίας[n].
Cicero also speaks of it as one of the most flourishing towns of Asia. (pro L. Flacc. c. 30.) It had
received various grants and privileges from the Roman senate, for the part it took in the wars with Antiochus and Mithridates. (Liv. XXXV. 42. XXXVII.
16, 54. XXXVIII. 39.) But it afterwards suffered
much from the siege sustained by Trebonius, one
of Cæsar's murderers, against Dolabella, who finally
overcame him, and put him to death. (Strab. XIV.
p. 646. Cic. Phil. XI. 2.. Liv. Epit. CXIX. Dio
Cass. XLVII. 29.) In the reign of Tiberius, eleven
cities of Asia pleaded before the senate for the honour of being allowed to erect a temple to the
emperor: the chief contest lay between Sardes and
Smyrna; but the merits of the latter city prevailed
with the judges, and she obtained the disputed favour. (Tacit. Ann. III. 63. IV. 56.) It continued
to flourish throughout the following reigns, (Plin.
V. 31.) and its schools of eloquence and philosophy
were in considerable repute. (Aristid. in Smyrn.)

[n] The epigraph on the coins
of Caracalla and other emperors, is CMΥΡΝΑΙΩΝ ΠΡΩΤΩΝ
ΑCΙΑC ΚΑΛΛΕΙ ΚΑΙ ΜΕΓΕΘΕΙ.
Sestini, p. 84.

The Christian church flourished also, through the zeal and care of Polycarp, its first bishop, who is said to have suffered martyrdom in the stadium of the city, about 166 years after the birth of our Saviour. (Iren. III. 3, 4. p. 176.) There is also an epistle from Ignatius to the Smyrnæans, and another addressed to Polycarp. Under the Greek emperors Smyrna experienced great vicissitudes. Having been occupied by Tzachas, a Turkish chief, towards the close of the eleventh century, it was nearly destroyed by a Greek fleet, commanded by John Ducas. It was, however, restored by the emperor Comnenus, but suffered again severely from a siege which it sustained against the forces of Tamerlane. Not long after, it fell into the hands of the Turks, and has remained ever since in their possession. It is now the great mart of the Levant trade. Chandler gives a detailed description of the ruins of this city. They consist " of the old wall, of which many rem-
" nants may be discovered, of a solid, massive con-
" struction; the stadium, stripped of its marble
" seats and decorations, between the western gate
" and the sea; a theatre on the side of a hill front-
" ing the bay. The port which shut up reached
" to the foot of the castle-hill, is now dry. Beyond
" the deep valley in which the river Meles winds,
" behind the castle, are several portions of the wall
" of the pomærium, which encompassed the city at
" a distance, but broken. The ancient sepulchres
" were chiefly in the pomærium without the city.
" These ruins have supplied materials for the public
" edifices erected by the Turks. Many pedestals,
" statues, inscriptions, and medals have been, and
" are still discovered in digging. Perhaps no place

" has contributed more than Smyrna to enrich the
" collections and cabinets of the curious in Europe[o].
" The Meles," according to the same traveller, " is
" a clear stream, shallow in summer, not covering
" the rocky bed, but winding in the deep valley be-
" hind the castle, and murmuring among the ever-
" greens, approaches the gardens without the town,
" where it is branched out by small canals. In
" winter, after heavy rains on the mountains, or
" the melting of snow, it swells into a torrent rapid
" and deep, often not fordable, or with danger. Old
" Smyrna was about twenty stadia, or two miles
" and a half from the present city, and on the other
" side of the river. It is described as near the sea,
" with the clear stream of the Meles running by,
" and existed in the second century. Perhaps some
" vestiges might be discovered even now in tracing
" the river toward the bay. This is less wide than
" it was anciently, and has been removed from the
" site by a large accession of low land, formed of
" soil washed from the mountains near, or of mud
" and slime brought down by the torrents[p]."

Smyrnæus, qui et Hermius sinus. We may remark that the bay in which Smyrna was situated, generally took its name from that city, but sometimes it was denominated Hermius, from the principal river which there united itself with the sea. (Hom. Vit. c. 2.)

Clazomenæ. Clazomenæ, which follows next on the coast, did not exist prior to the Ionian migration; it was founded, as we learn from Pausanias, by a colony of Cleonæans and Phliasians, who abandoned the Peloponnese at the time of the Dorian invasion, and joined the Ionians. They at first settled on a site

[o] Travels in Asia Minor, p. 76—79.　　[p] P. 87.

called Scyppium or Scyphia, (Steph. Byz. v. Σκυφία,)
in the Colophonian territory, but afterwards removed further north to a spot named Chytrium, or
Chytrum q, (Arist. Polit. V. 2. Strab. XIV. p. 645.)
under the conduct of Parphorus, or Paralus, a native
of Colophon. (Paus. Ach. 3. Strab. loc. cit.) Herodotus reports, that Alyattes, king of Lydia, having
attacked Clazomenæ, met with a determined resistance, and sustained finally a signal defeat. (I. 16.)
On the conquest of Lydia by the Persians, the Clazomenians abandoned the original site of their town,
and retired to a small island close to the land, where
they built a new city. This measure was adopted
from fear of the Persians. (Paus. loc. cit.) It was
not till many years after, that the latter obtained
possession of the island, and the town erected on it,
under the conduct of the two satraps, Artaphernes
and Otanes. This occurred at the commencement of
the Ionian revolt. (Herod. V. 123.)

Xenophon, in the Hellenics, speaks of Clazomenæ
as an island ; (V. 1, 28.) but in Strabo's time it appears to have been connected with the mainland ;
(XIV. loc. cit.) and Pausanias leads us to infer that
this was undertaken by Alexander the Great. (Ach.
3.) Thucydides relates that the Clazomenians, having revolted from Athens after the Sicilian disasters,
were employed in founding a place called Polichna,
on the continent, but the Athenians opposed the
work, and finally reduced them under their power.
(VIII. 14. 23.) After the defeat of Antiochus, Clazomenæ was declared independent by the Romans,
and received the little island of Drymusa, situated

---

q In Steph. Byz., who quotes
Ephorus, it is probable we ought
to read Χύτρον instead of Χυ-
τόν.

in its vicinity. (Liv. XXXVIII. 39. Polyb. XXII. 27. 5.) It was taken by the Cilician pirates in the time of Scylla. (App. Mithr. c. 63.) Clazomenæ derives further celebrity from having given birth to Anaxagoras the philosopher, whose disciple Archelaus taught Socrates and Euripides. (Strab. loc. cit. Diog. Laert. II. 16.) It had a treasury at Delphi, in which the magnificent offerings of Crœsus were deposited. (Herod. I. 51.) The Clazomenians joined the Phocæans, and some other states, in forming the emporium of Naucratis, in Egypt, (II. 178.) and first attempted to colonize Abdera, in Thrace. (I. 168.) Their town retained its name and existence throughout the Roman and Greek empires, (Plin. V. 31. Ptol. p. 119. Hierocl. Synecd. p. 660.) but towards the middle of the eleventh century it was much infested by pirates, and finally sunk under the power of the Turks, and has never risen from its ruins. These are to be seen somewhat to the northeast of *Vourla*, on a site corresponding with the descriptions of ancient authors. Chandler, who visited these remains, saw considerable vestiges of the work ascribed to Alexander. " The mole," says that traveller, " was two stadia, or a quarter of a mile in " length, but we were ten minutes in crossing it. " The width, as we conjectured, was about thirty " feet. On the west side, it is fronted with a thick, " strong wall, some pieces appearing above the " water. On the opposite is a mound of loose peb- " bles, shelving as a buttress, to withstand the fu- " rious assaults of storm and tempest. The upper " works have been demolished. We computed the " island to be about a mile long, and a quarter " broad. The city was small, its port on the

" N. N. W. side. Traces of the walls are found by
" the sea; and in a hill are vestiges of a theatre[r]."
Close to Clazomenæ is a cluster of small islands,
which Pliny names Pele, Drymusa, Anhydros, Scopelos, Sycussa, Marathussa, Psile, Perirrheusa. (V.
38.) Thucydides also notices Pele, Drymussa, and
Marathusa, (VIII. 31.) and we have already quoted
a passage from Livy, in which mention is made of
Drymusa. (Cf. Steph. Byz. vv. Πήλη, Δρυμοῦσσα,
Μαράθουσσα.) Chandler observes; " By Clazomene is
" a cluster of islets, all once cultivated, now neg-
" lected and barren. Their number was eight, but
" I could only count six[s]." Lampsus, according to
Ephorus, cited by Steph. Byz. was a portion of the
Clazomenian territory. (v. Λάμψος.) Thucydides
speaks of a spot called Daphnus, which seems to Daphnus.
have been in the vicinity of Clazomenæ, and dependent on that city. (VIII. 23 and 31.) I should
imagine that the temple of Apollo, mentioned by
Strabo, must have stood here. (XIV. p. 646.) Pliny
states that Daphnus no longer existed in his time.
(V. 31.) The same site was celebrated on account
of some warm springs, called the Agamemnonian
baths, from the circumstance of their having proved
beneficial to the Greeks who had been wounded in
an engagement with the troops of Telephus. (Phi-
lostr. p. 664. Strab. loc. cit.) Chandler discovered
several remains of the buildings near *Vourla;* he
says, " you descend by steps to the bath, which is
" under a modern vaulted roof, with vents in it for
" the steam; and adjoining to this is a like room,
" now disused. The current, which is soft and

---

[r] Travels in Asia Minor, p. 107, 108   [s] P. 109.

" limpid, is conveyed into a small round basin of
" marble, and runs over into a large cistern or re-
" servoir beneath. Our thermometer rose in the
" vein to one hundred and fifty[s]."

Resuming our periplus of the Ionian coast from
Clazomenæ, we have to point out a rugged promontory, which forms the north-west extremity
of the little bay of *Tcharpan*, which represents
Chytrium. This headland, now called *Esomeno*, is
probably the Apocremnus, or Hypocremnus, of
Strabo. (XIV. p. 645.) Beyond this, the coast advances still to the north, as far as cape Melæna, now
Kara-bouroun, near which, according to Strabo, was
a quarry, from which millstones were dug up.
(XIV. p. 645.) After doubling this point, we proceed along the coast to the south, as far as the bay
in which stood the ancient city of Erythræ. It will
be seen, from the map, that the sea forms a considerable peninsula in this part of Ionia, the neck of
which stands between Clazomenæ and the last mentioned town. A lofty ridge, known to the ancients
by the name of Mimas, occupies the centre of the
peninsula, and terminates in cape Melæna, its northern extremity. It is now called *Kara-vouno*. Mount
Mimas is described by Strabo as elevated and woody,
and well stocked with game. (XIV. p. 645.) Pliny
asserts, that its chain occupied an extent of 250
miles through the interior of Asia Minor; he adds,
that Alexander had conceived the project of cutting
a passage through the isthmus of Erythræ, and also
the mountain we are at present concerned with.
(V. 31.) The poets make frequent allusions to mount
Mimas.

Apocremnus sive Hypocremnus promontorium.

Mimas mons.

[s] P. 104.

ᵗΗ ὑπένερθε Χίοιο, παρ' ἠνεμόεντα Μίμαντα.
ODYSS. Γ. 172.

ᵗΙρις ἐπεὶ πάσῃσιν ἀφ' ὑψηλοῖο Μίμαντος
Σπερχομένη μάλα πολλὸν ἀπέτραπεν.
CALLIM. H. IN DEL. 157.

. . . . Cynthus et Othrys,
Et tandem Rhodope nivibus caritura, Mimasque.
. . . .
Ossaque cum Pindo. OVID. METAM. II. 221.

Mixtus Athos Tauro, Rhodopeque adjuncta Mimanti.
SIL. ITAL. II. 494.

(Cf. Thuc. V. 34. Ptol. p. 119.) Chandler, who crossed this mountain, represents " its shores as " covered with pines and shrubs, and garnished with " flowers. He passed many small pleasant spots, " well watered, and green with corn or with myrtles " and shrubs ᵗ." The view from the summit extends over the bays of Smyrna, Clazomenæ, and Erythræ, the islands of Samos and Chios, and several others.

Near cape Melæna was a small town, named Cy- Cybellia. bellia, or Cybelia. (Strab. XIV. p. 645. Steph. Byz. v. Κυβέλεια.) Thucydides points out a port called Phœnicus, on this coast, and under mount Mimas. Phœnicus portus. (VIII. 34.) Livy also notices it in his account of the naval operations of the Romans and their allies against Antiochus. He states that it belonged to the Erythræans (XXXVI. 45. Steph. Byz. v. Φοινικοῦς.) It is now called *Egri-limen*. Erythræ, one Erythræ. of the twelve states of Ionia, (Herod. I. 142.) is said, by Pausanias, to have derived its name and origin from Erythrus, son of Rhadamanthus, at the head of a Cretan and Lycian colony ; but it was subse-

ᵗ Chandler's Travels, p. 113.

quently strengthened by a body of Ionian emigrants, led by Cnopus [u], son of Codrus. From the latter chief it was sometimes called Cnopupolis ; (Steph. Byz. v. 'Ερυθρά. Polyæn. Strat. VIII.) but the original appellation always remained in use, and the other presently died away. (Strab. XIV. p. 633. Pausan. Ach. 3.) Athenæus quotes an interesting extract from Hippias of Erythræ, relating to the history of Cnopus. (VI. p. 259, 260.) Herodotus reports, that the Erythræans and Chians spoke the same dialect ; (I. 142.) but, notwithstanding this apparent tie, they are stated to have been early engaged in hostilities against each other. (I. 18. Anticl. ap. Athen. IX. p. 384. D. E.) The latter were however greatly superior in naval power, since they had 100 ships engaged at Lade, whilst the· Erythræans furnished only eight to the combined fleet. (VI. 8.) Erythræ revolted from Athens at the close of the Peloponnesian war. (Thuc. VIII. 14.) The Romans, on the conclusion of the war with king Antiochus, rewarded the citizens with grants of lands, and other marks of their approbation, for the zeal they had displayed in their service. (Liv. XXXVIII. 39. XXXVII. 11. 27. Polyb. XXII. 27, 6, XVI. 6, 5—8.) This city obtained further celebrity from the sibyl, who was said to have delivered prophecies there. Strabo distinguishes between the more ancient prophetess and another named Athenais, who flourished in the time of Alexander. (XIV. p. 645. Tacit. Ann. VI. 12. Lactant. Inst. I. 16.) We may trace the existence of this town, by means of coins and inscriptions, to a late

---

[u] Pausanias calls him Cleopus ; but this is doubtless a false reading.

period of the Roman empire [x]. Acts of councils,
and other ecclesiastical documents, prove it to have
been the see of a bishop in the province of Asia [y]:
In the Synecdemus of Hierocles, (p. 660.) Wesseling wishes to substitute Erythræ for Σατρώτη.
The territory of this city was rugged and mountainous; (Hom. Vit. c. 18.) but it produced good
wine, (Athen. I. 32. B.) and fine wheaten flour.

Ἐν δὲ φερεσταφύλοις Ἐρυθραῖς ἐκ κλιβάνου ἐλθὼν
Λευκὸς ἁβραῖς θάλλων ὥραις τέρψει παρὰ δεῖπνον.

ARCHESTR. AP. ATHEN. III. 112. B.[z]

A rivulet, called Aleos by Pliny, flowed into the
bay of Erythræ. (V. 31.[a]) The same writer states,
that its waters had the property of making the hair
grow. (XXXI. 10.) Pausanias reports, that there
was a very ancient temple of Hercules in this place.
(Ach. 5.) The site of the town retains the name
of *Ritré*. A modern traveller states, that " the
" walls were erected on two semicircular rocky
" brows, and had square towers at regular distances.
" They were very thick, the stones massive and
" rugged, the masonry that called *pseudisodo-*
" *mum*. In the middle is a shallow lively stream,
" clear as crystal, which turns a solitary mill, in its
" way through thickets of myrtle and bushes to the
" sea. This rivulet was anciently named Aleos.
" By a conical hill on the north are vestiges of an

[x] Nummi Imperatorii ΕΡΥ-
ΘΡΑΙΩΝ ab Augusto et Claudio,
indeque a Trajano usque ad
Otacilium, deinceps Valeriani
tantum. Sestini, p. 82. The
coins of Erythræ, anterior to the
Roman dominion, are very
scarce.

[y] Geogr. Sacr. Car. S. Paul.

p. 238.

[z] In the description of Greece
I have inadvertently applied
this quotation to Erythræ of
Bœotia.

[a] On the coins of Erythræ
the name of this stream appears
to be ΛΞΟΣ. Sestini, p. 82.

" ample theatre in the mountain side; and further
" on, by the sea, three pedestals of white marble.
" Beyond these is an old square fortress, standing on
" a low spot, a little island; and by it was a short
" sepulchral inscription. Erythræ has been long
" deserted, and, like Clazomene, stripped even of its
" ruins, except some masses of hard cement, a few
" vaults of sepulchres, a fragment of inscribed archi-
" trave, a broken column or two, and a large stone,
" on which is carved a round shield. The bare rock
" afforded a natural foundation for the houses and
" public edifices; and the materials, when they were
" ruined, lay ready to be transported to *Scio*, and
" other places which continued to flourish [b]." Erythræ possessed two ports; one situated close to the
town, the other somewhat to the south, and named
Cyssus, according to Livy. (XXXVI. 43.) Casystes
in Strabo, if the text of the latter is sound. (XIV.
p. 644.) The latter corresponds with the well-known
modern harbour of *Tchesmeh*, or *Chismeh*. Part of
the coast bore the name of Leopodon. (Hipp. ap.
Athen. VI. 259. A.) In front of Erythræ were four
small islands, named Hippi, now *Ogni* and *St.
George*. (Strab. loc. cit. Plin. V. 31.) The bay in
which the city was placed was closed by two promontories, the northernmost of which bore the name
of Coryne; the other, to the south-west, advancing
towards Chios, that of Mesate. (Pausan. Ach. 5.
Pomp. Mel. I. 19.) Thucydides assigns to Erythræ
two small towns, or fortresses, named Pteleum and
Sidussa. (VIII. 24. Cf. Steph. Byz. v. Πτελέον.) The
latter speaks of Embatum as a spot in this vicinity,
(v. Ἔμβατον,) also known from Thucydides. (III.

Coryne et Mesate promonto-ria.

[b] Travels in Asia Minor, p. 113, 114.

29.) To the south of Erythræ, a lofty mountain, anciently named Corycus, and connected with the range of mount Mimas, advances out to the west in the direction of Chios, and terminates in cape Ar- Argennum promonto-rium. gennum, which lies nearly opposite to cape Posi- dium, the easternmost point of that island : the strait which divides the two headlands is estimated by Strabo to be about sixty stadia in breadth. (XIV. p. 645.) Thucydides writes the name Arginus. (VIII. 34.) In Greek, 'Αργεννὸς and 'Αργινόεις denote the same idea, which is equally expressed by the modern Frank name *Capo Bianco*, or the *White Cape*. The high and rugged coast formed by mount Cory- Corycus mons. cus harboured formerly a wild and daring popula- tion, greatly addicted to piracy ; and who, by disguis- ing themselves, and frequenting the harbours in their vicinity, obtained private information of the course and freight of any merchant vessel, and con- certed measures for the purpose of intercepting it. The secrecy with which their intelligence was pro- cured gave rise to the proverb,

Τοῦ δ' ἄρ' ὁ Κωρυκαῖος ἠκροάζετο.

The modern name of this elevated ridge is the *Table Mountain*, but the ancient appellation is still preserved in that of *Kourko*, which belongs to a bold headland forming the extreme point of the Erythræan peninsula towards Samos. When Thu- cydides speaks of Corycus in the eighth book, I con- ceive he alludes to this cape. (VIII. 14. 33, 34. Cf. Liv. XXXVII. 12.) Pliny calls it Coryceon pro- montorium. (V. 31.) Between this headland and that of Argennum is a small island, close to the mainland, which Strabo names Halonnesus. (XIV. Halonne-sus insula. p. 645.) Beyond the Corycian promontory the shore recedes, and forms a considerable bay, advancing inland towards the north-east, and with that of Clazomenæ forming the neck of the Erythræan peninsula. Strabo places here some Chalcidians, who were contiguous to the isthmus, and who, as Pausanias reports, constituted a third part of the Erythræan state. He does not however quite agree with Strabo as to the name of this tribe, since he calls it Chalcitis. (Ach. 5.) He adds, that there was also a promontory so called, near which were some warm springs and baths, highly esteemed throughout Ionia for their medicinal efficacy. Above this district was a grove, consecrated to Alexander the Great, in which solemn games, named after that prince, were celebrated by the general states of Ionia. From this wood to the coast of Clazomenæ the distance by land was only fifty stadia, whereas by sea it exceeded a thousand. (Strab. XIV. p. 644.) Beyond the Chalcidian coast, and without the peninsula, was a port belonging to the city of Teos. Strabo writes the name Cherrœidæ, or Gerrhœidæ, (loc. cit.) but Livy Geræsticus. (XXXVII. 27.) There was also in the same vicinity a town called Eræ, or Geræ, and apparently a place of some strength. (Thuc. VIII. 19, 20. Strab. loc. cit.) Its site, if we may judge from the analogy of name, agrees with that now called *Erekevi*. In Scylax, I imagine we ought to substitute Γεραὶ for Ἄγρα. (p. 37.)

Teos had been originally colonized by a party of Minyæ from Orchomenus, led by Athamas; but it subsequently received great accession of strength from Athens at the time of the Ionian migration. The Athenian chiefs were Nauclus, son of Codrus, Apœcus, and Damasus; another reinforcement was

Margin notes:

Chalcis regio.

Gerrhœidæ sive Geræsticus portus.
Eræ sive Geræ.

Teos.

afterwards brought by Geres from Bœotia. (Strab. XIV. p. 633. Pausan. Ach. 3. Herod. I. 142. Scyl. p. 37. Steph. Byz. v. Τέως.) When Ionia was invaded by the armies of Cyrus after the overthrow of Crœsus, the Teians, despairing of being able to resist the Persian power, abandoned their native city, and retired to Abdera in Thrace. This colony became so flourishing in consequence, that it quite eclipsed the parent state. (Herod. I. 168. Strab. loc. cit.) Teos is celebrated in the literary history of Greece for having given birth to Anacreon, (Herod. III. 121.) and Hecatæus the historian, though the latter is more frequently known by the surname of Abderite. (Strab. loc. cit.) This town produced also Protagoras the sophist, Scythinus an Iambic poet, Andron a geographical writer, and Apellicon the great book collector, to whom literature is indebted for the preservation of the works of Aristotle. (Strab. loc. cit. Steph. Byz. v. Τέως.)

> Vitabis æstus, et fide Teia
> Dices laborantes in uno
> Penelopen, vitreamque Circen.
> Hor. Od. I. 17, 18.

Though deserted by the greater part of its inhabitants, Teos still continued to subsist as an Ionian city, as may be seen from Thucydides. (III. 32.) It revolted from Athens after the Sicilian overthrow, (VIII. 16, 19.) but was again reduced. (VIII. 20.) From Livy it appears, that, besides the harbour called Geræsticus, there was another port belonging to the city nearer to it, and more commodious. (XXXVII. 27. Cf. Polyb. V. 77. 5.) The chief produce of the Teian territory was wine ; (Liv. loc. cit.) and Bacchus was the deity principally revered by the inhabitants. It is singular that Pliny should rank Teos among the islands of Ionia; (V. 38.) at most it could only be reckoned as a peninsula. The site once occupied by this ancient city is now called *Boudroun.* Chandler says, " We found it almost " as desolate as Erythræ and Clazomenæ. The " walls, of which traces are extant, were, as we " guessed, about five miles in circuit; the masonry " handsome. It was with difficulty we discovered " the temple of Bacchus; but a theatre in the side " of the hill is more conspicuous. The vault only, " on which the seats ranged, remains, with two " broken pedestals, in the area. The city port is " partly dry, and sand-banks rise above the surface " of the water. On the edge are vestiges of a wall, " and before it are two small islets. On the left " hand, or toward the continent, is a channel, which " seemed artificial, the water not deep. The heap " of the temple of Bacchus, which was visible from " the theatre beneath on the right hand, lay in the " middle of a corn-field, and is overrun with bushes " and olive-trees. It was one of the most celebrated " structures in Ionia. The remains of it have been " engraved at the expense of the society of Dilet- " tanti, and published, with its history, in the Ionian " Antiquities [c]."

Myonne- sus.

To the south of Teos is another peninsula, in which was situated the town of Myonnesus, dependent on the former city. Livy describes it as " a promontory placed between Samos and Teos. " It is a hill rising from a base sufficiently broad to

[c] Travels in Asia Minor, p. 119, 120. We have gold and silver money of Teos; the legend is TION and THIΩN. The imperial series is traced from Augustus to Saloninus. Sestini, p. 85.

" a very pointed summit. The approach to it from
" the land is by a narrow path. On the sea-side it
" is girt by rocks, so worn by the waves, that in
" some parts the overhanging cliffs extend further
" out to sea than the ships which are stationed
" there." (XXXVII. 27.) Strabo also states that
the town was situated on an elevated peninsula.
(XIV. p. 643. Cf. Thuc. III. 32.) Strabo mentions
that certain mimes and players of Teos, having been
expelled from that city during a sedition, had been
afterwards settled at Myonnesus by king Attalus ;
but the Teians disliking their proximity, obtained
from the Romans that they should be removed to
Lebedos. (XIV. loc. cit. Steph. Byz. v. Μυόννησος.)
The hill of Myonnesus is now called *Hypsili-bounos:*
it is described by modern travellers as commanding
a most extensive view of a picturesque country, of
the sea-coast and islands [d]. Close to the shore was
a small island named Macris, near which the com- Macris in-
bined fleet of the Romans and Rhodians gained an sula.
important victory over that of Antiochus. (Liv.
XXXVII. 28, 29.) Pausanias seems to give the
name of Macria to the promontory of Myonnesus.
He states that there were some hot springs which
oozed out among the rocks on the sea-shore. Others
were used as baths, and decorated with elegant buildings. (Ach. 5.) Strabo notices another island between Teos and Lebedos : it was named by some
Aspis, by others Arconnesus. (XIV. p. 643.) " It Aspis, sive
" is now called *Carabash,* and stands about the sus insula.
" middle of the bay, stretching to the south-west [e]."

  Lebedos, which follows next, appears, accord- Lebedos.
ing to Pausanias, to have been originally held by

  [d] Chandler's Travels, p. 124.   [e] Ibid. p. 126.
                    A a 2

the Carians, who were expelled by an Ionian colony
under Andræmon, son of Codrus. The tomb of
this chief was to be seen on the road leading from
Lebedus to Colophon, across the river Hales. (Ach.
c. 3.) Herodotus mentions Lebedus as one of the
twelve Ionian cities. (I. 142.) It was afterwards
nearly destroyed by Lysimachus, for the sole purpose of aggrandizing Ephesus. (Pausan. loc. cit. et
Attic. c. 9.) but it became a place of some note as
the general rendezvous of all the Ionian stage-
players. They held a meeting once a year, and
celebrated games and sports in honour of Bacchus.
Strabo reports that they had originally occupied
Teos, but being expelled from thence on account of
a sedition, they withdrew to Ephesus. Attalus
afterwards placed them at Myonnesus, but on a representation from the Teians, who objected to them
as neighbours, the Romans finally fixed them at
Lebedos, the population of which was by this time
greatly reduced. (XIV. p. 643.) The latter fact is
confirmed by Horace.

> An Lebedum laudas, odio maris atque viarum ?
> Scis, Lebedus quam sit Gabiis desertior atque
> Fidenis vicus.   EPIST. I. 11. 7.

Pausanias observes, that the soil of Lebedos was
remarkably fertile : and he speaks of its mineral
baths as very salutary, and deserving admiration.
(Ach. c. 5.) The site of this town is marked by
some ruins, now called *Ecclesia*, or *Xingi*. They
consist of naked masses of stone and of brick, with
cement ; and a basement, with the entire floor of a
small temple. Nearer the sea are some traces of
ancient walls, and a few fragments of Doric columns[f].

f Chandler's Asia Minor, p. 125, 126.

Steph. Byz. reports, that between Lebedos and Colophon, which follows soon after, there was a place
named Dioshieron, (v. Διὸς ἱερόν,) and this position Dioshie-
seems to agree with the reference made to it by ron.
Thucydides. (VIII. 19.) But it must not be confounded with a Lydian town of the same name, •
situated near the Cayster.

Colophon, another Ionian city, and of greater cele- Colophon.
brity, was founded, as we learn from Strabo, by Andræmon, son of Codrus, who has been already mentioned more than once. (Cf. Pausan. loc. cit.) It
was situated about two miles from the coast, and
its port, called Notium, was connected with the city
by means of long walls. (Liv. XXXVII. 26. Thuc.
III. 34. Scyl. p. 37.) We learn from Herodotus
that it was through the Colophonians that Smyrna
was brought over to the Ionian confederacy. (I.
150.) The same historian relates that the Colophonians were however excluded, together with the
Ephesians, from the Ionian festival called Apaturia,
on account of some bloodshed in which they were
implicated. (I. 147.) Colophon is also stated by
him to have fallen into the hands of Gyges, king of
Lydia. (I. 14.) During the Peloponnesian war Colophon was occupied by a Persian force, but some of
the inhabitants retired to Notium, and being sup- Notium.
ported by Paches, an Athenian commander, were
enabled to maintain themselves successfully. (Thuc.
III. 34.) Strabo observes that Colophon at one
period possessed a flourishing navy, and its cavalry
was in such repute, that victory followed wherever
it was employed : hence the proverb τὸν Κολοφῶνα
ἐπέθηκεν, that is, " he has brought his work to a good
" conclusion ;" but the Scholiast of Plato gives

another version of the saying, which appears somewhat more probable, though his authority is not so
good. He states, that the Colophonians had the
right of a double vote in the Panionian assembly, on
account of the service they rendered the confederacy
in the matter of Smyrna. Hence they were frequently enabled to decide points left undetermined
from a parity of suffrages. (Schol. Plat. in Theæt.
p. 319.) Colophon is further celebrated from the
number of distinguished poets it has produced. It
was one of the rival claimants to the birth of Homer,
and was unquestionably the native city of Mimnermus, an elegiac poet, who flourished in the time of
Solon [g] ; of Polymnestus, a musician, noticed by Pindar ; Phœnix, an iambic poet, quoted by Athenæus
and Pausanias ; Hermesianax, a distinguished writer
of elegiacs, of which a celebrated fragment has been
preserved to us by Athenæus ; (XIII. p. 597. A.[h])
Antimachus, a well known epic poet ; Xenophanes, a
writer of (σίλλοι) silli on physical subjects ; and Nicander, who wrote Georgics, and poems on venomous
creatures, and their antidotes. He is also said to
have written a treatise on the poets of Colophon.
(Schol. Nicandr. Ther. 3.)

Colophon was destroyed by Lysimachus, together
with Lebedos, in order to swell the population of
the new town he founded at Ephesus ; a circumstance which we learn from Pausanias. (Attic. c. 9.
Ach. c. 3. Cf. Diod. Sic. XX. p. 483.) The Colophonians are stigmatised by several writers as very
effeminate and luxurious. (Athen. XII. p. 526.) In
the war with Antiochus, Colophon, or rather No-

[g] See Fabr. Bibl. Gr. tom. I.
p. 733. ed. Harles.

[h] See Ruhnk. Epist. Crit. II.
p. 374.

tium, was besieged by that king; but the siege was
raised by the Romans. (Liv. XXXVII. 26, 27.) The
conduct of the inhabitants of Notium on this occasion obtained for them the approbation of the Roman senate, and several privileges. (XXXVIII. 39.
Cic. Orat. Man. c. 12. Hor. Epist. I. 11, 3. Plin. V.
29.)

The little river Hales, which flowed near Colo- Hales fl.
phon, was noted for the coldness of its waters. (Pausan. Arcad. c. 28.) It is thought by some learned
critics that in the following fragment of Mimnermus, preserved by Strabo, (XIV. p. 634.) we should
read ‛Αλήεντος for ’Αστήεντος.

> ’Ες δ’ ἐρατὴν Κολοφῶνα βίην ὑπέροπλον ἔχοντες
> ‛Εζόμεθ’ ἀργαλέης ὕβριος ἡγεμόνες.
> Κεῖθεν δ’ ’Αστήεντος ἀπορνύμεοι ποταμοῖο
> Θεῶν βουλῇ Σμύρνην εἵλομεν Αἰολίδα.

This stream appears to flow from mount *Aleman*,
anciently called Gallesus, or Gallesium. (Strab. XIV. Gallesus
p. 642.) It was connected with the chain of mount mons.
Corax, or Coracium, (Strab. loc. cit.) which stretched
to the north in the direction of Smyrna and Clazomenæ. Chandler describes Gallesus as a vast mountain clad with pines, and abounding in rapid streams
and waterfalls [i]. Colophon derived further celebrity
from its vicinity to the oracle of the Clarian Apollo. Claros.
This famous seat of divination is supposed to have
been discovered soon after the siege of Troy, and
the poets relate many tales with regard to a contention of prophetic skill which took place here between
Calchas and Mopsus, which ended in the defeat and
death of the former. (Strab. XIV. p. 642.)

[i] Travels in Asia Minor, p. 130.

Παιπαλόεις τε Μίμας, καὶ Κωρύκου ἄκρα κάρηνα
Καὶ Κλάρος αἰγλήεσσα, καὶ Αἰσαγέης ὄρος αἰπὺ,
Καὶ Σάμος ὑδρηλή, Μυκάλης τ᾽ αἰπεινὰ κάρηνα.

HOM. HYMN. APOLL. 40.

῍Η θ᾽ ἵππους ἄρσασα βαθυσχοίνοιο Μέλητος,
Ῥίμφα διὰ Σμύρνης παγχρύσεον ἄρμα διώκει
᾽Ες Κλάρον ἀμπελόεσσαν, ὅθ᾽ ἀργυρότοξος ᾽Απόλλων
῏Ησται, μιμνάζων ἑκατηβόλον ἰοχέαιραν.

HYMN. IN DIAN. 5.

Οἷος δ᾽ ἐκ νηοῖο θυώδεος εἶσιν ᾽Απόλλων
Δῆλον ἀν᾽ ἠγαθέην, ἠὲ Κλάρον, ἢ ὅγε Πυθὼ,
῍Η Λυκίην εὐρεῖαν, ἐπὶ Ξάνθοιο ῥοῇσι.

APOLL. RH. I. 307.

. . . . . mihi Delphica tellus
Et Claros, et Tenedos, Pataræaque regia servit.

OVID. METAM. I. 515.

Trojugena, interpres Divum, qui numina Phœbi,
Qui tripodas, Clarii lauros, qui sidera sentis.

ÆN. III. 359.

(Cf. Pausan. Ach. c. 3, 5.) Tacitus gives us an account of the visit paid by Germanicus to this oracle. The priesthood was confined to certain families, principally of Miletus. The number and names of those who came to consult the oracle were announced to the seer, who, having descended into the cave, and drank of the spring, revealed in verse to each the subject of his secret thoughts. On this occasion, it is said that a speedy death was announced to Germanicus. (Ann. II. 54.) The oracle continued to flourish in the time of Pliny, (V. 29.) and as late as the reign of Constantine. Considerable vestiges are still to be seen at *Zille*, which occupies the site of the ancient Claros : these consist of several sepulchres; the prophetic fountain and cave, with marble steps leading down to it; also remains of a large temple, a theatre, and several churches [k]. A few wretched huts mark the position of the once flourishing city of Colophon. Notium has also entirely disappeared [l]. Beyond Colophon and Claros we come to the river Caystrus, and the marshes it forms Caystrus fl. at its mouth. The latter are doubtless the Ἄσιος Asiæ paλειμὼν of Homer, the favourite haunt of swans and lus. other water-fowl.

> Χηνῶν, ἢ γεράνων, ἢ κύκνων δουλιχοδείρων,
> Ἀσίῳ ἐν λειμῶνι, Καϋστρίου ἀμφὶ ῥέεθρα.
> IL. B. 470.

> Jam varias pelagi volucres, et quæ Asia circum
> Dulcibus in stagnis rimantur prata Caystri.
> GEORG. I. 383.

> Ceu quondam nivei liquida inter nubila cycni,
> Quum sese e pastu referunt, et longa canoros
> Dant per colla modos; sonat amnis, et Asia longe
> Pulsa palus. ÆN. VII. 699.

> . . . . non illo plura Caystros
> Carmina cygnorum labentibus audit in undis.
> OVID. METAM. V. 386.

> Sic niger in ripis errat quum forte Caystri,
> Inter Ledæos videtur corvus olores.
> MART. EP. I. 546.

Strabo speaks of two marshes, or lakes, near the mouth of the Caystrus, one of which was called Selinusia. They both belonged to the temple of Selinusia Ephesus, and were a source of considerable revenue. palus.

---

[k] Chandler's Travels in Asia Minor, p. 130, 131.
[l] Ibid. p. 132, 133.

The sovereigns of Asia had at one time sequestered
these funds, but they had been restored by the Romans. The revenue officers of the province, however, again endeavoured to appropriate these lands
to the purposes of the state. This led to a deputation on the part of the Ephesians to Rome, when
Artemidorus, the celebrated geographer, as we learn
from Strabo, pleaded the cause of his countrymen
before the senate, and obtained a fresh grant in their
favour. The Ephesians, in recompense for this
service, erected a golden statue to the orator in their
temple. At the end of the lake, which lies most in
a hollow, was a temple of Jupiter, or Pluto[m], said
to have been built by Agamemnon. (Strab. XIV.
p. 642.)

Pliny, describing the course of the Caystrus, says,
it rises in the Cilbian mountains, and after receiving
many streams, and among others the Pegasean
marsh which the river Phyrites brings down, waters
the plain of Ephesus. (V. 29.) The Phyrites seems
to be that stream which rises in the south-western
chain of Tmolus, and after passing by the village
of *Tourbali,* close to the ruins of Metropolis and
the foot of mount Gallesus, forms with the Caystrus
the marshes above alluded to. The Caystrus is
now called *Kutchuck Mendere,* or Lesser Meander,
by the Turks. We shall have to speak of the upper
valley of this river when we enter upon the description of Lydia. Near its mouth, and on the southern

Pegaseum
stagnum.

Phyrites
fluvius.

---

[m] Τῆς δὲ λίμνης ἐν τῷ κοιλο-
τάτῳ βασιλέως ἐστιν ἱερόν· φασὶ δ'
Ἀγαμέμνονος ἵδρυμα. The French
translators render it "un temple
"royal;" the Latin version "fa-
"num regis." I conceive Βασιλεὺς to mean here either Jupiter, (vid. Hesych. v. Βασίλειος
στοὰ, et not.) or Pluto, who is
styled by Homer ἄναξ ἐνέρων.

bank, was situated the renowned city of Ephesus.
Its foundation was so ancient as to be ascribed by
some to the Amazons, at which time it was called
Smyrna. (Callin. ap. Strab. XIV. p. 663. Steph.
Byz. v. "Εφεσος.) It also bore successively the
names of Samorna, Trachea, Ortygia, and Ptelea.
Bennamia and Sisyrba were parts of the town.
(Steph. Byz. vv. Βενναμία, Σίσυρβα.) The first inhabitants of the country, according to Strabo, were the
Leleges and Carians, who made way for the Ionian
colonists brought by Androclus, son of Codrus.
(XIV. p. 640.) The latter occupied also the island
of Samos. (Pausan. Ach. c. 2.) The colonists appear
not to have dwelt together in one place at first, but
to have been scattered throughout the Ephesian district till the time of Crœsus, when the city began to
assume an appearance of wealth and prosperity.
(Strab. loc. cit.) Herodotus relates, that the Ephesians, being invaded by that prince, dedicated their
city to Diana, by fastening a rope from their walls
to the temple of the goddess, a distance of seven
stadia. The historian remarks, that this applies to
the old town. (I. 26.) Not long after the Ephesians
quitted their former abodes, and drawing nearer to
the temple, built around it the new city, which subsisted till the time of Alexander the Great. (Strab.
loc. cit.) The shrine of Diana, as Pausanias affirms,
was already in great repute before the arrival of
the Ionians in Asia :

Σοὶ καὶ 'Αμαζονίδες, πολέμου ἐπιθυμήτειραι,
'Εν κοτε παρραλίη 'Εφέσου βρέτας ἰδρύσαντο
Φηγῷ ὑπὸ πρέμνῳ, τέλεσεν δέ τοι ἱερὸν 'Ιππώ.

CALLIM. HYMN. IN DIAN. 238.

Τάων ἀμφοτέρων γε βορειοτέρην ἐσίδοιο
Παῤῥαλίην Ἔφεσον, μεγάλην πόλιν Ἰοχεαίρης·
Ἔνθα θεῇ ποτε νηὸν Ἀμαζονίδες τετύχοντο.
Πρέμνῳ ἔνι πτελέης, περιώσιον ἀνδράσι θαῦμα.

DIONYS. PERIEG. 826.

and it was even affirmed that the Amazons, at a
remote period, had sacrificed to the goddess there.
The image of Diana, said to have descended from
Jupiter, (Act. Apost. XIX. 35.) was especially the
object of superstitious veneration. It had been preserved throughout all the vicissitudes and revolutions experienced by the city and temple, though
the material was only of wood ; it was affirmed by
Pliny, on the authority of Mutianus, who had in-
spected the idol himself, that nard, or some other
unctuous substance, was used to guard against decay, to which it would otherwise have been exposed.
(XVI. 79.)   It was richly adorned with embroidered
robes, and concealed from view, except during sacrifices, and other solemn occasions.   The service of
the temple was performed by priests, who were
eunuchs, named Megabyzæ, and accounted peculiarly sacred ; with these were associated a number
of virgins as priestesses, (Strab. XIV. p. 641. Xen.
Anab. V. 3, 7.) besides several other inferior officers
and retainers [n].   The annual festival of the goddess
was attended by all the Ionian states, and the month
Artemisius was moreover set apart as altogether to
be dedicated to her service [o].   The first temple was
planned and constructed by Chersiphron, a Cretan
architect, assisted by his son Metagenes, who con-

---

[n] Inscript. Ant. ap. Chand. p. 11.
[o] Chand. Inscr. Ant. p. 13.

trived a machine for conveying the huge marble blocks of which it was constructed from the quarries of mount Prion. (Vitruv. X. 6.) This edifice, which for its size and decorations was accounted superior to all other buildings of the kind, alone escaped the conflagration to which the other temples of Asia were doomed by Xerxes on his return from Greece. (Strab. VII. p. 273.) But several years after it was set on fire by a madman named Herostratus, and entirely destroyed, with the exception of the outer columns. This event is said to have happened the same night that Alexander the Great was born. (Plut. Alex. c. 3. Cic. de Nat. Deor. II. 27. Valer. Max. VIII. 14. Strab. XIV. p. 640.) The building remained in ruins till Alexander himself, on his arrival in Asia, offered the Ephesians to restore it, on condition that he should be declared the founder. The Ephesians however declined the proposal, alleging, in a style of flattery suited to the vanity of the monarch, that it was unbecoming in one god to erect temples to other deities. (Artemid. ap. Strab. loc. cit.) They therefore determined to rely. on their own resources, and those of voluntary contributors, to complete this great work, the execution of which was entrusted to Dinocrates [p], the architect who is reported to have entertained the gigantic and extravagant project of forming a statue of Alexander out of mount Athos. The ladies of Ephesus are said to have contributed on this occasion all their jewels and ornaments, and the wealthier ci-

[p] The name of this artist is variously given. Some MSS. of Strabo read Chirocrates ; Plutarch calls him Stasicrates ; (Alex. c. 52.) Eustathius, Dio- cles : (Il. O. p. 980.) but Vitruvius, (II. Præf.) Val. Maximus, (I. 4.) Pliny, (VII. 37.) and Strabo, according to some MSS., write Dinocrates.

tizens were not slow in devoting their property to
the service of the goddess ; a certain sum was also
raised from the sale of the materials of the former
building. These details were set forth in a decree
delivered by the Ephesians on this subject. (Artemid. ap. Strab. loc. cit.) The new temple greatly
surpassed the original building in dimensions and
magnificence ; being not only reckoned the most
beautiful sacred edifice of Ionia, but even of the
world, and accounted for that reason one of its seven
wonders. (Pausan. Ach. 5. Plin. XXXVI. 14.) It
was 425 feet in length, and 220 in breadth. The
pillars were 127 in number, and sixty feet in height,
and each of them had been the offering of a sovereign. Of these, thirty-six were carved ; one by the
celebrated sculptor Scopas. (Plin. loc. cit.) The
order is said to have been Ionic. The gates were
of cypress, highly polished, and the roof of cedar ;
the steps leading up to it of vine. The internal decorations corresponded with the size and external
appearance of the structure. The altar was almost
entirely adorned by the master hand of Praxiteles.
There were also some celebrated works of Thraso,
and Scopas, and a picture of Apelles, in which Alexander appeared armed with thunder. For this the
artist received the enormous sum of twenty talents
of gold. (Strab. loc. cit. Plin.) The asylum attached
to the temple was regarded with peculiar sanctity.
Alexander had extended it to a stadium, and Mithridates somewhat further ; Mark Antony nearly
doubled that distance : but the abuses to which this
privilege subsequently gave rise, caused it to be
abolished by Augustus. (Strab. loc. cit.) The city
itself had been gradually increasing with the cele-

brity and splendour of its fane ; to this Lysimachus
also contributed, by causing the inhabitants to remove from the old site, which was subject to disastrous inundations, to a better position, which he
had marked out and surrounded with walls. (Strab.
loc. cit. Dur. Epigr. ap. Steph. Byz. v. Ἔφεσος.)
This prince was desirous that the new town should
be called after his wife Arsinoe, but the attempt did
not succeed. (Strab. loc. cit.) Ephesus was considered in some sort the metropolis of Ionia, from
its having been originally founded by Androclus,
son of Codrus ; and the descendants of that prince
were, even in the time of Strabo, honoured with the
title of kings, and were decorated, on certain festive
occasions, with the purple robe and sceptre, and presided at the sacrifices of the Eleusinian Ceres. (Strab.
XIV. p. 633.)   After the defeat of Antiochus this
city was made over to the kings of Pergamum by the
Roman senate, (Liv. XXXVII. 4, 5. XXXVIII.
39.) and it seems to have enjoyed a considerable
degree of prosperity under the mild sway of these
sovereigns.   Attalus Philadelphus caused some extensive works to be made at the mouth of the Caystrus in order to prevent the alluvial deposit of that
stream from blocking up the harbour ; but the enterprise was injudiciously formed, and rather aggra-
vated the evil it was intended to correct.   Such was
however the advantageous situation of the city,
that, in Strabo's time, it was the great emporium of
all Asia. (XIV. p. 641. XII. p. 540.)   We know,
too, that at this period the temple of Ephesus had lost
nothing of its splendour and celebrity, though they
were destined, by the arrival of St. Paul, and the
power of the Gospel, to sustain a blow from which

they never recovered. The circumstances which
St. Luke has described in the nineteenth chapter of
the Acts illustrate so forcibly the history of this
period, and are so closely connected with the annals
of Ephesus, that it seems desirable to insert his
account here in his own words. The sacred historian, having in the eighteenth chapter mentioned
the first short visit paid by the apostle of the Gen-
tiles, and his departure for Cæsarea and Antioch,
after promising to return again, goes on to state the
arrival of Apollos at Ephesus, and the effect of his
preaching there. He then, at the beginning of the
nineteenth chapter, returns to St. Paul : " And it
" came to pass, that, while Apollos was at Corinth,
" Paul having passed through the upper coasts came
" to Ephesus : and finding certain disciples, he said
" unto them, Have ye received the Holy Ghost since
" ye believed ? And they said unto him, We have
" not so much as heard whether there be any Holy
" Ghost. And he said unto them, Unto what then
" were ye baptized ? And they said, Unto John's
" baptism. Then said Paul, John verily baptized
" with the baptism of repentance, saying unto the
" people, that they should believe on him which
" should come after him, that is, on Christ Jesus.
" When they heard this, they were baptized in the
" name of the Lord Jesus. And when Paul had
" laid his hands upon them, the Holy Ghost came
" on them ; and they spake with tongues, and pro-
" phesied. And all the men were about twelve.
" And he went into the synagogue, and spake boldly
" for the space of three months, disputing and per-
" suading the things concerning the kingdom of
" God. But when divers were hardened, and be-

" lieved not, but spake evil of that way before the
" multitude, he departed from them, and separated
" the disciples, disputing daily in the school of one
" Tyrannus.   And this continued by the space of
" two years ; so that all they which dwelt in Asia
" heard the word of the Lord Jesus, both Jews and
" Greeks.   And God wrought special miracles by
" the hands of Paul : so that from his body were
" brought unto the sick handkerchiefs or aprons,
" and the diseases departed from them, and the evil
" spirits went out of them.   Then certain of the
" vagabond Jews, exorcists, took upon them to call
" over them which had evil spirits the name of the
" Lord Jesus, saying, We adjure you by Jesus whom
" Paul preacheth.   And there were seven sons of
" one Sceva, a Jew, and chief of the priests, which
" did so.   And the evil spirit answered and said,
" Jesus I know, and Paul I know ; but who are ye ?
" And the man in whom the evil spirit was leaped
" on them, and overcame them, and prevailed against
" them, so that they fled out of that house naked
" and wounded.   And this was known to all the
" Jews and Greeks also dwelling at Ephesus ; and
" fear fell on them all, and the name of the Lord
" Jesus was magnified.   And many that believed
" came, and confessed, and shewed their deeds.
" Many of them also which used curious arts, brought
" their books together, and burned them before all
" men : and they counted the price of them, and
" found it fifty thousand pieces of silver.   So mightily
" grew the word of God and prevailed.   After these
" things were ended, Paul purposed in the spirit,
" when he had passed through Macedonia and
" Achaia, to go to Jerusalem, saying, After I have

" been there, I must also see Rome. So he sent
" into Macedonia two of them that ministered unto
" him, Timotheus and Erastus; but he himself
" stayed in Asia for a season. And the same time
" there arose no small stir about that way. For
" a certain man named Demetrius, a silversmith,
" which made silver shrines for Diana, brought no
" small gain unto the craftsmen; whom he called
" together with the workmen of like occupation, and
" said, Sirs, ye know that by this craft we have our
" wealth. Moreover ye see and hear, that not alone
" at Ephesus, but almost throughout all Asia, this
" Paul hath persuaded and turned away much
" people, saying that they be no gods, which are
" made with hands : so that not only this our craft
" is in danger to be set at nought; but also that the
" temple of the great goddess Diana should be de-
" spised, and her magnificence should be destroyed,
" whom all Asia and the world worshippeth. And
" when they heard these sayings, they were full of
" wrath, and cried out, saying, Great is Diana of
" the Ephesians. And the whole city was filled
" with confusion : and having caught Gaius and
" Aristarchus, men of Macedonia, Paul's companions
" in travel, they rushed with one accord into the
" theatre. And when Paul would have entered in
" unto the people, the disciples suffered him not.
" And certain of the chief of Asia, which were
" his friends, sent unto him, desiring him that he
" would not adventure · himself into the theatre.
" Some therefore cried one thing, and some another :
" for the assembly was confused; and the more part
" knew not wherefore they were come together.
" And they drew Alexander out of the multitude,

" the Jews putting him forward. And Alexander
" beckoned with the hand, and would have made
" his defence unto the people. But when they knew
" that he was a Jew, all with one voice about the
" space of two hours cried out, Great is Diana of the
" Ephesians. And when the townclerk had appeased
" the people, he said, Ye men of Ephesus, what man
" is there that knoweth not how that the city of the
" Ephesians is a worshipper of the great goddess
" Diana, and of the image which fell down from
" Jupiter? Seeing then that these things cannot be
" spoken against, ye ought to be quiet, and to do
" nothing rashly. For ye have brought hither
" these men, which are neither robbers of churches,
" nor yet blasphemers of your goddess. Wherefore
" if Demetrius, and the craftsmen which are with
" him, have a matter against any man, the law is
" open, and there are deputies : let them implead
" one another. But if ye enquire any thing con-
" cerning other matters, it shall be determined in a
" lawful assembly. For we are in danger to be
" called in question for this day's uproar, there being
" no cause whereby we may give an account of this
" concourse. And when he had thus spoken, he
" dismissed the assembly. And after the uproar
" was ceased, Paul called unto him the disciples,
" and embraced them, and departed for to go into
" Macedonia." It was probably to this tumult, and
to the danger which he then encountered, that the
apostle alludes in his Epistle to the Corinthians, (I.
xv. 32.) where he says, " If after the manner of men
" I have fought with beasts at Ephesus, what ad-
" vantageth it me, if the dead rise not." Many
respectable commentators are, I know, disposed to

take the words, εἰ κατὰ ἄνθρωπον ἐθηριομάχησα ἐν Ἐφέσῳ,
in a literal sense, as if the apostle had indeed been
compelled to engage with wild beasts in the arena ;
but I cannot help thinking, with Grotius and others,
that the metaphorical meaning is to be preferred ;
that is, " if I have fought against man at Ephesus,
" like unto a ferocious animal ;" for so remarkable a fact would not have been omitted by St.
Luke in his circumstantial narrative of the occur-
rences at Ephesus ; and it cannot be said that the
figurative sense is forced and unnatural.   This narrative fully agrees with the notions conveyed by
profane authorities of the idolatry and gross superstitions then prevalent at Ephesus.   But the great
apostle, during a three years' residence there, (Acts
xx. 31.) was enabled, with the divine assistance, to
establish there the faith of Christ, and to found a
church, which became, as it were, the metropolis of
Asia.   Of his great care of the Ephesian community we have a strong proof in the affecting charge
he delivered to their elders at Miletus, where he
had convened them on his return from Macedonia ;
(Acts xx. 16—38.) and still more in the Epistle he
afterwards addressed to them from Rome, and which
forms part of the sacred volume.   Tradition represents Timothy to have been the first bishop of Ephesus ; but there is greater evidence that St. John resided towards the close of his life in that city.   He
is also supposed, on good authority, to have composed his Gospel, and finally to have ended his life
there.   In the Revelations the apostle places the
church of Ephesus first among the seven ; and from
the gentle rebuke which it received from the Lord,
we may conclude that it was yet flourishing under

his care. (Rev. ii. 4, 5.)   As the Christian religion prospered, the worship of Diana diminished and sunk into insignificance.   Nero is said to have plundered the temple of many votive images, and great sums of gold and silver.   This edifice appears, however, to have remained entire in the second century; since we are told, by Philostratus, that a sophist, named Damianus, at that time expended great sums of money in erecting a portico, and other structures connected with its service. (Vit. Soph. p. 601.)   At a later period it was again spoiled by the Goths, and other barbarians, and time has so completed the havoc made by the hand of man, that, according to the reports of competent eye-witnesses, the mighty fabric has entirely disappeared [q].   Ephesus was governed, as we learn from Strabo, by a senate, with a select body of magistrates called Epicleti. (XIV. p. 640.)   The Asiarchs, mentioned in the Acts of the Apostles, were deputies chosen by the several towns of Asia to preside over the sacred games, and other affairs connected with religion. Among other distinguished persons who were natives of this city may be mentioned Heraclitus the philosopher, surnamed the Obscure; Hermodorus, from whom the Romans borrowed a part of their code; Hipponax the poet, Artemidorus the geographer, Alexander Lychnus, an orator, historian, and poet, and the two great painters Apelles and Parrha-

[q] Chandler's Travels in Asia Minor, p. 173. For further information respecting this celebrated temple and the worship of Diana, the reader may consult the great Thesaurus Gr. of Gronovius, tom. VIII. p. 2646. also Deyling. Obss. Sacr. p. iv. p. 283. and Polckius Diss. de Magn. Ephes. Diana, Lips. 1718, 4to.   Democritus, an Ephesian, had written a work in several books on the temple. Athen. XII. p. 525.

sius. (Strab. loc. cit.) Several spots are mentioned by ancient writers in connexion with the history of Ephesus. Of these may be noticed Lepre Acte, a part of the old town, situate near the base of mount Prion; some lands lying at the back of that acclivity were named Opistho-lepre. (Strab. XIV. p. 633.) Mount Prion was perhaps so called from its resemblance to a saw. Trachea was another portion of the old city on the slope of mount Coressus, in which stood the temple of Minerva, and the fountain Hypelæus. (Strab. loc. cit. Athen. VIII. p. 361.) We hear also of a temple sacred to Venus Hetæra, (Athen. XIII. p. 573.) an Olympeium and gate leading towards Magnesia. (Pausan. Ach. 2.) Pausanias speaks of mount Prion as a natural curiosity, and commends likewise the whole Ephesian district for its clime and fertility. (Ach. 5.) These advantages rendered the Ephesians as prone to luxury and voluptuousness as the rest of the Ionians. (Athen. XII. p. 525. XV. p. 688.) The ruins of Ephesus are to be seen near the Turkish town of *Ayasluck*, which seems to have risen about the middle of the fourteenth century. Chandler has entered into much detail in regard to these interesting remains, and the following extracts from his account may not be unacceptable to the reader. " Ephesus," says that traveller, was situated by the " mountains, which are the southern boundary of " the plain, and comprehended within its walls a " portion of mount Prion and of Corissus. Mount " Prion is a circular hill; Corissus a single lofty " ridge, extending northward from near mount Pac- " tyas, and approaching Prion; then making an " elbow, and running westerly towards the sea.

Marginal notes:
Lepre Acte.
Opistho-lepre.
Prion mons.
Trachea.
Coressus mons.

" We entered Ephesus from *Aiasluck*, with mount
" Prion and the exterior lateral wall of a stadium
" which fronted the sea, on our left hand. We
" measured the area, and found it 687 feet long.
" The vestiges of the theatre, (alluded to in the Acts
" of the Apostles,) which was very capacious, are
" further on in the side of the same mountain.
" Going on from the theatre you come to a narrow
" valley, which divides mount Prion from Corissus ;
" within the valley you find broken columns and
" pieces of marble, with vestiges of an odeum in the
" slope of Prion. Beyond the odeum the valley
" opens gradually into the plain of *Aiasluck*. Keep-
" ing round by Prion, you meet with vestiges of
" buildings, and come to the remains of a large edi-
" fice. This was the gymnasium. The street at
" the entrance of the city from *Aiasluck* was nearly
" of the length of the stadium. The opposite side
" was composed of edifices equally ample and noble.
" The way was between a double colonnade, as we
" conjectured, from the many pedestals and bases of
" columns scattered there. This street was crossed
" by one, leading from the plain to the valley. It
" had on the left the front of the stadium, and the
" theatre, with the portico adjoining. On the right
" are ample substructions, with pieces of massive
" wall. These remains reach as far as the portico,
" and have behind them a morass, once the city port.
" Opposite to the portico is a vacant quadrangular
" space, with many bases of columns, and marble
" fragments. Here, it is probable, was the agora,
" or market-place, which in maritime towns was
" generally near the port. At the end of the street,
" and near the entrance of the valley between Prion

B b 4

" and Corissus, turning towards the sea, you have
" the market-place on the right hand, on the left
" the sloping side of Corissus, and presently the
" prostrate heap of a temple. The extent of the
" city toward the plain, on which side it was washed
" by the Cayster, cannot now be ascertained; but
" the mountainous region has preserved its boun-
" dary, the wall erected by Lysimachus, which is of
" excellent masonry. It may be traced from behind
" the stadium over mount Prion, standing often
" above twenty feet high. It crossed the valley,
" and from thence it ascended mount Corissus, and
" is seen ranging along the lofty brow, almost entire,
" except near the precipice, where it ceases. On
" mount Prion are likewise remnants of an exterior
" wall. Near the entrance of Ephesus from *Aias-*
" *luck* are the vaults of several sepulchres, and others
" along the slope of Corissus shew that the Ephe-
" sians buried likewise within the city[r]."

Panormus. The port of Ephesus bore the name of Panormus; near it, at a little distance from the sea, was
Ortygia. a spot named Ortygia, thickly planted with cypresses
Cenchrius and other trees, and watered by the little river Cen-
fluvius.
chrius, where Latona was said to have been delivered of her twins. The grove was filled with
shrines, adorned with statues by the hand of Scopas
and other eminent sculptors. Above the wood rose
Solmissus mount Solmissus, where the Curetes, by the loud
mons.
din of their arms, prevented Juno from hearing the
cries of Latona. Splendid festivals and entertain-
ments took place annually in these sacred haunts.
(Strab. XIV. p. 639.) According to Chandler, this
part of the coast has undergone considerable altera-

[r] Travels in Asia Minor, ch. 35.

tions : Ortygia has disappeared, the land having encroached on the sea [s]. This process had already been carried on for some time when Pliny lived, since he affirms that the little island of Syria, at the mouth of the Cayster, was then in the plain. (V. 31.)

Continuing along the coast, the following places present themselves to our notice : Pygela, or Phygela, said to have been founded by some deserters of Agamemnon's fleet. Here was a temple sacred to Diana Munychia. (Strab. XIV. p. 639. Plin. V. 29. Pomp. Mel. I. 17. Steph. Byz. v. Πύγελα.) Xenophon writes the name Πύγελα. (Hell. I. 2, 2.) It is also alluded to by Livy. (XXXVII. 11.) Dioscorides (V. 12.) commends the wine of this town, a local circumstance which it has yet preserved, according to Chandler, who observed its remains on a hill between Ephesus and *Scala Nova* [t]. Further inland was Marathesium, ceded by the Samians to the Ephesians in exchange for Neapolis, a maritime town, situate nearer their island. (Strab. XIV. p. 639. Scyl. p. 35. Plin. V. 29. Steph. Byz. v. Μαραθήσιον.) Neapolis is represented by *Scala Nova*, distant about three hours from Ephesus. It is situate in a bay, and has some vestiges of antiquity [u]. Proceeding south we come to the celebrated chain of Mycale, which extends for some distance along the right bank of the Mæander towards the east, and to the west runs out into the sea, opposite the island of Samos. It was already known to Homer :

Pygela, sive Phygela.

Marathesium.

Neapolis.

Mycale mons.

---

[s] Travels in Asia Minor, p. 176. The coins with the epigraph ΦΥ. and ΦΥΓ. are ascribed to this town. Sestini, p. 83.
[t] Chandler's Travels, p. 176.
[u] Ibid. p. 178.

Μαιάνδρου τε ῥοὰς, Μυκάλης τ᾽ αἰπεινὰ κάρηνα :

Il. B. 869.

and became still more celebrated from the Panionium, or solemn assembly, of the Ionian states, held
in a temple situated at its foot; (Herod. I. 148.)
and also from the great victory obtained by the
Greek naval army, under the command of Leotychides, king of Sparta, against the Persian forces
encamped near the shore ; (Herod. IX. 97.) and
which wrested the whole of Ionia for a time from
the Persian dominion.   Herodotus describes the action as taking place near the temples of the Eume-
nides and that of the Eleusinian Ceres, founded by
Philistus, a follower of Neleus, son of Codrus.   He
also particularizes two spots, called Gæson and Sco-
lopoeis. (loc. cit.) The Persians had drawn up their
ships on shore, and fortified themselves with en-
trenchments and pallisades ; but they were forced
by the Greeks, after an obstinate resistance, and defeated with great slaughter.   Mount Mycale, according to Strabo, was well wooded, and abounded
with game ; a character which, as Chandler reports,
it still retains. This traveller describes it as a high
ridge, with a beautiful cultivated plain at its foot,
and several villages on its side [u].   Towards the
north-east it was connected with mount Pactyas,
belonging to the Ephesian territory; and its termination in the sea formed the bold promontory of
Trogilium Trogilium, nearly opposite to cape Posidium, in the
promonto-
rium. isle of Samos, and separated from it by a strait,
not more than seven stadia wide. (Strab. XIV.
p. 636.)   C. Trogilium is mentioned by St. Luke

[u] Travels, p. 179, 180.

in the Acts, in his account of St. Paul's voyage from
Troas to Miletus, by Mitylene, Chios, and Samos.
From the latter island they crossed over to Trogy-
lium, and after remaining there, it appears, one
night, they reached Miletus the following day. (Acts
xx. 15.) Strabo says there was a small island of
the same name off the point, and he reckons the
distance from thence to cape Sunium at 1600 stadia.
(loc. cit.) Pliny names three Trogilian islets, Psilon,
Argennon, Sandalion. (V. 31.) The modern appellation of Trogilium is *C. S*^{ta}*. Maria;* that of mount
Mycale, *Samsoun.* The Panionium, according to Panioni-
Strabo, was about three stadia from the shore, and um.
appears to have been resorted to by the Ionian cities
from the earliest period after their colonization.
Both the assembly and the temple itself, which was
dedicated to the Heliconian Neptune, were called
Panionium. The worship of Neptune had been imported by the Ionians from Achaia in Peloponnesus,
and the surname of Heliconian was derived from
Helice, one of their cities in that country. (Strab.
XIV. p. 639. VIII. p. 384. Pausan. Ach. 24.) But
the assembly was not merely convened for religious
purposes: it was also a political body, and met for
deliberative and legislative ends; and it appears
that some remnant of this ancient institution was
preserved till very late in the Roman empire, if it
be true, as Chandler imagines, that there is a medal
of the emperor Gallus, which gives a representation
of a Panionian assembly and sacrifice [x]. (Cf. Herod.
I. 148. VI. 7.) The site of this celebrated conven-
tion is supposed, with great probability, to answer
to that of *Tchangeli,* a Turkish village close to the

[x] Travels, p. 192.

sea, and on the northern slope of Mycale. Chandler, who explored this ancient spot but imperfectly, could discover only a few uninteresting remains [y]. Sir W. Gell subsequently observed an inscription, in which mention is made of the Panionium: this appears conclusive as to the identity of that site with *Tchangeli* [z].

Glauce.

According to Thucydides, there was a place or port named Glauce, near Mycale. It was in the narrow part of the strait which divides Samos from the continent. (VIII. 79.) Steph. Byz. calls it Glaucia. (v. Γλαυκία.)

Priene.

Priene, another considerable city of the Ionians, was founded at first by Æpytus, son of Neleus, but received afterwards a second colony, brought by Philotas of Thebes; hence it was sometimes called Cadme. (Strab. XIV. p. 633, 636. Pausan. Ach. 2.) It had originally belonged to the Carians. (Herod. I. 142.) The chief circumstances relative to its history are these. It was conquered by Ardys, king of Lydia; (Herod. I. 15.) but, after the defeat of Crœsus, it was forced to submit to the arms of Cyrus. (I. 142.) It could boast of having given birth to Bias, one of the seven sages, and an able statesman, as well as philosopher. (Herod. I. 27, 170. Diog. Laert. Cicer. Paradox. 1. Hippon. ap. Strab. XIV. p. 636.) After this, we find Priene a subject of contention between the Milesians and Samians; when the former, being worsted, applied for assistance to the Athenians. (Thuc. I. 115.) Strabo informs us, that the Prienians had the right of electing the president of the Panionian sacrifices. (XIV. p. 639.) Pausanias reports, that this town was at

[y] Travels, p. 196.   [z] Leake's Asia Minor, p. 260, 1.

one time greatly oppressed by Tabates, a Persian ;
and subsequently by Hiero, one of its own citizens. (Ach. 2.) The same writer speaks of a
temple of Minerva in this city, which contained a
very ancient statue of the goddess. (Ach. 5. Cf.
Polyb. XXXIII. 12. Plin. V. 29.) Scylax states,
that Priene had two ports, one of which might be
closed ; (Peripl. p. 37.) but Strabo reports, that
when he wrote, the town was forty stadia from the
sea. (XII. p. 579.) This was caused by the great
alluvial deposits made by the river Meander at its
mouth. The remains of this ancient city are to be
seen on the southern slope of Mycale, near the
Turkish village of *Samsoun*. Chandler says, " it
" was seated on the side of the mountain, flat be-
" neath flat, in gradation to the edge of the plain.
" The areas are levelled, and the communication is
" preserved by steps cut in the slopes. The whole
" circuit of the wall of the city is standing, besides
" several portions within it worthy of admiration
" for their solidity and beauty [a]." There are also
the ruins of several public edifices, including those
of the temple of Minerva Polias, which have been
engraved in the Ionian Antiquities. Near Priene
was a river named Gessus by Pliny, (V. 20.) but Gæson fl.
Gæsus by Mela. (I. 17.) We have seen that Hero- Gæsonis
palus.
dotus mentioned a site called Gæson, near Mycale ;
(IX. 97.) and Athenæus, in explaining these lines
of Archestratus,

Λάμβανε δ' ἐκ Γαίσωνος, ὅταν Μίλητον ἵκηαι
κεστρέα τὸν κέφαλον, κ. τ. λ.

observes, that Gæson, or Gæsonis, was, according
to Neanthes of Cyzicus, a lake between Priene and

[a] Travels, p. 200-2.

Miletus, which had a communication with the sea:
he adds, that Ephorus spoke of the Gæson as a river
which flowed into this lake. (VII. p. 311.)

Meander fluvius. We are now arrived at the Meander, one of the
largest and most celebrated rivers of Asia Minor, as
well from the fertility and richness of its valleys,
the number of flourishing cities situated along its
banks, as from the unusual sinuosity of its course;
whence even its name has been employed to denote
the tortuous channel of a stream.

> Non secus ac liquidus Phrygiis Meandros in arvis
> Ludit; et ambiguo lapsu refluitque fluitque:
> Occurrensque sibi venturas aspicit undas:
> Et nunc ad fontes, nunc in mare versus apertum,
> Incertas exercet aquas.   OVID. METAM. VIII. 162.

> . . . . qualis incerta vagus
> Mæander unda ludit, et cedit sibi
> Instatque; dubius litus an fontem petat.
>   SENEC. HERC. FUR. 683.

According to Pliny, Livy, and other writers, this
considerable river had its rise in a lake situated on
mount Aulocrene in Phrygia, close to the citadel of
Celænæ: being then joined by the Marsyas and
several other streams, it flowed through Phrygia,
Caria, and Ionia, and discharged itself finally into
the sea between the cities of Priene and Miletus.
(Plin, V. 29. Liv. XXXVIII. 13. Pausan. Corinth.
4. Arcad. 41.) Another remarkable feature in the
Meander was the great tendency it had to throw up
soil at its mouth. This had already proceeded to
such an extent, that, in Strabo's time, Priene, which
once was considered as a maritime town, was then
forty stadia from the sea; and when Pausanias
wrote, he states that the whole of the space between

the last-named city and Miletus had been by this
process reclaimed from the sea, and united to the
land. (Arcad. 24.) The same operation has been
still going on, and has produced perhaps the greatest metamorphosis of which we have any evidence
in comparative geography. These alterations will
be best explained when we come to examine the
topography of the country which surrounds Mile- Miletus.
tus. That once great and flourishing city, being
situated at the mouth of the Meander, and on the
left bank, must certainly be considered as belonging
to Caria; but it seemed more convenient to comprise it in the section which included the Ionian
cities, and not to detach from them one which held
so conspicuous a place in the confederacy. The
account which Ephorus, who is cited by Strabo,
(XIV. p. 635.) and corroborated by Pausanias,
(Ach. 2.) gives of the origin of the city is principally as follows. The whole of this part of Asia
was called Anactoria, from Anax, a native prince,
and was occupied by the Carians. On the arrival
of Sarpedon, brother of Minos, from Crete, with
some natives of that island, he was kindly received
by the Carians, and allowed to found a city, which
was called Miletus, either from a Cretan town, or
an individual of that name. (Cf. Steph. Byz. Μίλη-
τος. Plin. V. 29.) Herodotus does not appear to
have been acquainted with this tradition, since he
speaks merely of Sarpedon's establishment in Lycia.
(I. 173.) Homer also, though he mentions Miletus,
has recorded only the fact of its belonging to the
Carians:

Νάστης αὖ Καρῶν ἡγήσατο βαρβαροφώνων,
Οἳ Μίλητον ἔχον, Φθειρῶν τ᾽ ὄρος ἀκριτόφυλλον,

Μαιάνδοου τε ροὰς, Μυκάλης τ' αἰπεινὰ κάρηνα·
Τῶν μὲν ἄρ' Ἀμφίμαχος καὶ Νάστης ἡγησάσθην·

IL. B. 867.

When the Ionians subsequently arrived there, under
the conduct of Neleus, they put to death or expelled
the Carian inhabitants, and occupied the town. (Pausan. Ach. 2. Strab. loc. cit. Herod. IX. 97.) The
admirable situation of Miletus, and the convenience
of having four harbours, one of which was capable
of containing a large fleet, gave it at an early period
a great preponderance in maritime affairs. Its commerce was most flourishing, and the number of its
colonies probably exceeded that of any other city of
antiquity. Pliny reckoned no less than eighty, and
some modern critics have taken the trouble to identify them[b]; but it will be sufficient to name in this
place Abydos, Lampsacus, and Parium, on the Hellespont; Proconnesus and Cyzicus on the Propontis; Sinope and Amisus on the Euxine: others also
in the Chersonnese, the coast of Thrace, Tauris,
and on the Borysthenes. (Strab. XIV. p. 635, et
pass.) Among the ancients, Anaximenes of Lampsacus had given a list of the Milesian colonies, but
Strabo observes that it was incomplete. (XIV. p.
635. Athen. XII. p. 523.) The kings of Lydia
made several attempts to possess themselves of so
considerable a city: first Ardys, then Sadyattes,
who defeated the Milesians in two engagements.
In this war the Chians alone of the Ionians befriended them. After the death of Sadyattes, the
war was still prosecuted by his son Alyattes, who
falling sick, as it was affirmed, through the anger

[b] Rambach de Mileto ejus-   Larcher, Hist. d'Hérod. tom.
que Coloniis, Hal. Sax. 1790.   VIII. p. 344, 359.

of Minerva, whose temple had been burnt by his
troops at Assessus, in the Milesian territory, was
glad to make an atonement for the injury, and be
reconciled with the Milesians. (Herod. I. 17—20.)
The affairs of the latter were at this time administered
by Thrasybulus with sovereign authority, as
Herodotus states; and if we may judge from the
advice which he gave to Periander of Corinth, with
whom he was very intimate, he was a deep, but
unprincipled politician. (V. 92.) The historian asserts,
that it was chiefly through an artifice of his
that Alyattes consented to desist from his attempts
on Miletus. (I. 20.) The Milesians appear subsequently
to have made a treaty with Crœsus, in
which they probably acknowledged that sovereign
as their liege lord, and consented to pay him tribute.
The same treaty was also agreed upon between them
and Cyrus, when the latter had conquered Lydia;
and this saved Miletus from the disasters which
befell at that time the other Ionian states. (I. 141,
143.) But it was not always equally fortunate. In
the reign of Darius the whole of Ionia was excited
to revolt by the intrigues and ambitious schemes of
Histiæus, who had been raised to the sovereignty
of Miletus, his native city, by the Persian monarch,
in recompense for the services he had rendered during
the Scythian expedition. Aristagoras, his deputy
and kinsman, also greatly contributed to inflame
the minds of his countrymen. At his instigation
the Athenians sent a force to Asia Minor, which
surprised and burnt Sardis; but this insult was
speedily avenged by the Persian satraps, and, after
repeated defeats, Miletus was besieged by land and
by sea, and finally taken by storm. This beau-

tiful and opulent city, the pride and ornament of
Asia, was thus plunged into the greatest calamity;
the surviving inhabitants were carried to Susa, and
settled, by order of Darius, at Ampe, near the mouth
of the Tigris, on the Erythrean sea. The town
itself was given up by the Persian commanders to
the Carians. The Athenians are said to have been
so much affected by this event, that when Phrynichus, the tragic writer, introduced on the stage his
play of " the Capture of Miletus," the whole house
burst into tears, and the people fined the poet 1000
drachms, and forbad the performance. (Herod. VI.
6—21. Callisth. ap. Strab. XIV. p. 635.) The battle of Mycale restored the Milesians to liberty : this
however they only enjoyed in name, as they became, together with the rest of Ionia and Caria, dependent on Athens. (Thuc. I. 15. 115, 16.) Towards the close of the Peloponnesian war, they
revolted from that power; and, in a battle fought
under the walls of their town, they defeated the
Argive force which was opposed to them, whilst
the Athenians overcame the Spartan troops, and
prepared to besiege the town ; but on the approach
of the Peloponnesian fleet, Phrynichus, the Athenian
admiral, thought it advisable to abandon the enterprise. (Thuc. VIII. 25—27.) We learn from the
same historian, that the Milesians, not long after,
demolished a fort which Tissaphernes, the Persian
satrap, was erecting in their territory, with the
view of bringing them into subjection. (VIII. 85.)
When Alexander, after the battle of the Granicus,
appeared before Miletus, the inhabitants, encouraged
by the presence of a Persian army and fleet stationed
at Mycale, refused to submit to that prince, and

open their gates to his forces; upon which he immediately commenced a most vigorous attack on
their walls, and finally took the city by assault: he
however forgave the surviving inhabitants, and
granted them their liberty. (Arrian. Exp. Alex. I.
18—20. Strab. loc. cit.) The Milesians sided with
the Romans during the war with Antiochus. (Liv.
XXXVII. 16. XLIII. 6.) This city was yet flourishing when Strabo wrote; (loc. cit. Tacit. Ann.
IV. 63. IV. 55.) and still later, in the time of Pliny
(V. 29.) and Pausanias. (Ach. 2.) It appears, from
the Acts of the Apostles, that St. Paul sojourned
here a few days, on his return from Macedonia and
Troas, and summoned thither the elders of the
Ephesian church, to whom he delivered an affec-
tionate farewell address. (xx. 17, et seq.) The Milesian church was under the direction of bishops,
who sat in several councils, and ranked as metropo-
litans of Caria. (Hierocl. Syn. p. 687.) This continued as late as the decline of the Byzantine empire; (Mich. Duc. p. 41.) at which time, however,
the town itself was nearly in ruins, from the ravages
of the Turks and other barbarians, and the alluvial
deposits caused by the Meander. Miletus deserves
further mention as the birthplace of Thales, the
celebrated mathematician and philosopher; and his
successors, Anaximander and Anaximenes; also of
Cadmus and Hecatæus, two of the earliest historians
of Greece. (Strab. XIV. p. 635. Plin. V. 39. Suid.
v. Κάδμος.) The Milesians were equally voluptuous
and effeminate with the rest of the Ionians, though
they had once been brave and warlike; whence the
proverb cited by Athenæus from Aristotle:

Πάλαι ποτ' ἦσαν ἄλκιμοι Μιλήσιοι.

Heraclides Ponticus, in a fragment quoted also by Athenæus, affirmed that the serfs of the Milesians were called Gergithæ[c]. (XII. p. 523, 4.) The Milesians were in repute for their manufactures of couches and other furniture; and their woollen cloths and carpets were especially esteemed. (Athen. I. p. 28. XI. p. 428. XII. p. 540, 553. XV. p. 691.)

> Nec minor usus erit : quamvis Milesia magno
> Vellera mutentur Tyrios incocta rubores.
>
> GEORG. III. 306.
>
> . . Eam circum Milesia vellera Nymphæ
> Carpebant, hyali saturo fucata colore.
>
> GEORG. IV. 335.

Chandler reports, " that Miletus is a very mean " place, but still called *Palat,* or *Palatia,* the *Pa-* " *laces.* The principal relic of its former magnifi- " cence is a ruined theatre, which is visible afar off, " and was a most capacious edifice, measuring in " front 457 feet. The external face of this vast " fabric is marble. The seats ranged, as usual, on " the slope of a hill, and a few of them remain. " The vaults, which supported the extremities of " the semicircle, are constructed with such solidity " as not easily to be demolished. On the side of " the theatre next to the river is an inscription in " mean characters, rudely cut, in which the city " Miletus is mentioned several times. The whole " site of the town, to a great extent, is spread with " rubbish, and overrun with thickets. The vestiges " of the heathen city are pieces of wall, broken " arches, and a few scattered pedestals and inscrip-

---

[c] These were probably Carians; and the term seems to have been common to the Teucrians and Mysians, and should therefore be referred to the old Thracian tongue.

" tions. One of the pedestals has belonged to a
" statue of the emperor Hadrian, who was a friend
" to the Milesians, as appears from the titles of
" saviour and benefactor bestowed on him. An-
" other has supported the emperor Severus, and has
" a long inscription, with this curious preamble:
" ' The senate and people of the city of the Mile-
" sians, the first settled in Ionia, and the mother of
" many and great cities both in Pontus and Egypt,
" and in various other parts of the world [d].' "

There were several small islands off Miletus, of
which the most considerable was Lade, famous for Lade in-sula.
the battle fought there between the Ionian fleet and
that of Darius, in the revolt of Histiæus and Aristagoras. The former had 360 galleys, the latter
600. The victory which the Persians obtained decided the fate of the war. (Herod. VI. 14—16.)
Mention of this island is also made during the siege
of Miletus by Alexander, whose fleet was stationed
to blockade the port. (Arrian. Exp. Alex. I. 19.)
This island, like many others, has been joined to
the continent by the mud of the Meander; and its
place is only marked now by a hill, and village
named *Bautenau.* Strabo speaks of Lade as a station for pirates. (XIV. p. 635.) The mouth of the
river, according to Chandler, is distant about eight
miles; the plain smooth and level as a bowling-
green, except certain knolls extant in it, near midway before Miletus [e]. But the most remarkable
change in this vicinity, caused by the waters of the
Meander, is that which has taken place with regard
to the bay once called Latmicus Sinus, from mount
Latmus, the fabled seat of the adventures of Endy-

[d] Travels in Asia Minor, p. 181.   [e] Ibid. p. 219.

mion, and a small town of the same name situate
at its south-eastern extremity. This bay, which
Strabo describes minutely, with the different towns
and hills which lined its shores, was not less than
100 stadia in length from Miletus to Heraclea, a
port under mount Latmus; but it now exists only as
an inland lake, its mouth having been closed by the
slime which the Meander has thrown up. (Strab.
XIV. p. 636.)

One of the most interesting sites in the district of
Miletus is that called Didymi, where stood the celebrated temple and oracle of Apollo Didymæus. It
was served by priests named Branchidæ, from Bran-
chus, a favourite of Apollo, and it was already in
great repute in the time of Crœsus, who presented
many rich offerings to its shrine. (Herod. I. 46. 92.)
The historian adds, that it was very ancient, and
much resorted to by the Æolians and Ionians. (I.
157.)   Necho, king of Egypt, had sent presents to
the temple, when he took Cadytis in Palestine. (II.
159.)   This edifice was burnt by order of Darius,
together with the other temples of Asia Minor,
after the revolt of Miletus. (Herod. VI. 20.)   But
this appears to have been only partially executed,
for it was burnt more completely again by Xerxes
after the battle of Mycale, and the Branchidæ,
having accompanied him in his flight into Persia
with the sacred treasury, were settled by him in
Sogdiana.   Here they were found by Alexander
in the course of his conquests, and barbarously put
to the sword, as a punishment for their reputed
treachery. (Strab. XIV. p. 634. XI. p. 517. Quint.
Curt. VII. 5.)   The Milesians subsequently built

Didymi.

Apollinis templum.

e Travels in Asia Minor, p. 219.

another temple on the same site, which surpassed
all other edifices of the kind in magnitude. So
great was its size, that they were unable to roof it
in. The whole circuit, including the groves and
chapels annexed to it, was equal to that of a town.
It was in the latter that the oracles were delivered.
The interior of the temple was decorated with
splendid sculptures and paintings by the first artists.
(Strab. XIV. p. 634. Cf. Pausan. Ach. 2. 5. Plin.
V. 29.) The temple stood at the distance of twenty
stadia from the sea. (Strab. loc. cit. Plin. loc. cit.)
The tomb of Neleus, the founder of Miletus, was on
the road leading from Miletus to Didymi. (Pausan.
loc. cit.) There are yet some extensive ruins of this
celebrated edifice remaining, views of which have
been engraved in the volume of Ionian Antiquities
published by the Dilettanti Society. Chandler gives
a very animated and picturesque description of this
ruin. He states, that " it is approached by a gentle
" ascent, and seen afar off; the land toward the sea
" lying flat and level. The memory of the pleasure
" which this spot afforded me will not be soon or
" easily erased. The columns yet entire are so ex-
" quisitely fine, the marble mass so vast and noble,
" that it is impossible perhaps to conceive greater
" beauty and majesty of ruin. The whole mass
" was illuminated by the declining sun with a variety
" of rich tints, and cast a very strong shade. The
" sea, at a distance, was smooth and shining, bor-
" dered by a mountainous coast, with rocky islands[f]."
The promontory Posideum was in the vicinity of Posideum
Didymi, and terminated the Milesian territory and promonto-
Ionia to the south. (Strab. loc. cit. Plin. loc. cit. rium.

[f] Travels in Asia Minor, p. 188.

c c 4

P. Mel. I. 19.)　The modern name is cape *Arbora*. Somewhat more to the north is a little port called **Panormus portus.** *Kobella*, which probably answers to the Panormus of antiquity [g]. (Herod. I. 157.)　The ruins of the temple of Apollo are situated between the villages of *Oura* and *Jeronta*.　It appears that the name of Didymi was given to this spot from two hills, situated near it.　A fortress, named Melanudium, was erected there in the middle ages. (Pachym. Andr. Pal. p. 144.)　Limeneium was a place in the territory of Miletus, where, according to Herodotus, (I. 18.) the inhabitants of that city were defeated by the Lydians.

Myus.　Myus, another Ionian city, was situate apparently on the left bank of the Mæander, and about thirty stadia from the mouth of that river.　It was founded by Cydrelus, a natural son of Codrus, (Strab. XIV. p. 633.) and became one of the twelve states which sent deputies to the Panionian assembly. (Herod. I. 142. Cf. V. 37. VI. 8.)　Thucydides informs us, that this was one of the three towns granted to Themistocles by the Persian king, for his subsistence during his residence in Asia. (I. 138. Cf. Strab. loc. cit. Diod. Sic. XI. c. 57. Plut. Themist. c. 29. Athen. I. p. 29.)　The same historian mentions a check received by the Athenians near this place during the Peloponnesian war, from the Carians. (III. 19.)　Athenæus states, on the authority of Polybius, that Philip, son of Demetrius, king of Macedon, having obtained possession of Myus, ceded it to the Magnesians. (III. p. 78.)　Strabo reports, that in his time Myus was so much reduced

---

[g] Chandler noticed some vestiges of antiquity there. Ibid. p. 187.

that it had been annexed to Miletus. Pausanias accounts for this by the action of the Meander, which had choked up the bay in which it stood, and brought such a host of gnats around the place that the inhabitants were forced to abandon it, and retire to Miletus. The only edifice which this writer observed in Myus was a temple of Bacchus, of white marble. (Ach. 2. Cf. Plin. V. 29. Steph. Byz. v. Μυοῦς.) The little town of Pyrrha was between Pyrrha. Myus and Miletus, on the same side of the river, and near the entrance of what was the gulf of Latmus, but is now called the lake of *Oufa Bafi*. The distance from thence to Miletus, in a straight course, was thirty stadia. This site, which Strabo only notices, is supposed to agree with that of *Sarikomer*. Heraclea, which derived the surname of Heraclea Latmus from its vicinity to the mountain so called, was 100 stadia from Pyrrha, and rather more from Miletus. It had a port on the Latmicus Sinus. Latmicus (Strab. loc. cit.) The site of Heraclea corresponds Sinus. nearly with the village of *Oufa Bafi*, at the southeast extremity of the lake so called. Chandler mistook its ruins for those of Myus, and the lake also he erroneously connected with that town. He says, that " it is visible both from Priene and Mile- " tus, and is called by the neighbouring Greeks the " Sea. The water is not drinkable [h]." The site of Heraclea, which he miscalls Myus, he represents as highly romantic. " The wall encloses a jumble of " naked rocks, rudely piled, of a dark dismal hue, " with precipices and vast hollows, from which per- " haps stone has been cut." He observed " the " remains of a theatre hewn in the mountain, a quad-

[h] Travels in Asia Minor, p. 209.

" rangular area, edged with marble fragments, and
" a small temple. The city wall was constructed
" like that at Ephesus, with square towers, and is
" still standing, except toward the water[h]." Heraclea Latmi is mentioned as a town of Caria by
Polyænus, (Strat. VII. 2. Steph. Byz. v. Ἡράκλεια)
the scholiast of Apollonius, (IV. 57.) Hierocles
Synecd. (p. 687.) and the Acts of several councils.

Latmus
mons.

Mount Latmus, celebrated for the fable of Endymion, rises above the site of this town and its lake,
and is described by Chandler as remarkably wild
and craggy[i]. It is now called *Betchek parmak* by
the Turks. The cave and tomb of Endymion was
shewn to the curious in Strabo's time. (XIV. p.
635. Cf. Cic. Tusc. Disp. I. 38. Apoll. Rh. IV. 57.)

Οὐκ ἄρ' ἐγὼ μούνη κατὰ Λάτμιον ἄντρον ἀλύσκω
Οὐδ' οἴη καλῷ περιδαίομαι 'Ενδυμίωνι.

(Plin. V. 29. Pomp. Mel. I. 19.)

Grius
mons.

The name of Grius was applied to the chain
which ran parallel to mount Latmus, on the western
side of the Latmic bay. Strabo says it extended
from near Miletus to Euromus in Caria. It was
disputed which of the two chains should be identified with the Φθειρῶν ὄρος, mentioned by Homer. (Il.
B. 868.)

Phthira
mons.

Οἳ Μίλητον ἔχον, Φθειρῶν τ' ὄρος ἀκριτόφυλλον.

(Cf. Steph. Byz. v. Φθίρα.)

Assessus.

Assessus was a small place in the Milesian territory, with an ancient and much venerated temple
sacred to Minerva. (Herod. I. 19. Steph. Byz. v.
'Ασσησός.) The fountain of Biblis, mentioned by

Biblis
fons.

[h] Travels in Asia Minor, p. 205.
[i] He mistakes it, however, for mount Titanus throughout. (p. 202.)

Pausanias, (Ach. 5.) was also in this district. We must add to the list of Ionian towns the following, which are of uncertain position. Buthia, noticed by Steph. Byz. on the authority of Theopompus. (v. Βουθία.) Gambrium and Palægambrium, ceded by the Persians to Gongylus the Eretrian, on account of some services he had rendered them towards the end of the Peloponnesian war. (Xen. Hell. III. 1, 4. Steph. Byz. v. Γαμβρεῖον.) It was probably situated in the north of Ionia, if it did not belong to Lydia. Thebe, a place near Miletus. (Steph. Byz. v. Θήβη.) Carnia, a town mentioned by Nicolaus of Damascus. (Steph. Byz. v. Καρνία.) Myes and Sidele, which are given to Ionia by the same lexicographer, on the authority of Hecatæus. (vv. Μύης. Σιδήλη.) Sillyus (Id. v. Σίλλυος) was near Smyrna.) Trampe. (Id. v. Τράμπη.) We must now speak of the islands of Chios and Samos, which belonged to the Ionian league, and occupy a distinguished place generally in Grecian history.

Chios, as Pliny reports, bore anciently the names of Æthalia, Macris, and Pityusa, and was first inhabited by the Leleges and Carians, and a Pelasgian colony from Thessaly. (Strab. XIII. p. 621. XIV. p. 633.) Pausanias, who enters at some length into its antiquities, expresses his surprise that Ion, the tragic poet, a native of this island, and from whom he derives his information, should not have explained how the Chians came to be connected with the Ionians. (Ach. 4.) This connexion must be sought for, I imagine, in the colonies, which the island derived at an early period from the Abantes of Eubœa, who finally prevailed over the Carians under their king Hector. This prince is probably

Margin notes: Buthia. | Gambrium et Palægambrium. | Thebe. | Carnia. | Myes. | Sidele. | Chios insula.

the same as Egertius, mentioned by Strabo. (XIV. p. 633.) The Abantes are named by Herodotus among the mixed tribes which formed the Ionian states. (I. 146.) The Chians applied themselves early to maritime affairs, and were thus enabled to preserve their independence against the Lydian monarchs. (Herod. I. 18. 27.) They particularly distinguished themselves in the Ionian revolt under Aristagoras, and sent 100 ships to the combined fleet assembled at Lade. In the naval action which ensued they fought with great gallantry, but being ill seconded, and even deserted by the other confederates, they were forced to retreat, with the loss of a great part of their squadron. Having then taken shelter on the Ephesian coast, and advanced towards that city, they were mistaken by the Ephesians for pirates, and almost entirely destroyed. (Herod. I. 15, 16.) They were further barbarously treated by Histæus. (I. 26.) After these disasters the island was compelled to submit to the Persian yoke. (I. 31.) These appear to have set over it a tyrant named Strattis. (VIII. 132.) After the battle of Mycale, the Chians recovered their liberty, and readily joined the confederacy of Greek states for the prosecution of the Persian war. They remained faithfully attached to the Athenian interests during nearly the whole of the Peloponnesian contest, as it appears to have been the policy of Athens to pay them greater deference than their less powerful tributaries : (Thuc. III. 10.) but after the Sicilian failure, they were among the first to throw off the heavy burdens which oppressed them, and to declare for the Spartans. The feeble succours which the latter sent them, and the double policy of the Persian satraps, gave the Athenians time to collect an imposing force. Pedaritus, the Spartan commander, was defeated and slain, and the Chians, after sustaining repeated losses, were forced to remain subject to Athens. (Thuc. VIII. 14. et seq. 24. 55.) After the Lacedæmonians had been enabled, by the liberal aid of Cyrus, to dispute once more the empire of the sea, Chios was occupied by their fleet, and a squadron, which escaped from the defeat at Arginusæ, being stationed there, would have seized upon the town, if the plot had not been frustrated by the vigilance of Eteonicus, the commander. (Xen. Hel. II. 1.) When the successes of Conon had restored the naval ascendancy of Athens, Chios, and the other Ionian islands, reverted to that power; but the yoke proved so galling, that a vigorous effort was made by the Chians, in conjunction with the Byzantines and Rhodians, to set themselves free for ever from Athenian thraldom. In the war which ensued, and which is called the Social war, success seems rather to have favoured the confederates ; the Athenians being defeated in an attack on Chios, with the loss of some ships and their general Chabrias, were at length induced to sign a treaty, in which they renounced all authority and supremacy over the states allied in this war, and declared them free from contributions in ships and money. (Isocr. de Pace. Demosth. de Rhod. Lib. Diod. Sic. XVI. c. 7. 21. Corn. Nep. Vit. Chabr.)

Near the time that Roman affairs begin to be intermixed with those of Greece and Asia, we find the Chians acting in conjunction with the Rhodians as mediators between the Ætolians and Philip, king of Macedon. (Polyb. V. 24. 28. 100. Liv. XXVII. 30.)

They assisted the Romans in their naval operations against that prince and Antiochus, and received some lands in recompense for their services. (Polyb. XXII. 27. Liv. XXXVIII. 39.) When Mithridates had expelled the Romans for a time from Asia, he sent Zenobius, one of his generals, to Chios, who treated the inhabitants with the greatest severity; compelled them to deliver up their arms, to pay a heavy fine of 2000 talents, and, not content with this, he seized on the principal inhabitants, and sent them as slaves to Colchis. A portion of these unhappy men were however detained by the Heracleotæ of Pontus, and set at liberty. (Appian. Mithr. c. 24. Nicol. Damasc. et Posidon. ap. Athen. VI. c. 18.) The Chians were again plundered by Verres, (Cic. Act. II. 19.) and suffered from an earthquake in the reign of Tiberius. (Suet. Tib. c. 8.) We collect from Pliny that this island, and the principal city of the same name, was flourishing in his time, and we have coins which bring down its history to the decline of the Roman empire. The Chians were reckoned among the most opulent and wealthy of the Greek states, and their city was adorned in a manner suitable to their affluence. They had an abundance of slaves, and they are reproached with being the first who purchased their fellow-creatures. (Thuc. VIII. 24. 40. Athen. VI. p. 265.) Their mode of living was like that of the other Ionians, delicate and voluptuous. (Athen. I. p. 25, 26, 28.)

Chios laid great claim to the honour of having given birth to Homer; and if the hymn quoted by Thucydides (III. 104.) be genuine, the question would seem to be decided in favour of its pretension [k]. The author of the poet's life states, that he resided in the island for several years. (c. 25. et seq.) Strabo also reports that the Chians gave the name of Homeridæ to his descendants. (XIV. p. 645.) The other distinguished individuals who added to the renown of Chios, were Ion, the tragic poet, Theopompus, the historian, Theocritus, a sophist, Metrodorus, a physician, and Scymnus, the geographer. (Strab. loc. cit. Suid. vv. Θεόπομπος. Θεόκριτος. Athen. VI. p. 230. XIII. p. 603.) The isle of Chios, according to Strabo, is 900 stadia in circuit. (XIV. p. 645.) Pliny reckons 125 miles, or about 1000 stadia. (V. 31.) The general character of the soil was mountainous and rugged ; whence the epithet of παιπαλιέσση given to it by Homer ; (ap. Thuc. loc. cit.) but it produced the best wine of all Greece. (Strab. loc. cit. Athen. I. p. 26, et seq.) Its figs, mastic, and starch, were also much esteemed. (Var. de Re Rust. I. 41. Plin. XVIII. 7. Dioscor. I. 90.) An ancient poet says, that the women of Chios and Miletus were preeminent in beauty. (Crit. ap. Athen. I. p. 28.)

The principal city, which bore the same name Chios urbs. with the island, stood on the eastern side towards the Ionian coast, nearly in the same latitude with Erythræ. The modern *Chio* retains its rank and position. We have seen, from Thucydides, that it was a large and handsome city, adorned with numerous edifices, and noble works of art; several of the latter were plundered by Verres, (Cic. Act. II. 19.) The harbour was excellent, and could contain eighty galleys at once. South of *Chio* we have to point

[k] See, however, Ruhnken. Epist. Crit. I. p. 90.

Posidium prom.   out Posidium, a promontory nearly opposite to cape Argennum in the Erythræan territory. (Strab. XIV. p. 645.) A fort called after St. Helen, is situated on the brow of this headland, which is named *Catomeria*, and sometimes *Masticio*. Next follows

Phanæ portus et prom.   the harbour and cape of Phanæ, close to which stood a temple of Apollo, with a grove of palms. (Strab. loc. cit. Cf. Liv. XXXVI. 43. XLIV. 28. Steph. Byz. v. Φάναι.) The wine of this district was much esteemed, as appears from Virgil:

> Sunt etiam Amineæ vites, firmissima vina :
> Tmolius assurgit quibus, et rex ipse Phanæus.
>
> GEORG. II. 97.

Cape Phanæ is now called *Mastico*.

Notium portus. Laius - portus.   Beyond is a roadstead named Notium, the *Port Mastico* of modern charts. Laius, according to Strabo, was another port further north, in the same latitude with the capital of the island, and distant from it not more than sixty stadia across the land. This observation leads to the idea that Laius agrees nearly with the modern site of *Port Mesta*. The northern part of the island comprised chiefly the

Ariusia.   district of Ariusia, celebrated for its excellent wine.

> Vina novum fundam calathis Ariusia nectar.
>
> VIRG. ECL. V. 71.
>
> . . . . ambrosiis Arvisia pocula succis.
>
> SIL. ITAL. VII. 210.

Cf. Plin. XIV. 7.) Athenæus distinguishes three sorts. (I. p. 32. F.) The coast was rugged, and without a port for nearly 300 stadia. (Strab. loc. cit.) The district of Arvisia still goes by that name, and the village of *Volisso*, situated on the coast, represents

Bolissus.   doubtless the ancient Bolissus noticed in Thucydides,

(VIII. 24.) and the Life of Homer. (c. 23. Cf.
Auct. cit. ap. Steph. Byz. v. Βολισσός.) The cape,
which forms the north-western extremity of the
island, bore anciently the name of Melæna, and is Melæna
now known by that of *St. Nicolas.*   Strabo ob- Psyra in-
serves, that it faces the island of Psyra, distant from
it about fifty stadia, and forty in circuit. (XIV. p.
645.) The modern name is *Psara.*   Beyond cape
Melæna is mount Pelinæus, the most elevated sum- Pelinæus
mit of all the island, and famous for its marble quarries. (Strab. loc. cit. Plin. V. 31.)

Καὶ Χίος ἠλιβάτου Πελληναίου ὑπὸ πέζαν.
DION. PERIEG. 535.

Jupiter was worshipped on the summit. (Hesych. v.
Πελιναῖος. Steph. Byz. v. Πελλιναῖον.) It is now called
after *St. Elias.*   In a deep bay, more to the east,
Cardamyle, a place mentioned by Thucydides, with Cardamyle.
Bolissus and Phanæ, retains its name. (VIII. 24.)
The historian speaks in the same chapter of Leuco- Leuconi-
nium, the situation of which is unknown. But Del-
phinium, which he mentions (c. 25.) as a place fortified by the Athenians, (Cf. Steph. Byz. v. Δελφίνιον,)
is doubtless the present *Porto Delfino,* opposite the Delphini-
islands Œnussæ, now *Spalmadores,* or *Egonisi.* Œnussæ
This group belonged to the Chians, and Herodotus
affirms that the Phocæans, when driven from their
city by the arms of Cyrus, were anxious to purchase
them, in order to settle there, but the Chians refused
to cede them. (I. 165. Cf. Thuc. VIII. 24. Plin.
V. 31.)

Babras, or Babrantium, is cited as a small town Babras sive
of Chios by Steph. Byz. on the authority of Poly- tium.
bius. (vv. Βαβράντιον, Βάβρας.) Pliny enumerates several islets round Chios, such as Thallusa, or Daphnusa,

Elaphitis, Eurynassa; and towards Ephesus, the isles of Pisistratus; namely, Anthine, Myonnesus, Diarrheusa: to these he adds Halone, Lepria, Bolbulæ, Phanæ, Priapus, Melane, Sidusa, Anydros, Sycussa, and others which have been already named: some of these belong probably to the group of Hecatonnesi.

Samos insula. Samos, which yields little in extent, and nought in fame, to Chios, lies towards the southern part of the bay of Ephesus, and nearly opposite to the promontory of Mycale, or Trogilium. The channel which separates it from that part of the continent being not more than seven stadia in the narrowest part. (Strab. XIV. p. 637.) It is said to have borne in ancient times the names of Parthenia, Dryusa, Anthemisa, Melamphyllos, and others; that of Samos was derived either from a hero so called, or from the isle of Cephallenia, which formerly was known by that appellation, and may, as Strabo supposes, have sent a colony to its Ionian namesake. (XIV. p. 637. Cf. X. p. 437. Plin. V. 31. Heraclid. Fragm. p. 211. Steph. Byz. v. Σάμος.) The first inhabitants were Carians and Leleges, whose king Ancæus, according to the poet Asius, cited by Pausanias, married Samia, daughter of the Meander. The first Ionian colony came into the island from Epidaurus, having been expelled from thence by the Argives. The leader of this colony was Procles, a descendant of Ion. Under his son Leogoras the settlement was invaded by the Ephesians, under the pretext that Leogoras had sided with the Carians against Ephesus. The colony being expelled from Samos, retired for a time to Anæa in Caria, whence they again invaded the island, and finally expelled the Ephesians.

(Pausan. Ach. 4.) Samos is early distinguished in the maritime annals of Greece, from the naval ascendancy it acquired in the time of Polycrates, whose history is narrated at length by Herodotus. This chief raised himself by his talents from the condition of a private person to the government of his country, which he shared at first with his two brothers, Pantaleon and Syloson; but subsequently he caused the former to be put to death, and expelled the other; after which he reigned with undivided authority. His successes were great and rapid, and he acquired a power which made him dreaded equally by his subjects and neighbours; and his alliance was courted by some of the most powerful sovereigns of that period. He conquered the Lesbians and other islanders, and had a fleet of 100 ships, a navy superior to that of any one state recorded at so early a date. (Herod. III. 39. Thuc. I. 13. Strab. loc. cit.) The Samians attempted to revolt from him, but though they were assisted in the undertaking by the Lacedæmonians, they failed of success, and many were driven into exile. (Herod. III. 44, et seq.) The Spartans landed in the island with a large force, and besieged the principal city with vigour, but they were finally forced to abandon the enterprise, after the lapse of forty days. (III. 54, et seq.) The Samian exiles then retired to Crete, where they founded Cydonia. Here they remained for five years in a flourishing condition, but on the sixth year they were attacked by the Æginetæ, with whom they had formerly been at variance, and reduced to slavery. (III. 59.) Polycrates after this did not long enjoy the good fortune which had so constantly attended him, and the course of which,

by the advice of his ally Amasis, king of Egypt, he
had even attempted to break : he fell a victim to
cruel and artful designs of the Persian satrap Oroe-
tes, who lured him to his fate by the temptation of
immense wealth; and having got him into his power,
nailed him to a cross. (Herod. III. 125, et seq.)
Polycrates, though tainted by many vices, knew
how to estimate and reward merit.   He cultivated a
friendship with Anacreon, and retained the physician
Democedes at his court.   Pythagoras was also his
cotemporary; but unable to witness, as it is said, the
dependence of his country, he quitted Samos, in order
to cultivate science in foreign countries. (Herod. III.
121, 131. Strab. XIV. p. 638.)   After the death of
Polycrates, the government of Samos was held for
some time by Mæandrius, his secretary; but he was
expelled by the troops of Darius, who placed on the
throne Syloson, the brother of Polycrates, on account of some service he had rendered him in Egypt,
when as yet he was but a private person. (Herod.
III. 140. Strab. loc. cit.)   Strabo reports that the
yoke of this new tyrant pressed more heavily on the
Samians than that of Polycrates, and that in consequence the island became nearly deserted; whence
arose the proverb,

"Εκητι Συλοσῶντος εὐρυχωρίη.

(Cf. Heraclid. Pont. p. 211.) From Herodotus, however, we learn that the Samians took an active part
in the Ionian revolt, and furnished sixty ships to
the fleet assembled at Lade; but by the intrigues of
Æaces, son of Syloson, who had been deposed by
Aristagoras, and consequently favoured the Persian
arms, the greater part of their squadron deserted
the confederates in the battle which ensued, and

thus contributed greatly to the defeat of the allies.
(Herod. VI. 8—14.) On learning the result of the
battle many of the Samians determined to quit the
island rather than submit to the Persian yoke, or
that of a tyrant imposed by them. They accord-
ingly embarked on board their ships and sailed for
Sicily, where they first occupied Calacte, and soon
after, with the assistance of Anaxilas, tyrant of Rhegium, the important town and harbour of Zancle.
Æaces was replaced on the throne of Samos, and,
out of consideration for his services, the town and its
temples were spared. (VI. 22—25.) After the battle
of Salamis, the Samians secretly sent a deputation
to the Greek fleet stationed at Delos, to urge them
to liberate Ionia, they being at that time governed
by a tyrant named Theomestor, appointed by the
Persian king. (IX. 90.) In consequence of this in-.
vitation, Leotychides, the Spartan commander, advanced with his fleet to the coast of Ionia, and
gained the important victory of Mycale. (IX. 96, et
seq.) The Samians, having regained their independence, joined, together with the other Ionian states,
the Grecian confederacy, and with them also passed
under the protection, or rather domination, of
Athens. The latter power, however, having attempted to change the constitution of the island to
a democracy, had nearly been expelled by the oligarchal party, aided by Pissuthnes, satrap of Sardes.
For the Samians ventured even to engage by sea
with the Athenian fleet, and obtained some important advantages when blockaded both by sea
and land, during the absence of Pericles; but when
that able general returned to his command, they
were unable to resist the overwhelming force brought

against them, and submitted to the Athenians. They were compelled to destroy their fortifications, give up their ships, deliver hostages, and pay the expenses of the war by instalments. This occurred a few years before the breaking out of the Peloponnesian war. (Thuc. I. 115, 117.) After this, we hear little of Samos till the end of the Sicilian expedition, when the maritime war was transferred to the Ionian coast and islands. At this time Samos became the great *point d'appui* of the Athenian fleet, which was stationed there for the defence of the colonies and subject states; and there is little doubt that the power of Athens was alone preserved at this time by means of that island. We learn from Thucydides that the oligarchal party at Athens had at first overthrown the democracy in Samos, as they had done at home; but by the exertions of Thrasybulus and Thrasyllus, and other commanders, the supremacy of the people was again restored over that of the landholders. (γεώμοροι.) (VIII. 21, 72—74[1].) The Athenian army then making common cause with the Samian people, determined to prosecute the war with vigour, and to use every exertion to restore the democratic influence at Athens. They were induced by these steps to enter into negociations with Alcibiades, and by securing the assistance of that able leader, they contributed essentially to the successes which were afterwards obtained on the Hellespont. (VIII. 86, et seq.) We learn from Polybius, that, after the death of Alexander, Samos became for a time subject to the kings of Egypt.

---

[1] These appear to have been colonists sent by Athens, to the number of 2000, after the reduction of the island by Pericles. Strab. XIV. p. 638. Heraclid. Pont. Frag. p. 211.

(V. 35. 11.) Subsequently it fell into the hands of Antiochus, and on his defeat, into those of the Romans. The temple and worship of Juno contributed not a little to the fame and affluence of Samos. Pausanias asserts that this edifice was of very great antiquity; this, he says, was apparent from the statue of the goddess, which was of wood, and the work of Smilis, an artist contemporary with Dædalus. (Ach. 4. Callim. Epigr. ap. Euseb. Præp. Ev. III. c. 8. Clem. Alex. Protr. p. 30.) The temple, according to Menodotus, a Samian writer quoted by Athenæus, had been founded by the Carians and Leleges, the first inhabitants of the island. (XV. p. 672.) Herodotus affirms that it was the largest of any he was acquainted with. The first architect had been a Samian, named Rhœcus, son of Philes. In Strabo's time it was adorned with a profusion of the finest works of art, especially paintings, both in the nave of the building and the several chapels adjoining. The outside was equally decorated with beautiful statues by the most celebrated sculptors. Among these were three colossal figures forming one group, by Myron. Marc Antony had carried these away, but Augustus replaced two of them, which represented Minerva and Hercules; he reserved that of Jupiter to adorn the Capitol. (XIV. p. 637.) Besides this great temple, Herodotus describes two other works of the Samians, which were most worthy of admiration: one was a tunnel carried through a mountain for the length of seven stadia, for the purpose of conveying water to the city from a distant fountain. Another was a mole, made to add security to the harbour; its depth was

twenty fathoms, and its length more than two stadia.
(III. 60.)

The circuit of this celebrated island, which retains
its ancient name, is 600 stadia, according to Strabo.
Agathemerus reckons 630. Pliny eighty-seven miles,
which make upwards of 700 stadia. (Plin. V. 31.)
It yielded almost every kind of produce, with the
exception of wine, in such abundance, that a proverbial expression used by Menander was applied
to it; φέρει καὶ ὀρνίθων γάλα. (Strab. XIV. p. 637.)

The city of Samos, with which we shall commence
the periplus of the island, was situate to the south-
east, exactly opposite to the promontory of Trogilium and mount Mycale, the channel which parted
them being in width about forty stadia. The port
was secure, and convenient for ships, and the town
for the most part stood in a plain rising gradually
from the sea towards a hill situate at some distance from it. The citadel, built by Polycrates, was
called Astypalæa. (Polyæn. Strat. I. Steph. Byz.
Etym. M. v. ᾿Αστυπάλαια.) The Heræum, or temple
of Juno, was near the suburbs and the little river

Imbrasus Imbrasus ; hence the surname of Imbrasia given to
fluvius.   the goddess :

> . . . . ᾿Ιμβρασίης ἕδος ῞Ηρης.
> APOLL. RH. I. 187.

Callimachus affirmed that this stream was first called
Parthenius.

> ᾿Αντὶ γὰρ ἐκλήθης ᾿Ίμβρασε Παρθενίου.

(ap. Schol. Apoll. Rh. II. 868. Cf. Strab. loc. cit.
Plin. V. 31. Athen. VII. p. 283.) Besides the Im-
Chesius fl. brasus, Pliny mentions the Chesius and Ibettes.
Ibettes fl.
Chesium   According to the scholiast of Callimachus, Chesium
prom.

was a promontory of the island, where Diana was
worshipped. (Callim. Dian. 228.)

Χησιὰς Ἰμβρασίη, πρωτόθρονε.

(Cf. Apoll. Rh. ap. Athen. VII. p. 283. Steph. Byz.
v. Χήσιον.) There was an ancient and much revered
asylum attached to the temple of Juno. (Tacit. Ann.
IV. 14.) Virgil reminds us that the name of Juno
was nowhere so much venerated as at Samos, with
the exception of Carthage.

> Quam Juno fertur terris magis omnibus unam
> Posthabita coluisse Samo.   Æn. I. 15.

The ruins of the city and temple are to be seen
near *Megalochora*, the present capital of the island.

A little to the north is a promontory anciently
called Posidium, and dedicated to Neptune. Close Posidium
to this headland was the little island Narthecis, and prom.
the distance from thence to the mainland of Ionia
was only seven stadia. (Strab. loc. cit.) In the same
vicinity we must seek for Calami, a spot where the Calami.
Greek fleet was stationed before the battle of Mycale. (Herod. IX. 96.) Panormus and Palinurus, two Panormus.
havens noticed by Livy in his account of the naval Palinurus.
operations of Polyxenidas, admiral of Antiochus,
against Pausistratus, a Rhodian officer. (XXXVII.
11.)

Ptolemy places south of Samos the city, the promontory of Ampelus, but Strabo says it was oppo- Ampelus
site to the island of Icaria: the latter description prom.
would agree with *Cape Samos*, or *S. Dominico*;
the former would answer to *C. Colonni*, or *Bianco*.
There was also in the centre of the island a mountain, named Ampelus. It is easily recognised under
its modern appellation of *Ambelona*. (Strab. XIV.

p. 637.) Strabo, however, elsewhere speaks of the headland opposite to Icaria, under the name of Cantharium, (XIV. p. 639,) so that it will be safer to consider that as the ancient name of cape *S. Dominico*. Pliny names another mountain, Cercetius, which the poet Nicander also notices in the Alexipharmaca :

Κερκετέω νιφόεντος ὑπὸ σχοινώδεσιν ὄχθαις.

It answers to mount *Kerki*, near *C. Dominico*. Pliny adds the fountains Gigartho and Leucothea. Assorum was another mountain of this island, according to Steph. Byz., whence flowed a stream, named Amphilysus. (v. 'Ασσωρὸν.) Gorguia, a spot where Bacchus was worshipped. (Dur. ap. Steph. Byz. v. Γόργυια.) Ipnus, where a temple was erected to Juno. (v. 'Ιπνοῦς.)

Icaria insula.

The island of Icaria, which was said to derive its name from Icarus, the son of Dædalus, and to have transmitted it to the Icarian sea, is 300 stadia in circuit, according to Strabo. (XIV. p. 639.) The geographer adds, that it possesses no harbours, but a roadstead or two; the best of these was near a promontory called Isti, ('Ιστοὶ,) situate towards the west. The eastern point of the island, facing cape Cantharium of Samos, and distant from it only eighty stadia, was named Dracanum, now *Cape Phanari*, or *St. John*. (Strab. loc. cit.) Dracanum was also the name of a mountain in this island, where Bacchus, according to some traditions, was said to have been born.

Isti prom. et statio.

Dracanum prom. et mons.

Χαίροι μὲν Διόνυσος ὃν ἐν Δρακάνῳ νιφόεντι
Ζεὺς ὕπατος μεγάλαν ἐπιγουνίδα θήκατο λύσας.

THEOCR. ID. XXVI. 33.

'Αλλὰ τὰ μὲν δολιχῆς τε καὶ αἰπεινῆς Δρακάνοιο
'Ικάριον ῥήσσει κῦμα περὶ κροκάλαις.

EUPHOR. EPIGR. ANTH. PAL. VII. 651.

Icarus was much celebrated for its wine, especially that called Pramnian, though an ancient writer describes it as rough and harsh, and very strong. It was so called either from a hill named Pramnus, where it grew, or the particular vine which yielded it. (Eparch. ap. Athen. I. p. 30.)

Ancient writers agree in assigning to this island two towns : (Scyl. p. 22. Plin. IV. 12.) one called Dracanum, and situate near the cape of the same name; the other Œnoe, and placed in the opposite direction. (Strab. XIV. p. 639. Athen. loc. cit. Steph. Byz. vv. Δράκανον, Οἰνόη.) There was also in the interior a temple of Diana Tauropolos. Eparchides, the writer quoted above from Athenæus, and who seems to have compiled a history of Icaria, related that Euripides had at one time resided on the island. (II. p. 61.) Strabo informs us that in his time the island was nearly deserted : it was only frequented by the flocks which the Samians sent thither to pasture. Other islets round Samos were the Corassiæ, or Corseæ, (Strab. loc. cit. Plin. V. 31. Steph. Byz. v. Κόρσειαι.) now *Formiche* or *Ant* isles. A ship sailing from cape Trogilium or Mycale, to Sunium, passed these and Samos and Icarus on the right, but the rocks or shoals called Melantii to the left; these therefore must either have been near Patmos, or the islets named *Stapodia*, to the east of Myconus. Apollonius Rhodius seems to place the Melantian rocks in the Cretan sea. (IV. 1706.) Near Samos was also the little isle of Tragia, noticed by Thucydides on account of a sea-fight which

Dracanum urbs.

Œnoe.

Corassiæ sive Corseæ insulæ.

Melantii scopuli.

Tragiæ insula

took place in its vicinity, between the Athenians and Samians, when the latter were defeated. (I. 116.) Pliny reckons more than one islet of the name off the Ionian coast; perhaps they are the rocks called *Samopoulo*, close to the Ampelus promontorium. Strabo seems to place them near Lade. (XIV. p. 635.)

Camelides insulæ. In this direction Pliny names the two Camelides, Rhypara, Nymphæa, close to Miletus; and near to Samos, Rhypara, Achillea, insulæ. Nymphæa, Achillea. (V. 37.) At some distance from the coast, and nearly opposite to Panormus, the island called *Garthonisi* in modern charts is supposed Hyettusa insula. posed to represent Hyettusa, mentioned by Pliny. (V. 31.) *Farmaco*, opposite to cape Posidium of Pharmacusa insula. Miletus, is evidently the isle Pharmacusa, near which Julius Cæsar was once captured by pirates. (Plut. Vit. Cæs. Suet. J. Cæs. c. 4.) Steph. Byz. says Attalus was killed there. (v. Φαρμακοῦσσα.) Further Lepsia insula. ther out at sea we have to notice Lepsia, (Plin. loc. cit.) now *Lipso*.

Patmos insula. Patmos is a little to the west of Lipsia. This small island, so interesting to the Christian on account of the banishment of the apostle St. John, is mentioned by Strabo among the Sporades, (X. p. 488.) and by Pliny, who says it is thirty miles in circuit. (IV. 12.) It is the general opinion of commentators that St. John was banished to Patmos towards the close of the reign of Domitian. He himself declares, (Rev. I. 9.) "I John, who also am " your brother, and companion in tribulation, and " in the kingdom and patience of Jesus Christ, was " in the isle that is called Patmos, for the word of " God, and for the testimony of Jesus Christ." It is not known how long his captivity lasted, but it is thought that he was released on the death of Domi-

tian, which happened A. D. 96, when he retired to
Ephesus. (Iren. II. 22. 5. Euseb. Hist. Eccl. III.
18. Dio. Cass. LXVIII. 1.) The island, which is
now called *Patino,* contains several churches and
convents; the principal one is dedicated to the apostle. There are also the ruins of an ancient fortress, and some other remains [m].

LYDIA.

Having now finished the survey of the Ionian
coast and the adjacent islands, I shall next proceed
to inquire into the ancient state of the country
situate at some distance from that coast, and confined generally between the waters of the Hermus
and Meander on the north and south, whilst to the
east it was conterminous with the greater Phrygia.
Within these limits was included the kingdom of
the Lydian monarchs, before the conquests of Crœsus and of his ancestors had spread that name and
dominion from the coast of Caria to the Euxine,
and from the Meander to the Halys. The celebrity
of Crœsus, and his wealth and power, have certainly conferred on this part of Asia Minor a greater
interest than any other portion of that extensive
country possesses, Troas perhaps excepted; and
we become naturally anxious to ascend from this
state of opulence and dominion to the primitive and
ruder period from which it drew its existence. In
this inquiry, however, we are unfortunately little
likely to succeed; the clue which real history affords
us for tracing the fortunes of Lydia through her

[m] See Mr. Whittington's account of these remains, extracted from his journal, in Walpole's Memoirs of Turkey, tom.
II. p. 43.

several dynasties, soon fails, and we are left to the false and perplexing directions which fable and legendary stories supply. Some great and leading facts are certainly however to be elicited from all the authorities which have touched upon the history of Lydia; and though these facts are of a general nature only, they are such as may be considered useful in the chain of historical analogies, and at all events such as we must be satisfied with, for want of more specific information. The sum of what we learn is this, that Lydia, or that portion of Asia Minor specified above, appears to have been governed for a much greater space of time than any other part of that country, by a line of sovereigns, broken, it is true, into several dynasties, but continuing without interruption, it seems, for several centuries, and thus affording evidence of the higher civilization and prosperity of their empire. It is not to be supposed, however, that the country remained all this time undisturbed by revolutions and political changes; we have evidence to the contrary: and indeed it would have been opposed to analogy to imagine that the possession of a country so eminently favoured by nature should not have been a subject of dispute and contest, when almost every other province witnessed repeated changes of inhabitants during its progress to a permanent and settled state of things.

Our sources of information respecting the history of Lydia are almost entirely derived from Herodotus, and the high name which he bears doubtless attaches great respectability to his testimony; but as we have no opportunity of weighing his authority on this particular subject, from being unacquainted with the sources whence he drew his information,

and also from having no parallel historian with
whom to compare his account, it is evident we cannot place such dependence on his Lydian history as
on those of Egypt, Babylon, and Persia. Our suspicions will of course be increased, if we find that the
circumstances he relates are incredible in themselves,
and at variance also with other authorities. The
difficulties respecting these circumstances, both as to
facts and dates, have given rise to many disquisi-
tions on the part of learned men, without however
leading to any satisfactory solution of them, at least
in my opinion ; and this I imagine, because they
have strained at little points, without seeking to
clear away the real obstacles which beset our path.
Time has unfortunately deprived us of the Lydian
annals of Xanthus, a native of the country, somewhat anterior to Herodotus, and whose accounts
were held in great estimation for accuracy and
fidelity by sound judges[n] ; but from incidental
fragments preserved by later writers, we are led to
infer that he had frequently adopted traditions materially differing from those which Herodotus fol-

[n] Dionysius of Halicarnassus, in his Roman Antiquities,
(I. 30.) speaks of his history in
high terms of commendation.
Strabo also makes frequent cita-
tions from his writings. (XII.
p. 579. XIII. p. 628. XIV. p.
680, &c.) Nicolaus of Damascus appears to have derived
much information from him,
and Steph. Byz. quotes him repeatedly. Nevertheless, it was
pretended by some critics, that
the works ascribed to this ancient historian were spurious,
being really the productions of
Dionysius, surnamed Σκυτοβρα-
χίων ; but though there might
be forgeries among his writings, there can scarcely be any
doubt that many were genuine,
since Ephorus spoke of them as
well known to him, and represented Xanthus as more ancient than Herodotus, and even
as paving the way for him.
(Athen. XII. p. 515.) The
fragments of Xanthus have
been collected and published,
with those of other early Greek
historians, by Fr. Creuzer, Hei-
delb. 1806. 8vo.

lowed, and that his history also, as might be expected, contained several important facts unknown to the latter, or which it did not enter into the plan of his work to insert. Xanthus would probably have given us some valuable information on a subject which belongs especially to the nature of our enquiries, and on which Herodotus seems scarcely to touch, I mean the origin of the Lydian nation. Without his assistance, our means of information are of course very scanty and deficient ; but, such as they are, we must endeavour to compile and arrange them to the best advantage, for the benefit of our readers. The general account which we collect from Herodotus is this : he states, that the country, known in his time by the name of Lydia, was formerly called Mæonia, and the people Mæones. (I. 7. VII. 74.) This seems confirmed by Homer, who nowhere mentions the Lydians, but numbers the Mæonian forces among the allies of Priam, and assigns to them a country which is plainly the Lydia of subsequent writers :

Μῄοσιν αὖ Μέσθλης τε καὶ Ἄντιφος ἡγησάσθην,
Υἷε Πυλαιμένεος, τὼ Γυγαίη τέκε λίμνη,
Οἳ καὶ Μῄονας ἦγον ὑπὸ Τμώλῳ γεγαῶτας.

Iʟ. Β. 864.

Strabo also remarks, that many writers adopted this opinion, but that others looked upon these two nations as distinct : he himself adhered to the former. (XIII. p. 625.) Herodotus further states, that the name of Lydians was derived from Lydus, a son of Atys, one of the earliest sovereigns of the country ; (loc. cit.) and in this particular he closely agrees with Xanthus, quoted by Dionysius of Halicarnassus, (Ant. Rom. I. 30.) however he may differ from him in other considerable points. But the period to be assigned to this Lydus is a subject likely to baffle for ever the researches of the ablest chronologists. For Manes, according to Herodotus, being the first king of the country, (I. 94.) and father of Atys, consequently grandfather of Lydus, it would follow that the Mæonian name would have lasted only for two generations, and yet we find it the only one in existence when Homer wrote, or, at least, which he supposed to have existed at the period of which his poem treated. Some writers have reported that there was a prince named Meon, who was more ancient than Manes; (Diod. Sic. III.) but this is contrary to the testimony of Herodotus and Xanthus, whom Dion. Halic. probably copied [o]. (Ant. Rom. I. 30.) It is possible, however, that there may have been more than one sovereign who bore the name of Manes; for Herodotus speaks of one who was father of Cotys and grandfather of Asius, from whom the district, and subsequently the whole continent of Asia, is said to have derived its appellation. (IV. 45.) Now unless Cotys and Atys were brothers, which is not stated, it must follow that there were two Manes [p]. To this part of the subject seems to belong the question of the great Tyrrhenian migration recorded by Herodotus, which I have already discussed at some length

[o] This Manes appears to have been sovereign of Phrygia as well as Lydia; (Alex. Polyhist. ap. Steph. Byz. vv. Μανήσιον. 'Ακμόνιον. Plut. Is. et Osir.) and it is not improbable that he was worshipped in that country under the name of Men.

(Strab. XII. p. 556, 580.)

[p] This is also the opinion of the Abbé Sevin, in his learned dissertation on the kings of Lydia. (Mém. de l'Acad. des Inscr. et Belles Lettres, tom. V. p. 231.

in my work on ancient Italy, under the head of Etruria ; but I prefer making what further remarks I
have to offer on this point at a later period in the
present enquiry. Herodotus goes on to state, that
after a number of generations, which he does not
pretend to reckon, the crown passed from the line
of Lydus, son of Atys, to that of Hercules. This
hero had a son by a slave of Jardanus, who was then
apparently sovereign of Lydia ; and this son, suc-
ceeding to the throne by the command of an oracle,
became the author of a new dynasty, which reigned
through two and twenty generations, and during
the space of 505 years. (I. 7.) The introduction of
the name of Hercules indicates at once that we have
shifted our ground from history to mythology and
fiction. We know how the Greeks seized upon that
name as being exclusively their own, and how they
adapted the legends of other countries to the exploits and wonders achieved by the son of Amphi-
tryon. The doubts and suspicions, which this circumstance naturally creates in the mind, are rather
increased than lessened on inspecting the list of the
lineal descendants of Hercules, who reigned at Sardis. Well might Scaliger exclaim with astonish-
ment, when he saw the names of Ninus and Belus
following almost immediately after that of Hercules
their ancestor [q].

There seems to be here some extraordinary confusion of names, dates, and countries, out of which
it is hardly possible to extract any thing intelligible
or probable. For my part I cannot help imagining
that these names imply some distant connexion be-

[q] Scal. Can. Isagog. lib. III. p. 327.

tween the supposed Lydian dynasty of the Heraclidæ and the Assyrian empire. I confess that this
is only a surmise; but there are some curious traditions preserved apparently by Xanthus, in his
history of Lydia, which go some way towards supporting this hypothesis. Stephanus of Byzantium,
speaking of Ascalon in Palestine, states, that the
above historian affirmed that it had been founded by
Ascalus, an officer under the command of Aciamus,
king of the Lydians[s]. Nicolaus of Damascus repeated this story from Xanthus. (Steph. Byz. v.
Ἀσκάλων.) There is a further allusion to this part
of the Lydian traditions in Athenæus, who quotes
a fragment of Mnaseas in his work on Asia, where,
speaking of Atergatis, a Syrian queen, he adds, that
Xanthus reported that Atergatis was taken by Mopsus the Lydian, and thrown, with her son Ichthys,
in a lake near Ascalon. (VIII. p. 346.[t]) If there
is any foundation for these traditions, it must be
allowed, I think, that they belong to a period when
the Lydians occupied a very different situation in
the map of Asia from that which they subsequently
took up[u]. But, so far from the Lydians having
founded Ascalon, and other towns in Syria and
Palestine, I think it much more probable that they
derived, themselves, the original population of their
country from those parts, as did the Cilicians, Cappadocians, and Phrygians; and in that case we shall
no longer be surprised to find Ninus and Belus

[s] The name of this prince
appears to be Phœnician, or
Syrian; Achim, or Achiam.

[t] The Abbé Sevin observes,
that some writers identified
Atergatis with Derceto, mother
of Semiramis.

[u] The scriptural name of
Lud, or Ludim, may perhaps
have some connexion with these
traditions.

among the sovereigns of the country. It is also very possible, that the fable of Hercules and Omphale may have had its origin in some old tale imported by the Phœnicians, who laid an earlier claim, as Herodotus imagined, to the actions of that hero than the Greeks. (II. 44.) It would require a much longer space than we can devote to such an enquiry to attempt to establish a connexion between the Assyrian and Lydian empires, nor am I aware that it can be satisfactorily made out; but the surmises and hints which we have here thrown out, may perhaps be pursued by some more learned and laborious antiquarian, who will not lose sight of the great similarity which appears to have existed between the corruptions of Babylon and the conduct which history ascribes to the Lydian women : nor will it be forgotten, that the Lydians and Carians are said to have derived divinations and sacrifices from the Chaldees [x].

Whatever connexion may have existed between the Lydians and the nations to the east of the Euphrates, it must be confessed however that the ancients themselves were hardly aware of the fact. The testimony of Herodotus, who doubtless consulted the best authorities he could procure, would seem to shew that the Lydians regarded themselves as descended from the same stock as the Carians and Mysians. Now these being confessedly of Thracian origin, it necessarily follows that the former also must have been a branch of the same primitive race. (Herod. I. 171.) Menecrates of Elæa, and Xanthus, who are cited by Strabo, also confirmed the fact, as far as the affinity of the Mysians and Ly-

[x] See also Bochart, Geogr. Sacr. lib. II. c. 12.

dians is concerned, by the undeniable proof of a
strong similarity of language. (XII. p. 572.) But
by what name were these brethren of the Carians
and Mysians known before they settled in Lydia;
for I do not imagine that they imported that name
from Europe into Asia? Were they called Leleges
or Pelasgi? This is what cannot be now seriously
enquired into. All that we know is, that the intermixture of these various heterogeneous tribes already
named, constituted the nation which afterwards became known to the Greeks by the name of Lydians.
The confusion resulting from this intermixture being
such as to baffle, according to Strabo's observation,
all hope of discriminating between them. (XII. p.
572. XIII. p. 629.) In the time of Herodotus a
small remnant of the Mæonians, surnamed Cabelees
and Lasonii, yet preserved apparently some distinctive marks, in language and manners, from the
Lydians and the Carians, to whom they were contiguous. (III. 90. VII. 77.) Strabo, speaking of the
small district Cabalis, which must certainly be referred to this people, remarks, that many authors
looked upon it as the seat of the ancient Solymi of
Homer, who were doubtless of Phœnician origin;
(XIII. p. 630.) and that the Cabelees were so likewise, might be inferred from the fact, that their
arms and accoutrements were precisely those of the
Cilicians. (Herod. VII. 77.) The Torrœbi, who
once formed a considerable portion of the Lydian
nation, had long ago disappeared, since they are
neither mentioned by Strabo nor Herodotus; their
existence is only certified to us in a fragment of
Xanthus, preserved by Dionysius of Halicarnassus.
(Ant. Rom. I. 30.) According to that ancient his-

torian, the Torrœbi were so called from Torrœbus, brother of Lydus; their language did not differ much from that of the Lydians; but they had many terms in common, as the Dorians and Ionians have. Dionysius adduces this passage to prove that Xanthus knew nothing of Tyrrhenus, the brother of Lydus, and his pretended expedition into Italy; and certainly if the Lydian historian is correct, his authority would be decisive against the existence of that prince. But the great question with respect to this curious tradition preserved by Herodotus, and which must have had some foundation, is to ascertain whether it was really an Asiatic legend or an European one. What I mean is this : the Lydians, in the time of Herodotus, were no longer the indigenous or aboriginal inhabitants of the ancient Mæonia. They had come from Thrace and Macedon with the Phrygians and Carians and Mysians, and they were much intermixed with Pelasgi and Leleges and Caucones, and other primitive tribes. They may therefore have imported from those countries a tradition, which referred to events much anterior to their settlement in Lydia, but which was afterwards, by a natural confusion, adapted to their subsequent existence in that country, and was not countenanced by the more authentic records consulted by Xanthus. This mode of dealing with the tradition of Herodotus has this advantage, that it is perfectly consistent with those authorities which seem to place the original seat of the Tyrrheni in Thrace and Macedon, and in particular with that report mentioned by Plutarch, which stated that the Tyrrheni came first from Thessaly into Lydia. (Romul. c. 1.) It also removes the inconsistencies and difficulties attending its consideration as a legend purely belonging to the latter country, and in particular the strong objections brought against it by Dionysius.

Leaving now this obscure and uncertain field of enquiry, let us proceed to take a rapid sketch of the history of Lydia at a period when its records are more sure and faithful [y].

Candaules, whom the Greeks named Myrsilus, was the last sovereign of the Heraclid dynasty. He was assassinated, as Herodotus relates, by his queen and Gyges, one of his principal officers. The latter succeeded to the vacant throne, and became the founder of a new line of kings. (Herod. I. 8—14.) Under his reign it is probable that the mines of mount Tmolus, and other parts of Lydia, were first brought into activity; this would account for the fabulous stories which are related respecting him, (Plato de Rep. II. Cic. de Off. III. 9.) and his extra-ordinary wealth. He is said by Herodotus to have made very rich offerings to the temple of Delphi, both in gold and silver, (I. 14.) and his riches formed the theme of Anacreon, (Od. XV.) and Archilochus. (Frag. X. Cf. Theopomp. ap. Athen. VI. p. 231.) Under this sovereign the Lydian empire had already made considerable progress in several districts of Asia Minor. Its sway extended over a great part of Mysia, Troas, and the shores of the Hellespont; (Strab. XIII. p. 590.) and before his death Gyges had succeeded in annexing to his dominions the cities

[y] The reader who wishes to search further into the early Lydian history may consult the dissertation of the Abbé Sevin, above referred to, and also the researches of Freret on the Chronology of Lydia, which form a sequel to it.

of Colophon and Magnesia. (Herod. I. 14. Nicol. Damasc. Exc.) According to Herodotus he reigned thirty-eight years : but chronologists are not agreed as to the exact period of his accession to the throne ; some removing it back as far as 718 B. C., others bringing it down to 688.[z] He was succeeded by his son Ardys, who conquered Priene ; but for a time was stripped of his dominions and capital by an incursion of the Cimmerians. He reigned forty-nine years, and was succeeded by his son Sadyattes, of whom nothing is recorded except the bare fact that he occupied the throne for twelve years. Alyattes, who next follows, made war against the Medes, expelled the Cimmerians from Asia, conquered Caria and some of the Ionian cities, and after a prosperous reign of fifty-seven years, left the crown to his son Crœsus, whom he appears to have already associated with him in power some years previously. (Herod. I. -16—25. I. 92. Nic. Damasc. p. 243.[a]) Crœsus proved more ambitious and enterprising than any of his predecessors. He brought under subjection, or rendered tributary, all the Greek settlements in Asia, and all the barbarian nations west of the Halys, except the Lycians and Cilicians ; (Herod. I. 29.) and surpassed all the sovereigns of his time in the extent of his wealth and the splendour of his court. Ambition and vanity led him, however, to think that he could reduce the Persian power, which had lately risen on the ruins of the Median empire, under the youthful Cyrus. In an evil hour he

[z] See Freret, Recherches sur la Chronologie de l'Histoire des Rois de Lydie, Mém. de l'Acad. des Inscr. &c., tom. V. p. 280 —283. Clinton's Fasti Hellen. tom. I. Append. p. 296.

[a] See Clinton's Fasti Hell. Append. p. 298. tom. I.

crossed the Halys, and entered Cappadocia, then a
Persian province.   The first conflict was indecisive,
but Crœsus having withdrawn to his own dominions
to collect reinforcements for a second campaign, he
was speedily followed by his more quick-sighted
and active foe, and obliged to fight a second battle
nearly under the walls of Sardis.   Crœsus, after
sustaining a complete defeat, was soon shut up
within that city, which from its great strength
might have resisted for a long space of time, if acci-
dent had not put the enemy in possession of a secret
path, by which they stormed the citadel, and became
masters of the place. Crœsus was thus dethroned, and
Lydia became annexed to the Persian empire. (Herod. I. 75—84.)   The Lydians had previously been
a brave and warlike people, but from this time they
degenerated totally, and became the most voluptuous and effeminate of men.   (I. 79. 155—157.
Athen. XII. p. 515 et seq.)   They were celebrated
for their skill in music, (XIV. p. 617, 634.) and
other arts. (X. p. 432. III. p. 112.)   They are said
to have invented games, and to have been the first
to coin money. (Herod. I. 94.)   The conquest of
Lydia, so far from really increasing the power of the
Persians, tended rather to weaken it, by softening
their manners, and rendering them as effeminate as
the subjects of Crœsus ; a contagion from which
the Ionians had already suffered.   The great wealth
and fertility of the country have always caused it to
be considered as the most valuable portion of Asia
Minor, and its government was probably the highest
mark of distinction and trust which the king of
Persia could bestow upon a subject.   In the division of the empire made by Darius, the Lydians,

and some small tribes, apparently of Mæonian origin, together with the Mysians, formed the second satrapy, and paid into the royal treasury the yearly sum of 500 talents. (III. 90.) Sardis was the residence of the satrap, who appears rather to have been the king's lieutenant in Asia, and superior to the other governors. This was especially the case during the Ionian revolt, and indeed the whole of the reigns of Darius and Xerxes. (Herod. prop.) Lydia, somewhat later, became the principal seat of the power usurped by the younger Cyrus, and after his overthrow was committed to the government of his enemy Tissaphernes. (Xen. Anab. I. 1. Hell. I. 5. III. 1.) After the death of Alexander, we find it subject for a time to Antigonus; then to Achæus, who caused himself to be declared king at Sardes, but was subsequently conquered and put to death by Antiochus. (Polyb. V. 57, 4.) Lydia, after the defeat of the latter sovereign by the Romans at Magnesia, was annexed by them to the dominions of Eumenes. (Liv. XXXVIII. 39.) At a later period it formed a principal part of the proconsular province of Asia, (Plin. V. 29.) and still retained its name through all the vicissitudes of the Byzantine empire, when it finally passed under the dominion of the Turks, who now call its northern portion *Saroukhan;* the southern, *Aidin.* On the north, Lydia was contiguous to the territory of Pergamum, and that part of Mysia which was watered by the Caicus; on the east it bordered on Phrygia; and on the south it was separated from Caria by the tortuous Meander. Its western, or maritime portion was occupied by the Ionian colonies, which have been already treated of.

In describing Lydia it will be convenient to divide it into two portions ; the first consisting of the country between the Caicus and the Hermus, the second of that situated between the Hermus and the Meander.

Commencing then with the former, and setting out from Pergamum, Strabo notices to the east of that city a town named Apollonia, and situate on a height. (XIII. p. 625.) It is difficult to say whether this place was in Mysia [b] or Lydia, as Steph. Byz. names two in both provinces. If this is the Apollonia which Ptolemy places near the Cilbianus Campus, it would certainly belong to the latter. Beyond, continues Strabo, the road crosses a chain of hills, and then proceeds towards Sardes. The traveller has then on his left Thyatira, and on his right Apollonis, named after the wife of Attalus, a lady of Cyzicus. It was 300 stadia from Pergamum, and the same distance from Sardes. (Strab. loc. cit.) This town is frequently alluded to by Cicero. (Orat. pro Flacc. c. 21 et 32. Epist. ad Quint. I. 2. Cf. Tacit. Ann. II. 47.) In Pliny's time it was a place of little consequence. (V. 30.) The Ecclesiastical Notices mention it as the see of a bishop [c]. Some vestige of this ancient town is yet perceptible in that of *Bullene,* a hamlet whose situation agrees in other respects with Strabo's description. Strabo does not take notice of a river which it is necessary to cross after the Caicus. This is the ancient Hyllus, the principal tributary of the Hermus, according to Herodotus. (I. 80.) It rises in Phrygia Epic-

(marginal notes:) Apollonia. Apollonis. Hyllus fl. qui et Phrygius.

---

[b] It has therefore been noticed under that province.

[c] There are autonomous and imperial coins of Apollonis with the legend ΑΠΟΛΛΩΝΙΔΕΩΝ.

tetus, not far from the source of the Rhyndacus [d], and joins the Hermus a little above the site of the ancient Magnesia ad Sipylum. Strabo adds, that in his time this river commonly bore the name of Phrygius. Pliny, however, distinguishes between the Hyllus and the Phryx, or Phrygius; (V. 29.) and if he is correct, it is probable that, in his opinion, the Hyllus was the river of Thyatira; the Phrygius, the larger branch which comes from the north-east, and rises in the hills of the ancient Phrygia Epictetus. Livy also, in his account of the operations of Scipio prior to the battle of Magnesia, speaks of the Phrygians as being in the vicinity of Thyatira and Magnesia. (XXXVII. 37 and 38.[e]) Homer had carefully distinguished between the Hermus and the Hyllus.

$$. . . . . . τοι τέμενος πατρώϊόν ἐστιν,$$
$$Ὕλλῳ ἐπ' ἰχθυόεντι, καὶ Ἕρμῳ δινήεντι.$$

Il. Υ. 391.

The plain watered by the Hyllus, or Phrygius, bore
Hyrcanius anciently the name of Campus Hyrcanius. Strabo
Campus. accounts for the origin of the term by informing us, that a colony of Hyrcanians had been settled there by the Persians. (XIII. p. 629.) Xenophon probably alludes to these Hyrcanians. (Anab. VII.) Subsequently some Macedonians were settled here; whence Pliny and Tacitus term them, " Macedones " Hyrcani cognominati." (Plin. V. 29. Tacit. Annal. II. 47. Cf. Liv. XXXVII. 37. Steph. Byz. v. Ὑρκα-

---

[d] See Major Keppel's Travels in Asia Minor, tom. II. p. 261.

[e] Col. Leake conceives that Livy gives the name of Phrygius to the Hermus. Asia Minor, p. 267. At all events the historian is not accurate, in omitting to distinguish the two rivers.

νία.) There appears to have been also a town in this district bearing the name of Hyrcania. (Hieron. Chron. et Niceph.)

Mostene, according to Tacitus, was another town Mostene belonging to these Macedones Hyrcani. (loc. cit.) It is also mentioned by Ptolemy, Hierocles, (p. 671.) and the Ecclesiastical Notices[f]. Its situation, as well as that of Hyrcania, is not ascertained.

Thyatira stood further north, and on the borders Thyatira. of Mysia; Pliny reports that it was watered by the Lycus, a small stream apparently which joins the Hyllus, and adds, that it was anciently called Pelopia and Euhippa. (V. 29.) Strabo informs us that it was a Macedonian colony, (XIII. p. 625,) and Steph. Byz. confirms this account, while he adds to it by saying, that it was named by Seleucus Nicanor. (v. Θυάτειρα.) Antiochus was encamped in its vicinity when about to engage with the Roman army under Scipio, but retired to Magnesia on his approach. (Liv. XXXVII. 8. 21, 37.) It surrendered to the consul after the battle. (XXXVII. 44. Polyb. Frag. XVI. 1. 7. XXXII. 25, 10. Appian. Syr. Plut. Syll.) Thyatira is interesting to the Christian antiquarian, as one of the seven churches of the Apocalypse. The divine message which the apostle was commissioned to deliver unto the angel of the church in Thyatira was: " These things saith the " Son of God, who hath his eyes like unto a flame " of fire, and his feet are like fine brass ; I know " thy works, and charity, and service, and faith, " and thy patience, and thy works; and the last to

---

[f] There are imperial coins belonging to the Mosteni and the Hyrcani, the legends KAI- ΣΑΡΕΩΝ ΜΟΣΤΗΝΩΝ or ΜΟ-ΣΤΗΝΩΝ ΛΤΔΩΝ. and ΜΑΚΕΔ. ΤΡΚΑΝΩΝ. Sestini, p. 109, 110.

" be more than the first. Notwithstanding I have a
" few things against thee, because thou sufferest
" that woman Jezebel, which calleth herself a pro-
" phetess," &c. (Rev. ii. 18.) In the Acts, xvi. 14,
mention is made of Lydia, a purple-seller of Thyatira. The Ecclesiastical Notices give the names of
several bishops belonging to this see. We can trace
the history of Thyatira down to a late period of the
Byzantine empire, but it then appears under the
Turkish name of *Akhissar*, or " the white town,"
(M. Duc. p. 114.) which is its present appellation.
Mr. T. Smith was the first to give an account of
the antiquities of Thyatira, in his Notice of the
Seven Churches of Asia[g]. They consist chiefly
of inscriptions, and fragments of walls and pillars.

The Itineraries place between Pergamum and
Germa. Thyatira a station named Germa, twenty-five miles
from the former, and thirty-three from the latter.
(Anton. Itin. p. 335. Tab. Pent. IX. D.) This site
agrees nearly with that of *Somma*, on the road from
Bergamah to *Akhissar*. Somewhat to the north-
east, a site called *Bakhir* or *Bakri* was discovered
by Chishull to represent the ancient Nacrasa of
Nacrasa. Ptolemy[h]. Critics are of opinion that this town is
not different from the Acrasus of Hierocles and the

---

[g] P. 16—25. Lat. edit. See
also Wheeler and Spon, tom.
I. b. iii. p. 253. Chishull, Ant.
Asiat. There are numerous
coins, both autonomous and
imperial, belonging to Thyatira; the latter extend in a series from Augustus to Saloninus. The epigraph is ΘΥΑΤΕΙ-
ΡΗΝΩΝ. Sestini, p. 113.

[h] Chish. Ant. Asiat. p. 146.
The inscription he quotes has
for its preamble, Η. ΜΑΚΕΔΟ-
ΝΩΝ ΝΑΚΡΑΣΕΙΤΩΝ ΒΟΥΛΗ,
and the coins of Nacrasa confirm this orthography. Sestini,
p. 110. But the legend on the
coins of Acrasus is ΑΚΡΑΣΙΩ-
ΤΩΝ. Sestini, p. 105.

Ecclesiastical Acts; (Synecd. p. 670.) but, for the reason assigned in the note, this may be doubted.

To the west of Thyatira Ptolemy places Hiero- Hierocæ-
cæsarea, a town rendered somewhat remarkable for saren.
the worship of Diana Persica, said to have been
established there as early as the reign of Cyrus.
(Tacit. Ann. III. 62. II. 47. Pausan. Eliac. I. 27.)
This also appears on the coins of the city, which
bear the word ΠΕΡΣΙΚΗ[i]. In and about the valley
of the Hyllus, to the east and north-east of Thyatira, were several towns assigned to Lydia, though
closely bordering on Mysia. Of these, Gordus, a Juliagor-
place apparently at first not above the rank of a dus.
village, came afterwards to be a place of some consequence, and obtained the surname of Julia in com-
pliment to Julius Cæsar or Augustus. Ptolemy
names it Juliagordus. (p. 116.) In Hierocles (Synecd. p. 671.) it is simply called Gordus, as well as
in the Ecclesiastical Notices, and Socrates. (Eccl.
Hist. VII. 36[k].) According to the recent researches
of an intelligent traveller, aided by the learned
suggestions of Col. Leake, it would appear that
Julia-gordus, which retains some vestiges of its
name in that of *Ghiurdiz*[l], was situate near the
Hyllus, about twelve hours to the east of *Akhissar*.
Somewhat more to the north apparently was
Blaundus, which Strabo assigns to Lydia, but ob- Blaundus.
serves at the same time that it was near Ancyra, a
Phrygian town, seated in the upper valley of the

[i] Sestini, p. 108. The usual
legend is ΙΕΡΟΚΑΙCΑΡΕΩΝ.

[k] There are several coins of
Julia-Gordus. The legend is
ΙΟΥΛΙΑ ΓΟΡΔΟC, and ΙΟΥΛΙΕ-
ΩΝ ΓΟΡΔΗΝΩΝ. Sestini, p. 108.

[l] Major Keppel, the traveller
referred to, does not mention
any antiquities as observed by
him at this place. Travels, tom.
II. p. 272—281.

Macistus, a river which flowed through Mysia and joined the Rhyndacus. (Strab. XII. pp. 567, 576.) Blaundus appears, from its coins, to have been colonized by the Macedonians, who are usually termed in ancient authors Myso-Macedones; and it is further collected from the same monuments, that it was situated on a small river, named Hippurius[n]. It is probable that Balandus, an episcopal town of Lydia, according to the Ecclesiastical Notices, is no other than Blaundus[o].

South of the Hyllus, on the road from Thyatira to Sardes, we find the lake of *Mermere*, or *Gheul*, anciently known by the name of Gygæa Palus.

Gygæa, postea Coloe palus.

Μήοσιν αὖ Μέσθλης τε καὶ Ἄντιφος ἡγησάσθην,
Υἷε Πυλαιμένεος, τὼ Γυγαίη τέκε λίμνη.

IL. B. 864.

Κεῖσαι, Ὀτρυντείδη, πάντων ἐκπαγλότατ᾽ ἀνδρῶν,
Ἐνθάδε τοι θάνατος· γενεὴ δέ τοί ἐστ᾽ ἐπὶ λίμνη
Γυγαίη, ὅθι τοι τέμενος πατρώϊόν ἐστιν,
Ὕλλῳ ἐπ᾽ ἰχθυόεντι, καὶ Ἕρμῳ δινήεντι.

IL. Υ. 389.

Strabo observes that this lake, which was afterwards called Coloe, was forty stadia from Sardes. It was said to have been excavated by the hand of man, as a bason for receiving the waters which overflowed the neighbouring plains. (XIII. p. 627.) Near the lake, towards Sardes, was the tomb or tumulus of Alyattes, mentioned by Herodotus as one of the wonders of Lydia; he says, the foundation of this monument was of huge stones, but the

[n] They are thus described by Sestini, p. 106. BLAVNDOS. Autonomi. Epigraphe ΒΛΑΥΝ-ΔΕΩΝ. addito MAKE. ΜΑΚΕΔΟ-ΝΩΝ. Mentio situs a Fl. vel a Fonte Hippurio. ΙΠΠΟΥΡΙΟΣ. Imperatorii a Nerone ad Volusianum.

[o] Geogr. Sacr. Car. S. Paul, p. 244.

superstructure was a mound of earth. It was raised by the artisans and courtesans of Sardis. The historian adds, that in his time there were extant on the top of the mound five pillars, on which were inscribed the different portions of the work completed by the several trades; whence it appeared that the courtesans had the greater share in it. The circumference of this huge mound was six stadia and two plethra, and the width thirteen plethra. (I. 93.) Some writers affirmed it was called " the tomb of the " courtesan," and that it had been constructed by a mistress of king Gyges. (Clearch. ap. Athen. XIII. p. 573.) Strabo reports that there were other tombs of the Lydian kings, besides that of Alyattes; which has been confirmed by the observation of modern travellers. The same writer adds, that there was a temple sacred to Diana Coloene, on the banks of the lake, and an object of great veneration to the inhabitants. (XIII. p. 626.) Chandler describes the lake " as very large, it abounds in fish, its colour and " taste like common pond water, with beds of sedge " growing in it. The barrows (or tombs of the kings) " are of various sizes, the smaller made perhaps " for children of the younger branches of the royal " family; four or five are distinguished by their su- " perior magnitude, and are visible as hills at a great " distance: the lake, it is likely, furnished the soil. " All of them are covered with green turf; and as " many as I observed, in passing among them, re- " tain their conical form, without any sinking in of " the top. One of the barrows on the eminence, " near the middle, and towards Sardes, is remark- " ably conspicuous: it was the monument of Alyat-

" tes. It is much taller and handsomer than any I
" have seen in England, or elsewhere[p]."

In the valley of the Hermus were situated appa-

Hermo-
capelia.
rently the towns of Hermocapelia[q] (Plin. V. 30.
Hierocl. p. 670. Notit. Episc.) and Hermopolis, if
the two should not be considered rather as one[r].

Saettæ sive
Saittæ.
Saettæ, or Saittæ, to judge from the reference
made on its coins to the Hermus and Hyllus, was
situated near the junction of these two rivers[s]. Ptolemy writes the name Setæ, or Septæ, and fixes it in
the north-eastern part of the province. Hierocles
calls it Sitæ, (p. 669.) as do also the ecclesiastical
records, from which we learn that it was an episcopal see. (Act. Conc. Nic. II. p. 591.) Near the Pa-

Hyde.
lus Gygæa stood anciently a place to which reference was made by Homer in the Iliad, when he
said,

Τμώλῳ ὕπο νιφόεντι, Ὕδης ἐν πίονι δήμῳ.

Il. Υ. 385.

Some writers pretended also that the poet had made
mention of it in another line, which is not found in
our copies. Il. B. 783.

Χώρῳ ἐνὶ δρυόεντι, Ὕδης ἐν πίονι δήμῳ.

But Strabo is inclined to think there was no place
of this name in Lydia. (XIII. p. 626.) Plin. V. 28.

---

[p] Chandler, Travels in Asia
Minor, p. 325—27.

[q] The coins of Hermocapelia are numerous. Some are autonomous. The imperial coins
do not ascend higher than Hadrian. The inscription is usually
ΕΡΜΟΚΑΠΗΛΕΙΤΩΝ. Sestini,
p. 108.

[r] The only evidence for the
existence of this city are its
coins, which are allowed to be
dubious. Sestini, p. 108.

[s] Sestini, p. 3. Saetteni au-
tonom. Epigraphe ΣΑΙΤΤΗ-
ΝΩΝ etiam ΣΑΙΤΤΑΙ. Mentio
situs a binis fluviis ΕΡΜΟC. ΥΛ-
ΛΟC.

" A Mæoniis civitas ipsa Hyde vocitata est, clara
" stagno Gygæo."

To the east of the Gygæan lake, and on the Her- ^{Attalia.}
mus, is a village named *Adala*, which probably corresponds with the site of Attalia, a Lydian town,
known to us from Steph. Byz., who says it was
anciently called Agroira or Alloira. (v. Ἀττάλεια.)
The Ecclesiastical Notices have recorded some of its
bishops. A recent traveller passed through *Adala*,
on his way from Smyrna and *Cassaba*. " It is on
" the right bank of the Hermus, which flows at the
" base of a rocky mountain, through a chasm of
" which it disappears. The passage here is rather
" dangerous. The direct road from *Cassaba* to
" *Adala* is twelve hours[t]." The same traveller, to
whom we are indebted for the most accurate account
we have of the course of the Hermus, and the country through which it flows, discovered, somewhat
higher up that river, an inscription which fixes the
site of Bagæ, another Lydian town, on the right Bagæ.
bank of the river, and nearly opposite to *Sirghie*,
a Turkish village between *Kula* and *Jeni-sher*[u].
Bagæ is ascribed to Lydia by Hierocles (p. 670.)
and the Ecclesiastical Notices, and its coins are not
uncommon[x]. *Selendi*, a small village some miles
higher up the valley of the Hermus, has doubtless
taken the place of Silandus, an episcopal see of Ly- ^{Silandus.}
dia, as we collect from the Acts of the Council of

[t] Major Keppel, tom. II. p.
335. No vestiges of antiquity
were observed here. There are
coins however of Attalea. Sestini, p. 106. Attalia. Autonomi
Epigraphe ΑΤΤΑΛΕΑΤΩΝ. Nu-
mina. ΚΟΡΗ — ΒΟΡΕΙΤΗΝΗ.

Diana sic vocata.
[u] Travels, p. 367, 368.
[x] Sestini, p. 106. Bagæ. Autonomi Epigraphe ΒΑΓΗΝΩΝ
vel ΚΑΙϹΑΡΕΩΝ ΒΑΓΗΝΩΝ.
Mentio situs ab Hermo Fl. ΕΡ-
ΜΟϹ.

Chalcedonʸ, and its coins ᶻ. Beyond Silandus we approach the territory of Cadi, which formed part of Phrygia; we must therefore retrace our steps towards the west, in order to describe that portion of Lydia which lies south of the Hermus; and first we may enter upon that section which is intercepted by the parallel streams of the Hermus and Caystrus.

Magnesia ad Sipylum. The first town we shall notice will be Magnesia, distinguished by its proximity to mount Sipylus from its Carian namesake, seated in the valley of the Meander, (Strab. XIII. p. 622.) Plin. V. 29. Magnetes a Sipylo. (Cf. Tacit. Ann. II. 47.) We are not informed by whom or when it was founded; but its proximity to the Æolian cities leads to the conjecture that it was colonized by the Magnesians of Thessaly, not long after Cyme and Smyrna had been founded. Magnesia is most celebrated in history for the signal victory obtained under its walls by the Roman army, commanded by Lucius Scipio, assisted by the counsels of his brother Africanus, over the forces of Antiochus; a victory which drove the king of Syria for ever behind the chain of Taurus, and placed Asia Minor at the disposal of the conquerors. (Liv. XXXVII. 37—43.) Magnesia surrendered after the battle. (Ibid. c. 44. Appian. Syr. c. 35.) The Magnesians displayed great bravery in defending their town against Mithridates. (Paus. Attic. c. 20.) In the reign of Tiberius it was nearly destroyed by an earthquake, which shook and overthrew also several other cities in Asia. The emperor on this occasion granted considerable sums from the

---

ʸ Geogr. Sacr. p. 244.
ᶻ Sestini, p. 112. Silandus. Autonomi Epigraphe ΣΙΛΑΝ-

ΔΕΩΝ. Imperatorii Domitiani, Commodi, &c.

treasury, to repair the losses occasioned by this disaster. (Strab. XII. p. 579. XIII. p. 622. Tacit. Ann. II. 47.) We know from its coins that Magnesia continued to flourish at a late period of the Roman empire[a]. It is often alluded to by the Byzantine historians, and still preserves, under the corrupt appellation of *Manissa*, evident traces of its classical name. It was once the residence of the Turkish sultans, but is now much reduced[b].

Mount Sipylus rises to the south of *Manissa*, Sipylus mons. and is separated by a small valley from the chain of Tmolus to the south-east, and by another from mount Mastusia to the south. Sipylus is celebrated in Grecian mythology as the residence of Tantalus and Niobe, and the cradle of Pelops. These princes, though more commonly referred to by classical writers as belonging to Phrygia, must in reality have reigned in Lydia, if they occupied Sipylus, not in the Sipylus urbs. mountain merely, but a city of the same name situated on its slope, and which, according to traditions preserved in the country, had been swallowed up by an earthquake and plunged into a crater afterwards filled by a lake. The existence of this lake, named Sale or Saloe, is attested by Pausanias, who reports Sale pal that for some time the ruins of the town, which he calls Idea, if the word be not corrupt, could be seen at the bottom. (Ach. c. 24.) Strabo also confirms the destruction of this town by an earthquake. (I. p. 58.) Pliny reports that it had often changed its

[a] Sestini, p. 109. Magnesia. Auton. copiosi. Epig. ΜΑΓΝΗ-ΤΩΝ ΣΙΠΥΛΟΥ. Imperatorii ab Augusto cum Livia usque ad Saloninam. Conditor Tiberius, ΤΙΒΕΡΙΟΝ ΣΕΒΑΣΤΟΝ ΚΤΙ-ΣΤΗΝ. Mentio situs a Monte Sipylo et a Fl. Hermo.

[b] Chandler, Travels in Asia, tom. II. p. 332. Major Keppel's Travels, tom. II. p. 295.

name, and he mentions besides the destruction of two other places. (V. 29.) " Interiere intus Daphnus " et Hermesia, et Sipylum quod ante Tantalis voca- " batur, caput Mæoniæ, ubi nunc est stagnum Sale : " obiit et Archæopolis substituta Sipylo, et inde illi " Colpe et huic Lebade." Pausanias elsewhere calls this lake the marsh of Tantalus ; and he adds, that the tomb of that prince was conspicuous near it. (Eliac. I. c. 13.) The same writer adds, that the throne of Pelops was shewn on the summit of the mountain above the temple of Cybele, surnamed Plastene. It certainly was the prevailing opinion among the ancients that Pelops came from Sipylus. (Athen. XIV. p. 625. Strab. XII. p. 571.) Homer has made an allusion to this mountain as the scene of Niobe's metamorphosis :

Νῦν δέ που ἐν πέτρῃσιν, ἐν οὔρεσιν οἰοπόλοισιν,
'Εν Σιπύλῳ, ὅθι φασὶ θεάων ἔμμεναι εὐνὰς
Νυμφάων, αἵτ' ἀμφ' 'Αχελώϊον ἐρρώσαντο,
"Ενθα, λίθος περ ἐοῦσα, θεῶν ἐκ, κήδεα πέσσει.

Il. Ω. 614.

This passage has been beautifully imitated by Sophocles in the Antigone. (v. 822.)

'Ηκουσα δὴ λυγρόταταν ὄλεσθαι
Τὰν Φρυγίαν ξέναν.
Ταντάλου, Σιπύλῳ πρὸς ἄκρῳ
Τὰν, κισσὸς ὡς ἀτενὴς,
Πετραία βλάστα δάμασεν· καί νιν
"Ομβρῳ τακομέναν,
'Ως φάτις ἀνδρῶν,
Χιών τ' οὐδαμὰ λείπει,
Τέγγει θ' ὑπ' ὀφρύσι παγκλαύτοις
Δειράδας—

and Ovid. (Metam. VI. 310.)

Flet tamen, et validi circumdata turbine venti
In patriam rapta est. Ibi fixa cacumine montis
Liquitur, et lacrymas etiamnum marmora manant.

(Cf. Pausan. Arcad. c. 2. Apollod. III. 5, 6.) This part of the story of Niobe is to be accounted for by some optical phenomenon exhibited by the mountain. Pausanias states, " that he visited mount Si-" pylus, and witnessed this appearance himself: " when viewed close, he saw only the rock and pre-" cipices ; nothing whatever which resembled a " woman, either weeping, or in any other posture ; " but if you stood at a distance, you would fancy " that you beheld a woman in an attitude of grief, " and in tears." (Attic. c. 21.) " The phantom of " Niobe," says Chandler, " may be defined an effect " of a certain portion of light and shade on a part " of Sipylus, perceivable at a particular point of " view. The traveller, who shall visit Magnesia " after this information, is requested to observe care-" fully a steep and remarkable cliff, about a mile " from the town : varying his distance, while the " sun and shade, which come gradually on, pass " over it, I have reason to believe he will see " Niobe [c]." The same traveller elsewhere observes, that " the mountain, terminating on the north-east " in a vast naked precipice, has now beneath it a " very limpid water, with a small marsh, not far " from a sepulchre cut in the rock, and there per-" haps was Sale, and the site of Sipylus [d]." Pausanias speaks of the rock of Coddinus near Magnesia,

[c] Chandler's Travels in Asia Minor, p. 331. This remark has been confirmed by a subsequent traveller, who describes the phenomenon very fully. Emerson's Letters from the Ægean, tom. II. in fin.

[d] Travels, p. 331.

where was a most ancient statue of Cybele, said to be the work of Broteas, son of Tantalus. (Lacon. c. 22.) The modern appellation of Sipylus is *Saboundji Dagh*, and sometimes *Sipuli Dagh*. On the southern side of the mountain, and near the road leading from Smyrna to the ruins of Sardes, a spot named *Nif,* or *Nymphi*, recalls to mind the Nymphæum of the Byzantine emperors, a spot where they are represented by the historians of that period, to have enjoyed the fine season, apart from the cares of public life and the tumult of war. (G. Acropol. p. 56. G. Pachym. Andr. Pal. p. 153. M. Duc. p. 45.) The same writers often speak of Chliara, in conjunction with Nymphæum and the coast of Ionia. (Ann. Comn. p. 421. D. p. 429. C.) Judging from the name, it would seem to have been a place noted for warm springs and baths. It suffered from a disastrous earthquake in the time of Andronicus Palæologus. (G. Pach. p. 158.) In this direction Ptolemy places Ægara, which is unknown to all other geographers. It answers perhaps to *Dourgoutli,* or *Cassaba,* between Smyrna and Sardes. The river which passes near it and falls into the Hermus is perhaps the Cryon of Pliny. (V. 29.) From Smyrna and the Ionian coast there extends a continued chain of mountains throughout the whole length of Lydia. It commences, as Pliny remarks, with Mastusia, which answers to the modern *Tartali.* This, he says, is connected on one side with mount Termes [e], which joins the roots of Olympus; on the other with mount Draco, which joins Tmolus, this Cadmus, and that finally the central ridge

Nymphæum.

Chliara.

Ægara.

Cryon fl.

Draco mons.

[e] For Termes, we should perhaps read Temnus.

of Taurus. Mount Draco seems to answer to the
summit called by the Turks *Kizil-djeh Mousseh
Dagh*. Tmolus is a broad and elevated mass of Tmolus
mons.
mountains, which sends several tributary torrents
into the Hermus on the one side, and into the
Cayster on the other, and divides, in fact, the valleys through which those two rivers flow. It was
said to derive its name from Timolus, or Tmolus, a
Lydian king, having been previously called Carma-
norius. (Auct. de Fluv. in Pactol.) This mountain
was much celebrated for its wine. (Plin. V. 29.)

> Sunt etiam Amineæ vites, firmissima vina :
> Tmolius assurgit quibus, et rex ipse Phanæus.
>
> VIRG. GEORG. II. 97.

> Hinc nota Baccho Tmolus attollit juga.
>
> SENEC. PHŒN. v. 602.

> Deseruere sui Nymphæ vineta Timoli.
>
> OVID. METAM. VI. 15.

Hence the frequent reference to it in the Bacchæ of
Euripides.

> XO. Ἀσίας ἀπὸ γᾶς
> Ἱερὸν Τμῶλον ἀμείψασα, θοάζω
> Βρομίῳ. v. 64.

> ἀλλ' ὦ λιποῦσαι Τμῶλον, ἔρυμα Λυδίας.
> v. 55.

(Cf. Strab. XIV. p. 637.) It appears also to have
abounded with shrubs and evergreens. (Callim.
Frag. XCIII.) nor was it less noted for its mineral
productions. It yielded tin ; and Pactolus washed Pactolus fl.
from its cavities a rich supply of golden ore. (Strab.
(XIII. p. 610. p. 625.) This little stream, which is
so closely connected by the ancient poets with the
name and wealth of Crœsus, rose on mount Tmolus,

and after flowing beneath the walls of Sardes was received by the Hermus. Pliny reports, that it was sometimes called Chrysorrhoas, and its source Tarne. (V. 29. Conf. Athen. V. p. 203. C. Herod. V. 101. Auct. de Fluv. in Pactol.)

> Mæonia generose domo : ubi pinguia culta
> Exercentque viri, Pactolusque irrigat auro.
> VIRG. Æn. X. 141.

> Et qua trahens opulenta Pactolus vada
> Inundat auro rura.   SENEC. PHŒN. 604.

> Sed cujus votis modo non suffecerat aurum,
> Quod Tagus et rutila volvit Pactolus arena.
> JUVEN. SAT. XIV. 298.

A celebrated temple of Cybele rose on its banks, which is alluded to by Sophocles :

> Ὀρεστέρα παμβῶτι Γᾶ,
>   Μᾶτερ αὐτοῦ Διὸς,
> Ἁ τὸν μέγαν Πακτωλὸν εὔχρυσον νέμεις.
>   PHILOCT. 391.

This temple appears to have suffered in the burning of Sardes by the Ionians and Athenians. (Herod. V. 102.)

Callimachus and Dionysius Periegetes speak of the swans of Pactolus :

> Ἡ μὲν ἔφη· κύκνοι δὲ θεοῦ μέλποντες ἀοιδοὶ
> Μηόνιον Πακτωλὸν ἐκυκλώσαντο λιπόντες
> Ἑβδομάκις περὶ Δῆλον.   HYMN. IN DEL. 249.

> Μηονίη δ᾽ ἐπὶ τῇσιν ἐπ᾽ ἀντολίην τετάνυσται
> Τμώλῳ ὑπ᾽ ἠνεμόεντι· τόθεν Πακτωλὸς ὁδεύων
> Χρυσὸν ὁμοῦ δίνῃσιν ἐφελκόμενος κελαρύζει.
> Τοῦ δ᾽ ἂν ἐπὶ πλευρῇσι καθήμενος εἴαρος ὥρῃ
> Κύκνων εἰσαΐοις λιγυρὴν ὄπα, τοί τε καθ᾽ ὕδωρ
> Ἔνθα καὶ ἔνθα νέμονται ἀεξομένης ἐπὶ ποίης.
>   DION. PERIEG. 830.

The Turkish name of this poetical rivulet is *Ba-*

gouly. Some extensive ruins, belonging apparently to the temple of Cybele, were observed by Chishull in 1699; but Chandler, who visited them subsequently, found that they had materially suffered in the interval. There were, however, five Ionic columns still standing; the shafts fluted, and the capitals designed and carved with exquisite taste and skill [f]. Strabo. reports, that on the top of Tmolus there was a watch-tower erected by the Persians: it was of white marble, and commanded an extensive view of the surrounding country. (XIII. p. 625.) The mountain is called *Bouz Dagh* by the Turks. It is described by Chishull as " pleasant, " and garnished with an infinite variety of plants, " shrubs, and trees. Besides a fine prospect of the " country, the traveller is amused with impending " rocks, perpendicular precipices, and the murmurs " of a brook, probably the Pactolus. On the top " is a fruitful vale between two lofty ridges, with a " vein of marble as clear and pellucid as alabaster[g]." In the central part of the ridge, as the name indicates, was a town, or community, entitled Mesoti-molitæ, or Mesotmolitæ. They are mentioned by Pliny, (V. 29.) and the Ecclesiastical Notitiæ, together with Hierocles. (p. 671.) Tacitus speaks of a town named Tmolus, which was destroyed by an earthquake under Tiberius. (Ann. II. 47. Niceph. Call. I. 17.[h])

Mesotmolus sive Tmolus urbs.

Sardes, the capital of Lydia, was situated in a fertile plain at the foot of the northern slope of Tmolus. Pactolus flowed through the forum, and soon

Sardes.

---

[f] Travels in Asia Minor, p. 319.

[g] Travels, p. 16.

[h] Some coins are extant with the inscription TMΩΛΕΙΤΩΝ. Sestini, p. 114.

after joined the Hermus. (Herod. V. 101.) Its foundation, as Strabo reports, does not reach to the Trojan era, but it was nevertheless a city of great antiquity. (XIII. p. 625.) Herodotus informs us that it was first fortified by Meles, who, according to the Chronicle of Eusebius, preceded Candaules. That prince was ordered by the oracle of Telmissus to carry his infant son Leon round the fortifications of the city; but he neglected to do this, with respect to that part of the citadel which looks toward Tmolus, conceiving that this point was unassailable. It was nevertheless in this quarter that Cyrus succeeded in storming the place. (I. 84.) Herodotus however affirms, that Agron had reigned at Sardes, and this prince must have preceded Meles by several generations. (I. 7.) In the reign of Ardys, son of Gyges, this city was taken by the Cimmerians during the incursion they made into Asia; but they could not conquer the citadel, and they were finally expelled by Alyattes, father of Crœsus. (I. 15, 16. Cf. Callisth. ap. Strab. XIII. p. 627.) Under the reign of the latter, Sardes became a great and flourishing city, the resort of men of talent and learning, attracted thither by the fame and hospitality of Crœsus. (I. 29.) After the overthrow of this monarch by Cyrus, it still continued to be the chief town of the Persian dominions in this part of Asia, and the residence of the lieutenant of the great king. (V. 25. Pausan. Lacon. c. 9.) On the revolt excited by Aristagoras and Histiæus, the Ionians, assisted by an Athenian force, marched suddenly from Ephesus up the river Caystrus, and having crossed mount Tmolus surprised Sardes, except the citadel, which was defended by Artaphernes with a numerous gar-

rison.   Sardes on this occasion was accidentally set
on fire and burned to the ground, as most of the
houses were constructed of reeds ; even those which
were of brick had roofs made of the former substance.   After this event the Ionians and their allies
were forced to evacuate the place and retire to the
coast : but the burning of Sardes was long remembered by Darius, and it was to avenge this insult
that he invaded Attica, and fought the battle of Ma-
rathon. (V. 100—105.) It was at Sardes that Xerxes
passed the winter previous to his expedition into
Greece. (VII. 32—37.)   It was here also that the
younger Cyrus collected his army when about to
march against the king, his brother. (Xen. Anab. I.
2. 5.)   This prince had indeed made it his chief
residence ; and the beauty of his gardens is reported
to have excited the admiration of Lysander, especially when he learnt that he often laboured there
with his own hands. (Xen. Œcon. p. 830. C. Cic. de
Senect. c. 17.)

> .   .   .   quid Crœsi regia Sardis?
> Smyrna quid, et Colophon ?
>
> Hor. Epist. I. 11. 2.

Sardes surrendered to Alexander without resistance
soon after the battle of the Granicus.   Arrian reports, that he visited the citadel, and admired the
height and strength of its position, defended besides
by a triple line of fortifications.   He gave orders on
this occasion that a temple and altar should be erected
to Olympian Jove.   Alexander also commanded that
the Lydians should regain their freedom, and resume
their ancient laws and usages. (I. 17.)   On the death
of the king of Macedon, Sardes and Lydia came into
the possession of Antigonus, and after the defeat of

that general at Ipsus, into that of the Seleucidæ :
but Seleucus Ceraunus having been assassinated,
this part of his dominions was usurped by Achæus,
his relation by marriage. That officer at first con-
ducted himself with great prudence and moderation,
professing to hold the reins of government for Antiochus,
brother of Seleucus ; but, finally, urged by
his ambition, and emboldened by success, he threw
off the mask, and assumed the crown, and title of
king. (Polyb. IV. 48. V. 57.) Antiochus, however,
having ascended the throne of Syria, did not suffer
Achæus to enjoy long the principality of which he
sought to defraud him. He invaded Lydia, and
Achæus, being too weak to cope with the Syrian
forces in the field, was shut up in Sardes, where he
defied, for a whole year, all the efforts of the enemy
to become master of the town and citadel. At
length, however, Lagoras, a Cretan officer in the
service of Antiochus, having observed a part of the
fortifications called Prion, where the citadel joined
the town, unguarded, scaled the ramparts, and won
the city. (Polyb. VII. 4—7.) From the possession
of Antiochus, Sardes passed into that of the Romans,
having surrendered to the two Scipios after their
victory at Magnesia. (Id. XXI. 13. 1.) In the reign
of Tiberius, the Sardians preferred their claim to
the honour of erecting a temple to the emperor, and
alleged their connexion with Italy through the migration of Tyrrhenus ; but their arguments were
not thought so valid as those urged by the people
of Smyrna, and the latter city was preferred. (Tacit. Ann. IV. 55.) Sardes was indebted to Tiberius
for its restoration after a disastrous earthquake,which
had made it a heap of ruins. (Tacit. Ann. II. 47. Strab.

XIII. p. 627.)   We are not informed in the sacred
writings when Christianity was first established at
Sardes, but it was probably not long after St. Paul
had founded the church at Ephesus ; and there can
be little doubt that the metropolis of Lydia is included in the declaration made by St. Luke, that
" all they which dwelt in Asia heard the word of
" the Lord Jesus, both Jews and Greeks ;" (Acts xix.
10.) and in the salutation to the Corinthians from
all the churches of Asia. (1 Cor. xvi. 19.)   This is
rendered manifest by the Book of Revelations, where
Sardes is expressly named among the seven churches
of that province.   When the warning voice was
addressed to it by the mouth of the apostle, it was
then evidently already declining.   " And unto the
" angel of the church in Sardis write ; These things
" saith he that hath the seven Spirits of God, and
" the seven stars ; I know thy works, that thou hast
" a name that thou livest, and art dead.   Be watch-
" ful, and strengthen the things which remain, that
" are ready to die : for I have not found thy works
" perfect before God.   Remember therefore how
" thou hast received and heard, and hold fast, and
" repent.   If therefore thou shalt not watch, I will
" come on thee as a thief, and thou shalt not know
" what hour I will come upon thee.   Thou hast a
" few names even in Sardis which have not defiled
" their garments ; and they shall walk with me in
" white : for they are worthy." (Rev. iii. 1—5.)
Ecclesiastical history mentions more than one council held in this see.   From Pliny we learn that it
was the capital of a conventus juridicus. (V. 29.)
We trace the history of this once flourishing and

opulent city through the Roman emperors to the
close of the Byzantine dynasty. (Eunap. p. 154.
Hierocl. p. 669.[i]) The Turks took possession of it
in the eleventh century, and two centuries later it
was nearly destroyed by Tamerlane. (Ann. Comn. p.
323. Pachym. tom. II. p. 279. M. Duc. p. 39.) It
is now little more than a village, built in the midst
of extensive ruins, to which the name of *Sart* is
yet attached. Mr. Smith, in his Notice of the Seven
Churches, describes the remains of Sardis as very
considerable, and giving a great idea of the size and
magnificence of the city [k].

" The site of this once noble city," says Chandler,
" was now green and flowery. Coming from the
" east we had the ground-plot of the theatre at some
" distance on our left hand, with a small brook near
" us running before it. The structure was in a
" brow, which unites with the hill of the citadel,
" and was called Prion. Going on, we passed by rem-
" nants of massive buildings; marble piers sustain-
" ing heavy fragments of arches of brick, and more
" indistinct ruins. These are in the plain before
" the hill of the citadel. On our right hand, near
" the road, was a portion of a large edifice, with a
" heap of ponderous materials before and behind it.
" The walls are standing of two large, lofty, and
" very long rooms, with a space between them, as of
" a passage. This remain, it has been conjectured,
" was the house of Crœsus, once appropriated by
" the Sardians as a place of retirement to superan-

[i] The imperial coins of Sardis may be traced from Augustus to Salonina: the common
legend is ΣΑΡΔΙΑΝΩΝ. Some
are inscribed ΣΑΡΔΙΣ. ΑΣΙΑΣ.
ΛΥΔΙΑΣ. ΜΗΤΡΟΠΟΛΙΣ. Ses-
tini, p. 111.
[k] P. 27—31. Lat. ed.

" nuated citizens. It was called the Gerusia, and in
" it, as some Roman authors have remarked, was
" exemplified the extreme durability of the ancient
" brick. (Vitruv. II. 8. Plin. XXXV. 14.) The
" hill on which the citadel stood, appears from the
" plain to be triangular. It is sandy, and the sides
" rough. The fortress is abandoned, but has a
" double wall, besides outworks, in ruins. The
" eminence affords a fine prospect of the country,
" and in the walls are two or three fragments with
" inscriptions. Not far from the west end is the
" celebrated river Pactolus, which rises in the moun-
" tain behind, and once flowed through the middle
" of the market-place of Sardes. We passed the
" miserable village of *Sart*, which stands, with a
" ruinous mosque, above the river, on a root or spur
" of the hill of the citadel[1]." Before quitting Sardes
we may remark, that this city has given birth to
the poet Alcman, who is thought to have been contemporary with Gyges, and to have afterwards resided in Laconia. This is proved by an epigram of
Alexander the Ætolian. (Anth. Pal. VII. 709.)

Σάρδιες ἀρχαῖαι, πατέρων νομός, εἰ μὲν ἐν ὑμῖν
  Ἐτρεφόμαν, χέρνας ἦν τις ἂν ἢ βακέλας
Χρυσοφόρος, ῥήσσων καλὰ τύμπανα· νῦν δέ μοι Ἀλκμὰν
  Οὔνομα, καὶ Σπάρτας εἰμὶ πολυτρίποδος.
Καὶ Μούσας ἐδάην Ἑλικωνίδας, αἵ με τυράννων
  Θῆκαν Δασκύλεω μείζονα καὶ Γύγεω.

Strabo also mentions two orators, named Diodorus,
who were of Sardes; and we may add to them Eu-
napius, the historian. On the southern slope of

1 Travels in Asia Minor, p. and plan of Sardis in the Tra-
316—318. There is a view vels of Mons. Peysonnel.

mount Tmolus, and near the sources of the Caystrus, stood Hypæpa, a city of no extent, but frequently mentioned by classical authors. (Strab. XIII. p. 627.)

> . . . . riget arduus alto
> Tmolus in ascensu ; clivoque extentus utroque,
> Sardibus hinc, illinc parvis finitur Hypæpis.
>
> OVID. METAM. XI. 150.
>
> Orta domo parva, parvis habitabat Hypæpis.
> ID. VI. 13.

Pausanias reports, that sacrifices were offered here by some Lydians, who were of Persian extraction. The ceremony was performed by a magus (Eliac. I. 27.) The Hypæpeni claimed the honour of erecting a temple to Tiberius, probably on account of these local rites, but they were rejected. (Tacit. Annal. IV. 55.) The sex here was said to be remarkably beautiful. (Steph. Byz. v. ˝Υπαιπα.) The Lydian women generally were entitled to the same praise ; and their grace in the dance has been celebrated by Dionysius Periegetes, in these elegant lines. (v. 839.)

> Οὐ μὰν οὐδὲ γυναῖκας ὀνόσσεαι, αἱ περὶ κεῖνο
> Θεῖον ἕδος, χρυσοῖο κατ᾽ ἰξύος ἅμμα βαλοῦσαι
> Ὀρχεῦνται, θηητὸν ἐλισσόμεναι περὶ κύκλου·
> Εὖτε Διωνύσσοιο χοροστασίας τελέοιεν
> Σὺν καὶ παρθενικαὶ, νεοθηλέες οἷά τε νεβροὶ,
> Σκαίρουσιν· τῇσιν δὲ πέρι σμαραγεῦντες ἀῆται
> Ἱμερτοὺς δονέουσιν ἐπὶ στήθεσσι χιτῶνας.

Hypæpa is also noticed by Ptolemy, Pliny, (V. 29.) and the Ecclesiastical records and Acts of Councils[m].

[m] Geogr. Sacr. p. 236. The coins of this city are not rare : the epigraph is ΥΠΑΙΠΗΝΩΝ. The name of the Cayster is visible on some. Sestini, p. 108.

Its ruins are to be seen close to the little town of *Pirghé*, or *Birkhé*, probably a corruption of Πύρ-γιον. Chandler conjectures that a fortress was erected there to command the pass of mount Tmolus [n].

In the immediate vicinity of Hypæpa stood a village, named Caloe, where Leo Diaconus, the By-zantine historian, was born, as he himself informs us. He describes it as a beautiful spot on the slope of Tmolus, and near the source of the Caystrus. (Leo Diac. Hist. I. c. 1.) In Hierocles, it is probable we ought to substitute Caloe for Colose, (p. 660.) as mention is made of its bishops in the Acts of Councils. There is little doubt that the site answers to the spot marked in Lapie's map under the name of *Caliveh Khan*, on a mountain tract leading from *Birghé* to *Dourgoutli*. *{Caloe vicus}*

The Caystrus, on leaving the mountain, flows through a rich and beautiful plain, anciently called Cilbianus. This was divided into Upper and Lower; a fact which we learn from Pliny, (V. 29.) and also from the coins struck by the inhabitants of both valleys [o]. Strabo reports, that the Cilbianus Campus was extensive, fertile, and well peopled. (XIII. p. 629.) The lower plain, which belonged to the Ephesians, contained some mines of cinnabar. (Vitruv. VII. 8. Plin. XXXIII. 7.) The only Lydian town we have to notice in the western part of the province is Metropolis, whose ruins are to be seen near a place called *Cabadja*, at the back of mount Gallesus, which, as we have seen, rose above Colo- *{Cilbianus Campus.}* *{Metropolis.}*

[n] Travels in Asia Minor, p. 321.

[o] Sestini, p. 107. Cilbiani Inferiores, ΚΙΛΒΙΑΝΩΝ ΤΩΝ ΚΑΤΩ. Cilbiani Superiores, ΚΙΛ-ΒΙΑΝΩΝ ΤΩΝ ΑΝΩ. From the same numismatic writer we learn that there were other Cilbiani, styled ΝΕΙΚΑΙΕΙΣ, ΠΕΡ-ΓΑΜΗΝΟΙ, and ΚΕΑΙΤΟΙ.

phon and Notium. It is mentioned by Ptolemy and
Steph. Byz. (v. Μητρόπολις.) One of its bishops subscribed to the Council of Chalcedon [p].

Returning to Sardes and its territory, the Sardia-
nus Campus of Herodotus, (I. 80.) and proceeding
along the left bank of the Hermus towards its
source, we shall reach that district of Lydia, or

*Catacecau-
mene re-
gio.* Mæonia, which was named by the Greeks Catacecaumene, (Κατακεκαυμένη,) or " the Burnt," from its
volcanic appearance and character. Strabo observes,
that this country was traversed by the Hermus, and
by some was assigned to Mysia. He also states,
that Xanthus, the Lydian historian, and other
writers, placed here the Arimi of Homer, and the
scene of Typhœus' punishment. (XII. p. 579. XIII.
p. 628.) According to Strabo, this district was 500
stadia in length, and 400 in breadth : the valleys
were covered with ashes, and the rocks and hills
were blackened as with fire. This judicious writer
does not hesitate to ascribe this to the effect of extinct volcanoes, the three principal craters of which
were visible in his time, at a distance of about forty
stadia from each other. There were also hillocks,
formed of lava and other substances, which attested
the existence of igneous action at some previous period. The only produce of the country was wine,
which, however, was of an excellent quality ; hence
it was wittily observed, that it was with reason that
Bacchus was termed Πυριγενὴς, or born of fire. The
account which a recent traveller gives of this country, accords strikingly with the description given of
it by Strabo. Having crossed the Hermus at *Adala*,
Attalea, he says, " we continued to march in an

[p] Geogr. Sacr. p. 237.

" easterly direction, and traversed a range of moun-
" tains of white and coloured marble. As we ap-
" proached *Kula*, the road was entirely black, and
" strewed with cinder-looking substances. Wherever
" the rock was broken, it exhibited the same black
" appearance. The people here call this mountain
" *Kara dewit*, or Black Ink-stand. On the oppo-
" site side of the hill, the face of the country under-
" goes a complete change. Instead of a continued
" chain of mountains, like those we had quitted,
" was a succession of detached hills of a conical
" shape, and covered for the most part with vines.
" In the midst of these eminences, at the further ex-
" tremity of a circular plain, is the highly pictu-
" resque town of *Kula*, situate amidst huge black
" vitrified masses in the bed of an extinct volcano [q]."
Kula itself appears to represent some ancient city, Mæonia urbs.
being full of inscriptions and architectural fragments; and from one of the inscriptions, which contains the name Μηϊόνες, one might be inclined to
think that it has been built on or near the site of
Mæonia. Major Keppel, however, informs us, " that
" the inscription in question was brought from a
" village two leagues distant, actually bearing the
" name of *Megna*,[f] which closely resembles Mæonia."
He was informed also, that several of the surrounding villages abounded with inscriptions and monuments [r]. The wine which he drank here was observed to be the best he had tasted in the course of
his journey [s]. Mæonia is mentioned as a Lydian
town by Pliny; (V. 29.) also by Hierocles, and the
Episcopal Notitia : and it is further known from its

[q] Major Keppel's Travels in Asia Minor, tom. II. p. 340.
[r] P. 344.   [s] P. 355.

coins of the reigns of Nero, Hadrian, and others [t]. Vitruvius also speaks of its wine, called Catacecaumenites. (VIII. 3.)

Near *Kula* is a village called *Ghiuldiz*, which, from the vestiges of antiquity, consisting of foundations of houses and temples, fragments of marble, and numerous bas-reliefs, observed there by Major Keppel, must have been the site of some Lydian town [u]. From some analogy of the name it may be Daldes, or Daldia, assigned to Mæonia by Ptolemy, *Daldes vel Daldia.* (p.120.) and the Episcopal Notitiæ [x]. Artemidorus, the writer on dreams, who was a native of the place, (Oneirocr. II. c. ult.) mentions that Apollo Mystes was worshipped there. There are several existing coins of this town [y]. Tabula, another ob *Tabala.* scure town of the same province, appears from its coins to have been seated on or near the Hermus, and some vestige of the name may be traced in that of *Tonbaili,* a village on the left bank of the river, between *Adala* and *Kula.* In Hierocles the name is corruptly written Talaza, (p. 670.) and in the Ecclesiastical Notices, Gabala [z]: but the coins shew incontrovertibly how it should be written [a]. Hie rocles names, after Mæonia, Julianopolis, which is *Julianopolis.* unknown to other writers; and Aureliopolis, a see *Aureliopolis.* whose bishops are known to have subscribed to the councils of Constantinople and Nicæa [b].

---

[t] Sestini, p. 109. Epigraphe ΜΑΙΟΝΩΝ et ΔΗΜΟΣ ΜΑΙΟΝΩΝ. Imperatorii a Nerone, indeque ab Hadriano usque ad Etruscum.

[u] P. 356.

[x] Geogr. Sacr. p. 244.

[y] Sestini, p. 107. Daldis. Epigraphe ΔΑΛΔΙΑΝΩΝ. Imperatorii ab Augusto usque ad Philippum Jun.

[z] See a note of Wesseling on Hierocles, loc. cit.

[a] Sestini, p. 113. Tabala. Epigraphe. ΣΥΝΚΛΗΤΟΣ ΤΑΒΑΛΕΩΝ.

[b] See Wesseling on Hierocles, p. 670. Sestini produces

Apollonoshieron, so called from a temple of Apollo, Apollonos-
is noticed by Pliny as a place of little note. (V. 29.) hieron.
It appears to have been afterwards a bishopric;
(Hierocl. p. 670.) and if it is the place mentioned
by Aristides, (I. p. 625, 629.) it was seated on a
hill, and about 300 stadia from Pergamum, a distance which rather agrees with the Apollonias of
Strabo.

Ptolemy places in Mæonia, which he makes a separate district between Lydia and Phrygia, besides
Daldia, Septæ, or Settæ, of which we have already
spoken, and Sattala. (p. 120.) The latter is known Sattala.
also from Hierocles, (p. 670.) and the Acts of the
Council of Chalcedon, to which its bishop subscribed.
Reference is likewise made to it in the Dionysiacs
of Nonnus, (XIII. 474.) under the form Στάταλα.
The poet's description leads us to place it in the
heart of the volcanic district.

Καὶ Στατάλων κεκόρυστο πολὺς στρατός, ᾗχι Τυφωεύς
Θερμὸν ἀναβλύζων πυριθαλπέος ἄσθμα κεραυνοῦ
Ἔφλεγε γείτονα χῶρον.

It is either *Kula* itself, or one of the neighbouring
sites, where antiquities are found.

Sirghié, a place near which Major Keppel observed some antiquities [c], may perhaps correspond
with Cerasæ, a Lydian bishopric, named by Hie- Cerasæ.
rocles (p. 671.) after Bagæ, which we have seen,
from the traveller above quoted, to have been opposite to *Sirghié*. The bishops of Cerasæ are also
referred to in the Acts of the council of Chalcedon
and Nicæa. Nonnus speaks of Cerassæ, and gives a

some coins with the legend ΑΥ-   [c] Travels, tom. II. p. 363—
ΡΗΛΙΟΠΟΛΙΤΩΝ; they are not   365.
earlier than Commodus.

fanciful derivation of the name; at the same time he informs us that it was in the wine country. (XIII. 468.)

Καὶ χθόνα Βακχείην σταφυληκόμον, ἧχίτε κοῦρος
Ἀμπελόεις Διόνυσος, ἔχων δέπας ἔμπλεον οἴνου,
Ῥείη πρῶτα κέρασσε, πόλιν δ᾽ ὀνόμηνε Κέρασσας.

Philadel-
phia.

But the most considerable and important town in this part of Lydia was Philadelphia, which owed its foundation to Attalus Philadelphus, brother of Eumenes, king of Pergamum. (Steph. Byz. v. Φιλα-δέλφεια.) Pliny reports, that it was seated on the river Cogamus, at the foot of Tmolus. (V. 29.) Strabo places it on the borders of Catacecaumene, and observes, that it suffered repeatedly from violent shocks of earthquakes. The walls and houses were constantly liable to be demolished, and as the inhabitants were continually apprehensive of some disaster to themselves and their property, it had nearly become deserted. (XIII. p. 628. XII. p. 579.) Tacitus mentions it among the towns restored by Tiberius, after a more than ordinary calamity of this kind. (Annal. II. 47.) In the midst of these alarms Christianity however flourished in Philadelphia, a fact which is well attested by the Book of Revelations, where it is mentioned as one of the seven churches. (iii. 7.) " And to the angel of the " church in Philadelphia write; These things saith " he that is holy, he that is true, he that hath the key " of David, he that openeth, and no man shutteth; " and shutteth, and no man openeth; I know thy " works: behold, I have set before thee an open door, " and no man can shut it: for thou hast a little " strength, and hast kept my word, and hast not de-

d Note to Hierocles by Wesseling, p. 671.

" nied my name." And a little further, "Because thou
" hast kept the word of my patience, I also will keep
" thee from the hour of temptation, which shall come
" upon all the world, to try them that dwell upon
" the earth. Behold, I come quickly: hold that
" fast which thou hast, that no man take thy crown."
The zeal of the Philadelphians shone forth conspi-
cuously in the gallant defence they made against
the Turks on more than one occasion. (G. Pachym.
p. 290.) At length they were conquered by Bajazet
in 1390. (M. Duc. p. 70. Chalcond. p. 33.) It is
now called *Allah-sher*, and preserves some remains
of Christianity, and also a few monuments of heathen antiquity. Chandler states, " that it is now
" a mean but considerable town, of large extent,
" spreading up the slopes of three or four hills. Of
" the walls which encompassed it, many remnants
" are standing, but with large gaps. The materials
" of this fortification are small stones, with strong
" cement. It is thick and lofty, and has round
" towers. The bed of the Cogamus, which is on
" the north-east side, was almost dry. The number
" of churches is reckoned at twenty-four, mostly in
" ruins. Only six are in better condition, and have
" their priests [e]." The Table Itinerary lays down
a road leading from Philadelphia to Cotyæum in
Phrygia, and divided into four stages: the first is
Clanudda, distant thirty-five miles from Philadel- Clanudda
et Calyd-
phia. I conceive this spot to be the fortress which nium.

[e] Travels, p. 310, 311. The
coins of Philadelphia are very
numerous. The imperial series extends from Augustus to
Valerian. The epigraph is ΦΙ-
ΛΛΔΕΛΦΕΩΝ. On one of them
is the word ΠΗΓΗ, denoting
some spring, or fountain, near
the town. It is probably the
hot source observed by Chandler near the Cogamus, p. 311.

Strabo calls Callydium, and Eustathius, who quotes
him, Calydnium. The geographer speaks of it as
a place of great strength, long occupied by Cleon of
Gordus during his marauding expeditions in these
parts. (XII. p. 574.) We should expect to find
some remains of this post in the vicinity of *Ieñi-*
sher, where there are some antiquities, as we have
learnt from Major Keppel [f]. Aludda, or Attalyda,
as it should probably be read, is thirty miles beyond,
and seems to belong to Phrygia.

There remains now only to speak of that portion
of Lydia which lies between the Caystrus and the
Meander. Near the former river, and perhaps in
the Cilbianus Campus, was Dioshieron, or the temple of Jove, a town mentioned by Ptolemy, (p. 119.)
and Pliny. (V. 29.) Hierocles assigns it to Asia.
(p. 659.) Steph. Byz. says it was a small town between Lebedos and Colophon. (v. Διὸς ἱερὸν.) From
the mention of the Caystrus on its coins, it however
appears plainly to have been near that river [g]; and
Ptolemy's numbers accord with this idea. When it
became a bishopric, the heathen name was dropped
for that of Christopolis. (Concil. Constant. III. p.
500. ed. Labb.) *Tirieh,* on the left bank of the
Caystrus, about twenty miles above Ephesus, possibly corresponds with the ancient site of Larissa,
which Strabo says is 180 stadia from that city.
(XIII. p. 620.) The chain of mountains which

Marginal note: Dioshie-ron.

Marginal note: Larissa.

[f] Strabo seems to place Calydnium in Mysia, the limits of
which, it must be remembered,
were very indefinite, involving
districts which at other times
were assigned to Mæonia and
Phrygia. Col. Leake, in a note
appended to Major Keppel's
work, states, " having learnt
" that a coin exists in the pos-
" session of a gentleman at
" Smyrna, bearing the inscrip-
" tion Κλαινουδέων." p. 371.

[g] Sestini, p. 107. Epigraphe
ΔΙΟCΙΕΡΕΙΤΩΝ, mentio situs ad
Fl. Caystrum ΚΑΥCΤΡΟC.

divides the valley of the Caystrus from that of the
Meander begins above Ephesus, where its roots
form the hills of Pactyas and Coressus ; it then runs
parallel to Tmolus from west to east, under the ancient name of Messogis, till, having passed beyond Messogis
the head of the Caystrus, it bends to the north, to mons.
meet the great Lydian range. To the east it however continues to extend its ramifications with Phrygia beyond the sources of the Meander [h]. (Strab.
XII. p. 629.) In Ptolemy the name is faultily
written Misatis. (p. 119.) To the Turks it is known
by that of *Kestenous Dagh.*

   If a traveller proceeds from Ephesus to the south-
east, across mount Pactyas, and follows a small stream
which winds in a valley towards the Meander, he will Magnesia
reach, not far from their junction, the ruined site of drum.
ad Mean-
Magnesia, which took its surname from the latter
river. Founded by a colony of Magnesians from near
Dotium in Thessaly, who were joined by some Cre-
tans, (Strab. XIV. p. 636, 647.) it had attained to a
high rank among the surrounding cities of Greek
origin, and was able to cope with success against the
powerful city of Ephesus. (Callin. ap. Strab. XIV.
p. 647.) Subsequently, however, the Magnesians
were overcome by the Treres, a Thracian horde
which overran Ionia and Lydia, and were nearly
destroyed. The year following, the city being deserted was occupied by the Milesians, or, as Athenæus reports, by the Ephesians. (XII. p. 525.)
These disasters were alluded to by Archilochus. (ap.
Strab. loc. cit. Athen. loc. cit.) It is probable, however, that the Magnesians recovered from this ruinous

---

[h] The name of this mountain evidently refers to its extension toward the interior, ἐν
μεσογείᾳ.

condition, since we find their city assigned by Artaxerxes to Themistocles when residing in his dominions, for the purpose of supplying his table with
bread. (Plut. Vit. Themist. Thuc. I. 138.)

Its territory, indeed, was extremely fertile, and
produced excellent wine, figs, and cucumbers. (Athen.
I. p. 29. II. p. 59. Polyb. ap. eund. III. p. 78.) Before that period, it appears from Herodotus to have
been occasionally the residence of the Lydian satrap.
(III. 122. Cf. I. 161.) Strabo reports that there was
anciently a celebrated temple of Dindymene, or Cybele, at Magnesia, of which, as it is said, the wife
or daughter of Themistocles was once priestess.
But he adds that the temple no longer existed in
his day, the site of the town having been removed
to that occupied by the temple of Diana Leucophrys.
Strabo does not inform us of the cause which led to
this change in the situation of Magnesia, nor of the
period at which it took place; but it will appear to
have occurred posterior to the age of Xenophon,
who mentions in the Hellenics Leucophrys as a
spot distinct from Magnesia, which he does not
name at all; at the same time there can be no doubt
that it is the site which Strabo alludes to, for he
says, there is there a temple of Diana much venerated, and a lake more than one stadium in circuit,
with a sandy bottom, and producing a never failing
supply of water, fit for drinking, and warm. (Hell.
III. 2. 14.) And elsewhere he speaks of Leucophrys
as a town in the vicinity of Priene and the Meander. (Hell. IV. 8. 17.) The poet Nicander, speaking of the roses which bloomed on the spot, evidently connects it with Magnesia.

Οὐδ' αὐτὴ Λεύκοφρυν ἀγασσαμένης ἐπιμεμφὴς,
Ληθαίου Μάγνητος ἐφ' ὕδασιν εὐθαλέουσα.

GEORG. II. AP. ATHEN. XV. p. 683.

For the Lethæus is known, from Strabo and other Lethæus fl.
writers, to have flowed close to Magnesia, on its way
from mount Pactyas to join the Meander. (XIV.
p. 646.) The temple of Diana, though inferior in
size and riches to that of Ephesus, was allowed to
excel it in the beauty and skill of its architectural
contrivance ; and in magnitude it only yielded to
the edifice above named, and that of Apollo at
Didymi. (Strab. loc. cit.) The style was Ionic, and
the architect Hermogenes of Alabanda, who is said
to have invented the order. (Vitruv. VII. præf. Cf.
Pausan. Lacon. c. 18.) Magnesia, with the rest of
Lydia, was annexed to the kingdom of Pergamum
by the Roman senate, after Antiochus had been
driven beyond mount Taurus. (Liv. XXXVII. 45.)
And Strabo relates, that a poet named Daphidas,
having written some satirical lines on the new
sovereign, was crucified on mount Thorax, above Thorax
the town. (XIV. p. 647. Cf. Suid. v. Δαφίδας. Cic. mons.
de Fat. c. 3. Val. Max. I. 8. 8.) Little is known respecting this town after this period, but it is noticed
by Pliny (V. 29.) and Tacitus. (Ann. IV. 55.) Hierocles ranks it among the bishoprics of Asia, and
later documents seem to imply that it once had the
name of Meandropolis. (Concil. Constant. III. p.
666 ¹.) Magnesia is now well known to correspond
with the site and ruins of *Inek-bazar;* former tra-

---

¹ The coins of Magnesia prove
its existence in the time of Aurelius and Gallienus. The legend is MAГN. and MAГNH-
TΩN. Allusion is also frequently made to the worship of Diana Leucophryne, and the river
Meander. Sestini, p. 83.

vellers, as Pococke and Chandler, had identified it
with *Guzel-hissar;* but Mr. Hamilton was the first
to examine the remains of antiquity at *Inek-bazar,*
and to prove that the position of that place agrees
with the accounts of Strabo and other ancient
writers. This is demonstrated by the discovery he
made of the ruined temple of Diana Leucophryne,
views of which have been published by the Dilettanti society. We know besides, that Magnesia
was fifteen miles from Ephesus, (Plin. V. 29.) or
120 stadia, according to Artemidorus. (ap. Strab.
XIV. p. 663.) 'Pausanias mentions that there was
at Hylæ, a spot near Magnesia, a cave sacred to
Apollo, containing a very ancient image of the god.
(Phoc. c. 32.)

Anæa.· It is uncertain whether we should assign Anæa, a
town not unfrequently spoken of by ancient writers,
to Lydia, or Caria. Scylax is in favour of the former
location, but Ptolemy and Stephanus pronounce
for the latter. The Byzantine geographer adds,
that it was opposite to Samos; if so, it must have
been within the limits of Lydia, since no part of
the Samian coast extends south of the Meander.
Hierocles also, and the Ecclesiastical Notices, by
assigning it to the province of Asia, with Ephesus
and Magnesia, evidently lead us to suppose it was
on the right or Lydian bank of the river. Anæa is
often referred to by Thucydides, who mentions its
being occupied by some Samian exiles in the early
part of the Peloponnesian war. (IV. 75. Cf. III.
32.) That it was a maritime place, or at least accessible by water, is also clear, from (VIII. 19.) where
it is said that the Chians sailed there from their
island, in order to obtain intelligence about Miletus,

and draw other towns to revolt. If we examine another passage again in the same historian, it appears that an Athenian officer, named Lysicles, having sailed to Myus with twelve ships, landed with a detachment, and marched up the land through the Meandrian plain, but being attacked by the Carians and Anaiitæ, near a hill called Sandius, was Sandius collis. defeated and slain with most of his corps. (III. 19.) It will be seen therefore that the Anaiitæ, or people of Anæa, must have lived in the vicinity of the Meander, and between Magnesia and Priene, but on the high ground above the river, as the name seems to imply, and it is not improbable that their territory extended also on the other side of the hills towards Ephesus, and the coast opposite Samos. And they might have a port in that direction, where the Chians, in the passage from Thucydides above referred to, would naturally have landed, without going so far round as the mouth of the Meander, and then up the river beyond Priene and Myus. Stephanus says, on the authority of Ephorus, that Anæa was so called from an Amazon who was interred there. He adds, that it was the birthplace of Menelaus, a peripatetic philosopher, and considerable historian. In Hierocles, there is little doubt that for Ἐνέα we should substitute Ἀναία. In this vicinity we must also place Achilleum, a town or fort mentioned by Xenophon, in conjunction with Priene and Leucophrys, and other cities in the Meandrian plain. (Hell. IV. 8. 17. Cf. III. 2. 13.) Stephanus Byz. states more vaguely that it was a fortress near Smyrna. (v. Ἀχίλλειος Δρόμος.)

The plain of the Meander, " Meandrius Cam- Mæandrius Campus. " pus," is constantly referred to by ancient authori-

ties, as the richest and most fertile soil in all Asia
Minor. (Xen. Hell. III. 2. 13. Herod. I. 161.) It
was subject to be overflowed by the waters of the
river, which however fertilized it by means of the
mud and slime which it brought down. Strabo informs us that the inhabitants had a strange custom
of bringing actions against the Meander for changing its course, and thus altering the limits of their
lands. (XII. p. 580.) Herodotus appears to have
imagined that the whole of this plain was once a
gulf washed by the sea; (II. 10.) and Pliny does
not scruple to affirm that the sea even came up as
far as Magnesia, and that the islands named Dera-
sidæ, were joined to the land on its subsequent
retiring. (V. 29.) Strabo seems to restrict the Meandrian plain to the right bank of the river, and
remarks, that it was common to the Lydians, Carians, Milesians, and Magnesians. (XIV. p. 648.)
In the middle ages, this district appears to have received the name of Mænomenus Campus, (μαινόμενος,)
probably from the fertility of its pastures[k]. (Georg.
Pachym. Andr. Pal. p. 216. M. Duc. p. 46.) It was
then almost constantly the seat of war, and exposed
to destructive ravages. Beyond Magnesia to the
south-west, and somewhat nearer the Meander, was

Tralles. Tralles, one of the most flourishing cities of Asia
Minor in the time of Strabo, and noted for the
opulence of its inhabitants. It was said to have
been founded by some Argives, together with a
body of Thracians, from whom it took the name of
Tralles. (XIV. p. 649. Hesych. v. Τράλλεις. Diod.
Sic. XVII. 65. Plut. Ages. c. 16.) It had previously

---

[k] As in Sophocles, ἱππομανῆ
λειμῶνα (Aj. 143.) is explained
by some ἐφ' ᾧ οἱ ἵπποι μαίνον-
ται.

borne those of Anthea, or Euanthea, Erymna, Charax, Seleucia, and Antiochia. (Steph. Byz. vv. Τράλ-
λις, Χάραξ. Etym. M. p. 389. Plin. V. 29.)   The
shape of the town was that of a trapezium, and it
was defended by a citadel, and other forts.   The
river Eudon, or Eudonus, flowed near the walls, Eudon fl.
and another little stream or fountain, named The- Thebais
bais, traversed the city. (Plin. V. 29.)   It was situate on the high road leading from Ephesus, through
Lydia and Phrygia, as far as Cappadocia and the
Euphrates, and consequently must have been a place
of great traffick. (Cic. Ep. ad Att. V. 14. ad Fam.
III. 5. Q. Frat. Ep. I. 1. 6. Artemid. ap. Strab.
XIV. p. 663.)   The citizens of Tralles, on account
of their great wealth, were generally elected to the
office of asiarchs, or presidents of the games, celebrated in the province.   Pythodorus, who had held
this situation, was very intimate with Pompey, a
circumstance which exposed him to the vengeance
of Cæsar.   His estates, worth, it is said, more than
2000 talents, were confiscated in consequence; but
he was nevertheless enabled to redeem them, and
leave the whole to his children, of whom Pythodoris, princess of Pontus, was one.   Menodorus, a
man of learning and priest of Jupiter Larissæus,
was another distinguished individual who flourished
at Tralles in the time of Strabo; but he fell under
the persecution and false accusations of Domitius
Ænobarbus' party. (XIV. p. 648.)   The country
around Tralles was much subject to earthquakes,
and in the reign of Augustus several public edifices
were destroyed by a violent shock, which damaged
other cities also; these received a grant from the
emperor to repair the losses they had sustained.

(Strab. XII. p. 579.) The Trallians petitioned for the honour of erecting a temple to Tiberius, but without effect. (Tacit. IV. 55.) Mention of this city is likewise made in Polybius, (Exc. XXII. 27. 10.) Liv. (XXXVII. 45. XXXVIII. 39.) Cæs. (B. Civ. III. 15.) Juv. (Sat. III. 70.) and Hierocles. (p. 659.) In the middle ages it was repaired by Andronicus Palæologus. (G. Pachym. p. 320.) Chandler mistook the ruins of Tralles for those of Magnesia, as Monsieur Barbier du Bocage has well proved in his notes to the French translation of his work. They are situated above the modern *Ghiuzel-hissar*, in a position corresponding with Strabo's description. Pococke had also discovered there an inscription, in which mention was made of Tralles; and others were found afterwards by Mr. Sherard[1]. Chandler says he saw at *Ghiuzel-hissar* many fragments of architecture of the Corinthian and Ionic orders: on the castle, and a hill somewhat beyond it, were some massive remains of a wall and arches[m]. Vitruvius mentions a temple of Æsculapius at Tralles. (Præf. lib. VII.) Besides the Eudon, there was a stream named Characometes, which flowed in the vicinity of this city: the name has evidently some reference to a small place called Charax, which existed prior to the foundation of Tralles. (Steph. Byz. v. Χάραξ.) The river might be discovered by means of the hot spring which Athenæus refers to. (II. p. 43.) Nysa, another considerable city of Ly-

Characo-
metes fl.

Nysa.

[1] Col. Leake's Asia Minor, p. 246.

[m] Travels in Asia Minor, p. 258, 259. The medals of Tralles are to be found in every collection: the epigraph is ΤΡΑΛΛ. or ΤΡΑΛΛΙΑΝΩΝ; sometimes ΚΑΙΣΑΡΕΩΝ ΤΡΑΛΛ. in allusion, probably, to the restoration by Augustus. Sestini, p. 115.

dia, was situated to the east of Tralles, and between
mount Messogis and the Meander, backed by the
mountain, and divided by a torrent which descended
from it. Tradition assigned the foundation of Nysa
to three brothers, named Athymbrus, Athymbradus,
and Hydrelus, who came from Sparta, and founded
three towns in the Meandrian plain; but in process
of time Nysa absorbed them all. The Nysæans
themselves acknowledged more especially Athymbrus as their founder. (Strab. XIV. p. 650. Steph.
Byz. v. Ἀθυμβρα.) Their city was also once named
Pythopolis. (Id. vv. Νύσαι, Πυθόπολις.) Literature
seems to have greatly flourished here, and Strabo
mentions several distinguished philosophers and rhe-
toricians who taught in the place. Strabo himself,
when a youth, had attended the lectures of Aristodemus, a stoic and disciple of Panætius: another
Aristodemus, his cousin, also of Nysa, had been
preceptor to Pompey. (XIV. p. 650. Cf. Cic. ad
Fam. XIII. 64. Plin. V. 29.) Hierocles classes Nysa
among the sees of Asia, and its bishops are recorded
in the councils of Ephesus and Constantinople[n].
The vestiges of Nysa have been recognised by
Chandler and others, at *Sultan*, or *Eski-hissar*,
above the plain of the Meander, on a site much
resembling Strabo's account. He describes it as divided into two towns by a torrent, over which was
thrown a bridge: its waters also flowed under the
amphitheatre. Besides this public building, he notices a theatre, a forum, a gymnasium for youth, and
another for elders. (XIV. p. 649.) Chandler found
vestiges of a large theatre in the mountain side,

[n] Wesseling's note to Hierocles. The medals of Nysa are
inscribed ΝΥΣΑΕΩΝ. They exhibit a series of Roman emperors, from Augustus to Gallienus. Sestini, p. 89.

with many rows of seats, almost entire; also of the amphitheatre, gymnasium, senate-house, market-place, &c.[n] The country around Nysa, and generally in the vicinity of the Meander, bore evidence of the existence of subterraneous fires, either by exhalations and vapours, or the bursting forth of hot mineral springs. Between Nysa and Tralles, but nearer the former, was a place called Acharaca,

Acharaca. celebrated for a Plutonium, or a beautiful grove and temple of Pluto, and a cave, named Charonium, where some wonderful cures were performed under the influence of Pluto and Proserpine, and by means of remedies suggested in dreams to the priests. The patients were sometimes shut up in the cave for several days, fasting. Every year there was a great concourse at this place, during which a bull was driven by the youth of the gymnasium to the cave, where he presently expired. There was another cave

Limon. at Limon, about thirty stadia from Nysa, also dedicated to the same deities, and supposed to communicate with that of Acharaca. Some pretended that this meadow was the Asius Campus of Homer. (Strab. XIV. p. 650.) The slope of mount Messogis, above Acharaca, produced the best wine of the whole

Aromata. chain. It took its name of Aromeus from Aromata, (Ἀρόματα,) a small town near which it grew. (Strab. loc. cit. Steph. Byz. vv. Μέσσωγις, Ἄρωμα.)

Briula. Mastaura. Near Nysa Strabo also places Briula and Mastaura. These towns are likewise mentioned by Pliny, (V. 29.) Hierocles, (p. 659.) and the other Notices and Acts of Councils. Mastaura, as appears from Stephanus Byz. (v. Μάσταυρα,) was watered by

Chrysor-rhoas fl. a stream named Chrysorrhoas. Some vestiges, to-

[n] P. 261.

gether with the name of *Mastauro* attached to them, a little to the east of *Eski-hissar*, mark the site of this ancient town [o].

It is a matter of uncertainty where to look for the positions of Aninetum, Enara, and Arcadiopo- Aninetum.
Enara.lis, episcopal towns of Asia, according to Hierocles, Arcadiopo-
lis.whose authority is also confirmed by the records of various councils [p]. Aninetum, or Aninesum, in particular, has the additional evidence of coins in its favour [q].

The last town of Lydia we have to mention on the Meander was Tripolis, placed by the Itineraries Tripolis.on the road leading from Sardes by Philadelphia to Laodicea, and other towns of Phrygia. (Itin. Anton. p. 336. Cf. Tab. Pent.) It is not noticed by any writer prior to Pliny, who says, in his concise way, " Tripolitani iidem et Antoniopolitæ Mæandro allu- " untur ;" (V. 29.) whence it would appear to have been also called Antoniopolis. The name of Tripolis, however, is much more frequently used, being found in Ptolemy, (p. 119.) the Ecclesiastical Notices, and Hierocles. (p. 669.) This place must have been near the junction of the two roads leading from Lydia and Caria into Phrygia, and consequently in the vicinity of Callatebus, a Lydian town mentioned by Herodotus in his account of Xerxes' march from Cappadocia and Phrygia to Sardes. (VII. 31.) The Persian monarch, having left Colossæ in the latter

---

[o] Pocock's Travels. There are coins of Briula and Mastaura. The former are inscribed BPIOYΛEITΩN, the latter MAΣTAYPEITΩN; these are more numerous, and prove Mastaura to have been the more

considerable town of the two. Sestini, p. 106, 110.

[p] Wesseling on Hierocles, p. 659.

[q] Sestini, p. 105, Aninesum. Epigraphe ANINHΣIΩN.

province, reached Cydrara on the confines of Lydia, where the limits of the two provinces were marked by a pillar erected by Crœsus. Cydrara must therefore have been very near Hierapolis, now *Pambouk Calessi*, where the two routes indicated by Herodotus branch off. Xerxes, following the road to Sardes, took to the right, and, having crossed the Meander, came to Callatebus, where confectioners, says Herodotus, made honey from tamarisk and wheat.

Callatebus. Mannert is inclined to identify Callatebus with Philadelphia [r]; but the account of Herodotus leads one rather to seek for it nearer the Meander and the Carian frontier. In Mons. Lapie's map there are some ruins laid down to the north of Tripolis, at a place called *Eski Kaleh*, which is not unlikely to be the Callatebus of Herodotus. Steph. Byz. is the only geographer who names this place besides him, and he copies merely from his account. (v. Καλλά-τηβος.) Tripolis, according to some church traditions, is connected with the apostles St. Philip and St. Bartholomew. It is also frequently referred to by the Byzantine historians in the course of the Turkish wars. (G. Acrop. p. 38.) Its ruins consist of confused heaps of stones, with some vestiges of a theatre and castle [s].

Having now terminated the tour of Lydia, it only remains for me to close the section with the names of such places as have no fixed site assigned to them in it, and are consequently of a more dubious character than those hitherto mentioned.

[r] Geogr. t. VI. P. 3. p. 365-6. He inadvertently writes it Callabetus.

[s] Chandler's Travels, p. 305. There are coins of Tripolis of the reigns of Augustus and downwards to that of Gallienus. Allusion is made on them to the proximity of the Meander. Sestini, p. 90.

Acrasus has already been alluded to as differing Acrasus. from Nacrasa, though identified with it by some antiquaries [t].

Anolus is assigned to Lydia by Steph. Byz. (v. Anolus. Άνωλος,) and there are some coins which may possibly be referred to it [u]. We learn from Hierocles, (p. 670.) and other ecclesiastical documents, that it was an episcopal town.

Asia, according to Steph. Byz. was a city of Ly- Asia. dia, near Tmolus, (v. Άσία,) where the harp with three strings was invented. (Cf. Etym. M. v. Άσι-άτις.) According to Herodotus, it was a portion of Sardes. (IV. 45. Cf. Callin. et Demetr. Sceps. ap. Strab. XIII. p. 627.)

Assus, a meadow in the Cilbianus Campus, and Assus. near the Cayster. (Steph. Byz. v. Άσσος.) This is perhaps a mistake for Asius.

Astelebe and Asteria are ascribed to Lydia by Astelebe. Asteria. Steph. Byz. on the authority of Xanthus. (vv. Άστε-λέβη, Άστερία.)

Attalyda, according to the same lexicographer, Attalyda. was founded by Atys. (v. Άττάλυδα.)

Aphneium, a town of Lydia. (Steph. Byz. v. Άφ- Aphneium. νειον.) It is however probably the same place spoken of near Cyzicus.

Diospolis. Among other cities of this name Steph. Diospolis. Byz. assigns the sixth in his list to Lydia ; it is probably the same as Dioshieron.

Eupatria is given to the same province, on the Eupatria. authority of Xanthus. (v. Εὐπατρία.) There are two Heracleas in the list of Stephanus, which seem to Heraclea.

t The legend on its coins is ΑΚΡΑΣΙΩΤΩΝ. Sestini, p. 105.

u Sestini, p. 105. Anolus? Autonomi Epigraphe, $\frac{AV}{\Omega. \text{Æ.}}$

belong to Lydia. One was near Magnesia, and is noted for producing the magnet, called Magnes, or Heraclius, by the ancients[x]. (Eustath. ad Hom. Il. B.) Another is said to have been ἐν Λυδίῳ Ταύρῳ. If this reading is right, we should understand by this mountain Messogis, which joined Mount Taurus; but perhaps we ought to correct it to ἐν τῷ Ἀντιταύρῳ.

Thyessus. Thyessus, said to have been named after a trader so called, (Steph. Byz. v. Θυεσσός,) is known also from its coins[y].

Thymbrara, vel Thymbra. Thybarra, or Thymbrara, where the great battle was fought, according to Xenophon, which decided the fate of the empire of Crœsus, is assigned by Steph. Byz. to Lydia, and placed on the banks of Pactolus. But it is plain, from Xenophon's account, that Thymbrara, or Thymbria, (the MSS. differ very much about the orthography of the name,) (Cyrop. VI. p. 158, Leuncl.) was beyond Pactolus: he adds, that in his time it was the rendezvous of all the barbarian forces under the Persian monarch in Lower Asia. This seems to point also to the Castoli Campus. plain called in the Anabasis Castoli Campus, Καστω-λοῦ πεδίον, (I.1.) where it is said that Cyrus was appointed by his brother Artaxerxes governor of all the nations which assembled in the plain of Castolus. This was probably a river, but Steph. Byz. calls it a town. I do not understand the lexicographer, Καστωλοῦ πεδίον· Δωριέων ἐκλήθη δὲ ὅτι Καστωλοὺς τοὺς Δωριεῖς οἱ Λυδοί φασιν. There must be some confusion here.

---

[x] There are some imperial coins of the Lydian Heraclea. Sestini, p. 108.

[y] Sestini, p. 114. Thyessus, autonomus unicus. Epigraphe ΘΥΕΣΣΕΩΝ.

Ibeni, a people of Lydia, called also Iaonitæ. Ibeni. (Steph. Byz. v. Ἰβαῖοι.) According to the same lexicographer we have likewise an Itone in this province. Itone. It is also mentioned by Nonnus in conjunction with a torrent or river named Cimpsus:

Λυδῶν δ᾽ ἁβρὸς ὅμιλος ἐπέρρεεν, οἵτ᾽ ἔχον ἄμφω
Κίμψον ἐϋψήφιδα, καὶ ὀφρυόεσσαν Ἰτώνην.

DIONYS. XIII. 465.

Cyalus, a town of Lydia, founded by Cyalus, son Cyalus. of Jove. (Id. v. Κύαλος.) Cyne is assigned to the Cyne. same country on the testimony of Hecatæus. (Id. v. Κυνή.)

Lycapsus, a spot near Lydia, according to Eu- Lycapsus. phorion. (Id. v. Λύκαψος.)

Lycosthene, or Lycosthenea, a town of Lydia, Lycosthene. mentioned by Xanthus and Nicolaus of Damascus. (Id. v. Λυκοσθένη.)

Melampea, cited from Xanthus. (v. Μελάμπεια.) Melampea.

Oanus, a place noticed by Dionysius in the Bas- Oanus. sarica. (Id. v. Ὄανος) and Nonnus.

Καὶ σκοπιὰς Ὀανοῖο, καὶ οἱ ῥόον ἔλλαχον Ἑρμοῦ
Ὑδατόεν τε Μέταλλον, ὅπῃ Πακτώλιον ἰλὺν
Ξανθὸς ἀποπτύων ἀμαρύσσεται ὄλβος ἐέρσης.

DIONYS. XIII. 470.

Pelope, a village on the borders of Phrygia. Pelope. (v. Πελόπη.)

Progasia, so called from Progasus, son of Melam- Progasia. pus. (Id. v. Προγάσεια.) Procle, a town of Lydia. (Id. Πρόκλη.)

Strogola, cited from the history of Xanthus. (Id. Strogola. v. Στρόγωλα.)

Tarrha, a town of Lydia. (Id. v. Τάρρα.) the Etym. Tarrha, vel Tyrrha. Magnum calls it Tyrrha.

Tomarene.   Tomarene, a town known only from its coins, is assigned to Lydia by Sestini [z].

Torrhebus.   Torrhebus derived its appellation from Torrhebus, a son of Atys. It gave its name to the district Torrhebis, in which was Mount Carius, and a temple of the hero Carius, son of Jove and the nymph Torrhebia. There was also a lake, Torrhebia. All this seems derived from Nicolaus of Damascus, who copied Xanthus. (Steph. Byz. v. Τόῤῥηβος. Cf. Dion. Halic. Pont. and Nonnus Dionys. XIII. 467.)

$$Ο\text{'} τε Τορήβιον εὑρὑ, καὶ οἱ Πλούτοιο τιθήνας$$
$$Σάρδιας εὐώδινας ὁμήλικας Ἡριγενείης.$$

Hysbe.   Hysbe, a town of Lydia. (Id. v. ῞Υσβη.) Hierocles has, under the head of Asia, the following obscure

Algira.   sees, belonging either to Lydia or Ionia: Algiza,

Nicopolis.   Nicopolis, Palæapolis, Baretta, Auliucome, Neaule.
Palæapolis.
Baretta.   (p. 660.) Mostine, which Wesseling supposed to be
Auliu-
come.   a correction for Mystene, crept in from the margin,
Neaule.
Mossina.   (p. 671.) appears to be genuine, if its coins are so. They teach us that the true name of the town is Mossine, and that it was near a small stream, or fountain, called Aligomon [a]. The Table Itinerary places on a road leading from Sardes to Ephesus by Hypæpa, a station named Anagome, nine miles from the last mentioned town, and thirty-four from the former. The site seems to answer nearly to that of *Bainder*, near the Caystrus.

[z] Lett. Numism. II. 13. p. 81. Caput Herculis barbatum nudum, cum pelle leonis ad collum ΤΟΜΑ PHNΩN Leo gradiens. Æ. 3. p.

[a] Sestini, p. 110. Mossina, vel Mossinus. Autonomi epigraphe, ΜΟΣΣΙΝΩΝ ΛΥΔΩΝ; in alio ΘΕΟΝ ΣΥΝΚΛΗΤΟΝ. Fons sacer ΑΛΙΓΟΜΩΝ.

END OF VOL. I.

ERRATA.

VOL. I.

P. 28, l. 21, *for* Pomponius, Mela *read* Pomponius Mela.

P. 71, l. 1 and 10, *for* Arisba *read* Arisbe.

P. 87, l. 22, insert a comma after Ida.

P. 103, l. 28, *for* Θυμβαῖε *read* Θυμβραῖε.

P. 112, l. 12, *for* χρύσην *read* Χρύσην.

P. 180, l. 8, the quotations from Aristotle and Pliny probably refer to the Palus Ascania of Pisidia or Phrygia.

P. 193, l. 23, *for* P. Gythius *read* P. Gyllius.

P. 282, l. 8, *for* Chærades *read* Chœrades.

P. 412, l. 11, for *Garthonisi* read *Gaitonisi.*

P. 454, l. 15, *for* Tabula *read* Tabala.

VOL. II.

P. 24, l. 26, it is more correct to write Berecyntian, Berecyntii and Berecyntia.

P. 53, l. 4, *for*, it is not frequently, *read*, it is not unfrequently.

P. 85, l. 28, *for* Ambitrii *read* Ambitui.

Ibid. l. 30, *for* Thynbres *read* Thymbres.

P. 114, l. 26, *for* ψόφοοι *read* ψόφοι.

P. 150, l. 13, for *Turnberan* read *Turuberan.*

P. 196, l. 13, *for* Calynda read Calydna.

P. 209, last line, for *Gengere* read *Gongere.*

P. 275, l. 9, *for* Cydrema *read* Cadrema.

ImTheStory.com

Personalized Classic Books in many genre's

Unique gift for kids, partners, friends, colleagues

Customize:

- Character Names
- Upload your own front/back cover images (optional)
- Inscribe a personal message/dedication on the inside page (optional)

Customize many titles Including
- Alice in Wonderland
- Romeo and Juliet
- The Wizard of Oz
- A Christmas Carol
- Dracula
- Dr. Jekyll & Mr. Hyde
- And more...

Lightning Source UK Ltd.
Milton Keynes UK
UKHW02f1932110118
315984UK00013B/607/P